Exploring (Im)mobilities

ENCOUNTERS

Series Editors: Ana Deumert, *University of Cape Town, South Africa*, Zane Goebel, *University of Queensland, Australia* and Anna De Fina, *Georgetown University, USA*.

The Encounters series sets out to explore diversity in language from a theoretical and an applied perspective. So the focus is both on the linguistic encounters, inequalities and struggles that characterize post-modern societies and on the development, within sociocultural linguistics, of theoretical instruments to explain them. The series welcomes work dealing with such topics as heterogeneity, mixing, creolization, bricolage, crossover phenomena, polylingual and polycultural practices. Another high-priority area of study is the investigation of processes through which linguistic resources are negotiated, appropriated and controlled, and the mechanisms leading to the creation and maintenance of sociocultural differences. The series welcomes ethnographically oriented work in which contexts of communication are investigated rather than assumed, as well as research that shows a clear commitment to close analysis of local meaning making processes and the semiotic organisation of texts.

All books in this series are externally peer-reviewed.

Full details of all the books in this series and of all our other publications can be found on http://www.multilingual-matters.com, or by writing to Multilingual Matters, St Nicholas House, 31–34 High Street, Bristol BS1 2AW, UK.

ENCOUNTERS: 23

Exploring (Im)mobilities

Language Practices, Discourses and Imaginaries

Edited by
**Anna De Fina and
Gerardo Mazzaferro**

MULTILINGUAL MATTERS
Bristol • Jackson

To the memory of Jan Blommaert

DOI https://doi.org/10.21832/DEFINA5297
Library of Congress Cataloging in Publication Data
A catalog record for this book is available from the Library of Congress.
Names: De Fina, Anna, editor. | Mazzaferro, Gerardo, editor.
Title: Exploring (Im)mobilities: Language Practices, Discourses and
  Imaginaries/Edited by Anna De Fina and Gerardo Mazzaferro.
Description: Bristol, UK; Blue Ridge Summit: Multilingual Matters, 2021.
  | Series: Encounters: 23 | Includes bibliographical references and
  index. | Summary: "The chapters in this volume use
  ethnographically-based methodologies to address the interconnectedness
  between forms of mobility and immobility in international migratory
  processes or in discriminatory practices within the boundaries of
  national states, thus bringing to light a sociolinguistics responsive to
  21st century concerns"— Provided by publisher.
Identifiers: LCCN 2021034535 (print) | LCCN 2021034536 (ebook) |
  ISBN 9781788925280 (paperback) | ISBN 9781788925297 (hardback) |
  ISBN 9781788925303 (pdf) | ISBN 9781788925310 (epub)
Subjects: LCSH: Linguistic minorities. | Immigrants—Language. | Language
  policy—Social aspects. | Sociolinguistics. | LCGFT: Essays.
Classification: LCC P40.5.L56 .E97 2021 (print) | LCC P40.5.L56 (ebook) |
  DDC 306.44—dc23 LC record available at https://lccn.loc.gov/2021034535
LC ebook record available at https://lccn.loc.gov/2021034536

British Library Cataloguing in Publication Data
A catalogue entry for this book is available from the British Library.

ISBN-13: 978-1-78892-529-7 (hbk)
ISBN-13: 978-1-78892-528-0 (pbk)

Multilingual Matters
UK: St Nicholas House, 31–34 High Street, Bristol BS1 2AW, UK.
USA: Ingram, Jackson, TN, USA.

Website: www.multilingual-matters.com
Twitter: Multi_Ling_Mat
Facebook: https://www.facebook.com/multilingualmatters
Blog: www.channelviewpublications.wordpress.com

Copyright © 2022 Anna De Fina and Gerardo Mazzaferro and the authors of individual chapters.

All rights reserved. No part of this work may be reproduced in any form or by any means without permission in writing from the publisher.

The policy of Multilingual Matters/Channel View Publications is to use papers that are natural, renewable and recyclable products, made from wood grown in sustainable forests. In the manufacturing process of our books, and to further support our policy, preference is given to printers that have FSC and PEFC Chain of Custody certification. The FSC and/or PEFC logos will appear on those books where full certification has been granted to the printer concerned.

Typeset by Nova Techset Private Limited, Bengaluru and Chennai, India.

Contents

Contributors vii
Acknowledgements xi

Introduction 1
Anna De Fina and Gerardo Mazzaferro

Part 1: The (Im)mobilization of Language Resources, Repertoires and Practices

1 Multilingual Young African Migrants: Between Mobility and Immobility 17
  Mari D'Agostino

2 Sociolinguistic (Im)mobilities in Spaces of Migration 38
  Necia Stanford Billinghurst

3 Categorization and the Use of English as an (Im)mobile Resource in Service Encounters with Migrants in Flanders 60
  Katrijn Maryns and Stef Slembrouck

Part 2: (Im)mobilities, Technologies and Control

4 Controlling Migrants' (Im)mobilities through Telecommunications: Technopolitical Governance in Telephony Advertising Discourse 87
  Maria Sabaté-Dalmau

5 On Being Enregistered into the Matrix of Online Knowledge: An Ethnographic Exploration of an Internet-based Dismissal in an Asylum-seeking Procedure 116
  Massimiliano Spotti

6 From Language to Politics: Communication, Power and Migration in the Central Mediterranean 136
  Marco Jacquemet

Part 3: Spaces of (Im)mobility and Resistance

7 Everyday Communicative Practices and Repertoires in Contexts of Involuntary and Enforced Immobility   163
  Anna De Fina and Gerardo Mazzaferro

8 Beachspaces: Racism and Settler-Colonial (Im)mobilities at the Shoreline   183
  Ana Deumert

9 Language and Humanitarian Governmentality in a Refugee Camp on Lesvos Island   207
  Birgul Yilmaz

Part 4: (Im)mobilities, Subjectivity, Identity and Agency

10 Estrangement and Home in Queer Asylum Stories   229
   Mike Baynham, Bahiru Shewaye and Gomes O. Kayode

11 The Power of (Im)mobility: Irish Travellers' Agentive Identities in Transit and Permanency   247
   Roberta Piazza

12 Postscript: Immobilities Normalized   270
   Jan Blommaert

Index   274

Contributors

Mike Baynham is Emeritus Professor at the University of Leeds. His research focus includes language and migration and narratives of migration, including queer migration. With John Gray he has recently contributed a chapter entitled 'Narratives of queer migration' to the *Oxford Handbook of Language and Sexuality*.

Necia Stanford Billinghurst is a sociolinguist and international development professional with expertise in migration and sub-Saharan Africa. Necia researches the interplay of multilingual practices in 'southern' and 'northern' spaces. Currently at the University of South Australia, she is investigating the lifelong linguistic agency of refugee-background women resettled in Australia.

Jan Blommaert was a Belgian sociolinguist and linguistic anthropologist, Professor of Language, Culture and Globalization and Director of the Babylon Center at Tilburg University, the Netherlands. He is the author of *The Sociolinguistics of Globalization* (Cambridge University Press, 2010) and *Ethnography, Superdiversity and Linguistic Landscapes: Chronicles of Complexity* (Multilingual Matters, 2013).

Mari D'Agostino is a Full Professor of Italian Linguistics at the University of Palermo. She directs the School of Italian Language for Foreigners (ItaStra) and the 2nd level Master's (post MA) in 'Theory, Design and Didactics of Italian as L2/LS' at the same university and has coordinated the PhD in 'Literary, Philological and Linguistic Studies'. Mari's interests focus on Italian sociolinguistics, migration and transnational communities, literacy education and second language learning for adults.

Anna De Fina is Professor of Italian Language and Linguistics and Chair of the Italian Department at Georgetown University. Her interests focus on narrative, discourse and identity, immigrant and transnational communities and superdiversity. Anna has published widely on a variety of sociolinguistics topics, from the discourse construction of identities to the use of media among transnational communities, from narratives in immigrant discourse to the role of ethnography in sociolinguistic research. Her latest publication is the *Handbook of Discourse Studies*, co-edited with Alexandra Georgakopoulou (Cambridge University Press, 2020).

Ana Deumert is Professor at the University of Cape Town. Her research program is located within the broad field of African sociolinguistics and has a strong transdisciplinary focus. She has worked on topics in historical sociolinguistics, the history of linguistics, sociolinguistic and decolonial theory, as well as digital communication.

Gomes O. Kayode is the founder of *Love Planet*, an LGBTQI organization for African asylum seekers and refugees, providing services and addressing issues relating to health, rights and social well-being with focus on LGBTQI, people with disability, people living with STI/HIV/AIDS, commercial sex workers and migrants/refugees. He is a blogger and filmmaker.

Marco Jacquemet is Professor of Communication and Culture at the University of San Francisco. His scholarship focuses on the communicative mutations produced by the circulation of migrants and media idioms in the Mediterranean area. His most significant English publications to date are *Credibility in Court: Communicative Practices in the Camorra's Criminal Trials* (2nd edn, Cambridge University Press, 2009) and *Ethereal Shadows: Communication and Power in Contemporary Italy* (co-authored with Franco Berardi, Autonomedia, 2009).

Katrijn Maryns is Assistant Professor in the Department of Translation, Interpreting and Communication at Ghent University, Belgium. She examines discursive practices and linguistic inequality in institutional contexts of asylum and migration. Katrijn is the author of *The Asylum Speaker: Language in the Belgian Asylum Procedure* (Routledge, 2006) and co-editor of the book series Translation, Interpreting and Social Justice in a Globalised World (Multilingual Matters).

Gerardo Mazzaferro is Researcher in English Language and Linguistics at the University of Turin (Italy). He has carried out research in several fields of multilingualism and the sociolinguistics of immigration. Gerardo is the organizer of the International Conference on the Sociolinguistics of Immigration (Slimig). His most recent publication is *Translanguaging as Everyday Practice* (Springer, 2018).

Roberta Piazza is Reader in English Language & Linguistics at the University of Sussex, UK. Her research is in the area of discourse, ethnography and sociolinguistics as well as media discourse. Lately she has concentrated on aspects of narrative and identity with regard to mobile individuals with uncanonical relations to place, e.g. Travellers and Gypsies, squatters and diasporic groups. Roberta has published in international journals and is the editor of several volumes on various aspects of discourse. Her most recent publication is *The Discursive Construction of Identity and Space among Mobile People* (Bloomsbury, 2020).

Maria Sabaté-Dalmau (MA, Linguistic Anthropology, University of Toronto; PhD, English Studies, Universitat Autònoma de Barcelona) is Associate Professor at University of Lleida, where she conducts critical sociolinguistic ethnographic research on (im)mobilities and multilingualism. She is Chair of the board of the Catalan Sociolinguistics Society. Maria's published work includes *Migrant Communication Enterprises: Regimentation and Resistance* (Multilingual Matters, 2014).

Bahiru Shewaye is a filmmaker and storyteller from Ethiopia. He is the co-founder of *House of Guramayle*, a platform that advocates for respect and dignity for the LGBTI Ethiopian community. Bahiru's podcast, *Alen Show*, demystifies misconceptions about queer people and promotes counter-narratives in Ethiopia, Africa and throughout the world.

Stef Slembrouck is a Senior Full Professor in the English section of the Linguistics Department of Ghent University. His research concentrates on the role of language use and communicative practices in the construction of institutional identities (social welfare, health, administration, education), often with particular reference to the implications of migration and globalization-affected multilingualism.

Massimiliano Spotti is Senior Lecturer in the Department of Culture Studies at Tilburg University, the Netherlands. Further, within the same institution, he is Deputy Director of Babylon – Centre for the Study of Superdiversity. For a number of years, his ethnographic discourse-analytical work has focused on the topic of identity construction within learning environments characterized by the presence of ethnic, linguistic and religious diversity. Currently, Massimiliano's research line focuses on investigating the online-offline nexus and the implications this has for institutional encounters in asylum-seeking procedures in both the Netherlands and Flanders.

Birgul Yilmaz is a British Academy postdoctoral researcher at UCL, Institute of Education in the Department of Culture, Communication and Media. Her postdoctoral research project deals with refugees' language practices and their everyday lives in squats (and previously refugee camps). Birgul's research interests are language and migration, language and humanitarian governmentality and international law.

Acknowledgements

We dedicate this volume to Jan Blommaert. Without his work and the inspiration that it provided to all of us, this book would have not been possible. We are also forever indebted to him for having devoted precious hours of his life, which was by then already coming to an end, to write the postscript to the contributions.

Introduction

Anna De Fina and Gerardo Mazzaferro

Mobility has been a key term in a variety of disciplines including sociology, anthropology, migration studies, media studies and sociolinguistics in the last 20 years, so much so that according to Hannam *et al.*:

> The 'mobility turn' is spreading into and transforming the social sciences, not only placing new issues on the table, but also transcending disciplinary boundaries and putting into question the fundamental 'territorial' and 'sedentary' precepts of twentieth-century social science. (Hannam *et al.*, 2006: 1)

As we will discuss below, the construct itself is subject to multiple interpretations and understandings, but its preeminence in the social sciences indicates the importance of the phenomena that it tries to capture. Indeed, the rise of mobility has been connected with the overwhelming impact of flows of people, goods, technologies, capitals, information and cultural items that has come to be a reality in 21st century societies. These changes have been captured by scholars of modernity such as Appadurai (1996) and Bauman (1996). As noted by Salazar (2018: 154), a new vocabulary has been introduced to reflect on and describe different facets of mobility and its consequences. The idea of *flows* (Castells, 2000), for example, has been used to characterize ways in which movement of different entities happens, the prefix *trans* has been applied to a variety of adjectives or nouns (such as cultural, national, idiomatic, language), and contexts that are relevant to exchange and movement have been called *scapes* (Appadurai, 1996) and *pathways* (Lo & Park, 2017). In addition, there has been a surge of interest in borders and border crossing – as reflected in recent books and conferences – which is part of a new emphasis on the significance for social collaboration, conflict and change of so-called 'contact zones' (Pratt, 1991).

Research in the area of migration studies has been influential in pushing the idea that many individuals and groups on the planet do not inhabit single worlds and are not members of individual societies, but rather are part of transnational flows that involve not only economic processes such as the sending of remittances to their countries of origin, but also cultural processes and products. According to Glick-Schiller *et al.* (1992: 1), for example, transnational individuals actively 'build social fields that link together their country of origin and their country of settlement'; therefore, studying their identities, ideologies and ways of life involves analyzing processes and practices that are different from those that are relevant for people who are firmly grounded in one place. In particular, it requires an understanding of belonging as multiple, contradictory and deterritorialized rather than as unitary and rooted (on this point, see also De Fina & Perrino, 2013), and also a consideration of hybridity, a construct that had been widely employed in studies about identities. Indeed, as noted by Iyall Smith (2008: 5) 'Hybridity encompasses partial identities, multiple roles and pluralistic selves.'

At the same time as thinking about migration has evolved, our view of the way in which world relations and equilibria have changed in the last 30 years has also shifted because of the emergence of a variety of phenomena related to mobility. The new role played by international corporations in the conduct of economic affairs (Fairclough, 2006) and the growing reliance of developing countries on remittances by migrants and their relocation of significant resources across borders are just some of the phenomena that are seen as underlying economic globalization and dictating new relations between centers and peripheries (Heller, 2003). To these changes, we need to add the shifting of borders, the sudden emergence of new conflicts, ecological disasters and wars in different parts of the planet, with consequent readjustments in transglobal political and military equilibria. These transformations have gone hand in hand with a technological revolution initially introduced by the availability of mobile phones (see Vertovec, 2010), and later by growing access to electronic communication and media that has radically altered communicative practices, pop culture manifestations and the ways in which social networks are constituted and operate (Androutsopoulos, 2010; boyd, 2011).

The Turn to Mobility in Sociolinguistics

In sociolinguistics, the turn to mobility has spurred a profound reflection on the ways in which languages and identities are envisioned, on the role of language in relation to other resources and to the contexts in which it is used, on the relationships between social semiotics, times and spaces, and of course also on the methodologies for studying linguistic phenomena. These changes have been developing since the beginning of the new century and are now in full display. Two movements also greatly contributed to the shift towards mobility: the superdiversity orientation and the sociolinguistics of globalization. The influence of these approaches to the intersection of language and social life are clear in the contributions collected here, and for this reason we want to briefly discuss some of the main ideas that they have developed and inspired.

The concept of superdiversity came about initially as a direct response to the changes in the patterns and composition of migration flows to Europe. Vertovec (2010) recognized that migrants are not following the same routes as in the past, that they do not constitute stable and homogeneous communities in the countries in which they arrive, and that their trajectories of mobility can be very complex and so can be their networks as they establish ties and connections in different geographical areas. As a result of all of this, many urban but also some peripheral areas have become contact zones and have witnessed the intensification of occasions for different cultural and ethnic groups and individuals of varied origins to live side by side and to interact with each other.

For sociolinguistics these realities and the reflections put forth by superdiversity scholars (see, for example, Arnault *et al.*, 2015, Blommaert & Rampton, 2011; Creese & Blackledge, 2018; De Fina *et al.*, 2017) have been important in pointing to a number of consequences of these societal changes for the way we theorize and study language. One first consequence is the emphasis on mobility and plurality within languages, with a rejection of what Blommaert (2017: 95) has called 'sedentary models' of language and context.

Such a vision, to which traditional sociolinguistic models subscribed, regarded languages as rooted within communities, largely stable and homogeneous based on ethnic and often also territorial identities. Leaving aside the problems with the mechanisms for identifying speech communities (see Rampton, 2009, for a critique), this approach appears limited today because of the increasing presence of a variety of types of communities that share communicative (rather than simply linguistic) resources, many of which are virtual, and the increasing physical and digital mobility of individuals, which highlights the need to think of linguistic resources as also mobile and in continuous transformation.

A second trend in sociolinguistics that the superdiversity movement has highlighted has been precisely the rejection of a view of languages as stable and predefined entities and the analysis of linguistic phenomena in isolation from their interaction with other semiotic systems. This has brought about a stress on languages as assemblages of resources, as embodied, contextualized within physical and digital environments, mediatized and imbricated with other resources. Superdiversity scholars have also underscored how a view of languages as resources is fundamental to understanding and being able to analyze multilingualism as it has emerged under superdiverse conditions. Indeed, the diversification of human contacts and the access to global resources generates continuous innovations in communication patterns not only in the ways in which named languages are used and mixed, but also in the manners of incorporation of a variety of visual and multimodal resources. These insights are at the center of transformative trends such as the 'translanguaging' (Hua et al., 2017; Li, 2018) movement and the conceptualization of languages as parts of not only 'landscapes' but also other kinds of scapes (Pennycook & Otsuji, 2015). Within those trends there is now a recognition of the fact that translanguaging phenomena do not simply cover the mixing of different languages, but include combinations of registers and styles and the mobilization of varieties of resources.

The sociolinguistics of globalization (see Blommaert, 2010; Lo & Park, 2017) has also been influential in favoring a shift towards mobility by underscoring how communicative resources are not anchored to specific contexts, but rather are themselves mobile and acquire different values and meanings not only through time but also in connection with different spaces. Discourses get circulated as well and they are continuously subject to recontextualization. At the same time, linguistic and semiotic resources move with people, as they go along trajectories and spaces. The circulation of resources and discourses is at the center of processes of enregisterment (Agha, 2007, 2008) and of the spread of ideologies. Central to these understandings is the concept of scales (Blommaert, 2015) or ranges of scopes of different types on which the significance of phenomena is valued and understood. Scales allow linguists to think in terms of multiple ways in which linguistic resources are affected by and affect contexts rather than in terms of binary oppositions (for example, between micro and macro levels). Resources acquire different value when transported from one place to the other. For example, thinking of multilingual individuals, someone who has the ability to speak a certain variety of English may enjoy a certain prestige as that variety is highly valued at a local level, but that resource may be of no use in another area where, for example, another variety may have either more prestige or greater utility. Linguistic skills may be socially scaled up or down according to where and when they are used and they may be associated with different indexical orders as they get transported. By underscoring the importance of multiple contexts and scales, the sociolinguistics of globalization has also brought our attention to the dynamic relations between centers and peripheries in that globalization has shown that the processes that link centers and peripheries respond to power hierarchies, but are also subject to changes, shifts and readjustments. So not only the economies and social processes, but also the cultural and communicative practices located in or associated with peripheries, can suddenly become prominent or conquer the mainstream, especially thanks to the wide reach of digital technology. This has been shown, for example, with cultural phenomena such as rap music (Pennycook, 2007), but also with linguistic phenomena such as the diffusion of communicative practices and languages related to resistant minorities or protest movements, such as the examples of innovations of English in Hong Kong documented by Li (2020).

Another way in which the turn to mobility has manifested itself in sociolinguistics in recent times has been in the new focus on the interconnections between spaces, identities, communicative practices and resources. Indeed, the critical reconsideration of the fact that identities, communities and languages are no longer necessarily defined by their ties with well-demarcated spaces such as geographical areas, cities, neighborhoods and so forth has led to a reflection on the role of different kinds of spaces (including virtual or imagined ones) in the configuration and negotiation of identities and in the development of communicative practices. Work on migration and belonging (Horner & Dailey O'Cain, 2020) and on digital media and multilingualism (Androutsopoulous, 2006; Androutsopoulos & Juffermans, 2014) and recent reflections on linguistic landscapes (O'Connor & Zentz, 2016; Seargeant & Giaxoglou, 2020; Stroud & Mpendukana, 2009) have been central in demonstrating the evolving and mutual interconnections between the way spaces are constructed and lived, identities are configured and communicative resources are used. In a recent edited volume, Horner and O'Cain (2020) showcase work in which belonging is analyzed as expressed differently in relation to different spaces and in which spaces in turn are seen as constraining and influencing the way people (un)belong. Research on digital technologies and multilingualism has brought to light the importance of virtual spaces as domains in which mobile people construct social networks but also where new literacies and linguistic practices are developed. Recent research on linguistic landscapes has suggested an approach to the study of the interactions between places and semiotic resources in terms of a sociolinguistics of multilingual mobility, in the sense that it traces 'the passage and transport of discourses as the unit of analysis across sites and artifacts' (Stroud & Mpendukana, 2009: 363), while at the same time investigating 'how sites are differentially produced in the flow of messages' (2009: 363).

Finally, work on chronotopes has greatly contributed to demolishing static and territorially bound views of identities and social practices by positing the essential connectedness between space/time and identities. Starting from Bakhtin's (1981: 84) definition of the chronotope as expressing the 'intrinsic connectedness of temporal and spatial relationships', Blommaert and De Fina (2017) have argued that much of the identity work that participants in interactions do can be conceptualized in chronotopic terms in the sense that identities are not static or pre-given but are profoundly connected with specific configurations of time and space. Such a conception, which has seen a great deal of development in sociolinguistics (see, for example, De Fina et al., 2020; Karimzad & Catedral, 2018; Kroon & Swanenberg, 2020; Procházka, 2018), draws attention to the fact that identities and contexts are multiple, mobile and evolving, and that small changes in spatiotemporal frames can involve huge shifts in meaning-making practices and identities. Chronotopic analysis also emphasizes how participants in interaction bring to bear in their present communications semiotic chunks that are tied to different temporalities and scales.

In that sense, it is important to remember that time and space are embedded in discursive and ideological frames; that is, they are not neutral or void of power – by contrast, they are inscribed into webs of power relations and discourses, which are constitutive of specific subjectivities and identities (Foucault, 1980). Although identity is dependent on power relations, it is within the latter that individuals are able to construct resistive subjectivities and practices. As argued by Butler (1995: 46), 'to claim that the subject is constituted is not to claim that it is determined: on the contrary, the constituted character of the subject is the very precondition of its agency'.

Mobilities and Immobilities

Above we have summarized some of the ideas and concepts that underlie the contributions to this book. In this section we discuss our main focus – (im)mobilities – and we point to ways in which our volume can contribute to studying it. Much of the literature that has taken this construct as a fundamental point of departure has not, in our view, fully reflected on the definitions of mobility, the characteristics of different types of mobility and, importantly, on the dynamics between mobilities and immobilities.

Salazar (2018) eloquently points to some of these limitations when he notes that mobility is too often seen exclusively from a positive angle and:

> This translates into three assumptions, partly influenced by neoliberal and capitalist ideologies, which are widely spread via public discourses and images about globalization: (1) there is (increasing) mobility; (2)

mobility is a self-evident phenomenon; and (3) movement generates positive change, often conceived of as an improvement for oneself and one's kin (e.g., in the case of migrants) or for non-related others (e.g., in the case of NGO-workers). (Salazar, 2018: 154)

The other side of the coin is an excessive stress on immobilities in the case of certain social categories, prominently when it comes to economic and vulnerable migrants. Indeed, even though these migrants are seen as mobile in physical terms, they are also often portrayed as economically, socially and linguistically immobile. Much of the literature on migration presents them as passive recipients of policies and discourses, as victims of historical processes, which effectively leads to seeing them as immobile.

One point that we want to make through the collection of contributions in this book is that in order to understand mobile people and mobile phenomena it is important first of all to appreciate that there are different kinds of mobility and, second, that there is a continuous and complex dynamic between mobility and immobility. In terms of kinds of mobility: there is the commonsense understanding of the construct as referring to physically moving, particularly moving from one place to another and/or transiting through places as it happens when people migrate. But people can move with their imagination or they can move by virtually networking; they can move by ascending or descending the social ladder. At the same time, they can also be moved or forcefully removed. In the same way as languages can move with people or across objects, discourses and signs participate in flows of communication, and so forth. But none of these types of movements can be fully understood without considering the constant and continuing shifting relations between mobility and immobility. These are absolutely evident in this time of the Covid-19 pandemic during which we are writing, as people's unprecedented mobility across borders has facilitated the spread of a virus that has made us immobile. But being physically stuck in our places has also contributed to an unprecedented volume of virtual exchanges and communications. Thus, mobilities and immobilities are inevitably and intricately bound and related to each other. It is clear, for example, that the mobility of a group or an individual often represents the other side of the immobility of other groups or individuals and profound socio-economic differences are revealed through the ways in which physical, social and cultural mobilities and immobilities are distributed. The great economic inequalities in our era lead to forced mobilities for many while ensuring stability and permanence for others. At the same time, mobility and immobility are also linked by their occurrence together either concurrently or at intervals as we saw above. Economic migrants who look for a better life are pushed by their needs and or by their dreams to take to the road, but they are subject to hurdles and obstacles such as the closure of safe passage areas, the lack of money to continue their trips, incarcerations and illness that stop them in their tracks for short or very extended period. When they get to their destinations, they are often stuck through bureaucratic procedures. As Salazar (2020) notes:

> ... to assess the extent or nature of movement, or, indeed, even 'observe' it sometimes, you have to spend time studying things that stand still: the borders, institutions and territories of nation-states, and the (imagined) sedentary 'home' cultures of those that do not move. In other words, motion is always framed within a material and institutional infrastructure, and the circulation of people is constantly limited or promoted by economic coercions, political guarantees and sociocultural imaginaries. ... Even those who do not move are affected by movements of people in or out of their communities, and by the resulting changes. (Salazar, 2020: 770)

In this sense, it is also important to highlight the role of a critical approach to the phenomena we have been talking about. As many social scientists have noted (see, for example, Abram *et al.*, 2017; Casas-Cortes *et al.*, 2015; Salazar & Smart, 2011), the experience of mobilities and immobilities is not the same for everyone. Issues of gender, social class, geographical or ethnic origin, social status and so forth underlie the experience of different groups and individuals and there is a great deal that we still do not know about those differences and that we need to investigate in a socially sensitive way. Hence, our focus is on populations and individuals who have been or are marginalized, on bureaucratic and gatekeeping processes, on issues of power and resistance. In this volume we aim at advancing the investigation of issues of mobility/immobility in sociolinguistics by exploring how mobilities are affected by and in turn affect power dynamics and relations, the kinds of resources that people use and how they use them within communication processes that emerge within different types of (im)mobilities, and the role of agency in the management of (im)mobilities. Our contributors focus on the tensions between institutional blocks to physical and social mobility and the desires and aspirations of mobile people; they discuss how linguistic and semiotic resources are deployed in order to resist these obstacles or to perpetrate them, to counter discourses of immobility or to impose them. Thus, they also investigate subjectivities and agentive meaning-making practices through which (im)mobility is recontextualized and reconfigured by individuals and groups from their own perspective. With these considerations in mind, we now move on to describe the chapters within this volume in some detail.

Overview of the Chapters

Part 1 of this volume is devoted to the issues concerning the (im)mobilization of repertoires of language resources and meaning-making practices of individuals on the move, namely migrants, across different sociolinguistic timespace configurations. The focus is on how asylum seekers and refugees, who are both stuck in timespaces of enforced and involuntary (im)mobility and subject to border regulations and practices, are in some ways able to mobilize and negotiate repertoires of resources, which are encapsulated in their life and migratory trajectories. **Mari D'Agostino** explores young African migrants' linguistic repertoires across geographical and digitally interconnected spaces, characterized by different temporalities and spatialities. In line with Busch (2012), the author conceptualizes linguistic repertoires as lived and dynamic, that is, 'heteroglossic and contingent space[s] of potentialities [...] to which speakers revert in specific situations' (Busch, 2012: 521). By drawing on sociolinguistic and ethnographic fieldwork among migrant women living in South Australia, **Necia Stanford Billinghurst** offers a case study on the relationships between language and space in migratory processes. She focuses on Lingua (pseudonym), a South Sudanese woman, and her ability to construct language practices tactically (de Certeau, 1984) across various timespaces of (im)mobility in order to negotiate her sense of identity and belonging as well as to contrast social exclusion and inequalities. **Katrijn Maryns and Stef Slembrouck** address the issue of the management of language resources in institutional encounters between service providers, refugees and asylum seekers, who navigate governing systems that attempt to establish the conditions of their (im)mobility. The focus is on mediation of institutional literacies and practices through a globally (im)mobile language, namely English, and meta-communicative resources. The authors demonstrate how, even in situations where participants in the interaction are oriented towards mutuality and cooperation, lack of institutional literacies and language resources may affect processes of meaning-making.

As the chapters in **Part 2** illustrate, (im)mobility is tied to multiscale discourses and ideologies, which aim to regulate and control geographical and social (im)mobility of individuals and populations through bio-politics and neoliberal governmentality (Foucault, 1980, 2008), making 'mobility possible for some individuals and impossible for others' (Larsen, 2016: 28). **Maria Sabaté-Dalmau** takes a critical stance on information and communicative technologies regimes guided by the logics of market and tied to neoliberal governmentality. The author focuses on the strategies, instruments and processes of governance of 'illegal' migrants and transnational individuals and groups through advertisement discourse, aiming to categorize and construct migrants as socioculturally and emotionally passive and immobile subjects in need of 'communicative re-education', inspired by monolingual ideologies. **Massimiliano Spotti** explores national bordering policies and practices, by focusing attention on a story narrated by Bashir, an asylum seeker, during an asylum interview. The author notes how web-based information is used by asylum officers in order to enforce authenticity discourses on language varieties and geographical spaces, which may lead to both the misrecognition of migrants' voices and identities as well as aspirations to (im)mobility. **Marco Jacquemet** reflects on international migration processes within the Mediterranean Sea as discursively constructed and governed by institutional border-crossing policies. By drawing on Deleuze and Guttari's (1987) pragmatic approach to language as inherently political and performative, which is organized around two types of speech acts '*order-words*', or 'statements that "arrest," and *passwords*, statements that "move"' (Vallee, 2019: 74, emphasis in original), the author makes clear how order-words, namely anti-immigration media discourse, serve to legitimate and enforce restrictive national and European migration politics. On the other hand, passwords, in the form of non-standard language usage, namely slogans, are used to contrast and resist government's control over migrants and NGOs, who save migrants' lives attempting to cross the Mediterranean Sea.

In **Part 3** of this volume, contributors turn to issues concerning the relationship between power and resistance as both inextricably interwoven and spatiotemporally organized. They note how physically and discursively immobilized vulnerable individuals are able to carve out timespaces of resistance by constructing counter-conducts as well as language practices in order to contrast regimes of immobility. **Anna De Fina and Gerardo Mazzaferro** investigate resistance as constructed in and through everyday translanguaging practices conceived as communicative counter-conducts through which asylum seekers within temporary reception centers in Italy resist both social and physical immobilization and oppose monolingual ideologies and practices. **Ana Deumert** raises the question of settler colonialism as a spatial, economic and symbolic structure of dispossession. The author examines the case of recent media debates on beachplaces as spaces of symbolic domination and political struggle as well as resistance to ideologies of racial segregation and domination in post-apartheid South Africa. Central is the issue of the racially structured experiences of space, specifically control over movement of racialized bodies across spaces, and more specifically how 'micro-mobilities' of black beachgoers hinder 'white'-mobilities, which are part of the settler colonial project and imaginary. **Birgul Yilmaz** turns to the investigation of language teaching and learning as tools for the management and governing of vulnerable subjects within the 'panoptic' space of the refugees' camp in Lesvos Island, Greece. She explores how individuals within the camp construct certain behaviors or counter-conducts, which challenge neoliberal humanitarian governmentality and its attempt to normalize and conduct refugees' lives through the imposition of Greek-only language teaching and learning.

The interplays between spaces of (im)mobility and their indexical significance, perception and configuration in terms of individual subjectivities, identities and human agency are touched upon in the chapters in **Part 4. Mike Baynham, Bahiru Shewaye and Gomes O. Kayode** explore queer migration narratives with special attention to asylum seekers' backstories of sexual and gender identity construction and ideological becoming across heteronormative timespaces. The authors note how asylum seekers' past events and formative experiences, which shape the chronotope or timespace coordinates of their life story from child to young adult (Bakhtin, 1981), are key to both ambition and desire to move as well as capacity and possibility for human agency. **Roberta Piazza** provides insights into how Tracy, a female Irish traveler, constructs herself as an agentive and reflexive subject across experiential spaces of semi-mobility and immobility. The author points out that Tracy's agency is both spatio-temporally dependent and socially constructed or in need of social and institutional recognition. Tracy does not consider (im)mobility as inherently positive or negative. While she sees her actual condition of immobility as materially desirable, ensuring a certain degree of economic independence as well as self-dignity and security, semi-mobility, a safe timespace where she can act as a fully agentive and reflexive subject, remains a key factor for her recognition as an intelligible subject.

In his postscript, **Jan Blommaert** summarizes the most pertinent concepts to frame the volume by providing his own personal evaluations on the complex issue of (im)mobility. For Blommaert, (im)mobility is due to 'social and institutional power' as well as articulated around the two poles of possibility and impossibility. That is, (im)mobility is differently enacted and asymmetrically distributed across different scales and chronotopes.

References

Abram, S., Feldman Bianco, B., Khosravi, S., Salazar, N. and de Genova, N. (2017) The free movement of people around the world would be utopian. *Identities: Global Studies in Culture and Power* 24 (2), 123–155.

Agha, A. (2007) *Language and Social Relations.* New York: Cambridge University Press.
Agha, A. (2008) Voice, footing, enregisterment. *Linguistic Anthropology* 15 (1), 38–59.
Androutsopoulous, J. (2006) Multilingualism, diaspora and the internet: Codes and identities on German-based diaspora websites. *Journal of Sociolinguistics* 10 (4), 520–547.
Androutsopoulos, J. (2010) Localizing the global on the participatory web. In N. Coupland (ed.) *The Handbook of Language and Globalization* (pp. 203–231). Oxford: Wiley-Blackwell.
Androutsopoulous, J. and Juffermans, K. (2014) Digital language practices in superdiversity: Introduction. Special Issue Discourse, Context and Media, 4–5, 1–6.
Appadurai, A. (1996) *Modernity at Large: Cultural Dimensions of Globalization.* Minneapolis, MN: University of Minnesota Press.
Arnaut, K., Blommaert, J., Rampton, B. and Spotti, M. (eds) (2015) *Language and Superdiversity.* New York: Routledge.
Bakhtin, M. (1981) *The Dialogic Imagination: Four Essays* (C. Emerson and M. Holquist, trans.). Austin, TX: University of Texas Press.
Bauman, Z. (1996) From pilgrim to tourist: Or a short history of identity. In S. Hall and P. Du Gay (eds) *Questions of Cultural Identity* (pp. 18–36). London: Sage.
Blommaert, J. (2010) *The Sociolinguistics of Globalization.* Cambridge: Cambridge University Press.
Blommaert, J. (2015) Chronotopes, scales, and complexity in the study of language in society. *Annual Review of Anthropology* 44, 105–116.
Blommaert, J. (2017) Commentary: Mobility, contexts, and the chronotope. *Language in Society* 46, 95–99. doi:10.1017/S0047404516000841
Blommaert, J. and De Fina, A. (2017) Chronotopic identities. On the timespace organization of who we are. In A. De Fina, D. Ikizoglu and J. Wegner (eds) *Diversity and Superdiversity: Sociocultural Linguistic Perspectives* (pp. 1–15). Washington, DC: Georgetown University Press.
Blommaert, J. and Rampton, B. (2011) Language and superdiversity. *Diversities* 13 (2), 1–21.
boyd, d. (2011) Social networked sites as networked publics: Affordances, dynamics, and implications. In Z. Papacharissi (ed.) *A Networked Self: Identity, Community, and Culture in Social Network Sites* (pp. 39–58). New York: Routledge.
Busch, B. (2012) The linguistic repertoire revisited. *Applied Linguistics* 33 (5), 503–523. doi:10.1093/applin/ams056
Butler, J. (1995) Contingent foundations: Feminism and the question of 'postmodernism'. In S. Benhabib, J. Butler, D. Cornell and N. Fraser (eds) *Feminist Contentions: A Philosophical Exchange* (pp. 35–57). New York: Routledge.
Casas-Cortes, M., Cobarrubias, S., De Genova, N., Garelli, G., Grappi, G. and Heller, C. (2015) New keywords: Migration and borders. *Cultural Studies* 29 (1), 55–87.
Castells, M. (2000) *The Rise of The Network Society.* Oxford: Blackwell.
Creese, A. and Blackledge, A. (eds) (2018) *The Routledge Handbook of Language and Superdiversity.* New York: Routledge.
de Certeau, M. (1984) *The Practice of Everyday Life* (S. Rendall, trans). Berkeley, CA: University of California Press.
De Fina, A. and Perrino, S. (2013) Transnational identities. *Applied Linguistics* 34 (5), 509–515.
De Fina, A., Ikizoglu, D. and Wegner, J. (eds) (2017) *Diversity and Superdiversity: Sociocultural Linguistic Perspectives.* Washington, DC: Georgetown University Press.
De Fina, A., Paternostro, G. and Amoruso, M. (2020) Odysseus the traveler: Appropriation of a chronotope in a community of practice. *Language & Communication* 70, 71–81.

Deleuze, G. and Guattari, F. (1987) *A Thousand Plateaus: Capitalism and Schizophrenia*. Minneapolis, MN: University of Minnesota Press.
Fairclough, N. (2006) *Language and Globalization*. Abingdon: Routledge.
Foucault, M. (1980) *Power and Knowledge: Selected Interviews and Other Writings 1972–1977* (C. Gordon, ed.; C. Gordon, L. Marshal, J. Mepham and K. Sober, trans). New York: Pantheon.
Foucault, M. (2008) *The Birth of Biopolitics: Lectures at the Collège de France, 1978–1979*. Basingstoke: Palgrave Macmillan.
Glick-Schiller, N., Basch, L. and Blanc, C.S. (1992) *Towards a Transnational Perspective on Migration: Race, Class, Ethnicity and Nationalism Reconsidered*. New York: Annals of the New York Academy of Sciences.
Hannam, K., Sheller, M. and Urry, J. (2006) Editorial: Mobilities, immobilities and moorings. *Mobilities* 1 (1), 1–22.
Heller, M. (2003) Globalization, the new economy, and the commodification of language and identity. *Journal of Sociolinguistics* 7, 473–492.
Horner, K. and Dailey-O'Cain, J. (eds) (2020) *Multilingualism, (Im)mobilities and Spaces of Belonging*. Bristol: Multilingual Matters.
Hua, Z., Li, W. and Lyons, A. (2017) Polish shop(ping) as translanguaging space. *Social Semiotics* 27 (4), 411–433.
Iyall Smith, K. (2008) Hybrid identities: Theoretical examinations. In K.E. Iyall Smith and P. Leavy (eds) *Hybrid Identities: Theoretical and Empirical Examinations* (pp. 3–12). Leiden: Brill.
Karimzad, F. and Catedral, L. (2018) 'No, we don't mix languages': Ideological power and the chronotopic organization of ethnolinguistic identities. *Language in Society* 47 (1), 89–113.
Kroon, S. and Swanenberg, J. (2020) *Chronotopic Identity Work: Sociolinguistic Analyses of Cultural and Linguistic Phenomena in Time and Space*. Bristol: Multilingual Matters.
Larsen, M.A. (2016) *Internationalization of Higher Education: An Analysis through Spatial, Network and Mobilities Theories*. New York: Palgrave Macmillan.
Li, W. (2018) Translanguaging as a practical theory of language *Applied Linguistics* 39 (1), 9–30.
Li, W. (2020) Multilingual English users' linguistic innovation. *World Englishes* 39, 236–248.
Lo, A. and Park, J.K. (2017) Metapragmatics of mobility. *Language in Society* 46, 1–4.
O'Connor, B.H. and Zentz, L. (2016) Theorizing mobility in semiotic landscapes: Evidence from South Texas and Central Java. *Linguistic Landscape* 2 (1), 26–51.
Pennycook, A. (2007) Language, localization, and the real: Hip-Hop and the global spread of authenticity. *Journal of Language, Identity & Education* 6 (2), 101–115.
Pennycook, A. and Otsuji, E. (2015) Making scents of the landscape. *Linguistic Landscape* 1 (3), 191–212.
Pratt, M.L. (1991) Arts of the contact zone. *Profession* 1991, 33–40.
Procházka, O. (2018) A chronotopic approach to identity performance in a Facebook meme. *Discourse, Context & Media* 25, 78–87.
Rampton, B. (2009) Speech community. In N. Coupland and A. Jaworski (eds) *The New Sociolinguistics Reader* (2nd edn) (pp. 694–713). London: Red Globe Press.
Salazar, N.B. (2018) Theorizing mobility through concepts and figures. *Tempo Social, Revista de Sociologia* 30 (2), 153–168.
Salazar, N.B. (2020) On imagination and imaginaries, mobility and immobility: Seeing the forest for the trees. *Culture & Psychology* 26 (4), 768–777.

Salazar, N.B. and Smart, A. (eds) (2011) Anthropological takes on (im)mobility. *Identities: Global Studies in Culture and Power* 18 (6), i–ix. doi:10.1080/1070289X.2012.683674

Seargeant, P. and Giaxoglou, K. (2020) Discourse and the linguistic landscape. In A. De Fina and A. Georgakopoulou (eds) *Handbook of Discourse Studies* (pp. 282–305). Cambridge: Cambridge University Press.

Stroud, C. and Mpendukana, S. (2009) Towards a material ethnography of linguistic landscape: Multilingualism, mobility and space in a South African township. *Journal of Sociolinguistic*s 13 (3), 363-386.

Vallee, M. (2019) *Sounding Bodies, Sounding Worlds: An Exploration of Embodiments in Sound*. Singapore: Palgrave Macmillan.

Vertovec, S. (2010) Superdiversity and its implications. In S. Vertovec (ed.) *Anthropology of Migration and Multiculturalism: New Directions* (pp. 65–96). Abingdon: Routledge.

Part 1

The (Im)mobilization of Language Resources, Repertoires and Practices

1 Multilingual Young African Migrants: Between Mobility and Immobility

Mari D'Agostino

Introduction

This chapter is part of a broader study into new migration experiences and, in particular, that of young migrants who have recently arrived in Italy via the Mediterranean route. The main object under investigation is the linguistic and communicative resources available to these migrants at their point of departure, how these have been used and modified during their journey, and how they have been used and modified through the different phases of their life in Italy (see Amoruso & D'Agostino, 2017; D'Agostino, 2017, 2021a, 2021b; D'Agostino & Mocciaro, 2021). This is understood within the holistic entirety of an individual's repertoire, according to the individuations provided by Brigitta Busch (2012, 2017). We will thus look at both the history and the biography of each speaker, at their cognitive and emotional dimensions and the ideologies and practices of both the subjects themselves and others: 'The repertoire can thus be seen as a hypothetical structure, which evolves by experiencing language in interaction on a cognitive and on an emotional level and is inscribed into corporal memory and embodied as linguistic habitus and which includes traces of hegemonic discourses. These discourses are expressed in categorisations that are backed up by inclusive and exclusive language ideologies' (Busch, 2012: 521). Busch concludes the same work by describing the repertoire as a 'heteroglossic (...) space of potentialities' which includes 'imagination and desire':

> Drawing on a broad range of earlier voices, discourses, and codes, the linguistic repertoire forms a heteroglossic and contingent space of potentialities which includes imagination and desire, and to which speakers revert in specific situations. (Busch, 2012: 521)

The centrality held by a revised notion of repertoire within linguistic research today has been noted by many. Within a wide-spanning re-examination of the bases and methods of sociolinguistics, Hall *et al.* (2006: 232) defined repertoire(s) as 'conventionalized constellations of semiotic resources for taking action – that are shaped by the particular practices in which individuals engage' (see also Otsuij & Pennycook, 2010). Blommaert (2008, 2010) has also emphasised how the repertoire ought to be seen not from pre-established linguistic constructions (languages, dialects, variations) but through focusing our attention on resources in a continuous state of flux. In particular, Blommaert (2008: 16) refers to that which he calls a 'polyglot repertoire', which he claims cannot be associated to a particular national space, nor to a stable linguistic national order, but rather to the life of a single individual, following a particular human and social trajectory. This represents an important shift away from those models that bound (and bind) the concept instead to structure, system and regularity, moving instead towards approaches that put fluidity and creativity of individual and collective linguistic practice in the spotlight. This perspective is particularly important for the current research, which focuses on the analysis of linguistic behaviour among young people from African contexts, in which the complex expressed forms of multilingualism relating to the individual, space and discourse make it even more important to examine the fluidity of linguistic practices rather than abstract constructions and systems as such. This follows the suggestions of Lüpke and Storch (2013), who pick out two crucial questions for sociolinguistic studies of African contexts:

> The first is that speakers' profiles can be better described and understood in terms of registers and repertoires than in terms of discrete languages. The second observation is that just as there are no fixed languages or fixed linguistic identities, there is no fixed alignment of linguistic practice with ethnically or otherwise construed aspects of identity. (Lüpke & Storch, 2013: 2)

It is also important to bear a series of complex features in mind that characterise the forms of migration that we will be looking at in this study. For the young African migrants examined herein, the great experience of digital connection and spatial mobility is often accompanied by physical and spatial segregation. This first aspect has been frequently studied within the category of 'connected migrants', especially in Dana Diminescu's (2008) essay, 'The connected migrant: An epistemological manifesto'. The importance of this text is in non-defining migrants on the basis of physical and psychic experience alone, and on their un-rootedness. Over the past few decades we have learnt to think of the migrant as someone who lives in a double absence, excluded from the political and social order of both the locations they have inhabited and inhabit, and still more as someone who lives 'in between', in a no-man's land, both within and outside of the conflicts that they continually traverse. We must now, however, begin to recognise this new dimension of living: being simultaneously here and there. Rather than characterising migration therefore through Abdelmalek Sayad's (1999) famous image of the 'double absence', from both one's own home and that of one's host, the use of digital technologies seems to indicate a 'portability of the networks of belonging'. Connected migrants maintain a sense of co-presence, of their being 'here and there at the same time'.

Diminescu's perspective is situated within a line of inquiry that opens up a radical overcoming of the classic sociological model characterised by integration, assimilation and insertion in favour of a totally new line of inquiry that looks towards movement, participation and connection within range of social locations, within contexts both of departure and arrival:

> If it is true that these new patterns of migration can no longer be ascribed to social processes described in classic terms of integration, assimilation and insertion, then we find ourselves faced with a reversal of our perspective. Questions of integration are going to have to be rethought in the specific context of the multiplication of temporary displacements and the participation in a variety of social milieus. (Diminescu, 2003: 570)

This also necessitates a total revision of models of communication. Here we are not presented with the familiar model of conversation but with a new mode that contains a form of continuous presence leading to important changes in migrants' lives:

> The development of communication practices – from simple 'conversational' methods where communication compensates for absence, to 'connected' modes where the services maintain a form of continuous presence in spite of the distance – has produced the most important change in migrants' lives. Not only have migratory practices been revolutionized (in particular the activation of networks, remote organization, the monitoring of movements) but also the way mobility is experienced and implicitly the construction of relational settlement. (Diminescu, 2008: 572)

The possession of tools that connect people to other spaces and locations thus presents an extraordinary advantage for both organising journey during the months or years of the 'back way' – the terms that Gambians use for the difficult migration route that, so they hope, leads beyond the Mediterranean Sea – as well as reconfiguring models of living on arrival, in particular through the construction of transnational networks that help to sustain their movement within Europe.

Digital connections also play an important role – one that still requires investigation – in all of the phases of enforced immobility in sites of transit and arrival, in periods of physical and social isolation, during phases of segregation and in attempts to resist and overcome it. The last decades of the 20th century saw the development of considerations about how the era of globalisation may in fact be characterised by a growing restriction on movement, which cannot be seen or theorised as a mere 'malfunctioning'. In Bauman's (2000) celebrated *Liquid Modernity*, it is strongly emphasised how the majority of the world's population is more or less permanently immobilised and that differentiation in the possibility of movement is a strategy in and of itself, enacted by governments. This does not only include restrictions due to the costs of movement but rather that which has been called a 'mobility regime' or 'new mobility regimes'. The usefulness of the term lies in emphasising the role of policies, approaches, actions and perceptions in constructing the division between freedom of movement on one side and an illegality of movement on the other. The term 'bounded mobility' has a similar orientation, emphasising the fact that mobility is always bounded, regulated, mediated and intrinsically connected to forms of immobility and unequal power relations (Bougleux, 2016).

Segregation into 'connexions' and prisons in Niger and Libya, and the different forms of isolation in asylum-seeker hostels in Europe after this, in limited physical spaces located far from inhabited centres, is salient for understanding the specific character of current migration experience, including linguistic aspects. For example, there is the continuous learning of the travel and segregation companions' languages or, in Italy, the weak relation with the local dialect that, on the contrary, is present in the previous migratory experiences. What we see here is a regime of immobility and a physical separation that has few precedents in modern history and which – and this cannot be stressed too often – continues for many months following the famous boat landings. Below, we publish a few lines provided by a teacher that describe the reality of isolation in which these young people live for many months following their arrival in Italy, and which they only manage to break out of thanks to immersion in schooling:

> For young immigrants, the school becomes a threshold. It's a door that opens up a whole new world. You can live in Catania, closed up in an asylum seeker hostel for eight months, without knowing that the mountain which you spy from your window each morning isn't actually a mountain, but a volcano. This shouldn't surprise us. That's what isolation is like when there's no chance for conversation, if you can't speak even about pointless things with people 'outside'. (Teacher, Ragusa)

In the section titled 'Multilingualism and Segregation', we will see how immobility and segregation also have an important impact on the dynamics and modifications of the repertoire, just as much as mobility and large movements across earth and sea.

In what follows, we will describe the context within which the data were collected ('Research Context: From Linguistic Inclusion to Research, There and Back Again – the ItaStra Workshops') and analyse the complex issues related to the ethics of research in migratory realities such as those examined here ('Gathering Data Between Inclusion and Fear'). After describing the sample from a quantitative and qualitative point of view ('Methods of Data Gathering and Sampling'), we will focus on the main topic of the chapter ('Speaking Many Languages. But How Many? But Which? But With Whom? But Where?'), that is, the different forms of multilingualism exhibited and practised by young African immigrants ('Some preliminary data'), as well as the relationship between these forms and the long migratory journey ('Plurilingualism Investigation Through Teaching'). Finally, a topic of great importance will be mentioned, that is, the linguistic tools of mutual identification used by those who have passed through Libyan hell ('Multilingualism and Segregation'). Finally, we draw some conclusions.

Research Context: From Linguistic Inclusion to Research, There and Back Again – the ItaStra Workshops

The construction of a complex programme of research as well as the various phases of data collection (both quantitative and qualitative, as described in the section on 'Methods of Data Gathering and Sampling' below) took place for the most part within the remit of a project for linguistic inclusion at the Scuola di Lingua italiana per Stranieri (henceforth, 'ItaStra') at the University of Palermo, which has included thousands of immigrants in its classrooms from 2013 onwards, particularly young people who have recently arrived in Italy by sea.

All of this information, and the stories we draw on here, are taken from the young people who participated in the Italian language courses (some of which have been designed specifically for illiterate people and those with weak literacy), art and theatre workshops, storytelling workshops, projects for understanding the local area, specific training courses in different sectors (e.g. media, tailoring, carpentry) and public events which have gradually seen the increasing protagonism of young migrants themselves in management roles (see Amoruso *et al.*, 2015; D'Agostino, 2021b; Tobagi, 2016).

Without the 'open' space provided by the restored former convent which has formed ItaStra's centre, in which so many young people have spent months of their lives gradually immersing themselves in a cultural and linguistic environment markedly different from the one in which they had lived up until that moment, there would not have been the opportunity for the precise questions that slowly emerged and from which the research work and investigation took inspiration. This context allowed for the gathering of an important sample of quantitative data, produced through tests and questionnaires, but above all allowed for the gathering of hundreds of hours of recorded interviews and interactions of every kind, as well as a systematic investigation of Facebook interactions, which we describe in the section entitled 'Multilingualism and Segregation'.

Almost all of the qualitative data, and the majority of the quantitative data, were gathered once the didactic project was already consolidated and bonds of trust had been formed, i.e. once the space had been constructed not as an institutional one but as 'ItaStra', as the school is known. Many of the questions were asked once the person responding to the questions, simply engaging in conversation or using information from a Facebook profile, had already responded themselves to a range of questions in many different situations, and accompanied migrants through their pathway of social inclusion in Italy for a long time, thus creating bonds of faith, credibility and respect. The interviews were not carried out in the early months of attendance in ItaStra classes, but only after having established a relationship of mutual trust and sharing.

It is worth noting that an important part of the project of inclusion and research carried out over the years has been constructed through contact with the needs of a new kind of migrant who partly coincides with a new juridical category: the 'unaccompanied foreign minor' (herein, UFM). The EU directive 2011/95 defines an unaccompanied foreign minor as one: 'who arrives on the territory of the Member State unaccompanied by an adult responsible for him or her. By law or by the practice of the Member State concerned, and for as long as he or she is not effectively taken into the care of such a person; it includes a minor who is left unaccompanied after he or she has entered the territory of the Member States.' There are thus two parameters: being a child and arriving alone. These two elements have led international legislation to consider these young men as vulnerable subjects and thus in need of special attention. The migration context within which these young people are inserted is relatively recent and little known. The subjects themselves are nearly all young men, and for the most part between 16 and 17 years old, having arrived on the Italian, Spanish and Greek coastlines by boat. In the Italian context, following a high number of Bengali immigrants, there is now a strong presence of young men from The Gambia, Eritrea, Egypt and Nigeria, Senegal and

Mali, as well as other West African countries. The official statistics – as is indeed the case for all newly arriving immigrants – report only these indicators: sex, nationality and age.

UFM (who count for around 15% of the total number of immigrants arriving by sea in Italy between 2014 and 2018, a sum of more than 70,000 people, of whom 90% are between 15 and 17 years old) thus belong, first and foremost, to a juridical category, in the manner of 'asylum seeker' or 'refugee'. Their belonging to this category is established by a juridical/administrative action enacted by a state that attributes each individual with this particular status. The continuing proliferation of juridical/administrative labels is, among other matters, a new element that has grown up alongside these new migrations. In the past, people were simply immigrants and emigrants and then, from a certain point, simply 'migrants' (in Italian, *migranti*), yet today they are destined to very different approaches in their host country (and therefore life conditions) according to the juridical status that is attributed to them on arrival. This is a fundamental point because it determines their relation to the host society (the right – more or less – to language courses, school enrolment and much else besides) and is crucial for the processes of data construction. On the one hand, while having a juridical/administrative definition as a basis allows one to concentrate on some important elements for a sociolinguistic programme (young age, confronting the journey without an adult relative, the insertion into a state-run programme on arrival, etc.), on the other hand this should not mean that we forget how the complexity of migration is continually decomposed and re-aggregated in countries of arrival on the basis of pre-established juridical/administrative variables and parameters, ones that are often extremely difficult to grasp.

The data we have developed are based for the most part, if not exclusively, on information from young people who have been attributed the status of UFM on arrival (many of whom have by the time of writing turned 18). Alongside them we ought note the other young people who have the same migration experience and come from the same areas of sub-Saharan West Africa as their under-age peers. Very similar sociolinguistic profiles frequently correspond to different judicial statuses, and this is particularly evident for those who are (or are not) inserted in the UFM category.

The goal of the sociolinguistic research project has been, and continues to be, the improvement of pathways for inclusion through an increasingly detailed awareness of the different profiles of newly arrived migrants, which is fundamental for programming effective educational pathways and respecting rights, including linguistic rights. The connection between the project for inclusion and the construction of data, both quantitative and qualitative, has been central. The climate of trust and openness created over recent years has, in fact, had a strong impact on the quality of the data gathered.

Gathering Data between Inclusion and Fear

The particular features of this new and contemporary migration, caught between legality and illegality, forced mobility and forced immobility (in connexions, Nigerian and Libyan prisons, in isolated and confined European hostels) require continual additional work for constructing data, a process that is already complex for linguistic research that engages with information gathered in the field and generated through a continuous relation of exchange between the data gatherer and the speaker whose repertoire is being investigated. Each element recorded, even if only through the researcher's notes, cannot in this instance be seen outside of the entirety of the migration experience that the speaker is going through in that moment. The speaker-writer-migrant-'new-arrival' who needs to formalise their situation in Italy (as is the case across Europe) through an extremely complicated process, one that often ends in refusal, knows that their personal data and life story – i.e. the 'credibility' of their own story – can be determining factors for reaching this goal.

The provisional montage of personal life experiences assembled by each individual migrant in order to formalise their status in Italy, which begins prior to departure through a mixing of fragments of information often received over the internet, is the direct or indirect result of other migration experiences and moves between a series of extremely distant poles: on the one hand, there are the rules and regulations from the moment of the boat landing that tend to categorise people based on how much of their past is held to be 'credible' or 'acceptable' by the authorities and, on the other hand, there is one's own culture, one's own history. Continued requests for information and narratives of the migrant's story, received on an almost daily basis, move between these two very complicated and often distant points – requests that arrive from those working in the hostels, from different institutions (schools, health services, local council offices, regional and national authorities) and from other people with very different backgrounds and goals: journalists, video makers, documentary makers, members of NGOs and local groups working in the sector, etc.

The difficulty of manoeuvring within this space, in which any false move can bring ruin, is well understood by every migrant, by everyone around them constructing systems of mediation (and protection), by everyone who is trying to understand the situation with the care and attention it deserves as a field of research. The work of co-constructing data that usually occurs in a research context based on questionnaires and interviews designed to generate autobiographies and self-evaluations, representations and experience, fragments of languages and stories – as the current investigation is – cannot ignore the importance of this situation of insecurity and fear in which the migrant lives and, at the same time, the distance between their experiences and the pages to be filled, the questions to be answered.

The majority of investigations into these new migration experiences (and thus also of related linguistic research) happen in the phase in which the migrant's status has still not been defined, because the juridical process to which they are subjected on requesting international protection (or leave to remain as UFM, or another category) has still not reached a conclusion, or because the 'permit to stay' has a temporary or extremely limited duration. In the case of the current research, the data gathered took place, for the most part, before hearings by the Territorial Commission[1] for the evaluation of international protection, an important Italian administrative moment that occurs after an extremely variable time period (oscillating between one and three years) following the migrant's arrival. This is thus the period of the migrant's greatest 'sensitivity' and 'anxiety' in terms of the tools used (questionnaires, recording devices, questions about their life prior to their journey). The utmost attention to research ethics is required within this temporal arc. Every study within the realm of new migrations must, more than in any other field of investigation, have full awareness of responsibility in relation to the subjects being asked for information and above all of the 'special protection of minors and vulnerable subjects, their psycho-physical integrity, the protection reserved for them and for their private life'.[2]

An essential part of such protection is, in our opinion, the right to not have questions posed that cause embarrassment and anxiety or provoke painful memories, and the right to not have anything made public, even anonymously, that does not pertain to the research at hand. But above all, there is the 'right to lie', which belongs to those inserted into a system that constantly uses information against those who have provided it. We share the opinion of those working in the same field of research who have stated that: 'We could claim that lying is often the only possible reply to the hypocrisies that regulate migration, or the laws on the recognition of human rights' (Beneduce, 2015: 562). At no point within this project has a lie been covered over or has a request been made to correct information that is clearly in disagreement with other facts or versions. Simply put, such data can be placed outside of consideration in some phases while in others they become extremely useful.

At the same time, there is an important responsibility in such research not only in relation to the individual but also to migrants collectively, from which derives the duty to give back knowledge and awareness acquired from the community itself, which has produced it, so that pathways of inclusion as a whole can be improved, in particular didactic models for teaching the language of the host country. The research of which we provide an account below is the product of a long journey that also includes the training of many teachers (see Arcuri *et al.*, 2018) and multimedia courses in the Italian language for young illiterate adults (see the website www.pontidiparole.com).

Methods of Data Gathering and Sampling

The investigation, the first results of which are provided below, was conducted using a broad-ranging sociolinguistic questionnaire as well as two tests: a test of literacy and a test of Italian. More than 50 young migrants were asked to narrate their linguistic histories during the didactic workshops, as well as during individual and group interviews. In a following phase, some Facebook profiles were examined from the moment of their generation, which in the majority of cases occurred after arrival in Italy (for this phase, see section entitled 'Speaking Many Languages. But How Many? But Which? But With Whom? But Where?').

For this chapter, the sample used is composed entirely of young people from sub-Saharan Africa who had undertaken migration journeys across the central sub-Saharan route that begins in the Gulf of Guinea, passes through a fundamental fulcrum at Agadez in Niger and arrives in Libya. The group consisted of 531 newly arrived young migrants (the oldest being 35) living in hostels in Palermo, who attended a language course and courses for social inclusion at ItaStra between March 2017 and May 2018. The countries of origin of the participants, in order of relevance, were The Gambia (179 people), Nigeria (84), Ivory Coast (73), Mali (40), Senegal (40), Guinea Conakry (35), Ghana (31), and fewer than 10 people from Benin, Burkina Faso, Cameroon, Eritrea, Ethiopia, Guinea Bissau, Sierra Leone, Somalia and Togo. One important section of the sample was made up of UFM (around one-third).

Our key opening question is: 'Which languages do you speak?'. From a methodological point of view it is important to note how this question does not make reference to the concept of 'mother tongue', nor 'native tongue', nor 'first language', concepts that are problematic generally and particularly in the African context from which the young migrants arrive. As Lüpke and Storch (2013) note:

> The idea of 'mother tongue' and someone's 'first language' [...] has little relevance in many West African communities. There, and in many other parts of Africa, speakers use a number of different languages in different contexts, and live in multilingual families and multilingual neighbourhoods. Their multilingual skills are part of their cultural lives and social integrity. This is not only the prevailing situation in Africa, but also in many other parts of the world; it was once also a common praxis in most of Europe, and in urban environments still continues to be so. With the creation of the ideology of the nation state, implementation of uniform school systems, standardization of languages, etc., this has changed, however, in many people's minds. In the same vein, the power relations that had emerged in the nineteenth century (and before) made the European ideas about national language and societal monolingualism a dominant paradigm, which still continues to shape debates about underdevelopment and poverty. (Lüpke & Storch, 2013: 77–78)

The same scholars underline the dangerous and indeed culturally colonial character behind the idea of a 'mother language' as an ethnic group:

> This idea, and concept, almost completely negates the richness of linguistic variation and language use regardless of administered ethnocentrisms. Moreover, it creates an image of speakers as mere recipients of a tradition, namely of one ethnic language that is passed on from mother to child, within the boundaries of the tribal space. (Lüpke & Storch, 2013: 349)

Speaking Many Languages. But How Many? But Which? But With Whom? But Where?

Some preliminary data

In Table 1.1 we present the data relating to the number of languages spoken (besides Italian) by the sample of young people examined, giving a first representation – albeit quite approximate – of their linguistic situation on arrival in Italy. The first look, in which the vast majority (85%) of participants claim to speak between two and four languages (excluding Italian), becomes more interesting and radically complex once we make use of other knowledge tools.

A first, even if partial, element is the data from Table 1.2 in which the same replies are regrouped on the basis of not only a quantitative but also a relative basis according to labels indicated by the interviewee, distributed according to family linguistics (Wolff, 2019). As can be seen, these

Table 1.1 'What languages do you speak?': Answers by African language families

		Language [number of answers]
Niger-Kordofan		
Niger-Congo	West-Atlantic	Wolof [156]; Pular[a] [110]; Sere-sin[b] [1]
	Mande	Bambara [90]; Mandinka [223]; Maninka[c] [9]; Djoula [27]; Susu [4]; Soninké[d] [26]; Bissa [2]; Mahou [1]; Koyaga [1]; Guru[1]; Kono [1]; Xaasongaxango[e] [1]; Landuma [1]
	Volta-Congo	Mumuye [1]
	Gur	Tem [3]; Moore[f] [4]; Dagbani [2]; Kulango [1]
	Kwa	Twi-fante [50]; Ga [4]; Ewe [4]; Agni [2]; Akan [3]; Nzema[g] [3]; Abron[h] [2]
	Kru	Bassa [2]; Bété [2]; Wobé [1]
	Benue-Congo	Bini [7]; Edo [40]; Esan [14]; Yoruba [7]; Yekhee[i] [3]; Isha [4]; Igbo [6]; Isoko [3]; Ika [3]; Urhobo [1]; Igede [1]; Sanga [1]
	Bantoid	Gwa [3]; Kikongo [2]; Duala [1]; Manda [1]
Afro-Asiatic		
Semitic		Arabic [43]; Tigrinya [4]; Amharic [5]
Cushitic		Somali [7]
Chadic		Hausa [5]
Other languages: French [236]; English [470]; Krio [4]; Guinea-Bissau Creole [7]		

Notes: [a]Also Fula, Fellani, Ful(ah), Fulbe, Fulfede, Fulfude, Futa, Peul, P(o)ular, Pulaar, Tukolor, Toucouleur; [b]also Serer; [c]also Malinké, Maninké; [d]Also Aswanik, Aswanek, Maraka, Marka, Sarakole, Sarakolé, Sarakulé, Serahule; [e]also Kassonke, Khassonké, Xasonga; [f]also Mossi, Mòoré; [g]also Appolo; [h]also Bono; [i]also Auchi, Afemai, Afenmai.

Table 1.2 Number of languages spoken by interviewees (excluding Italian). Self-declared data

Number of languages spoken (besides Italian)	Absolute	%
1	43	8
2	225	42
3	154	29
4	75	14
5	28	5
6	3	0.6
7	2	0.8
8	0	0
9	1	0.2

bring together different African languages with colonial languages learnt in school contexts and beyond. Among the 470 people who claim to speak English and the 236 who claim to speak French, there were many subjects with a low or extremely low level of schooling, whose learning processes have taken place outside the classroom. As for the 49 participants who claim to speak Arabic, these were always people with less than five years of schooling who have in all likelihood learnt the language within forms of Arabic-Islamic schooling, whether formal or otherwise.

If we move from the data taken from the questionnaires to those gathered during the didactic process, the Italian language courses and the workshops, attended regularly for a period of months by each of the participants, within the remit of the social inclusion project as well as the sociolinguistic investigation, we see a very different reality. Not only does the complexity of the repertoire radically increase, but so does the plurilingualism endemic in sub-Saharan Africa, which increases in many areas, and finally that connected to the long journey away from home countries and through Libya. All of this is perfectly understandable once we look at the forms of socialisation (including linguistic socialisation) shared by the young people in our sample, who do not have (only) a location within a nuclear family – which in many societies is non-existent – but rather within a much wider context for which the peer group plays an essential role:

> Most of children's language socialization does not take place in a nuclear family – nonexistent in many contexts – and following Western scripts. From early on, children mainly interact among themselves, often minded by elder children, with whom they communicate much more than with adults. In addition, 'intergenerational' suggests that languages are transmitted from adults to children, and that language 'acquisition' (a term convincingly criticized by Mufwene 2008 for not adequately capturing the piecemeal process of imitating, reproducing and changing language by creating analogies based on limited input) stops at the onset of adulthood. In many African situations, languages are added to individuals' repertoires throughout their lives and occupy positions of varying centrality in them depending on a variety of factors. Adults continue to be socialized in languages they have 'acquired' before, and in new ones, when they move house, migrate, marry, divorce, retire, and foster children. (Lüpke & Storch, 2013: 308)

Plurilingual Investigation through Teaching

The classroom is one of the locations in which the expression of each person's repertoire takes on all of a 'heteroglossic space of potentialities' that includes 'imagination and desire', as Busch indicates in her 2012 article (see section on 'Research Context: from Linguistic Inclusion to Research, There and Back Again – the ItaStra Workshops'). We chose to investigate plurilingualism through didactic activity that would guide students – in spoken and written word, but principally through drawings and maps – to recount their linguistic biography. The narration of one's own life by focusing attention on the repertoire of the point of departure and the wealth of linguistic inputs to which they had been exposed during the journey brought to light not only 'mother tongues', 'father tongues', 'grandmother tongues' and 'aunt and uncle tongues', but also the many languages learnt outside of the family, 'neighbour tongues', 'friend tongues', those of playmates and co-workers. A large quantity of expressions emerged from infant experience and adolescence, which have then been used very little or left aside – and then occasionally brought back to life during migration experiences. This last category, which also included migration experiences within Italy itself, constitutes an important factor of linguistic enrichment. In narrating the months on the road, one finds – along with pain and hunger, violence and death – an experience of meeting with different people and languages. Extremely unstable drawings and designs narrate these months-long journeys, sometimes lasting years, with long pauses and frequent changes of direction. The use of maps turned out to be extremely useful for simultaneously showing the wealth of an individual's linguistic rucksack and for narrating their story:

> The main objective resulting from working on geographical maps to retrace the route of the journey was the association of languages used in each country. Thus, the creation of linguistic maps gives the students the chance to rethink languages as tools of communication and survival. Finally, students came to revaluate their personal skills and troubled experiences thanks to the appreciation of the linguistic knowledge used and improved during the journey. (Di Benedetto *et al.*, 2018: 104)

During the process of recounting their own biographies, aside from locating the different languages of the journey, the students positioned these languages within the outline of their own body, drawn out life-size. In the heart and stomach went Wolof, Mandinka, Bambara, Pulaar and many other languages. Often Italian went in the head but sometimes in the feet, perhaps to show the thousands of miles passed to arrive at listening and speaking it.

The appearance of 'other' languages, in various forms, both written and spoken, is another part of the narrating of the self that constitutes one of the strands of work that ItaStra has undertaken over the years, and that has produced important experiences of plurilingual narration and communication (see Amoruso *et al.*, 2015; ItaStra, 2018).

The same element clearly appears when one uses the tool of the open interview with young migrants able to move competently within the new language or by making use of translators. Indeed, an extremely interesting fact came to light, being the quantity of languages learnt in situations of extremely temporary 'full immersion'. Micro-migrations across borders characterise, for example, the linguistic richness of Mamadou (note: all names are pseudonyms), born in Senegal and currently 20 years old, who has been in Italy for the last two years. Aside from Pular/Fula, the language used within his family and particularly with his mother, he claims to know Wolof, Mandinka, Portuguese Creole, Bambara, English, French and Italian. Here are some extracts from an extremely long interview:

Mamadou: For example, the creole that I learnt with my friends, my school friends, is a language that I haven't used since I came to Italy, they were friends I played football with, in Senegal we share a border with Guinea, another with Mali, I played football in Guinea and then came home, in Mali and then came home... I played football for an under-16s team in Senegal, then for another in Ivory Coast, and I learnt another language there, there they call it Bambara...

Interviewer: So you also speak Bambara?

Mamadou: Yes, I speak it well and I learnt it like that (note: he refers to playing football), I'm good at speaking languages... I know (laughs) when I began making friends that came to ours in the holidays we organized something, a party... You don't know what you call it, a retreat, players came from The Gambia, they came to the sport centre where we used to play football and they came here, three or four days, then they went back... People also came from Guinea for a couple of days, a week, just like that... I began speaking their languages through spending time with these friends and some of them also started speaking my language... They started speaking Pular, they started speaking Mandinka.... It went on like that... But at first they didn't understand, they couldn't speak Pular or Mandinka... they can't speak (they don't understand), they speak only creole, the ones from Guinea, they speak creole, they only study Portuguese and speak creole.

Interviewer: But how come you know Mandinka?

Mamadou: I spoke Mandinka with friends from my town, but in a different neighbourhood, and they speak Mandinka there... But my family didn't want to speak it, my father doesn't speak Mandinka, nor does my mother ... Only I speak Mandinka, but this Mandinka has helped me a lot, because Mandinka and Bambara are very close to each other... I learnt Bambara in Senegal, but someone who understands Mandinka well also understands Bambara because they're very similar, if you speak Mandinka and you hear Bambara being spoken, you understand.

In this interview, as with many others, the expressions encountered through his life, often not demonstrated in the responses to the questionnaire, take on the role of a skill that can be activated in situations of necessity, when one needs to communicate something important, such as during the journey of emigration and still more during the experiences in Libya. In the majority of instances, this does not cover a full competence as such but a knife of 'truncated multilingualism' (Blommaert, 2010), i.e. a partial knowledge that can nevertheless be used in specific contexts and situations.

Among many possible examples, we can pick out that of Ibrahim, a young Gambian man from a village of a few thousand men and women, many children and young people, and a large diversity of ethnic groups and languages: 'a lot of people speak Mandinka and Wolof, some Jola, Manjako, Balanta, Karoninka, Sereer, Fula, Kasinko, Kasangko, Manojo, Soninke, Sarahule'.

In the questionnaire on different languages, Ibrahim picks out only Jola, Mandinka, Wolof and English. But in the long interview his linguistic heritage broadens out substantially, from the Fula (or Pular or Pulaar) he learnt from his neighbours through to expressions learnt through relationships with his peer group. He also explains how fairly marginal languages within his repertoire became useful during the journey. One of these is Manjako, which he learnt in a manner quite different from that usually described by our interviewees:

Ibrahim: At school I had a classmate who was Manjako, he taught me his language and the words and I wrote it in a notebook and I learnt it. 'Come and eat' is Billi ba dayla; tanding milik means 'give me water', and I wrote that down. No, I don't speak Manjako, but I understand it. One time on the road, when I was coming here, I'd hear someone speaking Manjako with someone else who spoke it, and I managed to understand them, they were talking about money.

Among the many idioms that do not belong (or only partially belong) to the pre-migratory life experiences, we often found – sometimes after precise questioning, at other times spontaneously – Algerian or Libyan Arabic.

Amadou, a young man from Mali (25 at the time of interviewing), who has been in Italy for five years, claims to speak the following languages, in the order provided by himself: French, English, Mandinka, Jola, Serahule, Bambara, Wolof and Italian. Following the intervention of the interviewer, who had already known him for some time, he also noted Arabic:

Amadou:	And Arabic, yes – but Libyan Arabic, because there are lots of kinds of Arabic. There are three or four kinds, so I only speak the one from Libya.
Interviewer:	Do you want to tell me that you don't understands the Tunisian guys?
Amadou:	Ok, there's maybe someone among the Tunisian guys who speaks Libyan Arabic, but there aren't many who understand it, because it's different... What you study at Koranic school and what you speak, it's not the same thing, because the Libyan one is more difficult that the one they do in the Koranic school... [...] Yeah, I understand them when they're talking, but I don't know how to respond... I was in Libya two months and six days, but before Libya I was in Sabha, which is a small town in Algeria, they speak the same language as in Libya, I did a year there, I learnt Arabic there in Sabha... It's a border with Algeria which they call Sabha but it's... Libya, Algeria... There are some people who come from Libya and some people who are from there, but they're always moving, so there are lots of people who speak Libyan there as well.... I learnt it there.

Amadou is entirely aware of the role that his migration experience, and his periodic pauses 'at the border' ('in frontiera' to use his own words), have had on the growth of his linguistic skills, because it is there that 'you speak and learn many languages'. But above all he is fully aware that this sharpened plurilingualism was extremely useful during his migration project:

Amadou:	I met a lot of people, different kinds of people come there, for business and other things, we don't have a stable job, so if someone calls you for a job, if you speak his language it's better, you know what you need to do, the situation, that's why we learnt these languages there...
Interviewer:	So you think that your linguistic skills helped you during your journey to Italy?
Amadou:	Yes, it helped me a great deal, because there are people who speak the same language, but you understand them. When I was speaking Libyan there was someone who helped me because I spoke his language, because they said, good! So this one speaks Arabic. Because if you speak the language, they help you out....

We often heard in the interviews that Arabic was extremely useful during the period of time spent in Libya, sometimes in prison, almost always in inhumane working conditions and during a troublesome period of waiting to embark on the boats. This aspect only occasionally appears in the questionnaires, an omission that is sometimes conscious, at other times not. Similarly, attendance at Koranic school – an experience common to the vast majority of young Muslim men – was sometimes declared and at other times even denied during a first moment governed by mistrust and fear; it then emerged when the climate of trust had been established. All of this seems explicable in the light of the complicated context in which the investigation took place, characterised by the extremely difficult political climate in both Italy and Europe more generally.

Multilingualism and Segregation

As we have seen, the migration journey works as an important factor for enriching an already extremely dynamic and fluid repertoire. These processes of reconfiguration and expansion happen within the different spaces in which young people find they have to live out their often very difficult experiences of forced immobility. By this we mean both the devastating experiences that many have gone through in Libya in sites of aggregation for migrants and prisons, as well as in the various hostels on arrival in Italy, often known by young migrants simply as 'camps' in continuation with their experiences prior to arrival.

In these different versions of segregation, and through the continued, forced interaction with other migrants, the management of an extraordinary multilingualism takes place, according to the model of 'receptive multilingualism' (see Singer, 2018; Thije & Zeevaert, 2007). Speakers with different linguistic backgrounds each use the language with a prominent role in their own repertoire and attempt to understand the languages of interlocutors who use very different idioms. The key concept for this communicative model is that of 'receptive language', i.e. the language sufficiently understood by the interlocutor. All of the participants keep up with a continuing process of adaptation and negotiation of the codes of communication and the continued control of overlapping zones between the repertoires of interlocutors in order to adapt to the codes being utilised. Through often very limited inputs, new languages – first and foremost Libyan Arabic – enter into and become part of the oral communication circuit, through processes of imitation and reproduction, beginning with very common forms of insult. *Anta kalb* ('you're a dog'), *anta clifti* ('you're mad') and other phrases penetrate within textual forms already marked by a high level of multilingualism, joining English and Mandinka,

French and Wolof, and many other languages. And they remain there – sometimes simply as fillers, sometimes as methods of recollection, even long after arrival in Italy, as a method of recognition between those who have 'passed through Libya'.

Conclusion

The young people described in this chapter – migrants from sub-Saharan Africa who have just arrived in Sicily, after a journey of years through Central Africa, Libya and the Mediterranean Sea – are of great interest not only for the sociolinguistics of migration but also for those who want to look at the dynamics of multilingualism in the present-day world and the different models of language acquisition.

They have, in extreme forms, the ability to move between different realities and worlds. Long before embarking on the long journey towards Europe, they have experienced countless short- or long-distance trips: to learn a job, to study, to know pieces of their family. They have travelled on foot, by bicycle, by bus, by pick-up truck along the African roads; they are able to move within the universe of multilingualism with the confidence of those who are not afraid of it and who know how to use all its resources. To the typical forms of African multilingualism, they have added mobility multilingualism and then again the experience of temporary communities built with the aim of segregating them in Africa and Europe.

The movement among many linguistic spaces is amplified by the great capacity of digital connections that make these young migrants not only prototypical connected migrants but prototypical connected people in a more general way. Such a connection ability appears to be a fundamental characteristic of successful men or women, that is, 'smart people', if we want to adopt an expression widely used in the language that emphasises and celebrates some forms of production, and even more of living, exhibited by fragments of the contemporary world. Yet these young migrants are still considered, in Italy as well as in most of Europe, as the prototype – and the symbol – of the migrant who is scary, who invades, who overturns values, who subverts the established order – the migrants we need to get rid of as soon as possible, without wasting time in understanding and knowing. The research in the field, in this as in many other cases, can help to build up a different narrative.

Notes

(1) In Italy, the 'Territorial Commissions for the Recognition of International Protection' were introduced through Law No. 189 of 30 July 2002 (the Bossi-Fini Law), Article

1-quarter; they are composed of four members: a representative of the local prefecture, a representative of the UNHCR, and two administrative staff. It is these two latter members, with rare exceptions, who actually interview the asylum seeker.
(2) The quotation is taken from the Commission for Research Ethics and Bioethics of the Italian National Research Council (www.cnr.it/it/ethics) 'Linee guida per l'integrità nella ricerca', revised on 11 April 2019.

References

Amoruso, M., Cipolla, N., Piraneo, C. and Salvato, V. (eds) (2016) *Odisseo Arriving Alone*. Palermo: Palermo University Press.

Amoruso, M. and D'Agostino, M. (2017) Teenage and Adult Migrants with Low and Very Low Education Level: Learner's Profile and Proficiency Assessment. In J.C. Beacco, D. Little, H.J. Krumm and P. Thalgott (eds) *The Linguistic Integration of Adult Migrants: Some Lessons from Research* (pp. 345–350). Berlin: De Gruyter Mouton (in cooperation with the Council of Europe).

Amoruso, M., D'Agostino, M. and Latif Jaralla, Y. (eds) (2015) *Dai Barconi all'università: Percorsi di inclusione linguistica per minori stranieri non accompagnati*. Palermo: Scuola di Lingua italiana per Stranieri.

Arcuri, A., D'Agostino, M. and Mocciaro, E. (2018) Teacher of Italian as a non-native language for low educated users: A new professional profile. In M. Sosinski (ed.) *Language and Literacy Teaching LESLLA Students* (pp. 33–42). Granada: Editorial Universidad de Granada.

Bauman, Z. (2000) *Liquid Modernity*. Malden, MA: Polity Press.

Beneduce, R. (2015) The moral economy of lying: Subjectcraft, narrative capital, and uncertainty in the politics of asylum. *Medical Anthropology* 34 (6), 551–571.

Blommaert, J. (2008) Language, asylum, and the national order. *Urban Language & Literacies* 50, 2–21.

Blommaert, J. (2010) *Sociolinguistics of Globalization*. Cambridge: Cambridge University Press.

Bougleux, E. (2016) Im/mobilities in subjects and systems. In M. Gutekunst, A. Hackly, S. Leoncini and I. Götz (eds) *Bounded Mobilities: Ethnographic Perspectives on Social Hierarchies and Global Inequalities* (pp. 13–16). Bielefeld: Transcript Verlag.

Busch, B. (2012) The linguistic repertoire revisited. *Applied Linguistics* 33 (5), 503–523.

Busch, B. (2017) Expanding the notion of the linguistic repertoire: On the concept of Spracherleben – the lived experience of language. *Applied Linguistics* 38 (3), 340–358.

D'Agostino, M. (2017) L'Italiano e l'alfabeto per i nuovi arrivati. *Testi e linguaggi* 11, 141–156.

D'Agostino, M. (2021a) Segregati e connessi. 'Nuovi migranti': Profilo sociolinguistico e costruzione dei dati. In A. Bertin, F. Gadet, S. Lehmann and A. Moreno (eds) *Réflexions théoriques et méthodologiques autour de données variationnelles* (pp. 45–64). Chambéry: Presses de l'Université de Savoie.

D'Agostino, M. (2021b) *'Noi che siamo passati dalla Libia': Giovani in viaggio fra alfabeti e multilinguismo*. Bologna: Il Mulino.

D'Agostino, M. and Mocciaro, E. (2021) Literacy and literacy practices: Plurilingual conncected migrants and emerging literacy. *Journal of Second Language Writing* 51 (3), 1–16.

Di Benedetto, L., Salvato, V. and Tiranno, C. (2018) The value of languages in linguistic autobiography. In M. Sosinski (ed.) *Language and Literacy Teaching LESLLA Students* (pp. 99–108). Granada: Editorial Universidad de Granada.

Diminescu, D. (2008) The connected migrant: An epistemological manifesto. *Social Science Information* 47 (4), 565–579.

Hall, J.K., Cheng, A. and Carlson, M. (2006) Reconceptualizing multicompetence as a theory of language knowledge. *Applied Linguistics* 27, 220–240.

Lüpke, F. and Storch, A. (2013) *Repertoires and Choices in African Languages*. Berlin/New York: Mouton de Gruyter.

Mufwene, S.S. (2008) *Language Evolution: Contact, Competition and Change*. London/New York: Continuum.

Otsuji, E. and Pennycook, A. (2010) Metrolingualism: Fixity, fluidity and language in flux. *International Journal of Multilingualism* 7 (3), 240–254.

Sayad, A. (1999) *La double absence*. Paris: Editions du Seuil.

Singer, R. (2018) A small speech community with many small languages: The role of receptive multilingualism in supporting linguistic diversity at Warruwi community (Australia). *Language & Communication* 62, 102–118.

Thije, J.D. and Zeevaert, L. (eds) (2007) *Receptive Multilingualism: Linguistic Analyses, Language Policies and Didactic Concepts*. Amsterdam: John Benjamins.

Tobagi, B. (2016) *La scuola salvata dai bambini: Viaggio nelle classi senza confine*. Milan: Rizzoli.

Wolff, H.E. (ed.) (2019) *The Cambridge Handbook of African Linguistics*. Cambridge: Cambridge University Press.

2 Sociolinguistic (Im)mobilities in Spaces of Migration

Necia Stanford Billinghurst

Introduction

In this chapter I explore how language contributes to (im)mobility within spaces encountered along the migration trajectory, particularly as it relates to Weber's affiliative agency or elective affinity (see Howe, 1978; McKinnon, 2010). With permission, I examine one woman's experiences of complex multilingualism and migration. Close study of a single case (Reissman, 2008) is used to suggest that geopolitical locations (internal displacement; refugee camp, settlement) intersect with sociolinguistic practices to establish spaces of (im)mobility. Adopting de Certeau's (1984, 2002) supposition that space is the convergence of practice and place, and superimposing Higgins' (2017) assertion that language shapes and is shaped by the spaces encountered, the research suggests that (im)mobility lies at the intersection of language and space.

Recent perceptions of an increase in human mobility, ethnolinguistic diversity and multilingualism have been endorsed by some (Arnaut *et al.*, 2015; Blommaert & Rampton, 2011; Vertovec, 2007) and contested by others (Edwards, 2012; Franceschini, 2012; Ndhlovu, 2016; Pavlenko, 2019; Wiley, 2014). Setting aside the question of novelty, current emphasis on human mobility and diversity appears to suggest a heightened acceptance of multilingualism as the norm (May, 2013). This has led to an unsettling of some conventional conceptualisations of language. For instance, traditional terms such as L1 for first language, mother tongue, home language or community language are now confounded. As multilingual individuals reveal the existence of more than one first language, the notion of an L1 becomes problematic. In addition, the term 'mother tongue' may not appropriately describe a first language that is based on a father's, grandparent's or community's language (see D'Agostino, this volume). Although home language may be used instead, there may be more than one home language in childhood, and then different languages used at home in adulthood. Issues such as these suggest the complexity, dynamism and plurality of language use and corresponding terminologies.

Likewise, conceptualisations around linguistic boundaries or 'named' languages have been disrupted (see Gal & Woolard, 1995, for an historic discussion). Academics such as Makoni and Pennycook (2007) and Otsuji and Pennycook (2010) argue that language boundaries are merely social constructs that negate the true fluidity of languages and perpetuate inequity. Agnihotri (2014: 364) proposes that 'human linguistic behaviour is marked by fluidity, rather than rigid compartmentalisation'. Others, such as Phipps (2013), have moved away from concepts of language as discrete and bounded, and argue instead for the unanchoring or 'unmooring' of language practices. These notions have led to the rise of terminology such as Agnihotri's (2007, 2014) multilinguality, as well as the (re)framing and popularisation of notions such as languaging (Becker, 1991; Mignolo, 1996; Swain, 2006) and translanguaging (García & Li, 2013; Williams, 1996).

While scholars such as Grin (2019) agree that languages are porous, they believe that boundaries are still present. Edwards (2012) suggests that while there may not be sharp delineations, separate languages do exist in the minds of the general public – 'for all ordinary intents and purposes, there *are* separate languages, and there *are* distinct varieties within them' (Edwards, 2012: 36, emphasis in original). These scholars fear that efforts to 'disinvent' language (Makoni & Pennycook, 2007) deny the very real perceptions of ordinary people for whom languages are separate and dialects distinct. Furthermore, Heugh (2019, personal correspondence) suggests that while the concept of language fluidity and 'multilinguality' may be useful in 'horizontal arrangements that secure affinity and conviviality', they may be less useful in vertical spaces that 'index unequal power functions and relations' (Heugh & Stroud, 2019: 3). Thus, concepts of linguistic fluidity may exacerbate social inequality rather than erasing it in certain sociolinguistic 'spaces'.

Henri Le Febvre (1974) and Michel de Certeau (1984) are credited with suggesting that space is the result of how humans perceive and use it. This is succinctly stated by de Certeau (1984: 117) as 'space is a practiced place' – dynamic and shaped by the purposes and activities in a location. That language may be one of the practices influencing a space seems evident. Higgins superimposes language on this conceptualisation of space, resulting in the assertion that 'space both shapes and is shaped by multilinguals' language practices'. She suggests that 'a dynamic view of space allows us to examine how migrants, transnationals, and other highly mobile populations experience a space, and how they use their language resources in their practiced places' (Higgins, 2017: 103).

Spaces reflect the practices of both individuals and societies moving into and mingling within those locations. For de Certeau (2002: 74), space consists of 'intersections of mobile elements', sites of struggle made up of both 'conflictual' and 'contractual' actions. They are places where inequalities can constrain permitted practices. Le Febvre proposes that spaces are established by social construct, and as such are rarely neutral, but rather manifestations of power inequalities and imbalances that mirror the actors in that space. Higgins (2017: 103–104) suggests that spaces are 'sites where power relations and inequalities are made visible'. Inequalities, therefore, may well constrain activities within a space.

Moreover, power affects human mobility into spaces, as in the case of migration. Nail suggests two assumptions when discussing human mobility. The first is an assumption of stasis or immobility – that individuals are normally located in 'place-bound social membership' and that they desire to remain there. The second assumption is that stasis should be bounded by a political state. Migrants, by definition, unsettle these two assumptions, having crossed borders and moved outside their home state. Indeed, migrants are defined by mobility, by 'becoming and displacement' (Nail, 2015: 3–4).

In addition to disrupting assumptions of stasis in a geopolitical location, migrants may disturb sociolinguistic assumptions in their new geopolitical 'place'. Here they may encounter what Clyne (2005) terms a monolingual mindset upon entering situations where language practice defines a space in a particular way, and where the host community is uncomfortable or unwilling to allow the space to be reshaped by the introduction of new linguistic practice. Higgins suggests a tendency for 'the imagining of spaces as belonging to particular ethnicities, religions, genders and languages' (Higgins, 2017: 102). However, this is much more than an imagining, particularly when spaces are revealed as sites of power inequality. In such spaces the imagining becomes reality. Reluctance to embrace the disruptive nature of a new wave of migrants may be expressed by communities already in the space. At a time when disruption is hailed in sectors like technology and business, it receives a lukewarm welcome in migration. Thus, migrants may bump up against an assumption of monolingualism or of existing language practices, and an unwillingness to welcome a new language. This is in addition to an assumption that that they should be static, but 'back where they came from'.

In the field of sociolinguistics, the concept of mobility is often equated with migration-related travel, including internal or external displacements, voluntary or forced, temporary or permanent (see Canagarajah, 2017). Mobility has, however, meanings beyond migration, such as social, economic, education, employment and even linguistic mobility. These mobilities present themselves in particular forms within the migration process, for example: (1) social: inclusion in and appreciation from host or ethnolinguistic communities; (2) economic: skill-matched employment or career advancement; (3) education: access to basic, higher or continuing education, or opportunities for upskilling; and (4) linguistic: opportunities for learning the language of a new community, for becoming literate, or for a dialect or accented variation of the host language being recognised as legitimate. Each of these manifestations plays out as a layer of mobility within the larger migration trajectory. Each poses the possibility of immobility as well. Limiting discussions of mobility to human movement erases these important aspects that occur within each stage of the migration process, whereas expanding the connotation acknowledges the complexity. This allows consideration of how multilingualisms interact in spaces within the various stages of forced or voluntary migration, as well as the overarching migration process.

There is limited research exploring the complex interweaving of multi-layered (im)mobilities within spaces along the migration trajectory and how these (im)mobilities are negotiated through multilingual practices. In this chapter, I expand on how conceptualisations of language, space and mobility in migrant situations illustrate the following propositions: (1) multilingualism is complex, dynamic and plural; (2) language shapes space; space shapes language; and (3) (im)mobilities can be either positive or negative, inclusive or exclusive. This is done to suggest that in situations of migration, (im)mobilities occur at the intersection of language and space. At these frontiers, conventions such as linguistic boundedness may serve positive as well as negative functions.

For this chapter, I draw on data collected through a mixed-methods study into language choices and affinities of 31 women with historic ties to South Sudan now residing in South Australia. Surveys, interviews, observations and auto-ethnography were used to elicit the role of language in experiences of displacement, asylum and settlement. Through orally administered surveys, the women shared their ethnolinguistic background, religious affiliations and migration journeys. They described everyday language use with family, friends and community, both in Australia and beyond. Five women participated in a follow-up interview to reflect on situations where language had advantaged or disadvantaged them at some time or place. Survey and interview data were combined with observations at gatherings of the South Sudanese community (including worship services, national conferences and language classes) collected between August 2018 and October 2019. The community observations are considered quasi-ethnographic due to the limited contact points and time period (Murtagh, 2007). The survey, interview and observation data were then compared with personal and professional observations gathered during my time working in South Sudan from 2008 to 2012 to support a reflexive (Bourdieu, 1989; Salö, 2018) research approach.

I focus here on experiences shared by one participant to suggest that mobilities are shaped at the intersection of space and language. Having passed through internal displacement, refugee camps, and now in resettlement, this individual moves among complex forms of mobility and immobility that are interconnected and linguistically framed/bounded. She finds herself in what Freire (2000: 102) terms 'limit-situations', spaces that involve political, social, linguistic, economic and educational constraints that do not necessarily disappear over time. Rather, these constraints morph into new forms that are shaped by the sociolinguistic spaces she now occupies. As she struggles to move through geopolitical spaces of power and social inequality, she encounters sociolinguistic spaces that illustrate immobility within mobility, and mobility within immobility. Having transitioned from displacement to settlement, she discovers that one space of immobility is often replaced by another (e.g. Heugh *et al.*, 2018; Maher & Cavalcanti, 2018), finding in her 'settledness' iterations of limiting practices that continue to be 'unsettling' in the new spaces she encounters.

In the first section ('Multilingualisms'), I introduce the participant, Lingua (pseudonym), a South Sudanese refugee who has been settled in Australia for more than a decade. Her multilingual background and migration journey are mapped out to illustrate that multilingualism is complex, dynamic and plural. Lingua speaks several South Sudanese languages, referred to as A, B and C throughout the chapter in order to safeguard anonymity. I do this with hesitancy, acknowledging that erasure of the African languages can be considered disempowering and a form of colonisation (see Smith, 2013). However, the sensitive nature of the stories Lingua shares prompts me to risk accusations of neo-colonialism in order to protect her identity. Moreover, circumventing specific language names may permit Lingua's linguistic world to represent multilingual women beyond the African context.

In the second section ('Spaces'), I examine the concept of space. I review four situations where language and space converge along Lingua's migration journey, to demonstrate how Lingua's geopolitical location (internal displacement; refugee camp, settlement) interacts with her sociolinguistic spaces and how language shapes and is shaped by the space she encounters. These examples illustrate how sites of power and inequality may be revealed, complicated and/or transformed through language.

In the third section ('Immobilities'), I discuss mobility in its several forms – physical, social, economic and linguistic. I purport that Lingua's experiences of language, space and mobility reveal that, like multilingualism, mobility is complex, diverse and plural. Lingua's (im)mobilities present in positive and negative forms, and result in increased inclusion or exclusion. Through Lingua's examples, I suggest that geopolitical and sociolinguistic (im)mobilities overlap and that migration comprises spaces of trade-off among mobilities and inclusions (Grin, 2019). While optimisation of mobility and inclusion may be illusive and imagined, it may be at the frontier of space and language where the most promise lies.

Multilingualisms

In this section I introduce Lingua, a multilingual South Sudanese woman resettled in Adelaide. With her permission, I share her linguistic background and migration journey in order to discuss notions of language, multilingualism and migration, and to illustrate how multilingualism is complex, dynamic and plural, and thus unique for each individual.

Lingua is of a mixed ethnolinguistic background. Her father (now deceased) is from one ethnolinguistic community (A) and her mother from another (B). Lingua was born in the land of her father's people, but soon shifted to her mother's community due to insecurity. There she grew up in a predominately B speaking area where Sudanese Arabic (a dialect of Arabic) was also used as a language of wider communication. When Lingua was first asked what language(s) she used as a young girl, before attending school, she indicated B and Sudanese Arabic (Arabic - S). However, in a subsequent interview she claimed A as another first language and reports using it with her mother and sister.

The example of Lingua's first languages illustrates complexities mentioned previously, namely questions of how to refer to her first language(s), and which one constitutes her home language. Lingua identifies a mother tongue (B). However, she also mentions a father tongue (A), as well as the local language of her mother's community (Sudanese Arabic), suggesting the existence of three L1s. Furthermore, she reports using the languages of both her father and mother at home as a young child. Thus, she has two home languages. Later, in Australia, Lingua's home languages shift to C, her husband's language, and English. She now has four home languages, although used at different times and places. The plurality of her first languages, and the dynamic nature of her 'home languages', makes it clear that current terminology does not accommodate Lingua's situation.

Lingua recalls that she spoke A with her father while he was alive. With her mother, who is still alive and currently in South Sudan, she speaks A and B. She has a sister who lives in Ethiopia, and with her she uses A and B; however, with her brothers living in South Sudan she uses only B. As a young woman living in the refugee camp, Lingua learned to speak C and later married a man of C ethnolinguistic background, using this language with him and her mother-in-law. Lingua has five children, all born in Australia. Here in Australia, C is the home language, and even though she is now estranged from her husband, she continues to speak C and some English to her children. They respond in English.

Lingua had limited opportunities for education. She completed three years of primary schooling in South Sudan with Sudanese Arabic as the medium of instruction. However, her education was disrupted as her family left South Sudan to seek security in a refugee camp in Ethiopia. There, she repeated these same school levels at the refugee camp using English. Because of this, her ability to read or write in any language is practically nil. She never completed further education in the camp, and when she arrived in Australia, she was 18 years old and already married.

Lingua shares that she speaks to friends on the phone in A, B and C, but only uses C for face-to-face visits. At church she uses English because she is the only South Sudanese attending her congregation. For social media she uses A, B, C, Sudanese Arabic and English, primarily through audio clips or YouTube videos, because of her limited literacy. Here in Australia, Lingua does not participate in any South Sudanese ethnolinguistic community and attributes this to the fact that her father, mother and husband come from different communities. Figure 2.1 shows a visual representation of Lingua's complex multilingual practice.

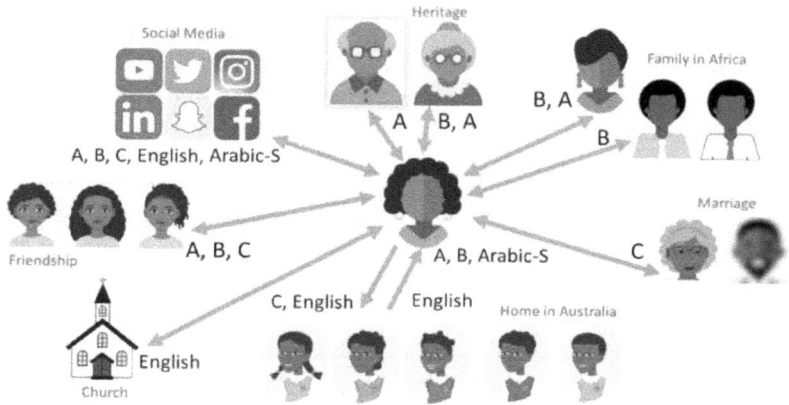

Figure 2.1 Lingua's multilingual world
Source: Billinghurst (2019).

When asked if she mixes her language (i.e. uses more than one language in a situation), Lingua shares that she sometimes gets mixed up. For example, if she is having a conversation in one language she may turn and speak to another person in that language, even though she knows he does not speak it. But she attributes this to age and says that it did not occur when she was younger. When asked if this is happening in Australia because of the many languages she uses, Lingua insists it did not happen before and that it is only due to age.

Lingua does, however, report using both B and some A to her mother and sister, and that she uses C and some English with her children. According to Lingua's self-perception, she rarely uses all of her languages together – this only happens in the home with her mother and sister and with her children. In such situations, she is engaging in what Heugh (2017) would call a horizontal language situation, namely a relatively power-neutral space, where conviviality and mutual understanding are the objectives. In other situations, Lingua does not use more than one language together – or at least she does not perceive that she does this. Whether this is entirely true or not, Lingua's self-perception indicates that she does not see those situations as ones where her multilingualism is needed, useful or appropriate.

While it is true that all of Lingua's languages are Nilotic, and therefore may be seen on a continuum, she clearly regards them as separate languages. As will be made evident through her stories of space and language, shared in the next section ('Spaces'), Lingua relies on the fact that each language is regarded as a separate entity in order to create opportunities for mobility, both physical and sociolinguistic. She uses the ideology of these 'named' languages to 'pass' (Bucholtz, 1995) as a member of different linguistic communities, paradoxically relying on fixed language ideology to support fluid ethnolinguistic identity. This fluidity, however, is stymied in certain spaces, which will be illustrated in the experiences Lingua shares. Hence, while language, and identity, may be porous and fluid, for Lingua it is also bounded and fixed.

As shown by Lingua's linguistic background and migration journey, three postulations about multilingualism are evident. First, multilingualism is complex. Establishing first languages, mother/father tongues and home languages is not simple or straightforward for many multilingual individuals. Conceptualisations of language that may work in some situations do not work in others. Perceived language use may differ from practice. Power and inequities create horizontal and vertical situations where language use may be fluid or bounded.

The second supposition is that multilingualism is dynamic. Lingua's multilingualism changes over time and space. Her linguistic repertoire and how she uses it has changed over the course of her life, with different languages taking precedence over others and new languages being added. In addition, her repertoire has shaped and been shaped by the locations she seeks out and moves in, as well as the 'spaces' she makes.

Third, multilingualism is plural, proposed by Heugh and Stroud (2019) to be a set of phenomena rather than a phenomenon. The multilingualism expressed by Lingua is exclusive to her, a type of linguistic 'footprint'. Each individual possesses a unique combination of language abilities that constitutes their multilingual capacity. As such, the complexity and dynamics of multilingualism at both the individual and community level make evident its plurality. Multilingualism is unique to each individual and, by correlation, to each community. There is no polarity between monolingualism and multilingualism. Rather, multilingualism is diverse; it is plural, a 'heterogeneity of experiences', phenomena rather than a phenomenon.

In this section, I have discussed multilingualism and how it is complex, dynamic and plural. Lingua's linguistic world provides examples of how purpose, place and space intersect with language. For instance, place influences language (e.g. English used at church where she is the sole person of African origin); purpose influences language (e.g. use of language C for speaking to mother-in-law); and space is influenced and influences language (e.g. 'home' space in Africa and languages spoken there versus 'home' space in Australia). These intersections will be further unpacked as more examples of Lingua's use of language in specific spaces are shared in the next section.

Spaces

In this section, I share examples of how language and space converge along Lingua's migration journey to demonstrate how Lingua's geopolitical location (internal displacement, refugee camp, settlement) interacts with her sociolinguistic spaces and how language shapes and is shaped by the spaces she encounters. Lingua's stories illustrate how purpose and place establish space and what happens when language and space intersect.

As discussed previously, space can be regarded as dynamic and experiential, born of purpose and place, and influenced by language practices. The spatial conceptions of Le Febvre, de Certeau and Higgins can be graphed using the theoretical triad of C.S. Peirce (1867), the North American philosopher and pragmatist, to visually show how these concepts interact. Peirce's three logical categories bear a striking resemblance to Le Febvre's spatial categories:

Peirce (1867)	Le Febvre (1974)
Firstness – the realm of natural order, concepts, uses	le conçu (conceived)
Secondness – physical representation, action, location	le perçu (perceived)
Thirdness – experiences and patterns emerging from first and second	le vécu (lived)

Drawing from the ideas of Le Febvre, de Certeau and Higgins, I map their concepts onto a Peircean grid to illustrate how purpose (firstness) and place (secondness) give birth to 'space' (thirdness) through language, and how language reciprocally influences all three (see Figure 2.2, linguo-spatial triad).

This triad borrows from Peirce's concepts of first, second and third and combines it with Le Febvre's triad of conceived space, perceived space and lived space. From Le Febvre and de Certeau I adopt the idea of space as dynamic, the idea that a place becomes a space as things happen there (first and secondness becoming thirdness). From Higgins, language is placed at the intersection of purpose, place and space, to illustrate how language shapes, and is shaped, by all three. Language lies at the centre of space-making.

Lingua's linguistic world provides examples of how purpose, place and space intersect with language. For example, place influences language (e.g. English used at church where she is the sole person of African origin);

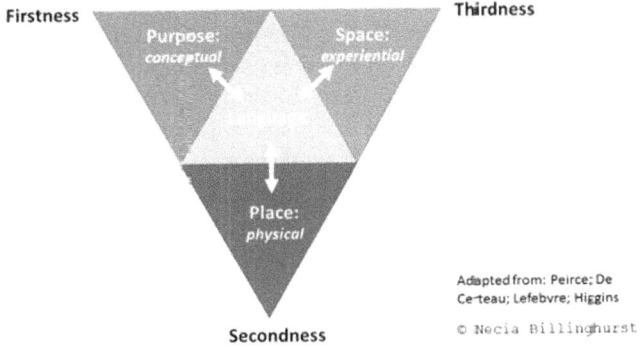

Figure 2.2 Linguo-spatial triad
Source: Billinghurst (2019).

purpose influences language (e.g. use of language C for speaking to mother-in-law); and space is influenced and influences language (e.g. 'home' space in Africa versus 'home' space in Australia). These intersections are further unpacked through additional examples of Lingua's multilingual practices in different spaces. The first occurs while Lingua is internally displaced within South Sudan. The second is from her time located in a refugee camp in Ethiopia. The final, two-part example is from her present situation, settled in Australia.

Example 1: 'She's Our Little Sister'

Lingua shares an experience from her period of displacement within South Sudan. As a child of seven or eight years old, Lingua is sent to the market to buy corn. In the market, boys are stealing people's money. Hearing the response of one victim she realises that the boys speak her mother tongue and are targeting other language groups. Being a young girl, she is an ideal target, and Lingua overhears their plans to snatch her money. She admits that all she wants to do is cry, but she knows she must figure a way out. Consequently, Lingua approaches a vendor who speaks a different language but uses her own mother tongue to ask the price. She hears the boys' surprise that she speaks their language. They discuss whether to take her money or leave her alone, ultimately reasoning that they cannot steal from a little girl of their same background because she is like their 'little sister'. Back home, Lingua recounts the story to her mother who asks how she knew to speak that language. Lingua shares that she had recognised that using any other language would allow the boys to rob her because she was not one of them. Using their language, especially to a vendor of a different language, would signal her belonging to their linguistic group. In this situation, Lingua successfully presents herself as a member of her own community in the market by using her mother tongue, what Bucholtz (1995) calls 'passing'.

In this first situation, Lingua is in the marketplace where the purpose is to buy and sell goods. Within the market, purpose and place interact with language to establish a multilingual 'space' for commodity exchange. However, within the same physical location of the market, the boys shift the purpose to stealing, thus creating a new 'space'. Language, which served an economic function in the market space, is now used for nefarious purposes as the boys use linguistic differences to identify their targets. With the change in purpose, the multilingualism in the market changes from a unifier to a divider. This example illustrates how purpose and place establish spaces, how language can support purpose and how language and space intersect.

Furthermore, within the new space created by the boys' thieving, Lingua uses linguistic differences to demarcate boundaries and establish a safe space for herself. She uses the dissimilarity between her mother tongue and the vendor's language to delineate a border between her linguistic space and that of the vendor, and of the market in general. Lingua thus establishes boundaries within the larger marketspace, and places herself within them. She uses the interaction with the vendor to expose this boundary and signal to the boys that she is one of them. Pennycook and Otsuji (2014: 161) refer to 'spatial repertoires – the linguistic resources available in a particular place'. Within the market scenario, Lingua selects languages from the greater spatial repertoire and plays them off against each other to reveal linguistic boundaries that are especially evident when inequality, power or insecurity are present.

Example 2: 'One Word Will Help You'

Lingua tells an experience from when she was a young teenager, around 13 or 14 years old. She travels on foot from the refugee camp to a town in Ethiopia without knowing that along the road her people are being attacked by bandits from another linguistic group. At the first shop, she speaks her mother tongue to the owner and is warned about the attacks. She realises the risk of returning home. Lingua explains that she knew some language of the bandits; thus, she goes to another shop and along the way follows several men in the road, chattering aloud in the language of the bandits. At the next shop, she uses only the language of the bandits. She recounts that the people in the shop question her ethnolinguistic identity and she replies, 'What do you mean, what language [do] I speak?' They press her and she responds that 'the language I speak is the language I speak. I don't know what you're talking about'. She tells me that because there are no distinguishing physical features, the only way to differentiate one community from another is via language. Lingua says that the people reason that there is no way a young girl from the targeted group would go along the road by herself, so she must be who she is making herself out to be. She is left alone and returns home. She muses that that even just 'one word will help you'. In this situation, Lingua uses her linguistic abilities to assume linguistic affiliation with the bandits, 'passing' as a member of a different ethnolinguistic community in the shop and along the road.

In this second example, Lingua again uses language to establish a safe space. Realising that speaking her mother tongue in the shops and along the road is not advisable, Lingua shifts language. In this example, language now serves two purposes in the same physical place, that of transacting her business and that of establishing an identity that will ensure safety.

In this situation, where power inequalities are evident, fluidity of language is not only unwelcome, but it may be unsafe. Lingua's need to use a language other than her mother tongue to ensure her safely walking back from shops in Ethiopia beyond the refugee camp clearly designates a situation where linguistic fluidity would be dangerous, as just one word could tip the bandits off to her ethnolinguistic origin. While it is true that sometimes migrants have the power to influence a space, in many situations that is not the case. Inequalities may manifest through language practices in a space where migrants hold no influence. Individuals or communities may use language practice as a tool for constraining and limiting the agency and movement of individuals within or trying to access that space (see De Fina & Mazzaferro, this volume, on the dangers of speaking in certain situations).

Example 3: 'Gentile'

Lingua shares that in Australia she doesn't participate socially in any of the three ethnolinguistic communities that would appear to be open to her due to her multilingualism. Rather, Lingua says that she and her children cannot belong to any or all of these 'spaces' because of her mixed background. She avoids community activities because she does not want her children to be called 'jur', a term she considers quite negative. She clarifies that it 'means gentile. You're from the other side, the other side, the other side, the other sides'. She further says, 'if you didn't speak my language that mean [sic] you jur'. She says it signals that you don't belong here. In order to protect her children from being mistreated at community events, she chooses instead to remain apart.

For Lingua, her multiple ethnolinguistic identity, and the identity she has passed on to her children, is not beneficial in Australia. She cannot move in any of the communities whose languages she speaks, including 'mainstream' Australia. Her children, who are Australian born, do not fit into either an African or an Australian community. In this supposed space of settlement, she is unsettled and faces rejection from those who could be her own people but who will not allow it. The possibility of affiliating with community A, B and/or C is blocked, rendering Lingua sociolinguistically immobile.

Example 4: 'I Don't Have a Place to Stand'

Not only is Lingua rejected, unable to enter into any group in Australia because of her ethnolinguistic background. Paradoxically, she also suggests a state of flux, feeling both ostracised, unable to belong to a community and, at the same time, that her identity is passed among the three

South Sudanese communities. She tells of how she is attributed to a different community depending on whether the community members approve of what she is doing. The As will refer to her as a B, the Bs as a C, etc. She laments, 'I don't have a place to stand'. Lingua is constantly in motion, simultaneously assigned an identity and denied a place of belonging. She seeks a place of equilibrium but instead has mobility forced upon her. Lingua references the Australian television documentary series, *Go Back Where You Come From*.[1] She explains that, for her, the way she is treated and usage of the word 'jar' signals the exact same sentiment. Not only does the term identify her as an outsider, it has the further connotation, at least to Lingua, of telling her to get out, to go back. In this instance, not only is she excluded, but she experiences dismissal. For this reason, she purposely avoids community activities, choosing to stay away rather than be sent away.

In the first two situations, at the market and along the road, Lingua uses language to establish new and distinct safe spaces, thus signalling her belonging and affiliation. In the first, she seeks inclusion in her mother tongue community and in the second in that of the bandits. Contrast this to the second two examples. Here Lingua is moving within the same linguistic space – that of the three South Sudanese communities in Australia; however, these examples show forms of exclusion. In the first she feels unable to access any of the communities because a part of her belongs to A and to B – 'my identity belongs to both of them' – and, through marriage, she and her children also belong to C. Yet, in that very same linguistic space Lingua also feels dismissed. Lingua shares how she feels unable to enter the communities, sent away and powerlessly assigned to any one of the communities without her input. In these first two situations she is able to assume the identity that she desires. In the final situation, she tries to negotiate her identity but finds it being imposed upon her. Lingua is unable to establish presence in the spaces that could be available to her. Not even her language skills will assist her.

Lingua's experiences of language and space suggest two things: (1) that recent critiques of the boundedness of 'named' language, and the proposition of fluidity of language, may not hold in certain practised places where power dynamics are at play; and (2) that (im)mobilities are revealed at the juncture of language and space.

First, in any given space, the actors and purposes/activities help determine whether a language situation is horizontal or vertical (Heugh, 2017). Horizontal or more power-neutral situations lend themselves to fluidity, while vertical or power-laden situations do not. The examples shared by Lingua occur in power-sensitive situations where the concept of language fluidity, language without borders, is of little use. I suggest, therefore, that linguistic fluidity is only possible and useful in power-neutral spaces and, in practice, space rarely exists in a power void. Language may be fluid in some few situations but is bounded in others.

While one might argue that Lingua's use of language is fluid – she makes choices to use certain elements of her repertoire in each situation – one might counter that the language elements in her repertoire have what Bourdieu (1989) calls symbolic power which link up to a named language. Drawing on these linguistic boundaries may be used positively or negatively to influence (im)mobility. Higgins suggests that space is where 'power relations and inequalities are made visible, but also where they can be transformed' (Higgins, 2017: 104). I argue that in spaces where power is revealed, one way to transform the power imbalance may be to play into linguistic boundaries, as Lingua does to confound the bandits and dissuade the boys in the market.

Second, Lingua's experiences suggest that (im)mobility occurs where language meets space. Building on Higgins' idea that language and space shape each other, in the next section I consider this nexus of language and space, proposing that (im)mobility lies at their intersection. I then explore how linguistically shaped spaces may result in greater mobility or increased constraints. Moreover, I discuss under what conditions a multilingual woman may craft desirable space and/or manoeuvre existing spaces she may wish to access or avoid.

(Im)mobilities

In this final section I review Lingua's experiences of language and space. I suggest that both geographic and sociolinguistic (im)mobilities lie at their intersection (see Figure 2.3). Multilingual language practices help shape space in ways that may increase or decrease motion. The conclusions drawn suggest that in linguistically shaped spaces, mobility and immobility present in positive and negative forms, and result in increased inclusion or exclusion. Borders between space and language can be frontiers that allow individuals to make imagined and desired mobility into reality.

For Lingua, her geopolitical mobility spanned 18 years and included multiple sites of internal displacement, two crossings into Ethiopia, five years in a refugee camp, and now 18 years settled in Australia. Within these spaces, some of her sociolinguistic mobilities have changed. Linguistically, she has added new languages (C, English); socially, she has married, borne children and separated. Other immobilities, however, have remained the

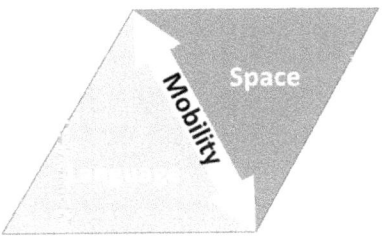

Figure 2.3 Intersection of language and space
Source: Billinghurst (2019).

same. She is still uneducated and illiterate in any language; she is unemployed and unable to get a job due to her illiteracy. Some (im)mobilities are more complex; for example, in the past she has experienced periods of physical closeness and distance from her immediate family. Currently she is distanced and without means of reuniting with her mother or siblings, either financially (purchasing a plane ticket) or politically (sponsoring them for immigration). Ethnolinguistically, she has moved from an A community (birth), to a B community (childhood and youth), to a C community (marriage), and now to an Australian/English community where she participates in her English religious community but does not participate in any of her South Sudanese communities. For Lingua and other migrants, (im)mobilities lie along the frontier of language and space. While it is true that language shapes space and space shapes language, it is also true that language ability can permit or prevent movement into a space, and actors in a space may accept or reject a language within its borders.

Each of Lingua's shared accounts illustrates a slightly different take on language, space and mobility, particularly as it relates to Weber's affiliative agency or elective affinity (see Howe, 1978; McKinnon, 2010) and inclusion (see Figure 2.4). In the first story, Lingua uses her first language to signal that she should not be harassed. She is a part of the boys' community and wishes to remain in that space. She does not want to move from the community of her birth: inclusive (positive) immobility. In the second, Lingua uses language to move to a different ethnolinguistic identity to protect her safety: inclusive (positive) mobility. In the third example, Lingua is trapped in an outsider position and called 'gentile'. Even though she has the linguistic skills to join in multiple communities, none of them will allow her to enter. She is left with nowhere to move: exclusive (negative) immobility. Finally, in the last scenario, Lingua shares that even beyond being denied a 'place to stand', she is constantly in motion, with identity imposed upon her and shifted from one community to another.

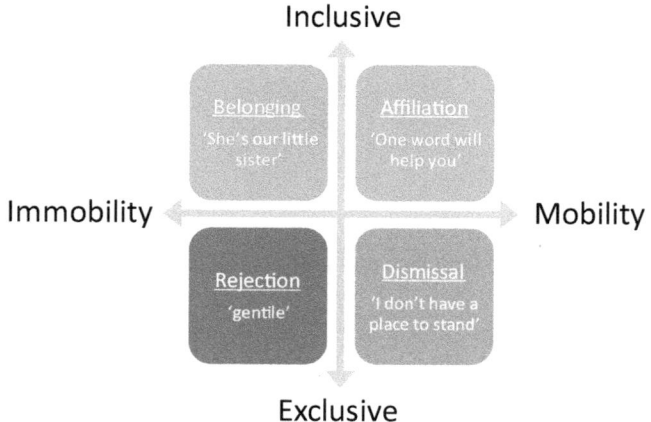

Figure 2.4 Mobilities and inclusions
Source: Billinghurst (2019).

She avoids her ethnolinguistic communities because she fears being told that she should leave: exclusive (negative) mobility. Exclusive mobility and immobility are entangled for Lingua. Indeed, all four classifications are intertwined and overlap.

The graphic suggests that immobility can be either an equilibrium or a stasis, positive or negative. It can be inclusive, having a 'place to stand', or exclusive. Likewise, mobility is not always positive but has a negative embodiment as well. Positive mobility allows freedom of movement; however, negative mobility may mean imposed and unfixed identity, or being told to 'go back to where you came from'. Positive immobility is strongly linked to belonging or inclusion, and is the converse of negative immobility or not being allowed to move into a group, not belonging. Negative mobility, however, goes one step further. Not only is an individual not allowed in, but she is sent away – told to 'go back' – or, as in the case of Lingua, passed among the communities, perpetually reassigned an identity. In these situations, mobility and fluidity present an 'unmooring' that is undesired. The accounts shared by Lingua support the assertion of Pavlenko and Blackledge (2004) that identity, in this case expressed through sociolinguistic mobility and inclusion, may be assumed, imposed or negotiated by the individual and/or the community members. Grin (2019) points out that 'more mobility may detract from inclusion, and more inclusion may hamper mobility'. This might be any of the types of mobility, including sociolinguistic mobilities. In the case of Lingua, her multilingual and multi-ethnic composition has increased her movement in some instances but decreased her inclusion in others. The paradox is that while mobility might be desired, so is positive immobility. There is a need for belonging, 'a place to stand', as well as an equally legitimate desire to move, to become.

Here Nail's (2015) two assumptions about migration – stasis and place-bound membership – are unsettled. As a migrant, Lingua has disrupted both assumptions, having crossed borders and moved beyond her place of birth, South Sudan. But while her life has been defined by movement, she does not desire this as a constant state. As observed from Lingua's experiences in settlement, stasis is what she desires. She seeks stability and belonging. However, because of forced migration, equilibrium must be established in both physical and social locations different from those of her birth. She must negotiate acceptance into new spaces, and this may meet with resistance, both by the host community and, surprisingly, within her own ethnic communities.

In new places of settlement, migrants such as Lingua may encounter new forms of (im)mobilities, perhaps rendering their 'settledness' more imaginary than realised. Yet, within the constraints of such spaces, mobile peoples may use the linguistic resources they bring with them to influence and open new possibilities. Lingua's stories illustrate how language both increases and decreases mobility when it intersects with various spaces. Her experiences reveal that named languages and their symbolic power may work for or against an individual who may be either butting against or relying on the 'imagining' of community space as belonging to only those of one particular language and identity. In Lingua's situation, this 'imagining' prevents her mobility into the three ethnolinguistic communities she might otherwise access. On the other hand, Lingua relies on the presumed connection of space, language and identity to indicate affiliation with the boys at the market and the bandits on the road. Lingua counts on the symbolic power attributed to language to enhance her mobility, sometimes to failure and at other times to success. Heugh (2019, personal communication) notes the paradox in Lingua's ability to 'judiciously' use her multilingualism in contexts of physical danger, but less so in the diaspora where the risk is perhaps more psychological than physical, and her positioning as an outsider subtler. I suggest that the difference may be less in the type of risk and more in the power dynamics of the space, including the actors' willingness to negotiate identity with Lingua.

In this section, I have suggested that mobility and immobilities are plural and present in both positive and negative, inclusive and exclusive forms. Lingua's experiences illustrate that different types of (im)mobilities layer up other (im)mobilities in spaces of migration. Mobility and inclusion may be at odds with each other, resulting in trade-offs between spaces of mobility and of belonging (Grin, 2019). Optimisation of mobility and inclusion may be illusive and imagined; however, possibility and opportunity may lie at the frontier of space and language.

Conclusion

In this chapter I have shared four encounters where language and space converge along Lingua's migration journey. This was done to demonstrate how Lingua's geopolitical position (displacement, seeking asylum, settlement) interacts with her sociolinguistic spaces. Through this I have proposed that (im)mobilities lie at the convergence of language and space. These limit-situations are complex, dynamic and plural, constraints or opportunities, resulting in increased inclusion or exclusion. Based on Lingua's experiences, I suggest that (im)mobilities lie within and layer on top other (im)mobilities, creating points where trade-offs between movement and inclusion occur (see Grin, 2019). At these sites, or 'spaces', power dynamics expose inequalities that may be enhanced or reduced by playing into neo-colonial boundaries between named languages and corresponding identities. In such spaces, the optimal balance between mobility and inclusion may be illusive or merely imagined.

The ideas presented in this chapter may prove useful for further research on the layering of (im)mobilities within other spaces encountered by multilingual migrants, such as education or employment. Incorporating aspects of time and space (chronotopes) would further illuminate the multi-layered mobilities encountered within spaces of migration. Moreover, additional research would be useful on how trade-offs between movement and inclusion are made by mobile multilinguals.

Finally, sociolinguistics could benefit from an exploration of how the concept of named languages may not be as obsolete as some may presume. As suggested by this research, linguistic boundaries and the symbolic power they convey may profit multilinguals in some situations of power imbalance. Freire cites Pinto as saying that limit-situations (constraints) are not 'impassable boundaries where possibilities end, but the real boundaries where all possibilities begin ... the frontier which separates being from being more' (Freire, 2000: 99). Thus, boundaries are not to be feared. They are lines that establish safe spaces, or the threshold to cross when starting a new journey. In fact, it is only by crossing borders into discrete spaces that inclusion may begin.

Note

(1) In the series, six Australians are taken on a reverse migration to the countries of origin of many Australian migrants so that the six might experience first-hand what the refugees may have experienced while seeking refuge in Australia and share that with a general Australian television audience.

References

Agnihotri, R.K. (2007) Towards a pedagogical paradigm rooted in multilinguality. *International Multilingual Research Journal* 1 (2), 79–88.

Agnihotri, R.K. (2014) Multilinguality, education and harmony. *International Journal of Multilingualism* 11 (3), 364–379.

Arnaut, K., Blommaert, J., Rampton, B. and Spotti, M. (eds) (2015) *Language and Superdiversity*. New York: Routledge.

Becker, A.L. (1991) Language and languaging. *Language & Communication* 11 (1/2), 33–35.

Billinghurst, N.S. (2019) Language, space, and (im)mobility: A case study of a South Sudanese woman in Adelaide. Paper presented at the Inclusion, Mobility and Multilingual Education conference of the Asia-Pacific Multilingual Education Working Group, British Council, Bangkok, Thailand.

Blommaert, J. and Rampton, B. (2011) Language and superdiversity. *Diversities* 13 (2), 1–22.

Bourdieu, P. (1989) Social space and symbolic power. *Sociological Theory* 7 (1), 14–25.

Bucholtz, M. (1995) From Mulatta to Mestiza: Language and the reshaping of ethnic identity. In K. Hall and M. Bucholtz (eds) *Gender Articulated: Language and the Socially Constructed Self* (pp. 351–373). New York: Routledge.

Canagarajah, S. (2017) *The Routledge Handbook of Migration and Language*. Abingdon: Taylor & Francis.

Clyne, M.G. (2005) *Australia's Language Potential*. Randwick: University of New South Wales Press.

de Certeau, M. (1984) *The Practice of Everyday Life*. Berkeley, CA: University of California Press.

de Certeau, M. (2002) Spatial stories. In A. Ballantyne (ed.) *What Is Architecture* (pp. 72–87). London/New York: Routledge.

Edwards, J. (2012) *Multilingualism: Understanding Linguistic Diversity*. London: Continuum.

Franceschini, R. (2012) History of multilingualism. *The Encyclopedia of Applied Linguistics*. Oxford: Blackwell.

Freire, P. (2000) *Pedagogy of the Oppressed* (30th anniversary edn; M. Bergam Ramos, trans.). New York: Continuum.

Gal, S. and Woolard, K.A. (1995) Constructing languages and publics: Authority and representation. *Pragmatics* 5 (2), 129–138.

García, O. and Li, W. (2013) *Translanguaging: Language, Bilingualism and Education*: New York: Springer.

Grin, F. (2019) Mobility, inclusion, and integrated language policy design. Paper presented at the Inclusion, Mobility and Multilingual Education conference of the Asia-Pacific Multilingual Education Working Group, British Council, Bangkok, Thailand.

Heugh, K. (2017) Re-placing and re-centring Southern multilingualisms: A de-colonial project. In C. Kerfoot and K. Hyltenstam (eds) *Entangled Discourses: South-North Orders of Visibility* (pp. 209–229). New York: Routledge.

Heugh, K. (2019) Personal correspondence.

Heugh, K. and Stroud, C. (2019) Diversities, affinities and diasporas: A southern lens and methodology for understanding multilingualisms. *Current Issues in Language Planning* 20 (1), 1–15. doi:10.1080/14664208.2018.1507543

Heugh, K., Stroud, C. and Scarino, A. (2018) Spaces of exception: Southern multilingualisms as resource and risk. *Current Issues in Language Planning* 20 (3), 1–20.

Higgins, C. (2017) Space, place, and language. In S. Canagarajah (ed.) *The Routledge Handbook of Migration and Language* (pp. 102–116). Abingdon: Routledge.

Howe, R.H. (1978) Max Weber's elective affinities: Sociology within the bounds of pure reason. *American Journal of Sociology* 84 (2), 366–385.

Le Febvre, H. (1974, 1984) *The Production of Space* (D. Nicholson-Smith, trans.). Oxford: Basil Blackwell.

Maher, T.M. and Cavalcanti, M.D.C. (2018) Unseen and unheard: Cultural identities and the communicative repertoires of Índios in Brazilian cities. *Current Issues in Language Planning* 20 (1), 50–66. doi:10.1080/14664208.2018.1503387

Makoni, S. and Pennycook, A. (eds) (2007) *Disinventing and Reconstituting Languages*. Clevedon: Multilingual Matters.

May, S. (ed.) (2013) *The Multilingual Turn: Implications for SLA, TESOL, and Bilingual Education*. New York: Routledge.

McKinnon, A. (2010) Elective affinities of the Protestant ethic: Weber and the chemistry of capitalism. *Sociological Theory* 28 (1), 108–126.

Mignolo, W.D. (1996) Linguistic maps, literary geographies, and cultural landscapes: Languages, languaging, and (trans)nationalism. *Modern Language Quarterly* 57 (2), 181–196. doi:10.1215/00267929-57-2-181

Murtagh, L. (2007) Implementing a critically quasi-ethnographic approach. *Qualitative Report* 12 (2), 193–215.

Nail, T. (2015) *The Figure of the Migrant*. Stanford, CA: Stanford University Press.

Ndhlovu, F. (2016) A decolonial critique of diaspora identity theories and the notion of superdiversity. *Diaspora Studies* 9 (1), 28–40.

Otsuji, E. and Pennycook, A. (2010) Metrolingualism: Fixity, fluidity and language in flux. *International Journal of Multilingualism* 7, 240–254.

Pavlenko, A. (2019) Superdiversity and why it isn't: Reflections on terminological innovation and academic branding. In B. Schmenk, S. Briedbach and L. Küster (eds) *Sloganization in Language Education Discourse: Conceptual Thinking in the Age of Academic Marketization* (pp. 142–168). Bristol: Multilingual Matters.

Pavlenko, A. and Blackledge, A. (eds) (2004) *Negotiation of Identities in Multilingual Contexts*. Clevedon: Multilingual Matters.

Peirce, C.S. (1867) *On a New List of Categories*. See https://en.wikisource.org/w/index.php?title+On_a_New_List_of_Categories&oldid=2154981.

Pennycook, A. and Otsuji, E. (2014) Metrolingual multitasking and spatial repertoires: 'Pizza mo two minutes coming'. *Journal of Sociolinguistics* 18 (2), 161–184. doi:10.1111/josl.12079

Phipps, A. (2013) Unmoored: Language pain, porosity, and poisonwood. *Critical Multilingualism Studies* 1 (2), 96–118.

Riessman, C.K. (2008) *Narrative Methods for the Human Sciences*. Los Angeles, CA: Sage.

Salö, L. (2018) Seeing the point from which you see what you see: An essay on epistemic reflexivity in language research. *Multilingual Margins: A Journal of Multilingualism from the Periphery* 5 (1), 24–39.

Smith, L.T. (2013) *Decolonizing Methodologies: Research and Indigenous Peoples*. London: Zed Books.

Swain, M. (2006) Languaging, agency and collaboration in advanced second language proficiency. In H. Byrnes (ed.) *Advanced Language Learning: The Contribution of Halliday and Vygotsky*. London: Continuum.

Vertovec, S. (2007) Super-diversity and its implications. *Ethnic and Racial Studies* 30 (6), 1024–1054.

Wiley, T.G. (2014) Diversity, super-diversity, and monolingual language ideology in the United States: Tolerance or intolerance? *Review of Research in Education* 38 (1), 1–32.

Williams, C. (1996) Secondary education: Teaching in the bilingual situation. In C. Williams, G. Lewis and C. Baker (eds) *The Language Policy: Taking Stock* (pp. 39–78). Llangefni: CAI.

3 Categorization and the Use of English as an (Im)mobile Resource in Service Encounters with Migrants in Flanders

Katrijn Maryns and Stef Slembrouck

Introduction

This chapter concentrates on the impact of linguistic diversity and the globally (im)mobile use of English on categorization practices in situations of institutional contact between service providers and foreign language speakers in Flanders (Belgium). Although English is not an official language in Belgium, it is frequently used as a contact language in multilingual service encounters, in which entitlements are being negotiated, denied or awarded and which, more generally, lead to outcomes with identity implications. This chapter raises the question of how we interpret and understand the use of mobility-related language resources in institutional contexts of service provision in today's globalized environments. Global English counts as a mobile language resource because of its status as a language with a worldwide distribution and its widespread occurrence as a mediating tool for contact between moving populations and members of local communities. At the same time, global English may lose its potential of meeting some of the inevitable necessities of real-world mobility in situations where its inherent diversity and heterogeneity of practice across settings of use is underestimated, and where it may cause mutual understanding and rapport to be wrongly assumed. The use of global English will be explored in the context of situated communicative practice, i.e. examined in relation to (a) the full repertoire of institutional agents and clients, including L1 use and the use of the locally dominant language, and

(b) the interactional alignment of institutional agents and clients and their orientations to 'local' communicative resources, purposes and interactional outcomes.

While research on English as a lingua franca (ELF) has always been primarily concerned with transnational encounters involving mobile populations (Jenkins & Wingate, 2015; Jenks, 2012; Seidlhofer, 2011), the encounters analyzed in this chapter differ considerably from those that have been typically addressed in research, i.e. informal conversational behavior in collaborative settings in which the main purpose is either to socialize (the prototypical context has been the international students' kitchen) or to accomplish mutually shared outcomes (e.g. international team work in a lab). It is important to recognize the institutional nature of the data being examined in this chapter. How do participant orientations to task and outcome pan out in asylum and migration encounters? How does the use of a 'boundary transcending' communicative resource, which is not the L1 of the client or the institutional agent, affect processes of categorization specifically, and meaning-making more generally? And how does the (im)mobility of global English as a meaning-making resource affect the ways in which clients access a procedure, actively participate in the negotiation of rights and resources and establish themselves as legitimate participants, e.g. as applicants for an entitlement to a service or status or, having been entitled, as users of an enacted service?

Building on qualitative sociolinguistic and linguistic ethnographic insight, our guiding principle is that the negotiation and co-construction of meaning in interaction are context-dependent processes. According to Gumperz (1982: 374), 'people use talk reflexively to build the very contexts in terms of which they understand what they are doing and talking about with each other'. In order to understand each other, interactants have to anticipate the balance between what is contextually shared, and can be presupposed, and what needs to be explicated/spelled out (cued) in interaction. Mutual understanding, in other words, depends in part on how much discursive effort the participants are *able* or *willing* to invest in the interaction. Different settings come with different targets, conditions and requirements for mutual intelligibility which are inextricably bound with the task-orientedness of the encounter and the consequentiality of its outcomes for the interactants. What is amenable to open negotiation in one setting may remain implicit or unspoken in another. For instance, legal-administrative encounters are clearly asymmetric contact zones involving inequalities between speakers in setting up the conditions of 'sayability' in terms of speaking rights and obligations, and determining what can or cannot be openly raised, divulged or talked about. Moreover, when an assessment of applicant credibility is involved, this may result in competing interactional orientations, where efforts at explaining a particular category by 'filling in' missing context may clash with institutional pressures to protect the integrity of the procedure (Slembrouck, 2021). In asylum interviews, for example, the dynamics of institutional categorization often lack transparency which may result in situations where asylum seekers' accounts are evaluated against criteria they cannot themselves anticipate (Maryns, 2006, 2013, 2017). Categorization refers to the discursive processes by which social and other realities are made relevant by being processed in terms of 'categories-with-consequences' (Mäkitalo, 2014). In asymmetric encounters, a lack of transparent communicative goals weighs heavily on any attempt at interactional alignment, even in the absence of a language barrier or in situations with the most advanced multilingual support. In less gatekeeping-oriented settings, such as legal or social service encounters with foreign language speakers, there may be more leeway to make transparent particular institutional categories, concepts and ways of going about things. Yet, here also, mutual understanding depends on the extent to which speakers manage, and actively choose, to align themselves interactionally and draw from the required contextual, linguistic and meta-linguistic resources to link up between perspectives and expectations. While these encounters are predominantly counselling oriented, they may also display gatekeeping sequences, and this mixture of advisory and evaluative stances may further complicate interactional alignment, even in situations where participants do their utmost to interactionally compensate for a shortage of contextual commonality. More specifically with regard to the use of English to bridge language difference, the practical problem-solving or socializing orientations that have been the hallmark of much ELF research will be different from the concerns that are central in a migration-related administrative contact zone where English is often used under unforeseeable and very complex conditions, including clients in precarious situations, intricate legal-administrative procedures that beg a considerable amount of explanation, and largely diverging institutional literacies.

Hence, one of the questions that comes within sight is how efficient a mobile resource such as 'global English' may be (or not) for bridging language difference in institutional encounters where speakers have to act in anticipation of certain local institutional or national procedural requirements and categorization processes. More specifically, we will focus on English use in service encounters with asylum seekers and refugees that deal with granting assistance and resources. We will concentrate on three social service encounters with asylum seekers and refugees in Flanders/

Belgium. The interactions are in English as a second or foreign language (not the first language of either the client or the professional). We will draw data from: (i) student administration services (the site is a university registration office for international students); (ii) frontline legal assistance (data from a regional welfare agency); and (iii) welfare support consultations (data from the social welfare department of a local authority). What the three cases have in common is that, apart from the fact that English is used as a more or less mobile resource in the communication between service providers and immigrant clients, the cases are concerned either directly or indirectly with client categorization. In Case 1, the administrator wants to ensure that the client meets the necessary criteria to register as an international Master's student. The social worker in Case 2 is concerned with fitting the client into the category of asylum seekers who qualify for a prioritized procedure. Case 3 brings to the fore an additional aspect of categorization, viz. the stage at which a category forms the input for resultant conduct within a network of institutional support. Before we turn to the data fragments, we will discuss the aspect of 'categorization', its relevance in institutional procedure, and how we suggest it can be approached conceptually and methodologically.

Categorization Practice

The functioning of institutions is hard to think about without the deployment of categories: the specific mechanisms for allocating social and other realities to categories, as well the ways in which they are acted upon once category membership has been determined and ratified. Mäkitalo (2014: 27–28) stresses how research into categorization practices highlights important elements of institutional practice, especially its role in the construction of a particular case, 'the process through which a person is transformed into a client of a particular kind'. While the deployment of a category in interaction allows the speakers to take certain things for granted, categorization is more often than not about rendering some aspect of social reality particularly relevant in terms of what is to happen next. For Mäkitalo, categorization is concerned both with knowledge that is processed and used, and resultant action within an institutional or professional framework (see also Verhallen et al., 2017).

Hall et al. (2006: 27ff.), drawing on Billig (1985: 82, 90ff.), view the dynamics of fitting social realities into categories in terms of pressures of both categorization (whether the properties of a particular situation, event or person fit a particular category) and particularization (what is specific or 'special' about a situation, event, person, etc. that may result in the category membership being undermined, open to negotiation, or an instance having to be treated as a special variant of the category, etc.). While the more popular, and bleaker, version of social reality is undoubtedly that in which the rigidity of categories prevails and clients and their realities either fit into them or they do not, or they are being forced to fit even when they do not and this has negative consequences, it remains important to remember that institutional activity is often also oriented to rendering categories 'malleable' so as to accommodate external realities and to enable work in the interest of the client, despite imperfections in category fit (Hall *et al.*, 2006: 37). Benefits to which one may be entitled are intended to address and accommodate real-life situations.

This two-faced reality of institutional functioning constitutes a terrain of possible interactional alignments, or possible 'lines' (Agha, 2005; Goffman, 1967, 1981), which clients may adopt as they enter into a procedure. This means that, continuing the tradition of Billig (1985), we argue that categorization practices need to be viewed as rhetorical practices, and not located exclusively in practices of (cognitive) perception. Categorization then depends on information exchange and its import. Sarangi and Slembrouck (1996: 87ff.) make a distinction between three possible client types, while recognizing that client stances may shift in the course of a larger procedure or one of its encounters: (i) 'naïve clients' tend to prioritize sincerity and provide agents with all the information they have and expect the agent to determine relevance and a matching category; (ii) 'professional clients' selectively supply (and withhold) information on the basis of strategic assumptions about what is relevant and decisive; and, finally, (iii) 'warrior clients' view particularization as a moral obligation of the institution and often put values of justice and fairness before the restrictive logics of the category regulators that apply for all practical purposes. In all of this, arguments may develop over the relative weight of particular features as compared to other features in determining category membership, as well as the degree to which the feature applies for it to warrant an allocation to the category. Following Billig (1985: 91), this can be summarized as the question of 'e-ness', whether there is enough of it, and how much weight is to be given to the feature. E-ness then stands for the situational application of one or more decisive and critical features that may hang in the balance. Finally, note that the two faces of institutional functioning, one oriented to client scrutiny and one oriented to client accommodation, are thus bound also to vary depending on where the encounter will be on the continuum from service/advice to gatekeeping and, even within that range, sequences of encounters and encounters in their own right may display shifting orientations towards/away from offering services, tailored advice and practical support, encouraging entitlement, establishing legitimacy, etc.

This chapter addresses itself to institutional encounters between participants with diverse sociocultural backgrounds, 'local' institutional literacies and local/global linguistic-interactional resources. In each of the cases examined, a degree of mediation or explication is required to determine category membership. A category may need to be translated, explained, and even compared to equivalent categories in other local/national contexts, before an application can be initiated. While this is happening, interactants are likely to anticipate how a category comes with entitlements and obligations and, more generally, how it is to be made relevant to their situation. Two plausible propositions therefore are: (i) that processes of categorization permeate the language mediation efforts of the institutional agent and/or the language worker who provides mediation, and (ii) that the successful deployment of mobile, difference-bridging language resources such as global English cannot be separated from the interactional and institutional dynamics of categorization.

Data and Methodology

In this chapter, we concentrate on a number of interactions recorded in Flanders with clients of international descent. We will draw data from different social service settings where English is used in consultations between Flemish service providers and their foreign language speaking clients: (i) student administration services (the site is a university registration office for international students); (ii) frontline legal assistance (data from a regional welfare agency); and (iii) welfare support consultations (data from the social welfare department of a local authority). A central concern in each of the three cases is that the correct procedures are followed for the client to obtain a particular status or access to particular resources. The institutional client in Case 1 is an asylum seeker who wants to enroll as an international student at university. His main concern is with ensuring that the required documents are submitted in order to qualify for inclusion in the category of 'admitted international student'. The client in Case 2 is an asylum seeker who solicits legal assistance in the preparation of his asylum interview. In an attempt to meet his client's urgent needs and help him out of his precarious living situation in Belgium, the social worker tries to anticipate how his client's experiences might fit into a category of asylum seekers who receive special treatment. The client in the third case is a refugee who has been granted refugee status on medical grounds and who receives assistance with the purchase of medication. The main concern here appears to be with ensuring that the correct financial procedure is followed, as prescribed by the type of financial aid. While the cases share a common ground of concern with categorization and procedural correctness, the analysis of the data will demonstrate how gradations in procedural literacies and institutional pressures may affect the ways in which the participants manage to achieve interactional alignment, using English, and meet the procedural requirements of the encounter.

The data in all three cases were collected through participant observation, field notes and audio-recordings of the observed consultations. No interview data were used, which means that attributions of communicative intent are based on analyses of externalized communicative behavior. The data in Case 1 have been collected by Sofie Permentier in the context of her Bachelor's paper (2012) which examines a total of 11 conversations in the student administration department of a university (seven were conducted in English, three in Dutch). The data in the second case have been drawn from Babette Weyns' Master's dissertation (2013), in which she investigates eight interviews conducted in English between Flemish social workers and immigrant clients at a regional welfare agency in a major city. The data in Case 3 have been selected from Nele Bauwens's and Glenn Branswijk's joint database (recordings in 2012, Bauwens's Bachelor's paper in 2013, Branswijk's Master's dissertation in 2014). This collection totals 13 conversations in a city's social welfare department (all conducted in English), with minority clients from diverse ethnic and national backgrounds.

Case 1: Task-Focusedness as Preventing Mutual Understanding while Securing that Things Get Done

In our first case, an international student with a Nigerian background (CLI in the transcription below) wants to enroll for a Master's program in Statistics at a Flemish university. He has brought along a friend (FRI). His main queries with the administrator (ADM) are about the timing of registration and his refugee status. A student-researcher is present as an observer of the interaction (OBS in the transcription).[1]

Excerpt 1

01 **ADM:** hello good afternoon what can I do for you?
02 **CLI:** I am searching for a ((hands over documents))
03 **ADM:** yes okay so can I have all your documents please? (7.0)
04 **ADM:** I just have one question as well (..) erm (..) this girl has to do her paper for her bachelor program (..) and she is following the conversations we have (..) and we need to have your authorization that she can follow and she can record this conversation (5.0)

05	CLI:	so *** (..) I don't understand what you what do you mean?
06	ADM:	[slower pace] well she needs to have some information some concrete data conversations to use in her paper – maybe she can explain a little bit more about the paper itself (..) yeah?
07	OBS:	it won't be about the content – it will just be the dynamics of theconversation (..) so I don't know if you have a problem with that – or that I can maybe use it for writing my bachelor paper for university (3.0)
08	CLI:	my university? (3.0)
09	OBS:	no
10	FRI:	no
11	ADM:	no it's for her
12	FRI:	[explains in L1 what was exchanged]
13	CLI:	oh actually I'm asking the question er I like to enroll in Master of Statistics
14	ADM:	mmhh
15	CLI:	I have (..) certificate
16	ADM:	yeah
17	CLI:	but I am a refugee
18	ADM:	mmhh
19	CLI:	can I keep admission
20	ADM:	admission
21	CLI:	yeah
22	ADM:	did you already start the admissions procedure?
23	CLI:	no
24	ADM:	no
25	CLI:	just (..) just (..) I have I have taken the form
26	ADM:	the form
27	CLI:	form
28	ADM:	yes and you have filled it out?
29	CLI:	I have yeah I have pli pri form what I printed what I have
30	ADM:	mmhh so you want me
31	CLI:	*** *** ***
32	ADM:	yeah?
33	CLI:	have I time maybe in June one think?
34	ADM:	erm normally yes (..) you have time until June the first
35	CLI:	yeah
36	ADM:	to hand in your complete application
37	CLI:	yeah
38	ADM:	package
39	CLI:	yeah
40	ADM:	you have all your documents?
41	CLI:	yeah I have all my documents
42	ADM:	yes (..) can I check your documents please?
43	CLI:	yeah (39.0 checking the documents)

68 Part 1: The (Im)mobilization of Language Resources, Repertoires and Practices

44	ADM:	and are you already recognized as a fugitive?
45	CLI:	I'm
46	ADM:	or are you still in the process
47	CLI:	I'm
48	ADM:	of being recognized as a fugitive?
49	CLI:	I have just this document (..) hold on
50	ADM:	so what you also need to add to your file is a letter from your counselor (..) so your lawyer who is defending your case to be recognized as a refugee erm that you are still in the process
51	CLI:	yeah
52	ADM:	yes you're not officially recognized yet he?
53	CLI:	yeah
54	ADM:	you're still in the process? (..) so we need to have a letter from your lawyer erm that you're still in the process
55	CLI:	yeah
56	ADM:	and these documents (..) they look okay to me but what you also erm can do is you can go to the court of first instance to have them legalized (..) they will translate into Dutch probably

This exchange is characterized by a rather striking contrast between, on the one hand, the lengthy opening sequence, with successive elaborations, in which the administrator and the student-observer together seek to establish the legitimate presence of the student-researcher (Turns 01–12) and, on the other hand, the rather straightforward and apparently unproblematic way in which the administrator's less-than-optimal formulation of categories is passed over without comment and appears not to affect mutual comprehension in the execution of the administrative task at hand.

When the administrator, after the initial transaction in which she asked for and received the documents, changes the topic of the talk to requesting permission for the researcher's presence, this results in an elaborated misunderstanding. The client signals his failure to understand in Turn 05, 'I don't understand'. Also the repetition in Turn 06 and the student-researcher's invited elaboration in Turn 07 are met with a display of non-comprehension in Turn 08, '[is this about] my university?' (with question intonation). At that point, the client's friend steps in and explains the situation in an L1-exchange between the two of them, and after the clarification, in Turn 13, the client switches back to English and states his request to enroll for the Master's program in Statistics.

Inasmuch as failed client comprehension despite the elaborations seems to characterize the opening sequence of the interaction, the same client does not appear to make an issue of the administrator's subsequent failure to make a distinction between a 'refugee' (the client's formulation in Turn 17) and a 'fugitive' (the administrator's subsequent reformulation in Turns 44 and 48) when checking the formal recognition of the client's civil status. While the two related terms come with fundamentally different entailments (a refugee is a victim, a fugitive not necessarily; 'refugee' is an officially recognized civil identity, whereas 'fugitive' is a classification in the social domain), the client may also be expected to take offence and object to the use of 'fugitive' to describe his social reality and status. Yet, the client allows this to pass. The use of the term 'fugitive' is not challenged or commented upon. In fact, upon the third mention, the administrator switches back to 'refugee' in Turn 50 and the exchange is concluded unproblematically with two pieces of advice: a letter is needed from the client's lawyer stating that he is in the process of seeking recognition, as well as a translation of the documents ratified by the court of first instance.

We suggest that the task-focusedness of the client in this particular exchange helps explain the apparently contradictory orientations between the two stages of the encounter. In the opening sequence, the administrator's use 'I just have one question as well' (Turn 04) has been unsuccessful in signaling a preliminary digression from the client's request to a permission-seeking routine for recording data. This is certainly suggested by the client's Turn 08: '[is this about] my university?', which suggests relevance in the student registration procedure. After the explanation, the client does not return to the permission question and, without further ado, returns to his administrative query (Turn 13). The same task-focusedness, and the observation that things are getting done, may be behind the client's move not to engage with the difference between 'fugitive' and 'refugee' – an illustration of the 'let-it-pass' principle (Firth, 1996). At the same time, the question may be raised if the client understands the difference between fugitive and refugee, or between refugee and asylum seeker. While we have no externalized conversational behavior to demonstrate the former, the data do show that the client makes no distinction between refugee and asylum seeker. Strictly speaking, and contrary to how he self-identifies (Turn 17: 'I am a refugee'), he is an asylum seeker in the process of being recognized as a refugee. The fact that he himself does not use the term with judicial currency to refer to his status may explain why he does not take offence at the use of the term 'fugitive'. But this does not detract from our overall point. The client's and the administrator's shared task-focusedness, despite apparent limitations in proficiency in English, positively affects the accomplishment of the institutional task. Arguably, the message seems to be: keep formulations short and be focused on the task to be done; elaborations cause difficulties. At the same time, the elaboration at the beginning turns out to be ineffective, possibly because the administrator did not succeed in establishing that this was going to be a detour from and preamble to the real institutional transaction: i.e. first seek permission to record, then deal with the client's administrative request.

Case 2: The Need to Perform Interactional Alignment at a Meta-communicative Level

Our second case is an interview between a Flemish social worker (SW in the transcription) and a Syrian asylum seeker (AS in the transcription) at a regional welfare agency[2] that offers frontline legal assistance to people with an uncertain residence status. The asylum seeker has made an application to the Belgian asylum authorities for international protection and he is now waiting to be invited for a second interview at the Office of the Commissioner General for Refugees and Stateless Persons (CGRS), the central asylum authority in Belgium. He has heard that the waiting period between the first and the second interview can take up to one year or more. As the asylum seeker expresses his concerns about this, the social worker decides to call the CGRS to check whether this is really the case. The CGRS confirms that the procedure may indeed take longer than usual due to the exceptionally high number of Syrian asylum applications at that time. Excerpt 2 starts at the point where the social worker tries to explain to the asylum seeker what the CGRS official has just discussed with her over the phone. The interview is conducted in English. While the social worker has a fair ability to express herself in English, the explanation of complex legal categories in English turns out to be really challenging. The asylum seeker is Arabic speaking and has a sufficient command of English to allow him to explain his situation and answer questions about his asylum application. Despite the social worker's suggestion of using an Arabic interpreter, the asylum seeker insists on doing the interview in English. But as it turns out, the social worker shares her office with an Arabic speaking intern (INT), and she is invited to step in when the asylum seeker cannot understand the social worker.

Excerpt 2

01　**SW:**　*Ja* it's true that it can take a long time because many people ask asylum who are from Syria so that's =euhm =and since =euh it's always one part of the *commissariaat* who does the interviews (0.1) They do the Middle-East section they do that =so it can take =they don't cannot say how long but euhm =and euhm =so it can take a year maybe =but euh if you want you can ask for to have a =euhm =quick euhm =that they ask =that they take your =euhm (0.1) demand for asylum before other ones (0.1) but you have you need to be =euh =you have to have a motivation (0.1) You need to say why

02　**AS:**　Uhu

03 SW: So what can you say
04 AS: Nothing what I can say
05 SW: Why you are more why yours is more urgent than ther ones?
06 AS: I don't understand
07 SW: So you can say yeah I want to have an interview soon for this reason (0.1) Wha =wh =why? For instance I don't know =give me an example =I don't know (0.2) euh =yeah =you don't have a place to stay (0.1) But then they will say yeah you can go to a center (0.1) So I don't know which reason you can give
08 AS: I don't understand you
09 SW: Ah
10 AS: ((addresses the intern in Arabic for clarification))
11 SW: ((addresses the intern in Dutch)) Ja wil jij nog eens =het is zo dat je =hij kan vragen voor een versnelling van de procedure maar dan moet hij een goeie motivatie hebben en ik weet niet welke motivatie dat hij kan= aangeven *(TRANSLATION INTO ENGLISH: Yes could you once more =the thing is that you = he could ask for an acceleration of the procedure but then he must have a good motivation and I don't know what motivation he can =point out)*
12 INT: ((interaction in Arabic between AS and SW in which the INT interprets what SW has explained so far))
13 INT: He said =euh the situation =wha =where he is =euh is enough for him to =so he cannot say (0.2)
14 SW: No that's not a good reason

Our analysis of this exchange starts from two main observations which are elaborated on below, viz. (a) the tension between experiential and institutional orientations to the task and outcome of the encounter, and (b) the significance of meta-communicative awareness and performance in bridging contextual gaps between speakers. First, the participants in the exchange clearly display different orientations to the institutional task at hand. These differences can be observed not only 'between' the speakers but also between the social worker's successive shifting stances on her professional role as counsellor. In the beginning of the consultation, the social worker adopted a supporting, even empathizing role in showing understanding for the asylum seeker's precarious situation arising from the protracted asylum procedure. This even prompted her to take further action by contacting the CGRS to inquire about the current state of affairs. As soon as the social worker starts conveying to the asylum seeker what the CGRS employee has just explained over the phone (Turn 01), her supporting role shifts into that of information provider. It is important to note here that 'providing information' actually implies the very complicated discursive task of rendering contextually dense input in a different language. The message she has to convey entails a complex line of argument, viz. that in order to work more efficiently, the CGRS is organized in geographical sections that examine applications with similar profiles (mainly based on country or region of origin), and that due to an increased influx of asylum seekers from Syria, the Middle-East section is overburdened with high numbers of applications, which in turn causes the waiting period to take up to one year or more. The social worker clearly struggles to get this line of reasoning across, as can be seen from her numerous false starts, word-finding problems and self-corrections in Turn 01. Terminology is either not translated (e.g. Dutch 'Commissariaat') or cover vocabulary is used (e.g. 'part' instead of 'geographical sections'). References lack explicitness (e.g. 'they' to refer to the asylum officers). Important links between the utterances remain implicit so that very little of the original message survives in the social worker's rendition.

The difficult task of getting across procedurally dense and complex information in a foreign language becomes even more challenging in the subsequent turns, at the point where the social worker actively shifts to an advisory role. Having established that the asylum seeker's concerns are indeed justified, the social worker suggests the possibility of applying for a prioritized treatment. The prioritized procedure was created at EU level to encourage Member States 'to favorably prioritize applications from persons with manifestly well-founded claims or vulnerabilities warranting special procedural guarantees' (ECRE, 2017: 2). As this procedure is rarely invoked in practice,[3] the criteria for applications to be processed by a prioritized procedure are not clearly stipulated. CGRS discourages priority requests from a concern that shorter procedures may affect 'qualitative, thorough and individual' assessments (CGRS website). The only specification provided for in the Regulation is that 'the application is likely to be well-founded or where the applicant has special needs' (Art. 23(3) of Directive 2005/85). The social worker tries to explain the procedure and its entry requirements but gets stuck on terminology: as she cannot find the English term 'prioritized procedure', she proceeds to paraphrase by explaining the procedure (Turn 01: 'they take your demand for asylum before others') and its eligibility criteria (Turn 01: 'you have to have a motivation', 'you need to say why'). It is interesting to see how the social worker lays bare the gatekeeping process in her attempt to match the asylum seeker's situation with the category of 'applications that deserve priority'. Also here, a lot of meaning remains implicit, as for example in Turn 03, where the seemingly straightforward question 'so what can you say?' actually implies 'so what could you possibly use as an argument to qualify as a candidate for prioritized treatment?'. Despite her numerous efforts to elicit from the asylum seeker possible criteria for category membership (Turn 05: 'why is yours more urgent than other ones?'), the asylum seeker appears not to understand (Turn 06). The social worker tries yet another approach in Turn 07, this time explaining the institutional category from a more experiential perspective, i.e. by putting herself in her client's position, animating a hypothetical line of reasoning for the asylum seeker, while leaving it up to the asylum seeker to complete. In the absence of a response, the social worker tries to give an example herself, but it soon becomes clear that it is very difficult to come up with a good reason on behalf of her client. Moreover, her repeated use of 'I don't know' ('k weet het niet hé') may be confusing for the asylum seeker (What is it that the social worker does not know? What if even the social worker does not know?). The social worker expresses uncertainty indeed, although this is not uncertainty or lack of knowledge about the procedure itself, but rather it expresses her reluctance to impose a possible motivation on the client as if she is saying, 'I don't know if this is the case for you because I don't know your situation that well'. The social worker eventually fills in a possible reason on behalf of the asylum seeker (Turn 07: 'you don't have a place to stay'), but immediately undermines her own example, adopting the perspective of the deciding authorities (Turn 07: 'but then they will say you can go to a center'). Despite the social worker's communicative efforts, the asylum seeker still does not understand (Turn 08), after which the social worker throws in the towel (Turn 07: 'I don't know which reason you can give').

Interestingly, the asylum seeker then turns to the Arabic speaking intern to accomplish clarification. The social worker supports this initiative (Turn 11: 'ja wil jij nog eens', meaning 'could you try' – the remaining part 'to explain this to him' is left implicit). The social worker now explains the procedure in Dutch instead of English. The contrast is striking: terminology is no longer an obstacle and, owing to the intern's familiarity with the asylum procedure, less needs to be explicated. The intern, now adopting the role of an ad hoc interpreter and despite visible limitations in method and formulation, concludes in Turn 13 that the asylum seeker is of the opinion that the pressing nature of his current situation in itself entitles him to get prioritized treatment so that no further argumentation is required. The social worker, however, realizes that what might be a good reason from an experiential point of view will not qualify as sufficient from an institutional perspective (Turn 14: 'no that's not a good reason'). While her supporting role allows her to fully align with her client, she also knows that only by acting in her capacity as legal advisor can she make a real difference to her client's situation. The most difficult part is to get the asylum seeker to make that switch as well. And there's the rub. She cannot make him understand that it is important for him to anticipate the institutional way of doing things and interpreting situations: personal situations have to fit certain categories and arguments will be verified.

Arguably, the main issue is a lack of institutional literacy on the part of the asylum seeker combined with a lack of interactional and (meta-)communicative resources on the part of the social worker to compensate for this. The asylum seeker, it appears, is not able to adopt the stance of a 'professional client' and make the switch from experiential to institutional reasoning, possibly because he lacks the necessary institutional knowledge. At the same time, the social worker and the asylum seeker lack linguistic-interactional common ground to explicate the institutional framework of a priority application. In circumstances such as the case outlined here, an intermediary explanation of why verifiable information is so important might have made a difference. Still, despite the interactants' sufficient command of English to perform straightforward communicative tasks, lingua franca use clearly falls short in getting across the contextually dense meanings that such a mediating explanation actually requires.

Case 3: Contesting the Action Implications of an Entitlement

In our third case, a client with refugee status from a West African country (CLI in the transcription below), who has been granted a residence permit on medical grounds, meets with the social worker (SW) to discuss various aspects of financial assistance from the local municipality's social welfare department (in particular, expenditure for rent and medication). The client is a new client in the local office: he has recently moved from another city. As is procedurally required, the local police have made the statutory visit to the client's home to confirm the change in address and residency, but this change has not yet been registered in the computer system (the client needs the registration of residence, among other things, in order to be able to enroll for a learning program). He has managed to secure some employment (part-time and on an irregular basis) but is experiencing cash flow problems (the sequence of monthly allowance payments is still to be enacted). The client's 'orange' residency card also makes it difficult to find work. The social worker undertakes to apply for a 'surplus exception', which will allow the client to earn something extra which is not held against his allowance (this is an incentive to secure employment). After that, 10 minutes into the conversation, the topic of the talk shifts to the medical prescription, which the client has brought along.

Excerpt 3

01	SW:	first and (..) I still have to take a copy of this one (..) this one I have
02	CLI:	yeah yeah have copy (..) er the medicine (..) I don't know I can get two pack from you
03	SW:	I told (..) erm (..) because I got a positive decision er (..) for that it's four hundred thirty-one (..) or something (..) tell me when you are going to get it and I try I do the payment in your account (..) so when do you needed it?
04	CLI:	I need it for (..) for this month (..) this month I also need medicine because I don't have this this
05	SW:	it's finished?
06	CLI:	it's almost (..) only one strip (..) for me there
07	SW:	and how long do you take (..) how long do you do with that?
08	CLI:	that that's for (..) erm that's for (..) ten days
09	SW:	ten days (..) yeah (..) okay (..) I'll try to make sure it's on your account next week(..) but I want the proof of
10	CLI:	no but you can buy it and give me here?
11	SW:	no I I I can't I don't buy
12	CLI:	and keep the receipt (..) I know
13	SW:	we're not allowed to do it we don't we don't do that (..) I give you the money and you just give me the proof of payment (..) mhm-okay? so I'm gonna put it in your account (..) you use that money and then you show me afterwards okay I use it then I know everything is okay
14	CLI:	you got my account already there (..) I think you buy it I just come for it (..) it will be okay
15	SW:	no but we don't (..) we don't (..) we don't do anything
16	CLI:	pass the money into my account (..) I don't really understand
17	SW:	no?
18	CLI:	yeah I don't understand how you do
19	SW:	it will be four hundred thirty-one euro extra
20	CLI:	you can (..) you can buy that in
21	SW:	but I got (..) I can I cannot go
22	CLI:	*** any money in my account always (..) I don't really really understand there (..) so
23	SW:	the only problem is I cannot go for you to the pharmacy (..) I can't do that
24	CLI:	yeah but then keep the money I come for I go and buy that and give receipt back or put money in my account later
25	SW:	or I'll make sure that it's there on Tuesday and Tuesday you go to the pharmacy and I call you
26	CLI:	yeah that's no problem
27	SW:	yeah? then you know that's that day it will be in your account
28	CLI:	*** go and get for it and buy the medicine
29	SW:	so you don't (.) yeah

30 CLI: when you put it there ... yeah it's
31 SW: it is it is you who will be responsible er for the buying of the medication
32 CLI: yes now but when I don't want for you to put it there for I don't know something and I *** ***
33 SW: I'm gonna call you yeah
34 CLI: yeah
35 SW: I'm gonna make sure
36 CLI: something e
37 SW: I'm gonna call you that day
38 CLI: okay
39 SW: yeah? so you know it's not money from nowhere ... I'm gonna take a copy of this one okay?
40 CLI: mhm (..) okay
41 SW: [more silently as if self-talk] okay so you have the right (..) amounts
42   [SW leaves room to take photocopies of the prescription]

The topic pursued in this exchange is not the entitlement itself, but how it is acted upon by the client and the social worker. When the client suggests an alternative course of action for its implementation, a disagreement unfolds over the action implications of the financial assistance entitlement. Following an initial exchange about the cost of the medication, how often it has to be bought and how far the client is in using up his current prescription, the social worker announces that the money will be made available through the client's bank account, but she will need proof of purchase after the client's visit to the pharmacy (Turn 09). To this, the client responds with the suggestion of an alternative routine (Turns 10–12): why doesn't the social worker buy the medication for him and keep the receipt? The client is cut short and there is overlapping talk. The professional brief for institutional agents is that they can mediate on behalf of clients, but they cannot go to the shop to buy things for clients (Turn 11). The social worker continues with an explanation of how things have to be done (Turn 13). The client repeats his suggestion (Turn 14) and expresses his disbelief that his suggested alternative course of action is not possible in Turns 16 and 18.

The disagreement continues after that and it can be noted how the social worker orients her talk to meeting the client half-way: following the voicing of another alternative course of action in Turn 18 (the client buys the medication and the money is claimed later, 'yeah but then keep the money I come for I go and buy that and give receipt back or put money in my account later'), the social worker announces that she will make sure the amount has been paid into the account by the following Tuesday and she will notify the client of this by telephone, so that 'you know it's not money coming from nowhere' (Turn 38). While the client initially appears to okay the suggested variant of the scenario (Turn 25, 'yeah that's no problem'), he nevertheless returns to his first suggestion in Turns 27, 29 and 31. This final voicing of the same suggestion is not responded to by the social worker. Instead, she persists with the scenario of notification by telephone. The client expresses agreement, albeit rather tokenistically (Turns 37 and 39). The exchange is concluded with the social worker leaving the room to make a photocopy of the prescription document.

Although some aspects of the formulations in this sequence remain unclear, the speakers do not signal gaps in understanding. The talk moves pretty fast. There is overlap and specific formulations invite 'gap filling'. For instance, that the client in Turn 23 suggests that he can pre-pay the medication does not really accord with his earlier line of talk about experiencing cash flow problems. It is one plausible interpretation of the turn, but this cannot be established with certainty. Perhaps the contradiction can be resolved by recognizing that the turn has to be read as coming from a 'warrior client', a voice of protest against the institutional scenario being unnecessarily cumbersome and complicated. In Turn 23, the client would thus suggest a way of doing things which both aligns with the institutional view (cf. the social worker cannot buy things for the client) and is less complicated (it involves fewer steps and exchanges). Read like that, the client's turn expresses indignation at institutional scenarios being unnecessarily cumbersome by suggesting: I can do it better even when I play it by your rules. One can think of other underlying motivations, for instance, a distrust of banking in his situation, or lack of clarity about which money he could then use for the medication. However, the motivation for the client's protest does not surface in his contributions to the talk. Nor does the social worker inquire into the specific reasons why the client objects to the institutionally prescribed way of proceeding, caught as the two interactants appear to be in the quick pace of a disagreement sequence.

Discussion

Our micro-analysis of institutional language data demonstrates how the use of global English as an (im)mobile resource in service encounters with asylum seekers and refugees in Flanders is closely related to the multilingual and interactional dynamics governed by underlying processes of institutional categorization. As institutional agents meet with minority clients from other national and/or ethnic backgrounds, it does not take long before they face the pressures of having to explain or make accessible particular 'local' institutional categories, concepts and ways of going about things. In some interactions, nation-specific concepts receive translations (e.g. 'the court of first instance' for 'rechtbank van eerste aanleg' in Turn 56 of Case 1). Some concepts are deemed more difficult to translate and are simply preserved in the institutionally dominant language (e.g. the use of Dutch 'commissariaat' in Turn 1 of Case 2). The choice not to translate often signals the need to understand the term technically and locally specific, and therefore as 'lost in translation'. In yet other situations, concepts are not translated nor preserved in L1, but their use is accompanied by a paraphrase or explanation (e.g. 'prioritized procedure' in Case 2), as a way around the possibility of translating straightforwardly. In addition to these more active forms of linguistic mediation that institutional agents, and possibly to a lesser degree also clients, engage in, one will equally note the effects of underlying L1 textualities as formal substratum effects that show in unfolding speaker formulations. This is especially the case when speakers struggle to translate and clarify categories and situations that they habitually talk about, not in English but in their L1 (e.g. the SW's repeated use of 'I don't know' in Case 2, Turn 07, as a literal translation of ''k weet het niet', to underplay the relevance of his outsider perspective). These observations corroborate more recent views in ELF research that emphasize the increasingly multilingual nature, and global/local interface, of lingua franca English (Jenkins, 2015). Textualities in languages other than English constantly play a role in ELF-conducted institutional contexts. As Canagarajah (2011: 5) stresses, understanding global English use may be just as much a matter of 'shuttling between the languages [...] to co-construct meaning' as it may be a matter of conducting one's business and affairs via a resource recognized and named as 'English'. The interplay between English and other language resources in the repertoire, an intricate interplay between 'local' and 'mobile' resources that may emerge during the interaction, will almost inevitably come with practices of 'translanguaging' (Canagarajah, 2013; García, 2009). The flexible drawing on and moving between resources in a speaker's repertoire which will be recognized as belonging to different languages can both occur as substratum effects, as active translation practice, or the opposite – e.g. when dealing with the reality that something cannot be translated, or a situation in which it is not desirable to do so. With specific reference to the third excerpt, one can draw attention to such details as the social worker's use of 'so you know it's not money from nowhere' (Turn 39). The turn amounts to saying, 'so you'll know where the money comes from', with underlying Dutch: 'zo dat je weet dat het geld niet van nergens komt'; this expression particularly indexes a more informal, even half-joking stance – a stance which is not necessarily picked up by the client here. Similarly, the social worker's Turn 05, 'it's finished', can be connected to underlying Dutch, ''t is op', meaning 'have you finished it?'. However, substratum effects are equally detected beyond the lexico-grammatical level. Again with reference to the third case, the social worker's non-fluency markers in Turn 31 (signaling 'have you got it?'), are arguably used in a way that is influenced by the agent's L1.

At the same time, the data cases have demonstrated that different encounters clearly come with different conditions and requirements for effective communication. In Case 1, it could be seen how different types of linguistic and interactional resources compensated for each other. Limited language proficiency at the level of formulation was compensated for by advanced interactional skills and a shared task-focusedness. Case 2 was initially built on cooperation between the participants (both parties wanted to find a solution for the asylum seeker's precarious situation), but interactional alignment was lost when the speakers did not succeed in responding to limitations in understanding. They seemed to lack the required linguistic and interactional common ground to meet the high contextual demands of the exchange. What could remain implicit, vague or even incorrect in Case 1 caused incomprehension in Case 2. In Case 3, on the other hand, the use of English as a multilingual resource turned out to be successful. Despite substantial differences in communicative resources, the interactants openly performed their 'dance of disagreement' and achieved a common understanding on what they disagreed upon.

It is therefore instructive to attend to both the verbal and the interactional dimensions of communicative behavior. Hence, following Canagarajah (2013: 14), the 'focus should not be on a shared form, but on the pragmatic strategies people use to negotiate difference and achieve intelligibility'. Whether or not lingua franca use can contribute successfully to the accomplishment of an adequate and fair procedure depends, in line with Canagarajah (2013: 836), not only on the sharedness of the language resource but equally on reciprocity. Relevant interactional strategies to this end may be listener initiated (e.g. lexical anticipation, lexical suggestion, lexical correction, not give up, repetition, request clarification, let it pass, listen to the message, participant paraphrase, participant prompt, etc.) or speaker initiated (spell out the word, rephrase, repeat, be more explicit, paraphrase, hedge on the use of local/idiomatic references, take the trouble to repair oneself, provide backchannel, rely on checking mechanisms, accommodate to client linguistic proficiencies and assumed pre-knowledge, orient explicitly to institutional expectations, etc.).

It is worth noting how each of the three analyzed fragments above underlines the need to highlight contextualization practice (Gumperz,

1982, 1999), both in terms of understanding behavior from the participant's point of view and as a form of analytical-interpretative practice (Bauman & Briggs, 1990). Interactional alignments are evident from the deployment of particular contextualization cues, which may also provide important indices for understanding an interactant's orientation to situated requirements of clarity, explicitness and precision. Situated here means: at this particular moment of speaking in this particular procedure. And, perhaps even more noteworthy is that it can go both ways: more of it, or less of it. It is to be questioned whether the 'more relaxed circumstances', in which none of the participants is a native speaker, do actually come with an assumption that, being equally (dis)advantaged, understanding will be sorted out between the speakers, as it is recognized mutually that neither of the two are native speakers. In the case of Excerpt 3, there is the client's animated voice that signals the urgent insistence with which he suggests an alternative scenario for expediting the medical prescription and in the ensuing disagreement over what is procedurally (im)possible. Any interactional display of mutual sensitivity to what the other really says has certainly disappeared from sight. In Case 2, on the other hand, the social worker's hedging (hesitations, false starts, self-corrections, use of 'euhm'), imprecision (deictic ambiguity, terminological inexactitude) and lack of meta-communicative display (not managing to explain the importance of an institutional perspective) overshadow his attempts to express his engagement with the asylum seeker. The social worker's elaborate interactional display seems to fail in its purpose. This may be due to the social worker's imprecise wording, probably in combination with the asylum seeker's limited administrative and procedure-related knowledge. But, even when the Arabic speaking intern steps in to help explain the social worker's proposal, the asylum seeker does not respond to the worker's intended reasoning.

Therefore, the next question to be raised is whether interactional understanding can be separated at all from the interactants' situated orientation to the state of play in the institutional task at hand. Mutual (in)comprehension, the (lack of) display of it, and of any expectations one may have at that particular point, appears itself very much a function of the social-actional position at the moment of speaking: it is a positioning that needs to be understood in terms of other interests than mutual (in)comprehension being more centrally at stake. It is a position not intrinsically oriented to accomplishing mutual understanding, but it is one oriented to the categorization processes that are taking place. The three cases selected for analysis each illustrate this. Although all three interactions take place in cooperative institutional settings, where service providers and their clients collaborate to obtain the best possible outcome for the client and where the interactional conditions are right for the participants to negotiate meaning, gradations in language proficiency, in procedural literacies and in underlying institutional pressures affect the ways in which the participants manage to achieve interactional alignment and meet the procedural requirements of the encounter.

Interactional understanding is closely linked to the transparency of the communicative and institutional goals pursued. As Cases 1 and 3 have demonstrated, communication can be successful, even with very limited communicative resources (Case 1) and different views on how things should be done (Case 3), as long as the dynamics of categorization are transparent to the interactants. However, when there is a lack of common 'need-to-know' (which may be caused by a digression from the institutional task at hand as in the opening sequence of Excerpt 1, or the introduction of an alternative institutional track in Case 2), successful speaker alignment may require complex communicative tasks such as anticipation of institutional literacies, and explication and meta-communication of contextually dense knowledge. And the complexities of the communicative event seem to increase as the underlying institutional pressures increase. While all three clients in the examined service encounters appear to experience little direct institutional pressure, the asylum seekers in Cases 1 and 2 find themselves in an institutionally much more precarious situation than the recognized refugee in Case 3. The insecurity inherent in their refugee identity also makes them more vulnerable in their interactions with host institutions, even if that interaction is intended to support them.

Moreover, gradations in institutional pressure tie in with the nature of the entitlement and the stringency of the eligibility criteria to be included in the category. Case 3 is about ensuring that the correct financial procedure is followed by the client for the purchase and reimbursement of medication. Entitlement itself is not an issue here: as a refugee, the client is entitled to medical support. Also, in Case 1, the eligibility criteria are fairly straightforward: asylum seekers have the right to study in the host country as long as they submit the required documents. Importantly, the documents that need to be submitted are independent of the refugee status of the client. Case 2 is more complicated because what is at stake here is the capacity of the asylum seeker to make his application meet the criteria of prioritized treatment. Entitlement here involves much more than a mere administrative formality (ensuring that the correct procedures are followed), as it depends on more subjective processes of evaluation and an assessment of the asylum seeker's personal motivation, which is inseparable from the insecure nature of his refugee status.

Concluding Remarks

This leads us to the conclusion that, even in cooperative institutional settings where interactants experience little direct institutional pressure, variable factors can get in the way of accomplishing mutual understanding. The combined effect of these situated variables is often hard to predict and may need to be addressed interactionally. In other words, even when the institutional conditions are apparently right for the interactants to communicate at a meta level, contextual differences (sociocultural, institutional, discursive) may remain unaddressed. The feasibility of English as a mobile, context-bridging resource in these encounters is closely related to how speakers interactionally align themselves in ways that may balance out potential contextual differences between them. While sufficient reciprocity between speakers can compensate for a lack of discursive resources, absence of reciprocity and alignment sets harder targets for linguistic and meta-pragmatic performance. In situations such as these, traditional center-periphery inequalities between global English varieties can emerge when the localized upward mobility associated with Western elite multilingualism takes precedence over the mobility of immigrant Englishes (Maryns, 2017). The linguistic heterogeneity and mobility of the participants in the institutional encounter may not only reflect but also consolidate global relations of inequality by which immigrant varieties of English get (re)valued against local regimes of language, identity and institutional legitimacy (Blommaert, 2016; Irvine & Gal, 2000; Park & Wee, 2009). These ideological implications of global English use may reduce the immigrants' capacity for linguistic mobility in the institutional process and, connected with it, their opportunities for upward social mobility and inclusion in the host society. In writing this, we stress the importance of conducting research at intersecting fields of inquiry in a globalized age. The sociolinguistics of multilingualism, the study of globalized varieties of a language (e.g. lingua franca English), the interactional analysis of institutional encounters, and translation/interpretation studies equally bear on our understanding of how contemporary institutions are responding to migration-affected conditions and the challenges that these pose to their functioning, including how successful the strategy may be for mobilizing globalized language resources.

Notes

(1) Transcription conventions:
 ***   unclear
 ===   latching, overlaps, self-corrections

(..)	pause
(3.2)	timed pause
Italics	use of another language

(2) Centrum voor Algemeen Welzijnswerk (CAW) – Centre for General Welfare work.
(3) Unlike the 'accelerated procedure', which was established for exactly the opposite purpose, viz. to allow 'manifestly unfounded applications' to be treated under an accelerated and 'less protective procedural regime' (ECRE, 2017: 2).

References

Agha, A. (2005) Voice, footing and enregisterment. *Journal of Linguistic Anthropology* 15 (1), 38–59.
Bauman, R. and Briggs, C. (1990) Poetics and performance as critical perspectives on language and social life. *Annual Review of Anthropology* 19, 59–88.
Bauman, Z. (2000) *Liquid Modernity*. Cambridge: Polity Press.
Bauwens, N. (2013) ELF in service encounters in Flanders: Social hierarchy reflected in discourse. Bachelor's paper, Ghent University.
Billig, M. (1985) Prejudice, categorization and particularization: From a perceptual to rhetorical approach. *European Journal of Social Psychology* 15, 79–103.
Blommaert, J. (2016) From mobility to complexity in sociolinguistic theory and method. In N. Coupland (ed.) *Sociolinguistics: Theoretical Debates* (pp. 242–259). Cambridge: Cambridge University Press.
Branswijk, G. (2014) Securing mutual understanding when English is used as a lingua franca: A study of practices in an OCMW-office. Master's dissertation, Ghent University.
Canagarajah, S. (2011) Translanguaging in the classroom: Emerging issues for research and pedagogy. *Applied Linguistics Review* 2, 1–28.
Canagarajah, S. (2013) *Translingual Practice: Global Englishes and Cosmopolitan Relations*. London: Routledge.
CGRS (Office of the Commissioner General for Refugees and Stateless Persons) (n.d.) *Explanation to the Asylum Seekers about the Waiting Periods*. See https://www.cgra.be/en/news/explanation-asylum-seekers-about-waiting-periods.
ECRE (European Council on Refugees and Exiles) (2017) *Accelerated, Prioritized and Fast-track Asylum Procedures: Legal Frameworks and Practice in Europe*. See https://www.ecre.org/wp-content/uploads/2017/05/AIDA-Brief_AcceleratedProcedures.pdf.
EU Council Directive 2005/85/EC of 1 December 2005 on Minimum Standards on Procedures in Member States for Granting and Withdrawing Refugee Status.
Firth, A. (1996) The discursive accomplishment of normality: On conversation analysis and 'lingua franca' English. *Journal of Pragmatics* 26, 237–259.
García, O. (2009) Education, multilingualism and translanguaging in the 21st century. In A. Mohanty, M. Panda, R. Phillipson and T. Skutnabb-Kangas (eds) *Multilingual Education for Social Justice: Globalising the Local* (pp. 128–145). New Delhi: Orient.
Goffman, E. (1967 [reprint 2017]) On face work. In *Interaction Ritual: Essays in Face-to-Face Behaviour* (pp. 5–47). Chicago, IL: Aldine.
Goffman, E. (1981) Footing. In *Forms of Talk* (pp. 124–159). Philadelphia, PA: University of Pennsylvania Press.
Gumperz, J. (1982) *Discourse Strategies*. Cambridge: Cambridge University Press.

Gumperz, J. (1999) On interactional sociolinguistic method. In S. Sarangi and C. Roberts (eds) *Talk, Work and Institutional Order: Discourse in Medical, Mediation and Management Settings* (pp. 453–471). Berlin: Mouton de Gruyter.

Hall, C., Slembrouck, S. and Sarangi, S. (2006) *Language Practices in Social Work: Categorisation and Accountability in Child Welfare*. London: Routledge.

Irvine, J.T. and Gal, S. (2000) Language ideology and linguistic differentiation. In P.V. Kroskrity (ed.) *Regimes of Language: Ideologies, Polities, and Identities* (pp. 35–83). Santa Fe, NM: School of American Research Press.

Jenkins, J. (2015) Repositioning English and multilingualism in English as a lingua franca. *Englishes in Practice* 2 (3), 49–85.

Jenkins, J. and Wingate, U. (2015) Staff and student perceptions of English language policies and practices in 'international' universities: A UK case study. *Higher Education Review* 47 (2), 47–73.

Jenks, C. (2012) Doing being reprehensive: Some interactional features of English as a lingua franca in a chat room. *Applied Linguistics* 33 (4), 386–405.

Mäkitalo, Å. (2014) Categorisation. In C. Hall, K. Juhila, M. Matarese and C. van Nijnatten (eds) *Analysing Social Work Communication* (pp. 25–43). London: Routledge.

Maryns, K. (2006) *The Asylum Speaker: Language in the Belgian Asylum Procedure*. London: Routledge.

Maryns, K. (2013) Disclosure and (re)performance of gender-based evidence in an interpreter-mediated asylum interview. *Journal of Sociolinguistics* 17 (5), 661–686.

Maryns, K. (2017) The use of English as ad hoc institutional standard in the Belgian asylum interview. *Applied Linguistics* 38 (5), 737–758.

Park, J. and Wee, L. (2009) The three circles redux: A market-theoretic perspective on World Englishes. *Applied Linguistics* 30 (3), 389–406.

Permentier, S. (2012) The role of English in the coordination of professional behaviour and conduct. Bachelor's paper, Ghent University.

Sarangi, S. and Slembrouck, S. (1996) *Language, Bureaucracy and Social Control*. London: Longman.

Seidlhofer, B. (2011) *Understanding ELF*. Oxford: Oxford University Press.

Slembrouck, S. (2021) Bureaucracy. In J. Stanlaw (ed.) *The International Encylopedia of Linguistic Anthropology*. Wiley Online. doi:10.1002/9781118786093.iela0043

Verhallen, T., Hall, C., Slembrouck, S. and Kirkwood, S. (2017) Managing arguments in social work encounters. *International Journal of Child and Family Welfare* 17 (1/2), 85–104.

Weyns, B. (2013) English as a lingua franca in service encounters with migrants in Belgium: Moving away from the social vacuum. Master's dissertation, Ghent University.

Part 2
(Im)mobilities, Technologies and Control

4 Controlling Migrants' (Im)mobilities through Telecommunications: Technopolitical Governance in Telephony Advertising Discourse

Maria Sabaté-Dalmau

Introduction: The Emergence of Technopolitical Institutions Targeting Migrants

Neoliberal governance: Controlling migrants through ICT-mediated mobility regimes

Current forms of social organization are dependent on, and regulated through, information and telecommunication technologies (henceforth ICT) (Castells, 2000 [1996]), which are key for transnational mobility, and which have become a crucial source of economic, political and social networking power, at the turn of the 21st century (Castells, 2009).

In economic terms, ICT have become the 'new petroleum' (Harvey, 2005: 159) of the globalized economy, as they are now the main source of productivity growth and of accumulation of economic value (Clifton *et al.*, 2011). Present-day telecommunications businesses seek to protect their shares in 'domestic' markets in the face of supranational competition in a deregulated market (Pujolar, 2007), by using newer commercial strategies that draw upon the (im)mobility conditions and needs of transnational populations. These business practices include the ICT sector's capitalization on commercial information concerning the calling behaviors of emergent consumer groups, particularly migrant citizens, who are targeted as a new market niche, as they invest en masse in ICT when trying to access resources such as health, schooling, employability or socioeconomic advancement (Castells *et al.*, 2007).

With regard to political power, ICT have become a fundamental resource for 'technologized governments' (Diminescu, 2008: 567) to navigate international mobility policies and secure their monopoly of sovereignty and demographic control within their territorial borders. Newer 'mobility regimes' (Deumert, 2020: 236) have emerged that regulate cross-border mobility by limiting and directing people's (freedom of) movement. These regimes crucially hinge upon the governments' policies regulating the conditions of access to the ICT available in the market, particularly mobile phone cards (Sabaté i Dalmau, 2014). Thus, ICT have consolidated as *a governance apparatus* to police demographic mobility and access to 'national' citizenship statuses (Inda, 2006).

In terms of networking power, ICT have become the 'social glue' (Vertovec, 2009: 54) for all sorts of civil organizations and networks of individuals – particularly for (un)documented migrants, who have developed myriad strategies (subversive and otherwise) to be at the cutting edge in ICT adoption (Panagakos & Horst, 2006). This is so because they require engagement with the ICT market in order to manage transnational family life and to get incorporated into host societies (Ros *et al.*, 2007) (see Jacquemet, this volume, on this point).

Departing from this approach to ICT as an unprecedented source of socioeconomic power, political control and networking capital, in this chapter I approach ICT-mediated mobility regimes as a *citizenship gatekeeping mechanism*, that is, as an unequally distributed and socially stratifying governance tool that is at the epicenter of modern legality regimes (see Horner & Dailey-O'Cain, 2020). These mobility regimes have led to network societies sustained upon social inequality, as they enhance the gap between the 'technology-haves' (e.g. businesspersons, international students or tourists), whose opportunities for mobility have intensified (Urry, 2007), and the 'technology-have-nots' (Bertot, 2003: 185) with curtailed chances for demographic movement (e.g. undocumented migrants or refugees profiled as 'non-citizens'), who find themselves spatially and socioeconomically immobilized.

These citizenship regimes speak of newer complex governance practices of advanced liberal societies which are operationalized through neoliberal market-oriented technopolitical governance bodies. These consist of regulatory nation-state/market partnerships that have displaced welfare modes of governance in favor of the 'financialization' (Harvey, 2005: 33) of individual well-being, putting political practice at the service of the economy, with the help of media corporations who give them a voice. One of the most powerful technopolitical blocks of governance is the nation-state/ICT-sector 'tandem', which remains largely under-explored, but which is essential to understand present-day im/mobility regimes that govern transnational societies (see section on 'Theoretical background and research aims').

In this study, I try to show how (macro) technopolitical governance concerning the execution of im/mobility regimes takes shape in the public arena and is made available in (micro) commonplace discourse – more specifically, in migrant-tailored telephony advertising discourse. I suggest that advertising discourse analysis focalizing on migrants' marketed narrative identities is an effective mechanism to understand how nation-state authorities and ICT-market corporations activate and justify the current practices that curtail the ICT-mediated transnational-living conditions of the 'illegals'.[1] In particular, I argue that commercial discourse, in the ICT realm, allows for the problematization of the institutionalization of racialized profilings of migrants whose opportunities for mobility 'off the radar' of regulatory institutions pose a challenge to the integrity of 'national' sovereignty, but whose economic power is much needed for 'local' telecommunications companies. Overall, this analysis of technopolitical governance in politicized telephony advertising, mobilized for both political and profit-making purposes, contributes to the critical exploration of the legitimization of xenophobic discourses concerning migrants' im/mobilities that keep penetrating our everyday life, through exclusionary narrative constructions of migrants' 'place identities' (Ribbens-Klein, 2020: 63), as detailed below.

The Study: A Contribution to Technopolitics through the Analysis of Migrant-tailored Advertising Discourse on Im/mobilities

Theoretical considerations and research aims

From a critical sociolinguistics perspective (Duchêne *et al.*, 2013), in this chapter I problematize current ICT-mediated mobility regimes which are established by '*neoliberal governance institutions*' (Martín-Rojo & Del Percio, 2019: 3) in order to both control and profit from transnational populations, now conceptualized as economicized bodies whose opportunities to access basic resources in given nation-states (healthcare services, work permits, 'national language' certificates, mobile telephony, etc.) depend on their engagement, and compliance, with productivity-oriented 'self-governmentality' (Del Percio, 2018: 239). Self-governmentality is based on the tenets of self-discipline and self-control of one's personal/professional (migratory) trajectories and of one's (mobility) life choices to attain legality. Such neoliberal logics place the responsibility for fully fledged citizenship rights upon the self-made individual, under a meritocracy rhetoric of 'freedom' and 'equality of opportunities' that does not consider the prior unequal possibilities of access to legality conditions, in the first place. On the basis of this, I consider *neoliberal governmentality* institutions as market-driven governance blocks whereby nation-states concede governance authority to private (and privatized) institutions, in order to keep the monopoly of citizenship control (crucially here, ICT-access control) by following economic 'imperatives' (Martín-Rojo, 2019: 184).

I focus on one of such 'win-win' public-private political institutions, the technopolitical governance block, which constitutes an interested nation-state/telecommunications sector body: a regulatory entity exercising power through 'a politics that is mediated by technologies' (Khan & Kellner, 2005: 95; Sabaté-Dalmau, 2021).[2] I do so by zooming in on the ways in which market-driven neoliberal governance is played out in the ICT domain, where governments regulate the requirements for ICT access and where, simultaneously, ICT-business corporations target 'the undocumented' with legal coverage and governmental funding. I analyze technopolitics because it allows me to explore the intersections between neoliberal citizenship control, ICT-market power and public migrants' discriminatory profilings.

I contextualize the study in Catalonia (see section titled 'The Context: Technopolitical Governmentality in Spain'), a Catalan/Spanish speaking society of about 7.5 million inhabitants in Spain, for three reasons. First, the Spanish nation-state epitomizes how 'the real battle regarding migration' today is played out 'in the information domain' (Ros *et al.*, 2007: 5). This allows us to explore the emergence of dataveillance systems targeting migrants through the use of ICT as technologies of power. Second, the Spanish telecommunications sector illustrates how this industry approaches '*el segmento inmigrante*' ('the immigrant segment') as one of the most profitable 'target groups' for selling 'integration' services (e.g. international calling cards). This unpacks the market's activation of a strangerizing neoliberal metadiscourse (a 'message') that goes beyond profit-making rationalities, because it also tries to foster particular migrant identity projections as well as to 'conduct the[ir] conduct' (Martín-Rojo & Del Percio, 2019: 7), seeking to discipline migrants' (consumption) behaviors by drawing on commercial mobility-based social categorizations. Finally, at the time at which the study took place, Spain had one of the highest rates of undocumented migrants (Sànchez, 2008), which put the Ministry of the Interior in the spotlight of supranational institutions like the European Union. This political pressure strengthened the alliance between Spanish authorities and telecommunications companies for the modernization of 'legalization' policies via the regulation of migrants' conditions of access to ICT. This allows us to understand the political economy (i.e. the historicized socioeconomic processes and political structures) that propelled the technologization of the border control practices which are discursively (re)shaped and publicized in telephony advertising discourse.

In line with Martín Rojo and Del Percio's proposed research venues, I focus specifically on how technopolitical governmentality targeting migrants 'is constructed in discourse, what knowledge is generated thereby, and what technologies of power are employed to do so' (Martín Rojo & Del Percio, 2019: 9). Following suit, I zoom into the analysis of politically informed migrant-tailored telephony advertising discourse concerning im/mobilities as a route into the workings of the Spanish technopolitical governmentality block and into what it entails for migrants' access to citizenship. I provide a critique of what the telecommunications sector/Spanish nation-state partnership can tell us about the ways in which migrants' transnational-life practices (particularly, demographic movements) get objectified as a commercial resource, and about the ways in which they are publicly marketed as displaced '*extranjeros*' ('foreigners').

I narrow down the exploration of technopolitical techniques for migrants' regimentation and clientelization to the analysis of *narrative-identity constructions* that emerge in multimodal discourse in telephony advertising. I understand migrant-tailored advertising as a window into the commonplace constructions of 'transnational communication' that unfold how the technopolitical tandem operationalizes and accounts for Spain's restrictive ICT-mediated mobility regimes for foreigners. I argue that this unfolds newer (projected) (re)presentations of the (im)mobility trajectories that are attributed to, and expected from, this segment of society, which unpacks the extent to which the Spanish technopolitical institution makes use of power technologies to prosecute irregular migration. In this sense, I approach these merchandized identities and projected im/mobility trajectories as a research space in which to observe how neoliberal practices of social difference and discrimination penetrate media-sponsored publicity through ethnocentric, essentialist notions of migration.

The frameworks employed to conceptualize narrative (re)presentations of migrant identities in multimodal advertising discourse are the following. Departing from Bamberg *et al.*'s (2007) and Baynham and De Fina's (2005) approaches to narrative identity (specifically, unsettled/

dislocated selves), I conceive of commodified place identities as sites in which to explore how migrants are authoritatively ascribed who they are, with whom, where and why (and whom they call, how, etc.), in a particular projected time and space. These demography-oriented narrative categorizations 'come into being' when they are publicly activated – in this case, unidirectionally to a generalist audience, albeit with a clear focus on transnational clienthoods.

Departing from Kress and van Leeuwen's (2006) framework for visual-communication analysis, I understand telephony advertising discourse as encompassing hybrid text-and-image narrative identities presented through different multimodal practices across diverse media spaces (Cook, 2001). These practices are politicized meaning-making acts (Thurlow & Jaworski, 2006) which establish profit-making models of reality that reveal how migrants are fetishized in publicity discourse. Following suit, I 'read' these identity compositions by considering them calculated 'representational structures' (Kress & van Leeuwen, 2006: 59) that have Western-specific ideational, interpersonal and textual metafunctions. The ideational metafunction (re)presents (conceptualizes, classifies) particular personhood profiles; the interpersonal metafunction projects particular expected (normative) social relationships among these profiles (it constructs who shall interact and/or is interacting/reacting to what/whom); and, finally, the textual metafunction (re)creates how the depicted (absent/present) participants (shall) get *emplaced* in society.

Given that Kress and van Leeuwen's (2006) 'macro' framework involves all sorts of visual textual typologies, I have adapted Fuertes-Olivera *et al.*'s (2001) model of 'micro' *multimodal* discourse analysis which, also assuming that public visual communication is both informative and manipulative, narrows down the object of investigation to *advertising discourse*, particularly politically charged slogans. This model revisits the following six elements of commercial communication (Fuertes-Olivera *et al.*, 2001: 1293): (1) the addresser (the ICT company advertiser and its brand identity), who is the key mobilizer of the persuasive functions of language in ads; (2) the addressee or message-receiver/'viewer' (the target audience), whose projected/expected consumption behaviors are approached through the use of conative (i.e. directive, appellative, disciplining) language functions; (3) the reality (the advertised product/service), which is associated to referential functions of language that provide interested information or 'facts' about the 'good' on sale; (4) the channel (written/spoken; printed/online, etc.), which considers the commercial spaces where addressee(s) may be reached; as well as (5) the code or particular composition combining text and image layouts (involving language choices, position of images in texts, etc.), which focuses on the poetic functions or 'aesthetic' components of ads; and, finally, (6) the general message of the whole publicity campaign (the 'metadiscourse'; Fuertes-Olivera et al., 2001: 1296), the macro ideological schema where the particular advert gets inserted, which provides information on the overall aim of the marketing technique and on the business model chosen by ICT companies to sell their products and services, here with the complicity of the nation-state.

This analytical framework allows me to focus on how the merchandised place-oriented migrant identities that emerge in situated commercial discourse provide information on the neoliberal technologies of power that naturalize and consolidate exclusionary governmentality rationalities, exacerbating the rise of anti-migrant (discursive) practices in Europe. I basically show that migrants are stereotyped as non-fitting 'outsiders' in need of resocialization, through pejorative discourses that make use of racist profiling to present them as dislocated nation-state 'inbetweeners' and as ICT misusers (see section on 'Analysis and Findings'). With this, I hope to contribute to the study of the larger socioeconomic and political processes whereby anti-migrant technopolitical governance grounded upon neoliberal (im)mobility regimes penetrates mundane institutional discourse in one of the most powerful economic sectors in Southern Europe (see 'Concluding Remarks' section).

Data sources

Five data sets are employed for the analysis of '*extranjero*' identities in telephony advertising, which were gathered within a larger project that investigated migrants' life trajectories in 'ethnic' (migrant-tailored) call shops in Barcelona, between 2007 and 2009 (see Sabaté i Dalmau, 2014). These are: (1) 20 advertisements distributed in newspapers or commercial magazines by the 30 ICT company addressers that were operating at that time in Spain; (2) seven media corporation statements that developed on these companies' campaigns; (3) six interviews with social agents working for these 30 businesses, including mobile phone operator entrepreneurs, automatic translators catering for multinationals, and call center assistants in mobile phone operators; (4) ethnographic visits to phone shops in Barcelona, and to commercial events such as the Mobile World Congress (2008 edition); and, finally although crucially, (5) policy documents concerning mobility regimes and telecommunications laws issued by the Spanish government, responsible for the regulation of citizenship granting and ICT access in Catalonia (Parlament de Catalunya, 2007).[3]

The Context: Technopolitical Governmentality in Spain

The nation-state

Following the 2006/24/CE Directives for data storage approved by the European Parliament and the Council of Europe as a reaction to the terrorist attacks in the United States in 2001, the Spanish Cabinet passed a telecommunications bill called *Ley 25/2007* (October 2006), with the support of the multinational Telefónica. This regulation aimed at the technologization of public administration by adapting it to the European system (Plan Avanza, 2012). This law had a direct impact on transnational migrants, because it obliged operators to register the identity of all clients via personal identification (via proof of legal residency) by 2009.

Spain, before passing this law, had also experienced attacks such as the Madrid bombings in 2004, which killed 193 civilians. No known mastermind for the bombings was found, and 21 people from nationalities other than 'Spaniard' were charged (LegalToday, 2007). *Ley 25/2007* was passed as a 'national security' measure *'para la protección de las personas [...] y el mantenimiento de la seguridad pública'* ('for the protection of people [...] and the maintenance of public security') (BOE, 2007: 42520). It was presented by Social Democrat Pérez Rubalcaba, the then Spanish Minister of the Interior, as part of the global war on 'terrorism', as follows: *'Identificar al dueño de cada número es una tarea de vital importancia en la lucha contra el terrorismo y el crimen organizado'* ('To identify the owner of every telephone number is of crucial importance in the fight against terrorism and organized crime') (El País, 2009). This official statement addressed some media claims, presented in the form of 'informative' assertions (i.e. as discursive 'truths'; Fuertes-Olivera *et al.*, 2001: 1297), that 'migrant Muslims' were behind the bombings, despite the fact that no direct involvement of the al-Qaeda group (pointed out as the main suspect) was found. *Ley 25/2007* was also called 'Compulsory registration plan for prepaid calling card users', as it put emphasis on the storing of data of prepaid SIM cards, which could previously be sold without the provision of any legality document. It in fact established that SIM card users would have their account numbers cancelled, with automatic disconnection from the network by the company providers, if they remained unidentified. The 'Plan' was executed by making use of the infrastructure provided by Telefónica, who then became a privileged technopolitical partner of the nation-state in the unfolding of neoliberal ICT-related mobility regimes. This 'compulsory registration' affected many of the undocumented migrants whose only option to access mobile telephony was through unregistered SIM cards (about 15 million users were affected by this disconnection; Avui, 2009). The way in which this law was presented, with the imperative '¡*Identifícate!*' ('Identify yourself!'), together with the fact that it was issued by the Ministry of the Interior (*not* by the Ministry of Industry, upon which telecommunications depend), provides evidence that the nation-state was trying to incapacitate undocumented migrants and to curtail their mobility opportunities to access Spanish territory by making use of ICT, in a new dataveillance system (a technology of power) for technopolitical citizenship regimentation. As shown in the section on 'Analysis and Findings', this law also entailed a covert monolingual Spanish-language regime, necessarily required for migrants to access 'legalization' through the new 'technologized' administration.

The telecommunications sector

The ICT sector comprises multinational corporations (MNCs), mobile network virtual operators (MNVOs), small/medium-size enterprises (SMEs) and financial lobbies. A brief historicization of the Spanish telecommunications sector (expanded in Sabaté-Dalmau, 2018) shows that it followed the phases that are characteristic of economic liberalism: liberalization, expansion, stagnation and specialization (Heller & Duchêne, 2012). In 2006, the formerly publicly owned monopoly, Telefónica, was obliged to comply with the liberalization rules of the European Commission and to 'open' the industry to other MNCs. The sector then took the shape of an oligopoly (Guillén, 2005), that is, of a monopoly conformed by three MNCs (Telefónica, Orange and Vodafone), which was also later forced to share the market with other emerging competitors. This phase of expansion resulted in a total of 30 operators in 2009 (CMT, 2011). In order to avoid stagnation in the face of market saturation, nine of these ICT companies specialized in the migrant niche. This customer 'segment' was then of 'strategic importance' (ACPI, 2007: 2), since market studies indicated that 'foreigners' were spending 40% more on ICT than 'locals', with a high connectivity rate among the 15–29 age group, who initiated twice as many phone calls, text messages and internet connections as local populations (FOBSIC & Idescat, 2010; Robledo, 2008). As Vargas, Head of Orange's Migrant Customer Department, put it: '*La inmigración es en España el mercado emergente más importante*' […] '*los ingresos medios que generan [los inmigrantes] son muy superiores a los que proporciona un cliente autóctono*' ('Immigration in Spain is the most important emergent market' […] 'The average income that they [immigrants] generate is much higher than that which an autochthonous client can offer'[1] (CiberP@ís, 2007: 1). These nine operators, which established partnerships with the three MNCs in order to access the telecommunications infrastructure (e.g. Lebara contracted Vodafone's network; Happy Móvil contracted Orange's; Digi. Mobil contracted Telefónica's), presented themselves, in branding, as 'ethnic' businesses offering *'un servicio de telefonía móvil diseñado especialmente para extranjeros'* ('a mobile telephony service specially designed for foreigners') (MóbilZona, 2020). This phase of specialization consolidated the *clientelization* of migrant customers, under macro homogenizing categories such as *'extranjeros'*, *'inmigrantes'*, 'Spanish ethnic communities' or 'ethnic minority customers'. This approach to migrants in clienthood terms was normalized with events such as *'Integra Madrid'* ('Madrid Integrates'/'Integrate Madrid'), the Products and Services for the Immigrant Fair, one of the most important commercial meeting points for more than 150 companies, including Telefónica, Vodafone, Lebara, Western Union and Banco Popular, sponsored by the Secretary of State for Immigration and Emigration (IFEMA, 2008). This provides further evidence of the use of ICT as economic tools to target migrants under the conditions of technopolitical governance, via a nation-state/ICT-sector alliance.

Analysis and Findings: The Construction of *'Extranjeros'* as Unsettled Others

This section zooms into the ways in which 'foreigners' are (re)presented/(re)created in commercial identity narratives, in migrant-tailored advertising discourse circulated by 30 ICT operators in Spain between 2007 and 2009. I focus on how migrant addressees are constructed as: geographically immobilized, temporary 'outsiders' (section titled 'Deterritorialized passers-by'); socioeconomically stagnated and 'backward' populations ('Monetized parenting, expensive relatives and racial profiling'); and emotionally distressed and in need of re-education on how to communicate transnationally, within a Spanish-language regime ('Emotionally weak migrants in need of re-education through a Spanish-language regime'). I try to understand what these socioeconomically and linguistically stereotyping identities can tell us about the public presentations of mobility regimes that revolve around the neoliberal technologies of (self)-regimentation and orders of reason (including morality values concerning im/mobility practices) with which migrants are profiled.

There is one aspect that shall be taken into consideration as a point of departure for the analysis, which concerns market understandings of 'communication'. All advertisements analyzed below follow a metadiscourse (a 'macro' circulating message) which naturalizes the idea that ICT-mediated communication is 'inherently good' and 'always empowering' (Donner, 2008). In fact, access to ICT is consistently mobilized, in discourse, as an addressee's goal: as a necessary *rite of entrance* into host societies and as a precondition for transnational living. In this sense, the ideational social identities represented here approach migrant selves as 'homo consumentus' (Lindgren *et al.*, 2002: 28) who are expected to become fully fledged consumerist selves and to attain 'integration' basically through an investment in ICT products – the wished-for/salvation 'reality' projected in ads.

Deterritorialized passers-by

A key advertising technique for companies to represent migrants is the ideational narrative use of particular place identities which draw on the essentializing nation-state paradigm, often in compositional layouts that make figurative use of flags, metonymic of official 'nationalities'. This paradigm 'profiles' migrant customers by associating particular bounded territories ('countries') to homogenized groups of monolingual 'native' speakers of a nation-state language, also recreated as having a 'fixed' culture and religion. This nation-state paradigm is the predominant circulating metadiscourse which allows for the construction of migrants as strangerized 'others' (Barth, 1969) or outsiders, with narrative devices that accomplish the textual metafunction of establishing a sharp, categorical identity boundary between 'locals' and 'migrants'. These othering practices are accomplished through the following textual devices (emphasis marked in bold in the examples below is mine):

(1) the systematized use of dichotomous deictic person pronouns (the relational person markers 'we' – 'Spaniards' versus 'they' – 'foreigners'), as seen in the logo 'the mobile to call **your** country' (Happy Móvil, 2008a), with representational frames where migrant addressees are emplaced outside the nation-state and are offered a list of calling destinations that are only 'international';
(2) the ascription of 'informative' (census-based) demonyms other than 'Spaniard' to migrants, as seen in the logo 'For the **Romanians** in Spain' (Digi.Mobil, 2010), or their assignment of one single 'country' or place-belonging except 'Spain', as in '*Comunidad* **Mi País**' ('Community My Country') (Vodafone, 2009), which also precludes representations of migrants as fully fledged citizens in host societies;
(3) the assignment of single pan-national cultural traits or religions to conceptually 'classify' heterogeneous migrant group representations under an 'anchoring' (Kress & van Leeuwen, 2006: 157) 'foreigner'

identity, as seen in *'Promoción **Ramadán** 2008'* ('Ramadan Special 2008') (Happy Móvil, 2008b), targeting callers to Morocco, Senegal, Nigeria, Pakistan and Bangladesh, all essentialized by constructing 'Ramadan' as the 'logical connective' (Fuertes-Olivera et al., 2001: 1296) that links diverse demographic taxonomies under the 'macro' category 'Muslims'.

The offers mentioned above are based on information taken from market studies which aim at investigating migrants' calling behaviors according to their (presumed) im/mobility practices and at exerting some influence on and regulating them. For example, Vodafone's 'Community My Country' promotion consisted of an offer for calls to one out of 70 African and Asian countries with different flat rates for specific weekdays and calling times (one of the options, for example, was a promotion whereby calls to Mali from 8am to 10pm cost 184.44 eurocents/minute, whereas they cost 132.24 before or after this timeframe, in 2009). This provides evidence that, under technopolitical conditions, companies have gained access to information on migrants' consumption needs and have been able to generate commercially interested knowledge on their calling 'tactics'. This is exemplified in media-sponsored public discourses presented as assertions (i.e. as metadiscursive 'evidentials'; Fuertes-Olivera et al., 2001: 1296), such as: *'El africano llama cada día, mientras que el latino lo hace en fin de semana'* ('The African calls every day, whereas the Latino does so at the weekend') (Timmerhuis, former Managing Director of Lebara; CiberP@ís, 2007: 6).

The nation-state paradigm also allows the sector to present migrants' mobilities as an ordered sequence of temporary visits to two compartmentalized nation-states – the 'home' and 'host' countries, with the contextualizing textual discursive 'there' (e.g. 'your country', above; or 'home', in the section on 'Monetized parenting, expensive relatives and racial profiling') versus 'here' (e.g. 'in Spain') in ads. This naturalizes the idea that migrants are 'uprooted' or self-isolated passers-by who cannot (or do not seek to) attain social incorporation, which reinforces the assumption that they are not expected to become 'naturalized' citizens (as we have seen, they are presented as 'foreigners' and are not offered any flat rates for 'local' calls). In turn, it places the responsibility for 'immobilization' and 'non-integration' upon migrant customers, presented as 'passive agents' (Kress & van Leeuwen, 2006: 64) not being involved in 'local' affairs – in fact, none of the migrant-tailored adverts mobilizes narratives of interaction between 'foreigners' and 'Spaniards', but of interaction within outsider (intra-migrant) 'Community My Country' groups instead.

These migrant identity displays as deterritorialized are also linked to understandings of geographic mobility as being *enforced* or motivated strictly for economic reasons. This naturalizes the metadiscourse that migrants are basically invested in the 'return back home' – constructed as their expected 'reactional process' or behavior, in Kress and van Leeuwen's (2006: 75) terms – as exemplified in Figure 4.1.

Figure 4.1 presents two ICT customers ('actors') who recreate and are indexical of two particular 'nationalities' whom the addresser (Lebara) tries to target: 'the Moroccans' and 'the Pakistanis', connoted through the metonymic use of the Moroccan and Pakistani flags and of two (repeated) prototypical Moroccan and Pakistani common names. These two

Figure 4.1 Market constructions of migrants as displaced passers-by. Advertisement by Lebara (Metro, 2008a: 17).

demography-based identities are endophorically entextualized through the images of two 'satisfied consumers' (endorsing Lebara's SIM cards) that are placed on the left-hand side of the ad, where the new, most relevant information is 'read'. The whole composition, therefore, takes the shape of two customers' 'testimonials', one of the most effective marketing techniques for brand-trust development and promotion (Martin *et al.*, 2008), which here takes the form of two short (theoretically informative) 'biographies'. These are aimed at enhancing credibility and attractiveness through the mobilization of affection (since the represented motive of mobility is fatherhood/bridegroom 'love'), following the prototypical simple discursive structure and patterns of omniscient storytelling, presented as 'truths' (Fuertes-Olivera *et al.*, 2001: 1303). In this case, the biographic stories are about a Moroccan breadwinner leaving his home alone to support his family in Morocco, and about a Pakistani man migrating to Spain to save money for his wedding 'back home'. These fetishized mobility trajectories, which display a personalized contextualizing 'situationality' (Fuertes-Olivera *et al.*, 2001: 1297) that draws on temporary economically driven displacement, read: 'Mounir from Morocco does not lose contact with his daughter, who lives in Tangier with her mother' and 'Tashkir from Pakistan does not lose contact with his girlfriend Aishwarya, whom he will marry at the end of the year'. The multimodal optimistic overtones (or 'attitude markers'; Fuertes-Olivera *et al.*, 2001: 1296) that accompany these stories of success are the smiles indexing the reactional endorsement of 'happiness' which 'approves of' (Kress & van Leeuwen, 2006: 67) and extols the 'affordable' product (note the repeated assertion 'does not lose money').

Figure 4.2 is a flat-rate offer for calls between Morocco and Spain named *'Tarifa Juntos'* ('Plan Together'), written in Modern Standard Arabic, which provides a modernized metaphoric image of the displaced passer-by presented in Figure 4.1. In Figure 4.2, the Spanish and Moroccan states (along with their respective metonymic official flags) are joined as a whole bounded unit on a seemingly 'old' travelers' map indexing an ongoing 'timeless narrative process of mobility' (Kress & van Leeuwen, 2006: 59). This is done not only through the careful blurring of territorial lines but also through the message *'Maghribesbanya'* (the main 'vector' or most salient element of the composition), which translates into 'Morocco-Spain', written as a single word and emulating the aesthetics of handwriting, which bears poetic (attention-gathering) functions. The part of the text reading *'Esbanya'* ('Spain'), though, is unambiguously placed (figuratively 'stamped') upon Moroccan territory, and the Strait of Gibraltar, which separates Africa from Europe and is an area of shipwrecks for

Figure 4.2 Market constructions of migrants as two nation-state cosmopolitan inbetweeners. Advertisement by Movistar (Metro, 2008b: 13)

migrants who try to access Spain in precarious boats, is missing. This is a cartographic representational explicit erasure (Byszewski, 2014) which constructs and naturalizes the 'Moroccan' addressees' socioeconomic (history of) 'displacement'. The visual imagery on the right-hand side of the ad shows three 'smiling' customers (directing their gaze to the targeted 'viewers') who encode young cosmopolitan personhoods that are 'Westernized' as 'global citizens', but racialized through non-Caucasian skin complexion. This imagery may be intended as a celebratory metaphor of 'binding nations', 'unity-in-diversity' and 'inclusiveness' (Krzyanowski & Wodak, 2011), despite the fact that the interpellated Arabic-reading customers are expected to call to two 'fixed' territories: either 'here' (Spain) or 'there' (Morocco). This 'social cohesion' message adds 'acceptability' (Fuertes-Olivera *et al.*, 2001: 1297) to this postcolonial cartography practice, which illustrates how the use of maps as technologies of nation-state formation and of demographic control (Craib, 2000) are taken up by current MNCs who support present-day governmental mobility regimes (presented in the section titled 'The nation-state') in ads.

Besides, this hybrid text-and-image composition establishes a neoliberal morality order of 'information rich' nation-states (Sabaté i Dalmau, 2014: 2) which reappropriates the use of a paternalistic discourse on 'doing good' to former colonies (by providing them with ICT), now called 'immature technology' markets of 'developing economies' (e.g. by ITU; see ITU, 2020: 9) constructed as being invested in equipment production for the (local) 'poor' (O'Neil, 2003: 85). Overall, Figure 4.2 shows how postcolonial regimes of mind get reframed and actualized in technopolitical governance discursive practices that permeate free-delivered daily newspapers.

Monetized parenting, expensive relatives and racial profiling

With moralistic messages that read *'Para llamar a casa sólo tienes que querer'* ('To call home you only need to want to'), *'un móvil para ellos, menos gasto para ti'* ('A mobile for them, fewer expenses for you') (Telefónica's promotion; Sabaté-Dalmau, 2014: 99) or *'un amigo es alguien con quien no te cuesta hablar'* ('a friend is someone with whom talking does not cost a thing' (Hits Mobile; ADN, 2008: 15), the market monetizes transnational family/friendship ties, with neoliberal metadiscourses that frame (im)mobilities in economic terms while trying to foster particular calling behaviors in a judgmental manner. That is, intimate relationships are recreated as interested and rationalized relations of production (Castells, 1999), in line with the economization of the 'responsible' individual self (see section on 'Theoretical considerations and research aims'). More specifically, unidirectional communication, established from North to South, is presented as a strong moral obligation and as an economic duty or 'burden' (an 'expense') for migrants, via conative (directive, indoctrinating) discourse markers, in transnational-family projections based on financial dependency, as illustrated in Figure 4.3, which epitomizes the monetization of family ties. This consists of an image of a 'smiling' non-Caucasian girl and her grandmother, represented through a 'close shot' picture, which is a visual strategy to signal affective 'personal/intimate' relationships (Kress & van Leeuwen, 2006: 148). These two 'pictures' are joined by a coin located in the viewers' frontal angle, directly interpellating migrant addressees. The back of the ad (not visible here) reinforces this message through a textual narrative (directly 'speaking to'

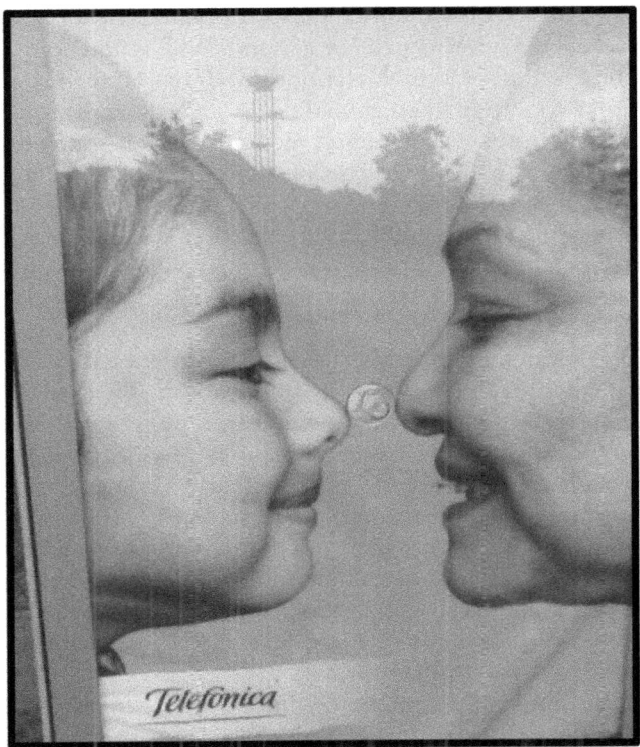

Figure 4.3 The monetization of transnational-family relationships. Advertisement by Telefónica (Sabaté-Dalmau, 2014: 98)

customers), reading '*Tu gente a sólo un céntimo de distancia*' ('Your people at only one cent's distance').

By drawing on the neoliberal logics of equality of access to a free market offering the best choices to autonomous consumers, intimate communication is intentionally presented as a matter of 'willingness'. Consequently, the responsibility for the successful management of transnational-family organization is seen as being dependent on migrating individuals; failure to communicate transnationally is presented as being the result of not wanting (or not being able) to navigate the market, via strong conative (appellative) markers employing 'direct' (second-person) deictic pronouns, as seen above in 'you only need to want to'. By providing a narrative representation of what a relative or what a ('proper') friend *is* and by referring to what these *do*, companies categorize non-frequent callers as irresponsible or careless relatives, and as hypocritical friends – in short, as 'unethical' or 'immoral' persons – via intentional discursive omissions (of who a 'non-relative' or a 'non-friend' is and does).

The monetization of family relationships draws on the metanarrative that migrants' 'countries' are technologically and economically 'underdeveloped' (as shown above), also employed in the nation-state's categorization of migrants as a group at 'risk of digital exclusion' (Plan Avanza, 2012). This is illustrated in Figure 4.4, which reads 'Talk to your country from your mobile'. A non-manipulated element of nature, a conch shell, is utilized as a metaphoric substitute for technology (a mobile phone handset) by another smiling non-Caucasian girl. This 'innocent' girl, who entextualizes 'fragility', 'purity' and 'docility' (Kress & van Leeuwen, 2006: 157), is located in a warm place, with a 'situationality' (i.e. discursive context) that locates her possibly in the South. This othering image actualizes and exacerbates an infantilizing view of migrant-sending societies based on racialism, in a non-ambiguous, unmitigated manner. In fact, the overall message (the metadiscourse) may be read as encoding a modern version of the 'noble savage' (Pennycook, 1998: 57) which draws on postcolonial mindsets that recreate 'home' societies as backward and as in need of 'help' from presumably wealthier relatives in the North (the use of similar paternalistic images mobilizing 'backwardness' recreation abound in the work of many ICT specialists; see, for example, Jones & Marsden's, 2006, book front cover).

This 'help' makes use of the neoliberal philanthropic rhetoric of 'moral rightness' and 'altruism' which grants acceptability to the selling intentionality that lies behind the ad in Figure 4.4 (see also Yilmaz, this volume, for a discussion of humanitarianism in dealing with migrants and refugees). This is seen in the following discourses, which use conative assertions directing the addressees' behaviors, in the form of strong

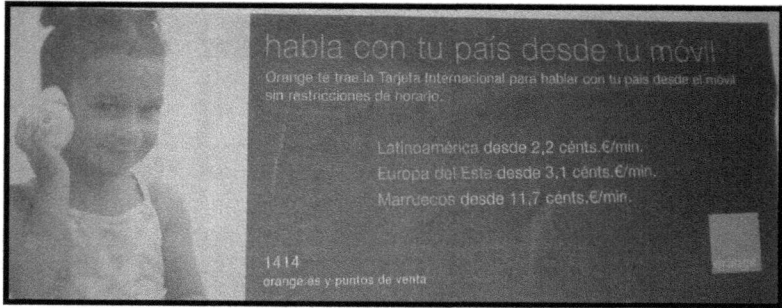

Figure 4.4 Market constructions of migrant-sending societies as 'underdeveloped'. Advertisement by Orange (20 Minutos, 2008: 5)

recommendations, instructions or commands, like: '*Si no tienen saldo, recarga su móvil desde España*' ('If they do not have credit, top up their mobiles from Spain') or '*Elige el móvil que les vas a regalar*' ('Choose the mobile you are going to give them as a gift') (Telefónica's offer; Sabaté i Dalmau, 2014). These textually represent the 'reality' (the product) both as a 'necessity' and as a 'gift', mobilizing the 'informative' and 'affective' components of advertising discourse.

Overall, this legitimizes a socially stratifying mode of self-disciplining among economically disadvantaged migrants, as they are morally instructed to be the ICT purchasers/providers for their transnational families. It also institutionalizes a place-oriented categorization regime based on deep-seated racist profiling practices, where migrants' places of birth are not only recreated as 'backward', but also as inhabited by powerless people incapable of managing or overcoming technological, geographic and socioeconomic stagnation.

Emotionally weak migrants in need of re-education through a Spanish-language regime

The advertisements analyzed (except for the one in Figure 4.2) are presented in a monolingual manner, in Peninsular Spanish. This is a language choice that is in line with dominant views of Spanish as the taken-for-granted language of migrants' social incorporation: a linguistic 'passport' and a 'barometer of integration'. The institutionalization of Spanish as the language to access 'legalization', now necessarily conducted via ICT, was established with *Ley 25/2007* (described in the section on 'The nation-state'). Apart from the new dataveillance system seeking to modernize the government's 'national security' mobility measures to target the 'undocumented', this technopolitical law also aimed at 'facilitating integration' and at 'clarifying legality procedures' for those whom the authorities represented as '*ciudadanos inmigrantes*' ('immigrant citizens') (Plan Avanza, 2012). This was done through the establishment of *a covert language regime*, because all the online information in the official website that was needed in order to conduct administrative tasks was provided solely in Spanish, turning this language into a requirement for ICT-mediated bureaucracy procedures, such as for accessing the official forms for temporary residence authorizations.[4]

At the time when the study was conducted, language economists working for the nation-state/ICT-sector technopolitical block (i.e. paid by the oligopoly and funded by the government; see Sabaté-Dalmau, 2021) also constructed Spanish as the 'natural' language of commerce, and justified this in productivity-oriented market terms. They did so by presenting Spanish as the language with the most important 'economic weight' (Del Valle & Gabriel-Stheeman, 2002: 196) for Spain's gross domestic product (GDP). This language choice was also a political strategy to keep the 'integrity' of what came to be called 'Spanish-speaking condominium' in the global telecommunications marketplace (García Delgado *et al.*, 2007: 21), then 'challenged' by a powerful lingua franca, English, and by the increased linguistic diversity of mobile populations, presented as a commercial hindrance (as a 'Babel's Tower'; García Delgado *et al.*, 2007: 117).

In public, though, all ICT companies claimed to have incorporated 'multilinguistic models' (Nekvapil & Sherman, 2013: 8) into their business strategies, presenting their brands as indisputably 'multilingual', as seen in: '*Somos multilingües [...] los servicios van a tener que tener la posibilidad de ser multilingües*' ('We are multilingual [...] services will have to have the possibility of being multilingual'), stated by a Telefónica consultant, in our interview at the Mobile World Congress; Sabaté-Dalmau, 2012: 143). This neoliberal rhetoric follows a metanarrative which constructs the management of linguistic diversity via 'multilinguistic models' as an index of efficiency, innovation, modernity and 'respect' (Hogan-Brun *et al.*, 2009). Following suit, most operators have adopted 'multilingual' corporate identities and claim to offer services 'in their clients' languages', as found in media discourses that employ the same 'reality' by describing the companies' ICT services as de facto multilingual, like: '*A cada cual en su idioma. Esa es la clave para llegar a la comunidad extranjera en España*' ('Everyone in their own language. This is the key to reaching the foreign community in Spain') (Metro, 2008c: 15).

A linguistic analysis of the 30 businesses, though, revealed that, in actual practice, operators offered their services monolingually in Spanish, in their shops, call centers and websites (Sabaté-Dalmau *et al.*, 2017). English was used by 14 of them, but as a commercial/branding technique to index 'professionalism', 'internationalization', 'success' and 'leadership' (Cenoz & Gorter, 2009: 57). However, the instances of English that I found were 'linguistic fetishes' (Kelly-Holmes, 2010) or tokenistic attention-gatherers mobilized for poetic ('aesthetic') rather than for informative functions, as seen in slogans like: 'Calling yours never was so easy' (see Sabaté i Dalmau, 2014: 53). Minority languages in Spain, like Catalan, Basque or Galician, were only offered by Catalan, Basque and Galician operators.[5] Migrants' languages were *totally absent*, with the exception of some presence of Romanian and Arabic, used by five 'ethnic' operators very unsystematically, only for particular customer services (e.g. Movistar and Orange claimed to offer call center customers services in Romanian in 2009; Sabaté-Dalmau, 2012: 146), or during particular advertising campaigns (e.g. during the 2008 winter, Lebara issued leaflets in many Barcelona call shop centers which included their slogan in Moroccan and Urdu; Sabaté i Dalmau, 2014).

The CEO of the translation services venture that was then working for Telefónica explained this absence of migrants' languages both in economicist and in political terms, in an interview that took place when he was assembling a Spanish-Arabic automatic translation system for that MNC which, in the end, was scrapped (29 April 2009). He stated that the incorporation of migrants' languages into customer services was not profitable enough for ICT companies to make extra investments in them, and that the sector did not have a particular interest (*'preocupació'*, 'concern') in catering for migrants who could not access languages other than those provided for local customers, as follows: *'Això [...] demostra la la falta de preocupació dels operadors per aquest tipus de gent pues potser perquè per aquest tipus de negoci pel volum que genera és poc'* ('This demonstrates [...] the the lack of concern for these sort of people by operators may be because of this type of business the turnover it generates is small'). Therefore, in terms of multilingual services provision, *a linguistic regime of clienthood in the nation-state language* was institutionalized which regulates the ICT marketplace (as attested in Gomariz & Lloberes, 2007) and, in fact, most commercial sectors in Catalonia (Solé Camardons & Torrijos, 2011). This strengthens the government's metanarrative that migrant populations shall get (re)socialized in the Spanish language in order not to be 'immobilized' in the host society.

The sector's construction of migrants as being in need of (self)-disciplining in the nation-state language is framed within a more general view of these 'deterritorialized' customers as being in need of transnational-communication (re-)education. This is seen in commercial and media discourses which construct transnational-family communication as inherently difficult and problematic due to migrants' inability to cope with the 'emotional distress' caused by the 'distance', naturalized as a 'reality' in promotions like '¡*Nostalgia zero!*' ('Zero nostalgia!') (Sabaté-Dalmau, 2014). The discursive mobilization of emotional affliction and anxiety presents migrants as being lonely, docile and emotionally weak, which positions them as non-competent ICT users. This is particularly so for migrant women, who bear the stigma of the 'disloyal mother' (Hondagneu-Sotelo & Avila, 1997), as shown in media statements like: '*Madres [...] aprenden cómo utilizar internet para estar en contacto con sus hijos*' ('Mothers [...] learn how to use the internet in order to be in touch with their children') (ADN, 2010). This shows the extent to which technopolitical governance to 'conduct the [communicative and linguistic] conduct' of 'deviant' transnational populations is unfolded in advertising discourse, as further illustrated in the example below, concerning the re-education of 'Latina' mothers.

In 2008, a 'self-help' book entitled *Educar desde el locutorio. Ayuda a que tus hijos sigan creciendo contigo*' ('Raising your children from the call shop. Help your children keep growing up with you') (Rodríguez, 2008) was published, which taught unsettled mothers to 'learn how to communicate transnationally' in order not to miss their children's education. This manual provided 'communication tips' (including self-discipline bodily dispositions) like: 'Avoid words like *"deberías"* ([you should]), *"no debes"* ([you should not/must not]), *"tienes que"* ([you have to/must])'; 'smile', 'don't cry', 'use loving language' and 'avoid silence' (Rodríguez, 2008: 24–25). These pieces of 'advice' were taken up by ICT ventures, as this 'self-help guide' is now found on many operators' websites (see, for example, the online 'Solidarity' section in Eroski Móviles; García, 2008). Besides, the book became a business opportunity, since, on the day of its presentation in *Casa América* (Madrid), an emblematic institutional building which belongs to the Spanish Ministry of Foreign Affairs, the company Orbitel sold 1000 prepaid SIM cards for 'only' one euro, on-site.

Overall, this unpacks neoliberal discourses that, in governmental spaces, present migrants as culturally deficient with regard to 'proper' family talk and 'rational' management of emotions. This is accomplished through technopolitical governance techniques which, through the use of multimodal narrative discourses in ads, impose a monolingual language regime that naturalizes stigmas and stereotypes of mobile populations, with the recreation of migrants as non-fully fledged neoliberal personas.

Concluding Remarks: The Normalization of Anti-migrant Neoliberal Governance

In this chapter, I have explored current modes of managing, controlling and profiling migrant populations through the use of advertising discourses revolving around the mobility regimes established by neoliberal governmentality institutions, which have mercantilized the organization of transnational public and private life under the conditions of the globalized new economy. These newer political-economic regulatory blocks are constituted by advanced liberal governments that struggle to keep their monopoly on sovereignty in the supranational arena, in interested alliances and 'win-win' partnerships with key market ventures (particularly, oligopolistic ICT businesses) with whom they share technologies of power for citizenship governance.

I have specifically focused on the technopolitical (nation-state/ICT-sector) block, which has ICT at its epicenter. ICT today is the new citizenship 'wall' for governmental authorities to control people's freedom of movement and access to 'legality' across nation-state borders. On the other hand, ICT are also the most 'crisis-resistant' (ITU, 2012) lucrative source of economic revenue (and a nation-state source of GDP income) required by 'domestic' markets to compete in the global arena, where the information-based economy prevails.

I have claimed that the investigation of technopolitics as a market-driven governmental practice and as a neoliberal rationality may generate new knowledge about how governmentality is currently exerted through newer mobility regimes upon 'foreign' populations, whose transnationally grounded professional and personal life trajectories hinge upon ICT.

I have narrowed down the analysis of technopolitical citizenship regimentation to the study of migrant-tailored advertising discourse, with a critical sociolinguistics multimodal analysis of the social meanings of representational structures that control and 'profile' migrant populations, in 20 telephony advertisements. This has included the investigation of what commercial place-based migrant identities (and discourses around them) get activated and are made operational in the political, commercial and media realms, and of what knowledge on migrants' transnational-life conducts gets circulated and why, and with what newer technologies of power and technologies of the self – particularly public metadiscourse generation.

I have focused on the emergence of technopolitical governance in a particular society in Southern Europe, Catalonia, involving the Spanish government and the Spanish telecommunications sector, both known for a management of migrants through citizenship-gatekeeping mechanisms based on socioeconomic and linguistic difference, inequality and exclusion. This management includes, for example, the establishment of mobility regimes that allow for the immediate 'disconnection' of the 'undocumented' if they remain unidentified, or for the imposition of monolingual language regimes in the nation-state language as a precondition for social incorporation and settlement.

I have shown that transnational populations are systematically represented as strangerized others and as geographically and socioeconomically immobilized outsiders. They are also constructed as 'immature' capitalist selves, deskilled, pauperized and technologically backward, who shall self-actualize as consumerist personas, as a rite of entrance to and emplacement in Europe. In this line, transnational-family or intimate relationships are monetized, in circulating metadiscourses that reinforce the neoliberal regime of morality which allows for the public construction of non-frequent callers as reprimandable 'non-persons'. Fetishized market identities also allow for the normalization of representations of spatially entangled migrants as culturally deficient, emotionally weak, distressed, and in need of re-education on how to communicate transnationally.

As I have shown elsewhere (Sabaté i Dalmau, 2014), migrants are invested in the consumerist culture and successfully engage with the logics of technopolitics, but they do not simply submit to them. They navigate and resist nation-state norms in alternative migrant-regulated spaces of communication (like 'ethnic' call shops) where they can access real multilingual ICT 'off the radar' of technopolitical authorities. They strategize with a diversity of ICT companies, simultaneously use many different devices across several calling spaces, and have many tactics to 'adapt communication technology to their own needs' (Castells *et al.*, 2004: 239). Expanding their mobility contacts, they collectivize ICT gadgets (SIM cards, etc.) among their transnational social networks, and they practice multidirectional communication with their transnational families, actually calling more frequently to host-society mobile phone numbers than 'internationally', overcoming their ascribed 'technology-have-nots' immobilized positionings.

And yet, this chapter provides a picture of the extent to which nation-states and the market have attained an unprecedented degree of control upon the exercise of power, the monopolization of knowledge and the generation of interested 'information' concerning migrants, which has allowed for their indoctrination into ICT-mediated mobility regimes and for the scrutinization of their transnational-life practices.

I have argued that, overall, neoliberal technopolitical governance has opened the doors for the normalized use of unmitigated racist rhetoric and overt postcolonial profilings, constructed, reproduced and exacerbated in mundane metanarratives, which saturate the general public. This contributes to understanding the emergence of anti-migrant 'legality' regimes and frames of mind in Europe, calling for the problematization of market-driven supranational regulations and citizenship profiling techniques concerning im/mobility that allow for the increased legitimization and penetration of xenophobic discourses in everyday life.

Acknowledgements

I would like to thank this book's editors as well as the anonymous reviewers, for their insightful comments on earlier drafts of this manuscript. This chapter also benefited from the feedback provided by the participants in the seminars *Dynamics of Im/mobility and Discursive Practices in the 21st century* (Bern, 8–9 November 2018) and *Migration, Language, and Practices: Challenges in the 21st Century* (Barcelona, 17–18 June 2019). Any shortcomings are mine.

This work was supported by the Spanish Ministry of Economy, Industry and Competitiveness, under Grants FFI2016-76383-P and FFI2011-26964; and by the Catalan Ministry of Economy and Knowledge, under Grant 2017SGR1522.

Notes

(1) Inverted commas are used to index emic social categorization practices and identities.
(2) Technopolitical governance blocks are not new, since partnerships between governmental authorities and the telecommunications sector may be traced back to the 19th century. The first oft-quoted technopolitical entity is the International Telecommunications Union (ITU), funded in 1865. This is the United Nations Agency that sets the standards for, and coordinates, the global access and use of the radio spectrum worldwide, with 193 nation-state members (including 'information-rich' countries like Canada, the United States and Japan, but also 'emergent' powers such as Azerbaijan, Cambodia or Ghana), 800 private-sector institutions (the world's largest vendors, manufacturers, telecom operators, SMEs and financial lobbies), and academia (ITU, 2019). For a historicization of the term 'technopolitics', see Kahn and Keller (2007).
(3) Oral data were collected with informed consent and were anonymized. Confidentiality was ensured by the Ethics Committee at the Autonomous University of Barcelona (CEEAH; registration file 725H). The Cooperative of lawyers Col·lectiu Ronda ensured that there was no conflict of interest and that copyrights were respected in the reproduction of the public telecommunications advertisements presented in this chapter. All translations from documents written in languages other than English are mine.
(4) Today, this language testing regime is overt, because proof of a basic command of Spanish is now required for 'naturalization' (BOE, 2015: 105524).
(5) The rest of the companies infringed *Llei 22/2010* of the Catalan Statute of Consumers, passed in 2011, which establishes that all co-official languages shall be of use in commerce (Sabaté i Dalmau, 2014).

References

20 Minutos (2008) Orange, advertisement (Section: *Elecciones 9M 5*), *20Minutos.es*, 6 March. Madrid: 20 Minutos Editora S.L.
ACPI (2007) *Estudio de medios para inmigrantes. Resumen general EMI 2007*. Madrid: Asociación para el Conocimiento de la Población Inmigrante. See http://www.fct.urjc.es/oicam/enlaces/docs/emi2007.pdf.
ADN (2008) *Hits Mobile*, advertisement (Section Deportes: 15), 16 December. Barcelona: Grupo Planeta.
ADN (2010) *Madres desde el locutorio*. ADN, 11 May. Barcelona: Grupo Planeta.
Avui (2009) *800.000 catalans no han identificat encara el mòbil*. *Avui*, 10 November. Tecnologia 28. Barcelona: Hermes Comunicacions S.A.

Bamberg, M., De Fina, A. and Schiffrin, D. (eds) (2007) *Selves and Identities in Narrative and Discourse*. Amsterdam: John Benjamins.

Barth, F. (ed.) (1969) *Ethnic Groups and Boundaries: The Social Organisation of Cultural Difference*. Boston, MA: Little, Brown & Company.

Baynham, M. and De Fina, A. (2005) *Dislocations/Relocations: Narratives of Displacement*. London/New York: Routledge.

Bertot, J.C. (2003) The multiple dimensions of the digital divide: More than the technology 'haves' and 'have nots'. *Government Information Quarterly* 20, 185–191.

BOE (2007) *LEY 25/2007, de 18 de octubre, de conservación de datos relativos a las comunicaciones electrónicas y a las redes públicas de comunicaciones*. No. 251, 19 October (pp. 42517–42523). Madrid: Gobierno de España, Ministerio de la Presidencia.

BOE (2015) *Real Decreto 1004/2015, de 6 de noviembre, por el que se aprueba el Reglamento por el que se regula el procedimiento para la adquisición de la nacionalidad española por residencia*. 7 November. Madrid: Gobierno de España, Ministerio de Justicia. See https://www.boe.es/diario_boe/txt.php?id=BOE-A-2015-12047.

Byszewski, B. (2014) Colonizing Chaco Canyon: Mapping antiquity in the territorial Southwest. In A. Goldstein (ed.) *Formations of United States Colonialism* (pp. 57–86). Durham, NC/London: Duke University Press.

Castells, M. (1999) Information technology, globalization and social development. UNRISD Discussion Paper No. 114. See http://www.unrisd.org/.

Castells, M. (2000 [1996]) *The Rise of the Network Society*. Oxford: Blackwell.

Castells, M. (2009) *Communication Power*. Oxford/New York: Oxford University Press.

Castells, M., Tubella, I., Sancho, T., Díaz de Isla, M.I. and Wellman, B. (2004) Social structure, cultural identity, and personal autonomy in the practice of the internet: The network society in Catalonia. In M. Castells (ed.) *The Network Society: A Cross-cultural Perspective* (pp. 233–248). Cheltenham: Edward Elgar.

Castells, M., Tubella, I., Sancho, T. and Roca, M. (2007) *La Transició a la Societat Xarxa*. Barcelona: Ariel.

Cenoz, J. and Gorter, D. (2009) Language economy and linguistic landscape. In E. Shohamy and D. Gorter (eds) *Linguistic Landscape: Expanding the Scenery* (pp. 55–69). London/New York: Routledge.

CiberP@ís (2007) El africano llama cada día, mientras que el latino lo hace en fin de semana. *El País Semanal* 477, 1–6.

Clifton, J., Díaz-Fuentes, D., Fernández-Gutiérrez, M. and Revuelta, J. (2011) The making (and un-making) of markets from public services: The case of telecommunications multinationals. *NABTMA Working Paper No. 34*. National University of Singapore: Centre on Asia and Globalisation.

CMT (2011) *Informe económico sectorial: Comunicaciones móviles*. See https://www.cnmc.es/expedientes/mtz-20112607

Cook, G. (2001) *The Discourse of Advertising*. London: Routledge.

Craib, R.B. (2000) Cartography and power in the conquest and creation of New Spain. *Latin American Research Review* 25 (1), 7–36.

Del Percio, A. (2018) Engineering commodifiable workers: Language, migration and the governmentality of the self. *Language Policy* 17 (2), 239–259.

Del Valle, J. and Gabriel-Stheeman, L. (2002) *The Battle over Spanish between 1800 and 2000*. London/New York: Routledge.

Deumert, A. (2020) Mobilities and struggle: A commentary. In K. Horner and J. Dailey-O'Cain (eds) *Multilingualism, (Im)mobilities and Spaces of Belonging* (pp. 234–243). Bristol: Multilingual Matters.

Digi.mobil (2010) *Nueva telefonía móvil al precio de la telefonía fija*. See http://www.digimobil.es.

Diminescu, D. (2008) The connected migrant: An epistemological manifesto. *Social Science Information* 47 (4), 565–579.

Donner, J. (2008) Research approaches to mobile use in the developing world: A review of the literature. *The Information Society* 24, 140–159.

Duchêne, A., Moyer, M.G. and Roberts, C. (eds) (2013) *Language, Migration and Social Inequalities: A Critical Sociolinguistic Perspective of Institutions and Work*. Bristol: Multilingual Matters.

El País (2009) ¿Usas tarjeta prepago de móvil?¡Regístrala! *El País*, 4 March. See http://www.elpais.com/.

FOBSIC & Idescat (2010) *Enquesta sobre l'equipament i l'ús de les Tecnologies de la Informació i la Comunicació (TIC) a les llars de Catalunya 2010. Usos TIC individuals*. See http://www.idescat.cat/pub/?id=ticll10.

Fuertes-Olivera, P.A., Velasco-Sacristán, M., Arribas-Baño, A. and Samaniego-Fernández, E. (2001) Persuasion and advertising English: Metadiscourse in slogans and headlines. *Journal of Pragmatics* 33, 1291–1307.

García, A. (2008) Derechos humanos. *Eroski Consumer*, 17 May. See http://www.consumer.es/web/es/solidaridad/derechos_humanos/2008/05/17/177047.php.

García Delgado, J.L., Alonso, J.A. and Jiménez, J.C. (2007) *Economía del Español: Una Introducción*. Barcelona: Ariel; Madrid: Fundación Telefónica.

Gomàriz, E. and Lloberes, M. (2007) L'ús del català a les companyies de telefonia mòbil estatals. *Llengua i Ús* 40, 55–63.

Guillén, M.F. (2005) *The Rise of Spanish Multinationals: European Business in the Global Economy*. Cambridge: Cambridge University Press.

Happy Móvil (2008a) ¿Quiénes somos? See http://www.happymovil.es/.

Happy Móvil (2008b) *Promoción Ramadán*. See http://www.happymovil.es/.

Harvey, D. (2005) *A Brief History of Neoliberalism*. Oxford/New York: Oxford University Press.

Heller, M. and Duchêne, A. (eds) (2012) *Language in Late Capitalism: Pride and Profit*. New York: Routledge.

Hogan-Brun, C., Mar-Molinero, C. and Stevenson, P. (eds) (2009) *Discourses on Language and Integration: Critical Perspectives on Language Testing Regimes in Europe*. Amsterdam: John Benjamins.

Hondagneu-Sotelo, P. and Avila, E. (1997) 'I'm here but I'm there': The meanings of Latina transnational motherhood. *Gender and Society* 11 (5), 548–571.

Horner, K. and Dailey-O'Cain, J. (eds) (2020) *Multilingualism, (Im)mobilities and Spaces of Belonging*. Bristol: Multilingual Matters.

IFEMA (2008) *Integra Madrid. III Feria de Productos y Servicios para Inmigrantes*. See https://www.ifema.es.

Inda, J.X. (2006) *Targeting Immigrants: Government, Technology and Ethics*. Malden, MA: Blackwell.

ITU (2012) *Measuring the Information Society*. Geneva: International Telecommunication Union.

ITU (2019) *About ITU*. See https://www.itu.int/en/about/Pages/default.aspx.

ITU (2020) ITU-R R19-WP5C Contribution 122: Proposal regarding the update of Resolution ITU-R 59-2 – Studies on availability of frequency bands and/or tuning ranges for worldwide and/or regional harmonization and conditions for their use by terrestrial electronic news gathering systems. See https://www.itu.int/md/R19-WP5C-C-0122.

Jones, M. and Marsden, D. (2006) *Mobile Interaction Design*. Chichester: John Wiley & Sons.

Kahn, R. and Kellner, D. (2005) Oppositional politics and the internet: A critical/reconstructive approach. *Cultural Politics* 1 (1), 75–100.

Kahn, R. and Kellner, D. (2007) Globalization, technopolitics, and radical democracy. In L. Dahlberg and E. Siapera (eds) *Radical Democracy and the Internet* (pp. 17–36). London: Palgrave Macmillan.

Kelly-Holmes, H. (2010) Markets and languages: Sociolinguistic perspectives. In H. Kelly-Holmes and G. Mautner (eds) *Language and the Market* (pp. 20–29). London: Palgrave Macmillan.

Kress, G. and van Leeuwen, T. (2006) *Multimodal Discourse: The Modes and Media of Contemporary Communication*. Oxford: Oxford University Press.

Krzyanowski, M. and Wodak, R. (2011) Political strategies and language policies: The European Union Lisbon strategy and its implications for the UE's language and multilingualism policy. *Language Policy* 10 (2), 115–136.

LegalToday (2007) Sentencia de la Audiencia Nacional, sala de lo penal sección segunda, de 31 octubre 2007. See https://www.legaltoday.com/historico/jurisprudencia/jurisprudencia-penal/sentencia-de-la-audiencia-nacional-sala-de-lo-penal-sec-2-de-31-octubre-2007-2007-10-31/

Lindgren, M., Jedbratt, J. and Svensson, E. (2002) *Beyond Mobile: People, Communications and Marketing in a Mobilized World*. New York: Palgrave.

Martin, B.A.S., Wentzel, D. and Tomczak, T. (2008) Effects of susceptibility to normative influence and type of testimonial on attitudes toward print advertising. *Journal of Advertising* 37 (1), 29–43.

Martín Rojo, L. (2019) The 'self-made speaker'. In L. Martin Rojo and A. Del Percio (eds) *Language and Neoliberal Governmentality* (pp. 162–189). London: Routledge.

Martín Rojo, L. and Del Percio, A. (eds) (2019) *Language and Neoliberal Governmentality*. London: Routledge.

Metro (2008a) *Lebara, advertisement* (in *Publicitat* 17). *Metro*, 26 February. Barcelona: Metro News S.L.

Metro (2008b) *Movistar, advertisement* (in *Profesionales* 13). *Metro*, 17 June. Barcelona: Metro News S.L.

Metro (2008c) *El éxito es móvil* (in *Noticias* 15). *Metro*, 29 April. Barcelona: Metro News S.L.

MóbilZona (2020) *Talkout: Información y tarifas Talkout*. See https://www.movilzona.es/talkout-informacion-y-tarifas-talkout/.

Nekvapil, J. and Sherman, T. (2013) Language ideologies and linguistic practices: The case of multinational companies in Central Europe. In E. Barát, P. Studer and J. Nekvapil (eds) *Ideological Conceptualizations of Language: Discourses of Linguistic Diversity* (pp. 85–118). Frankfurt am Main: Peter Lang.

O'Neil, P.D. (2003) The 'poor man's mobile telephone': Access *versus* possession to control the information gap in India. *Contemporary South Asia* 12 (1), 85–102.

Panagakos, A.N. and Horst, H.A. (2006) Return to Cyberia: Technology and the social worlds of transnational migrants. *Global Networks* 6 (2), 109–124.

Parlament de Catalunya (2007) *Constitució Espanyola*. Barcelona: Forma Color S.A.

Pennycook, A. (1998) *English and the Discourses of Colonialism*. London/New York: Routledge.

Plan Avanza (2012) *Estrategia general 2011–2015*. See https://avancedigital.mineco.gob.es/programas-avance-digital/Paginas/plan-avanza.aspx

Pujolar, J. (2007) Bilingualism and the nation-state in the post-national era. In M. Heller (ed.) *Bilingualism: A Social Approach* (pp. 71–95). London: Palgrave Macmillan.

Ribbens-Klein, Y. (2020) The embodiment of place: Boorlinge, Inkommers and the struggle to belong. In K. Horner and J. Dailey-O'Cain (eds) *Multilingualism, (Im)mobilities and Spaces of Belonging* (pp. 60–82). Bristol: Multilingual Matters.

Robledo, J. (2008) Generación-i: La transición multicultural. *El País Semanal*, 6 July. See http://elpais.com/diario/2008/07/06/eps/1215325611_850215.html.

Rodríguez, N. (2008) *Educar desde el Locutorio. Ayuda a que tus Hijos Sigan Creciendo Contigo*. Madrid: Plataforma.

Ros, A., González, E., Marín, A. and Sow, P. (2007) Migration and information flows: A new lens for the study of contemporary international migration. *Working Paper Series No. WP07-002*. See http://www.uoc.edu/.

Sabaté-Dalmau, M. (2012) 'The official language of Telefónica is English': Problematising the construction of English as a lingua franca in the Spanish telecommunications sector. *ATLANTIS Journal of the Spanish Association of Anglo-American Studies* 34 (1), 133–135.

Sabaté i Dalmau, M. (2014) *Migrant Communication Enterprises: Regimentation and Resistance*. Bristol: Multilingual Matters.

Sabaté-Dalmau, M. (2018) Multilingualism in migrant-tailored businesses: The case of telecommunications multinationals and 'ethnic' call shops. In A. Creese and A. Blackledge (eds) *The Routledge Handbook of Language and Superdiversity* (pp. 361–376). London: Routledge.

Sabaté-Dalmau, M. (2021) Ens cal desemmascarar les accions de governança neoliberal: Reflexions entorn de l'exclusió lingüística imposada 'des de dalt'. In C. Junyent (ed.) *El Català, Llengua Efervescent: 77 Visions sobre el Terreny* (pp. 147–149). Barcelona: Viena, Carta Blanca.

Sabaté-Dalmau, M., Garrido Sardà, M.R. and Codó, E. (2017) Language-mediated services for migrants: Monolingualist institutional regimes and translinguistic user practices. In S. Canagarajah (ed.) *The Routledge Handbook of Migration and Language* (pp. 558–576). London: Routledge.

Sànchez, J. (2008) 15 consideracions sobre la immigració estrangera a Catalunya en perspectiva comparada. *IDEES Revista de Temes Contemporanis* 31, 249–254.

Solé Camardons, J. and Torrijos, A. (2011) Els estudis sobre empreses i llengua a Catalunya: Balanç i perspectives. In M. Strubell and I. Marí (eds) *Mercat Global i Mercat Local: Implicacions per al Multilingüisme de l'Empresa. Actes del Seminari del CUIMPB-CAL 2008* (pp. 79–111). Barcelona: Universitat Oberta de Barcelona.

Thurlow, C. and Jaworski, A. (2006) The alchemy of the upwardly mobile: Symbolic capital and the stylization of elites in frequent-flyer programmes. *Discourse & Society* 17 (1), 99–135.

Urry, J. (2007) *Mobilities*. Cambridge: Polity Press.

Vertovec, S. (2009) *Transnationalism*. London: Routledge.

Vodafone (2009) *Comunidad Mi País*. See http://www.vodafone.es/.

5 On Being Enregistered into the Matrix of Online Knowledge: An Ethnographic Exploration of an Internet-based Dismissal in an Asylum-seeking Procedure

Massimiliano Spotti

Introduction

Linguistic ethnographic studies dealing with the so-called 'long interview' taking place between asylum-seeking applicants and host country officials have been led to powerful notions like trans-idioma (Jacquemet, 2005, 2013) and, more broadly, to uncover the normalcy that veils narrative inequality (Blommaert, 2005). In a nutshell, these studies showed this interview to be a moment of meaning-making *synchronised* and *crystallised* in the moment to moment unfolding of verbal, written and pictographic interactions between institutional figures and asylum-seeking applicants in a given power-saturated environment (Blommaert, 2009). The point, back then, was that whenever human beings communicate, they deploy a range of semiotic resources such as topics, chronology, toponymy, languages and their varieties, pictograms and accents, all of which are part and parcel of a much larger process of institutional enregisterment (Agha, 2003) into 'ergoic' discourses of identification and authenticity. One of the resources that had been neglected back then, mainly due to the paucity of its use in institutional encounters, was the internet and with that the resources that this infrastructure of globalisation brings into play (Spotti, 2015). Against this background, the present contribution wishes to explore the process of institutional enregisterment of the story narrated by an asylum-seeking applicant and the identity (mis)recognition that derives from it through internet-based knowledge. In so doing, the contribution advances considerations on how, in power-saturated communicative events of this kind, the knowledge held by a migrating subject is enregistered into an administrative prescriptive matrix of what someone should say, what someone should know and – within that – how someone should name things in order to give proofs of identity and gain legal mobility. Yet again, these proofs now ought to bridge the gap between the offline local knowledge of the applicant and the online support lent to institutional figures by internet-based knowledge.

The EU, Migration and the Diversification of Diversity

To anticipate briefly: the editors of the present volume have urged all contributors to this volume to think about immobility, a concept that increasingly seems to be settling its roots in present-day sociolinguistics and linguistic ethnographic conceptual armours. (Im)mobility, as we all have seen during the current pandemic, is ingrained in our *conditio humana*. As human beings, we move, we ought to move, we detest not moving and, when we do not move when we could, we are pointed at as suffering from 'hut syndrome' in that it is normal to move and thus to leave one's daily place of residence for either short or prolonged period of times. Asylum seekers who try to reach Europe's soil are no exception to the endemics of movement. Yet, these migrants who knock at Europe's doors are an issue that poses urgent questions. For instance, the EU as well as its nation-state members' authorities cannot any longer allow themselves to regard migrants as people engaged in a linear move 'from the rest to the West' (Hall, 1992). Rather, present-day migratory flows are among the most tangible testimonies of superdiversity. These flows, in fact, do not fall any more into the 'ethnic minority paradigm' of an earlier era in migration studies. Instead, they are tangible instances of the 'diversification of diversity'. That is, they are a tangible manifestation of 'an increased number of new, small and scattered, multiple-origin, transnationally connected, socio-economically differentiated and legally stratified immigrants' (Vertovec, 2007: 124). Aside from the shibboleths placed at the entry gates by border protection and national security (Detailleur & Spotti, 2012) people's history of migration, and then making use of it in assessing the truthfulness of their narratives (see also Jacquemet, this volume, on the surveillance of migrants). These proofs of identity often rest on an 'ergoic'[1] equation, where ergoic here stands for the fact that once the applicant knows facts X and Y about his self-proclaimed country of origin Z and uses (a territorially bounded variety of) national language W, then the applicant has managed to match the institutional expectations that move him into a safe area beyond suspicion, in that she or he has given the necessary grounds for identity recognition.

With the above in mind, the present contribution presents a linguistic ethnographic investigation of what I have decided to term the (internet-based) matrix of suspicion held by institutions. Our case in point deals with an asylum application filed in Flanders, the Dutch speaking part of Belgium, by an unschooled illiterate young man, whom I have decided for our purposes here to call Bashir. This young man claims to be originating from Guinee Conakry, and more specifically from its capital city, Conakry. The textual artefact that we will take into examination, the embodiment of the discourse of suspicion mentioned above, is the letter of rejection the applicant received from the Belgian Federal authorities during my stay in 2013 at the asylum-seeking centre in question. From there, using the text of the letter as a unit of analysis, this contribution teases apart the motivation that led the authorities to conclude that the applicant was not from Guinee Conakry. Core to this rejection is the issue of naming things right and, with that, of matching the narrative matrix and expectations held by the authorities (see also Spotti, 2018). In fact, any of us who might have encountered an institutional figure, say, for instance, a police officer inquiring about our conduct, has been confronted with questions about their name, surname, address and the actual name of the place where the event being reported has taken place. These are all matters of identification and verification that bring along with themselves issues of suspicion about someone's claim, against which we find (mis)recognition. The analysis of the authorities' letter is then further corroborated by a long open-ended interview carried out with another asylum-seeking applicant, whom I decided for the purpose of this chapter to call Malidi, who also was from Guinee Conakry. Given that he was Bashir's roommate and that he had already managed to give proof of coming from Guinee Conakry, Malidi functions here as an ethnographic means of *tertium comparationis*, showing how he understands the narrative matrix expected by the authorities and how he perceives the mismatches between that and Bashir's narration. The chapter concludes by reflecting upon the conceptual and societal implications of Bashir's case. These reflections are conceptually relevant in that they display the influence of the internet and its authority in the process of asylum approval and with that the discrepancy between the web-based (toponymic) knowledge that authorities expect to hear and the local (albeit unschooled) register used for the naming of places (see also Haas, 2015). Such reflections are also socially relevant in that they show how a discrepancy between the register used by the applicant and that expected by the authorities' narrative matrix is taken to be a valid proof that corroborates the politics of suspicion that characterises the institutional side of asylum-seeking applications in present-day Europe.

Registers of Authenticity and the Online-Offline Nexus in Asylum-seeking Applications

The analysis of those processes embedded in institutional encounters between authorities and asylum-seeking applicants have given way to ground-breaking concepts. For instance, among these we find close examinations of institutional encounters between authorities and applicants (Haviland, 1989), where the latter have to prove the truthfulness of their migration story and 'speak out' their language proficiency as tangible valid identity proof (Maryns & Blommaert, 2002), becoming thus 'asylum speakers' rather than asylum seekers alone. Further, we find the concept of voice (Blommaert, 2005) and, more broadly put, that of Hymesian narrative inequality. In sum, previous linguistic ethnographic work has showed that the encounter between the authorities and the applicant gives birth to a turn-taking communicative event where discourses of suspicion, and of identity recognition and/or rejection, are flagged up showing that, as Blommaert *et al.* (2006) point out:

> Ways of speaking are socially positioned, some discourses have more 'weight' than others [...]: the 'meaning' articulated in discourses is a function of the relative 'value' of these discourses socially. The words of some, providing that they match the criteria of appropriate production, are perceived as more reliable and important than those of others, and discourses can be mapped in terms of power and impact. (Blommaert *et al.*, 2006: 39)

From the above, we can extrapolate that whenever human beings interact, they deploy a range of resources, these being topics, chronology, toponymy, naming, languages and their varieties, pictograms and accents, which they try to map onto the communicative function they see as being requested at that very moment by their interlocutor. The discursive production that goes on at the moment when someone narrates a migration story then manages (or does not manage) to make him/her part of a much larger process of institutional enregisterment into discourses of authenticity and indigeneity. While, following Agha's definition (2003: 231), enregisterment should be understood as a set of 'processes through which a linguistic repertoire becomes differentiable within a language as a socially recognized register of forms', the careful opening up of this very notion allows for introducing a new facet to the enregisterment process. What is performed, at a given time and in a given space such as during the moment to moment unfolding of an applicant interview with the authorities, as an 'indigenous' repertoire of sociolinguistic and sociocultural knowledge, becomes a socially recognised register of forms that functions as proof of someone's truthfulness of words and deeds and of 'authenticity'. It follows that the assessment of someone's sociolinguistic repertoires and sociocultural knowledge, such as, for instance, the assessment of how someone maps sociolinguistic forms onto sociolinguistic functions and what he knows about a country, gives a glimpse into whether this mapping is mapping done by an 'authentic' inhabitant of Country X, in order to provide tangible proof of indigeneity, e.g. that someone is authentically from where s/he claims to be coming from.

One of the resources that was neglected in the early days of sociolinguistic ethnographic work on asylum, mainly due to the paucity of its use and the consequent absence of an online-offline nexus in people's lives, was the internet and its affordances for retrieving knowledge. It is through these affordances that this infrastructure of globalisation comes to play a key role in the 'ethnoscape' (Appadurai, 1996) of moving subjects and in the 'legalscape' and 'technoscape' of those institutions assessing asylum-seeking applications for refugee status adjudication. At present, the internet has become much more than a straightforward enabler and enhancer of people's interactivity. Rather, it has become a sociolinguistic and sociocultural field of knowledge in its own right and, as such, it has become a shibboleth at the gate, triggering the mobility of some and the immobility of others. Although the empirical part that follows will not venture a fine-grained analysis of the actual interview between the Belgian immigration authorities and the applicant, the analysis unveils the fact that – in such a power-saturated environment – what counts as a widely accepted display of someone's local sociolinguistic and sociocultural knowledge results in being at odds with the internet-based knowledge matrix that the authorities expect to hear and apprehend from the applicant at hand.

Method

This study, part of a larger ethnographic interpretive inquiry called Asylum 2.0 which started its first exploratory fieldwork in 2012, aims at unravelling the implications of the internet and in particular of its socio-technological platforms in the lives of asylum seekers. In doing so, it builds on three rounds of fieldwork taking place between 2012 and 2014 at an asylum-seeking centre in Flanders, the Dutch speaking part of Belgium. This ethnographic interpretive endeavour combines insights, methods and epistemological stances stemming from linguistic ethnography (Blackledge & Creese, 2009; Copland & Creese, 2014; Rampton *et al.*, 2007) and socioculturally rooted discourse analysis (Gee, 1999). In both frameworks, there is the underlying assumption that the way individuals speak as well as speak about things reflects their culturally embedded understanding of the human beings around them and their perception of the world. The data upon which the present contribution draws were collected in October 2013, during my first round of fieldwork at the centre. My positioning there was that of a buffer between: 'the assistants', i.e. staff members regularly employed by the centre but who did not play any role – at least officially – in either the recognition or dismissal of the applicants' claims; the volunteers who were coming in weekly for an array of activities; and the 'guests', a term used by the director to address all the residents of the centre which was taken from the official discourse employed by the federal authorities when dealing with asylum seekers (for a similar use of the word 'guest', see Yilmaz, this volume). When asked by 'the guests' who I was and what I was doing there, I candidly explained to them that I was writing a book about what it means to be an asylum seeker in contemporary times and what asylum seeking implies, and that I was interested in their daily lives. All the participants embraced my interest and, although they were given the opportunity to opt out of being included in the study, none of them did so. Possibly because I myself am a non-native speaker of Dutch with a national background other than the mainstream one, they reacted enthusiastically as they imagined that another foreigner who had somehow gained a voice wanted to use his voice to write about their lives and their experiences at the centre and beyond during their asylum-seeking routes.

Rather than using either nationality or ethnic grouping as criteria for assigning rooms, the director of the centre back then had opted – where he and his team members felt it not to be a risk – to put together people of different ethnic, linguistic and religious backgrounds. During this round of ethnographic fieldwork, the centre catered for 61 'guests'. They appear to be a multi-ethnic and multilingual group of migrants, yet still rather homogeneous regarding further aspects of diversity, such as age group, gender and legal status. Following the information gathered at the centre during their intake talks, guests were from the following (often self-claimed) national backgrounds: 13 from Afghanistan; 12 from 'The Russian Federation' – mostly from Armenia and Chechnya; nine from Guinea Conakry; nine from Bangladesh; and seven from the Democratic Republic of Congo. Following the unofficial statistics kept at the centre, the remaining 11 guests originated from what had been categorised as 'other'. These were, respectively, two from Senegal, one from Somalia, one from Togo, three from China, one from Albania and one from Ukraine. Forty of these guests were male; 21 were female. Eleven of them fell under the category of unaccompanied minors, although three of them still needed to give proof of age through bone investigation. Only two guests had passed their 50s. All names given in this case study are pseudonyms so as to grant the participants protection and privacy. My chats with them were informal, although I wrote synopses of the topics and the key points we discussed at the end of my fieldwork day. Although video-recording was not possible, audio-recording occurred when I felt that a talk I had just had was particularly interesting because it revealed a facet of their daily doings in asylum seeking. In that case, while permission had already been gained by the centre, I asked whether they felt like telling me their story again while being audio-recorded. Access to their files – granted by the centre director and by the applicants themselves – has helped me shed light on the same people but this time not from their first-hand lived perspective of doing asylum but through the institutional/legal lens. Here too, guests at the centre were told of my access to their procedural files and were given the opportunity to either agree or disagree with it. No disagreement was reported.

The Asylum Application

According to the Dublin Regulation, the asylum applications for which Belgium is responsible are transferred to the *General Commissariat for Refugees and Stateless People* (henceforth under the Dutch language acronym CGVS). The CGVS, an independent administrative authority, exclusively specialises in asylum decision making. In a single procedure, the CGVS examines first whether the applicant fulfils the eligibility criteria for refugee status and whether they are eligible for subsidiary protection status. There is no Belgian law imposing an obligation on the CGVS to decide within a given time in the regular procedure. Before we enter our applicant's life story, we must first make a very basic point. Bashir's life story is a narration put together by someone who is a young adult, who has gone through violent events that have characterised his country of origin and, in particular, his family. Further, this is the story of someone who – like many other asylum applicants – was asked to produce a coherent factual narrative about his country of origin and place of living. Although this request may seem to any literate individual easy to perform, Bashir has no formal schooling and even though he can read the Qu'ran because of his Qu'ranic schooling, he has very limited reading and writing skills in the Latin script through which all institutional documents are mediated.

The texts used as primary data sources here are extracts taken from the letter that sums up the findings that have emerged from Bashir's narrative during the long interview in which the CGVS asked him to give evidence of his identity as a Guinean from Conakry. It was impossible for me to gain direct access to the actual interview or to the immediate transcription produced by the CGVS. This meant that the object I had at my disposal for analytical purposes was the letter Bashir received and that his roommate, Malidi, read out loud to him. In the letter, typewritten and signed by a representative of the CGVS, we find first the negative result of Bashir's application. This is followed by a detailed report of the knowledge Bashir has failed to show and upon which evidence rejection has taken place (see Figure 5.1). This letter, though, is not only a document but also the product of a long and complex process of textual elaboration of someone's life story. The letter, in fact, funnels the findings that emerged during the long interview and renders Bashir's rejection indisputable in that it is based on a lack of factual knowledge. As the asylum procedure is a matter of assessing someone's claims of origin, being understood as a Cartesian matter of direct matching between applicants' knowledge and their identity claims, it was concluded that Bashir's story had to be truly false. The letter, in fact, reads as shown in Figure 5.1.

De nationalité guinéenne et d'origine ethnique peul par votre mère et malinké par votre père, vous êtes arrivé sur le territoire belge le 7 février 2012 et avez introduit une demande d'asile le lendemain en tant que mineur d'âge.

Vous invoquez les faits suivants à l'appui de votre demande d'asile :

Votre père est malinké et votre mère est peule. Les familles respectives de vos parents voulaient que vos parents se séparent en raison de leur différence ethnique. Le 5 janvier 2012, votre père a été poignardé par les membres de votre famille maternelle. Vous avez emmené votre père à l'hôpital de Donka, mais comme il était tard et que le service était fermé, les médecins vous ont fait attendre jusqu'au lendemain. Le lendemain matin votre père est décédé. C'est également depuis ce jour que vous n'avez plus revu votre frère qui était allé chercher des médicaments pour votre père. Lors de l'enterrement de votre père, les frères de votre mère ont dit qu'ils vous tueraient. Vous et votre mère n'avez plus osé rentrer chez vous et avez vécu dehors. Le 14 janvier 2012, votre mère vous a confié à Khalil Camara, un policier qui était ami avec votre père. Vous êtes resté chez cette personne jusqu'au 2 février 2012, jour où il vous a fait quitter la Guinée.

Figure 5.1 First excerpt from the letter from the CGVS

Given the lack of space here, I will take you through the most salient elements and passages of this textual artefact without giving its full transcript. The original text of the rejection letter is in the standard variety of French, the procedural language through which the authorities corresponded with Bashir. In the excerpt above (Figure 5.1), we first read Bashir's national and ethnic identity affiliation as somebody of Guinean nationality and of Peul ethnic origin, through being offspring of a Malinka father and a Peul mother. While going through the excerpt, we see that Bashir's story serves as testimony of the profound division amongst two major ethnic groups in Guinee Conakry, a division that is deeply entrenched in Bashir's family and in its misfortunes. Bashir's maternal side of the family was in profound disagreement with Bashir's father, and there was pressure for his parents to separate due to their ethnic backgrounds, which at the time was also associated with the political conflicts tearing apart the country. The inner family tensions escalated to an episode of violence on 5 January 2012, when Bashir's father was beaten by his mother's siblings. After having been taken to the Donka's hospital, in central Conakry, and having discovered that the hospital was closed, Bashir's father passed away a day later due to the injuries received during the beating. Bashir reported that after his father's burial he was threatened by his mother's siblings. Because of this, Bashir and his mother never went back to their home, and on 14 January 2012 Bashir's mother gave him into the custody of a policeman who had been friendly with his father. Bashir then stayed at Khalil's place until 2 February 2012, on which date he was made to leave. His asylum application on the basis of unsafety due to ethnic background was received in Brussels on 8 February 2012 and examined on 24 April 2012. His hearing at the CGVS took place on 6 July 2012. Figure 5.2 below reports the second excerpt taken from the CGVS' letter of rejection.

The second excerpt, reported in Figure 5.2, is mainly an evaluation of Bashir's story authored by the CGVS. The text, in summary, takes the form of a checklist and, more specifically, a checklist that recaps the information that Bashir did not manage to produce and that ended up disqualifying him as someone from Guinea and more precisely from its capital city, Conakry. Bashir's knowledge fell short when he was asked to name the four 'quartier' – *Hamdallaye* being the one Bashir claims to have lived in – that make up '*la commune de Ratoma*'.[2] This lack of knowledge was compounded by the applicant not knowing the (official) name of any big mosque in Conakry, a lack of knowledge deemed astounding (*etonnant*) as he claimed to have studied the Qu'ran every day, although without being specific about the whereabouts of his studies. Further, this astonishment came from the fact that the biggest mosque in West Africa – the *Mosquee du Fayçal*, an official name retrieved by the authorities from the

document de réponse gui2012-103w du 6 juillet 2012). Ensuite, alors que vous avez dit avoir vécu toute votre vie dans le quartier de Hamdallaye, qui se situe dans la commune de Ratoma, vous n'avez pu citer que quatre quartiers de cette commune (voir p. 14) et n'avez pas été en mesure de préciser dans quel quartier de Hamdallaye vous viviez (voir p. 13) alors qu'il en existe quatre : Hamdallaye I, Hamdallaye II, Hamdallaye Mosquée et Hamdallaye Pharmacie. Ensuite, vous avez dit que vous avez dormi avec votre mère pendant dix jours dans une mosquée, mais vous avez été incapable d'en citer le nom (voir p. 13). De même, vous n'avez pu citer le nom d'aucune grande mosquée à Conakry ce qui est étonnant dans la mesure où vous dites étudier le Coran tous les jours et que la grande mosquée Fayçal de Conakry, qui est la plus grande d'Afrique de l'Ouest, se situe en face de l'hôpital de Donka où vous dites avoir emmené votre père (Voir documents joints à votre dossier administratif : article *Le gouverneur de Conakry s'en prend aux mendiants qui occupent l'alentour de l'hôpital Donka et la Mosquée Faycal* du 10 mai 2012 publié sur aminata.com, carte de google maps et article *L'avis du Petit futé sur la mosquée Fayçal* publié sur petitfute.com). Par ailleurs, si vous avez pu citer de façon exacte le nom de la bouteille d'eau la plus répandue, la monnaie utilisée en Guinée, le camp Alpha Yaya, le nom de deux opérateurs mobiles ou dire ce qu'est un « magbana » (voir pp. 15, 16), vous n'avez cependant pas pu décrire correctement le drapeau guinéen ou citer le nom de l'équipe football guinéenne. De même, si vous dites être allé au marché avec votre père (p. 7) vous n'avez été en mesure d'en citer le nom et à la question de savoir si vous connaissez des noms de marchés, vous vous êtes contenté de répondre « ça s'appelle en ville » (voir p. 15). Ensuite, vous avez dit regarder la télévision (voir p. 10), or, vous n'avez été en mesure de citer le nom d'aucune chaîne guinéenne, répondant que vous regardiez *« les chaines guinéennes. Et aussi des films. J'écoute la musique »* (voir p. 15). Il vous a ensuite été demandé si vous connaissiez le nom du grand stade de foot central de Conakry, ce à quoi vous avez répondu par la négative et avez dit qu'un terrain est en train d'être construit à Cosa (voir p. 15). Or, il est étonnant que

Figure 5.2 Second excerpt from the letter from the CGVS

internet – is located right in front of the hospital where the applicant had brought his badly beaten father. The link the authorities make in the text above runs as follows. If you really studied the Qu'ran then it means you should have studied in a mosque. Further, if you are really from Conakry you should be able to give the official name of the mosque you used to attend. Given that you cannot do so and given also that – as we have retrieved from the internet – this mosque is the biggest mosque in West Africa, then we can cast serious doubts on the truthfulness of your identity claims. The case of the naming of the mosque is of further interest because the authorities rely here on web-based knowledge that uses the official name of this mosque: the first one is aminata.com – a site giving news about Guinee; the second is Google Maps; and the third and most intriguing one is petitfute.com – a website that gives handy tips to French speaking tourists wishing to explore faraway exotic countries. The testing of Bashir's factual knowledge that serves to prove his 'being indigenous' (or lack thereof) continues. As we read, Bashir was not able to produce the name of the bottled water most sold in Guinea. He was not able to name the money used in Guinea, the phone operator present in Guinea or to explain what a *'magbana'* is, i.e. the percussion drums used across Senegal and Guinea, as well as the official name of the military camp called 'Alpha

Yaya' which has been Guinea's governmental headquarter since 2008. Further, he failed to describe the Guinean flag or to name the members of the Guinean national football team. The final disproof of identity was his inability to name the market where he went with his father as well as the proper name of any market in Conakry, where he replied *'ca s'appelle en ville'* (that is called a city). He did not know the name of any Guinean TV channels, to which Bashir responded *'Je regard le chaine guineensis. Et aussi des films. J'ecoute la musique'* (I watch the Guinean channels, and films as well. I listen to music). Last, he did not know the name of the big football stadium in Conakry. As explained in the final part of the letter, the authorities considered all these questions manageable for a young man of Bashir's age and educational level.

A Chat with Bashir's Roommate

Given that Bashir relied almost blindly on his roommate, Malidi, for everything that concerned literacy, I have had the chance to 'hang out' with Malidi quite often after Bashir had fled into illegality due to his rejection. From there, I decided to have a chat with Malidi about Bashir's rejection, as he was the one who had read the rejection letter out loud to Bashir. In my conversation with him, I came to discover that Malidi comes from a well-known Quranic preachers' family in Guinee Conakry. Malidi's application had already been approved by the CGVS. Being aware that this could also have led to a chat about sensitive information, I obtained Malidi's consent to have my audio-recorder on. In what follows, I present two extracts in English from my conversation with Malidi, which took place in French. The first extract deals with Malidi having to speak to Bashir's mother on Bashir's mobile phone. The episode runs as follows:

Extract 1

Malidi: One day Bashir came into the room.
Max: hm
Malidi: He called his mother with Skype.
Max: hm
Malidi: So, his mother asked him whether he did his prayers.
Max: hm
Malidi: Daily.
Max: Yes, yes, yes
Malidi: He said yes (but) his mother did not trust him.
Max: Right!
Malidi: He gave me [...] to reassure his mother, he gave me the phone, so I had occasion to talk to his mother, so I then I spoke to his mother. So when I spoke to his mother, she asked me directly [...]

Max: Sorry I don't understand.
Malidi: She told me, my origin is Guinean, I, I [...] I, myself, have been born in Conakry, she told me, I myself am originally from Télimélé.
Max: From Télimélé what, you?
Malidi: Yes, she told me Ah! Me too I am from Télimélé, which family in Télimélé do you come from? Which family? The [XXX]'s family. So she said fine, I know them, the [inaudible], that family is well known there, and I believe you.
Max: Well known?
Malidi: Well known.
Max: Okay, your family, his family?
Malidi: My family.
Max: Your family.
Malidi: So, we spoke, she asked me whether Bashir was doing okay and whether he said his prayers, and whether he did this while I was there, because I [inaudible] here, so I do every [inaudible]
Max: hmm.

In the above, although the reported speech centres around Bashir's mother making sure that her son has done his daily Quranic prayers, we see more things emerging. The mother of Bashir, who first claims to be from Conakry, but then asserts to be from Télimélé, a city of 15,000 people 170 km away from Conakry, is building trust with Malidi because of his being the son of a well-known family there in Télimélé. Further, the conversation with the applicant's roommate unfolds as follows:

Extract 2

Max: But, but also, Bashir's language, you told me that Bashir's language is not Malinka, it is not the same as the one reported on the letter (the letter from the CGVS: MS)
Malidi: No, I have said, I did not confirm that he does not come from there, I say that he does not speak the language spoken there.
Max: He does not speak the language spoken there?
Malidi: Exactly, he speaks better the language of the capital, the Susu language.
Max: Oh, yeah?
Malidi: Me too, I speak better Susu than my mother tongue, the language of my mother and of my father, because I grew up in Conakry, you are forced to speak that language. But I speak French well too, that's better here in Belgium.
Max: Is Susu very different from your mother's and father's language?
Malidi: Yes, very different, *very* (stresses the e: MS) different, very very different, there is no link between my language, but the language of [inaudible], the other is the language of the market. The language of fishermen.

Max:	Hmm (...) of fishermen.
Malidi:	Yes, people who catch fish.
Max:	Oh right, so that is Susu.
Malidi:	Yes.
Max:	Okay, but, but, but, but [...] but I spoke to Bashir, once or twice and his French is way different from your French.
Malidi:	But yes, of course, it is not the same thing, I myself have studied, I have finished my studies, Bashir has not been to school.
Max:	He has not been to school?
Malidi:	He entered school here.
Max:	Oh yeah?
Malidi:	Yes! I am convinced [of that: MS] because it is me, to whom he went to, when there was a letter to send or to read he asks me whether I can read it for him. He knows absolutely nothing in French.
Max:	Oh yeah?
Malidi:	Yes!
Max:	Okay, okay, so writing is also extremely difficult for Bashir, right?
Malidi:	No! He cannot write!
Max:	hmm.
Malidi:	His papers are negative.
Max:	Yes, I know.
Malidi:	There you go. For him the motivation, they have asked him how many communes there are in Conakry [...]
Max:	Yes, I know, I know, I have seen the report.
Malidi:	There you are. He started to recite the quarters in Hemedaille and he did not understand.
Max:	Right, right.
Malidi:	He did not understand the difference between *quartier* and *commune*
Max:	He did not understand the difference, hmm.
Malidi:	Between *quartier* and *commune*. But it has only to do with the fact that Bashir has not gone to school and not because Bashir does not come from Guinee.
Max:	Hmm, okay, okay.
Malidi:	The same thing goes for everything, the Mosque, the market. The market is at the centre of town so for him that is 'town' and the Mosque, well, that is one big Mosque, but there at home we call it the big Mosque.

Extract 2 shows how well Bashir knew Malidi and how close they were; asking him to read or write letters on his behalf implied a fair deal of trust. Second, we discover that Bashir, because of his lack of schooling, did not know certain (basic) notions like the difference between *quartier* and *commune*. Even more interesting is Malidi's insight into Bashir's language repertoire. Aside from claiming that Bashir's proficiency in French is very limited, French being the language in which the report was written and in which Bashir had decided to give his answers during the interview, we also find another interesting sociolinguistic element. That is – following Malidi's self-reported language proficiency and metalinguistic judgement of Bashir's language repertoire – Bashir is mostly proficient in a language called Soussou, the language of trade and more specifically the language used by fishermen and fish traders, a language that one who grows up in Conakry would know. This language, also known as Susu or Soso, stems from the Mande language family, the same family as the Malinka language – the language of Bashir's father. Soussou is one of the official languages of Guinea Conakry, although also used in Senegal, and is in fact the language of trade mostly used in coastal areas like Conakry. Although I did not have the chance to gather data on Bashir's own sociolinguistic repertoire as he had already left the centre, Bashir's reported sociolinguistic repertoire and lack of schooling give an interesting insight in what might have gone missing with the naming of things during the interview which was fully carried out in French. Aside from the issue of the language in which Bashir was most proficient, it is also interesting to notice Bashir's failure to differentiate between *quartier* and *commune*, as well as his inability to give the proper names for the market and mosque, all things that did not surprise Malidi. In Extract 2, the names Bashir gave to places like the market and the mosque – to which Malidi too refers as 'the big mosque' (*la grand mosquee*) – are reported to be common naming practices 'there at home'. These are naming practices that do not match the register that the CGVS's authorities, from their immobility standpoint, drew on through the websites they used.

Register Discrepancies

As shown in the extract above, as well as in the letter explaining Bashir's rejection, much of the doubt cast by the authorities on Bashir's identity comes not only from his incapacity to articulate knowledge about Conakry, but also from his inability to name places correctly compared to the knowledge that the authorities had accrued on the internet. However, Bashir's lack of knowledge could easily be attributed to what McDermott names inarticulateness:

> [S]ituations that organise inarticulateness are legion, and it is easy to name the most obvious occasions. Funerals, police inquiries, job interviews, class and race border encounters, tax interrogations, sex talk with children, group therapy, television interviews, and first dates – all are potential tongue-stoppers. A folk account would have it that whenever our words can be immediately consequential and long remembered, the pressure can get to us, and new heights of eloquence and new lows of inarticulateness are frequent. (McDermott, 1988 38–40)

We feel there is more to it than that. The ambiguous relationship between names and the things they refer to, e.g. places, has been a matter of interest for linguistic anthropology for decades and it has informed inquiries into the question of whether the name of a given thing is given from the point of view of the individual or of the collective. The relationship is not just reflective: rather, there are processes of enregisterment at play there that construct the practice of naming as local knowledge praxis. Given that enregisterment is the sociolinguistic process through which someone establishes the desire to be recognised as a specific someone (see Agha, 2003; Karrebaek, 2011), we shift the analysis here from differences between 'languages' to differences within languages, e.g. 'ways of speaking', 'ways of narrating' and 'ways of naming things'. In sum, we take a close look to all those elements within language that characterise someone as a legitimate user of a language, in that s/he narrates things the way they should be narrated and s/he names things the way they should be named. Bashir's letter exemplifies that it is not only the process of naming but within that the process of enregistering knowledge (Agha, 2003: 231–235) in the names of things, like a mosque, that matters here. More specifically, the process of naming is not solely an arbitrary process of making denotational and connotational meaning match one another. Rather, the process of naming comes with a history of use (inter-textuality), as well as with a history of sociocultural evaluation and assessment (a notion termed pre-textuality, see Maryns & Blommaert, 2002: 13). In the case of proper names, as Agha shows (2003: 247), the speech chain structure in which the action of naming is involved serves to maintain the coupling of a name with a referent, e.g. the association of a certain name with a given person or object. The fact that a name refers to that specific person or object is, at first, something shared by those who were involved in the immediate naming ceremony, e.g. an inauguration. It is then through the process of name transmission across sociocultural networks that other members become acquainted with somebody's or something's proper name even though they were not present at the naming ceremony. The naming ceremony therefore produces a continuous speech chain, as exemplified and verified by the story reported by Malidi in the utterance, 'The same thing goes for everything, the Mosque, the market. The market is at the centre of town so for him that is "town" and the Mosque, well, that is one big Mosque, but there at home we call it the big Mosque', that needs neither to be attended or verified but that needs to be known by those who term to belong to that network. To link the above to my data, inasmuch as Agha (2003) in his case in point about enregisterment draws on a particular phono-lexical register of a language variety as a socially recognised register of forms, here too the local variety used for the naming of public spaces of interest in Conakry – the one drawn upon by the authorities and the one drawn upon by the applicant – come to construct discrepant registers of forms. In the case of the co-presence of a speaker (in this instance, an individual naming things) and of a hearer (in this case an authority figure hearing how things are named), the issue of matching register is key to understanding the breakdown which is then reported by the authorities in this letter of rejection.

Unfortunately, I could not be present at this interview, nor I could get hold of the whole transcript of the interview as it was not in possession of the asylum-seeking centre. However, the text of the rejection letter reported in Figures 5.1 and 5.2 and the counter-evidence provided by Malidi are both telling elements that help us make sense of the processes at hand. First, they show how Bashir repeatedly fails to match the register that is expected of him, that is, the official register he should draw upon in order to have his voice recognised by the authority as indexing his indigeneity, an indigeneity embodied in the naming of things in the right way. Further, what emerges clearly is that the sites the authorities used are sites generated by highly mobile and highly educated people – one of them even being a tourist site that appears to actually be directed towards Western, French speaking tourists who likely have certain expectations for how place names should be labelled and described, i.e. with their official names. It then follows that what emerges from the letter is an act of internet-based knowledge misrecognition in which the CGVS – an institution that clearly operates on behalf of the State – sees a lack of verification of the identity of the applicant. As Benedict Anderson (1993) states in his work on nations as imagined communities, this register embodies a set of prescriptions of what the other under scrutiny should say and know in order to have his identity match what the authorities believe that someone who is indigenous should say and know. The fact that Malidi fills in the pre-textual gaps that caused the immigration officials to reject Bashir's account is indicative of his greater upward mobility in his country of origin, combined with his situated knowledge of the local spaces where Bashir has circulated, allowing him to make the clarifications that Bashir was unable to give due to the pre-textual gaps between the officers and himself.

Conclusion

As Shannahan (2015: 77) puts it, institutional interviews are places where the voice of an asylum-seeking applicant – in this case an asylum-seeking applicant operating in standard French while not being proficient in that variety of French – finds himself confronted with the institutional voice – in French or at least in one of its vernacular varieties – produced by the officer(s) who is assessing the case. The communicative situation that unfolds follows clear patterns of questioning as well as clear patterns of understanding and answering along the institutionally favoured matrix of what is considered valid 'country talk', that is, talks that give away proofs of origin and of national/ethnic identity. Consequently, the applicant does not only need to understand the language that is being used as a vehicle of what is being questioned. Rather, in order to fit the institutionally held frame of valid knowledge (cf. Bohmer & Shuman, 2011: 7), the applicant must also strive to match the register used by those who are asking the questions. These registers, within the social interactions involved in the asylum interview, play a significant role in the processes of origin assessment, in that they enable the authorities to determine the applicant's identity according to the attributes of their story. As Goffman warns us:

> [W]e lean on anticipations that we have, transforming them into normative expectations, into righteously presented demands. [...] It is [when an active question arises as to whether these demands will be filled] that we are likely to realize that all along we had been making certain assumptions as to what the individual before us ought to know to be members of a society. (Goffman, 1963: 2)

The letter analysed here is therefore the last ring in a textual chain that has rendered 'faulty answers' into a bureaucratic text that stands to symbolise lack of knowledge, that is to say, into a text that homogenises what someone of Bashir's age, origin and educational level is expected to know about the country he claims to be from. Yet, as Gee reminds us:

> [t]he fact that people have differential access to different identities and activities, connected to different sorts of status and social goods, is a root source of inequality in society. [...] Since different identities and activities are enacted in and through language, the study of language is integrally connected to matters of equity and justice. (Gee, 1999: 13)

The naming register used to define markets and mosques, as well as everyday items like money and bottled water, is a model of factual knowledge that links naming and knowing to indigeneity, leading to the sociocultural recognition of the applicant as someone who is telling the truth. To rage against the bureaucratic oddity that is at the core of this study is of very little use. Rather, Bashir's case evaluation should serve to provide us with a glimpse into the valence of factual information for the assessment of identity claims in an asylum-seeking procedure (see Ochs, 1996: 417–419, on the indexical value of language). That is, Bashir's application is based on a complex set of associative networks that underpin the ideological expectations of what someone who claims to be from a certain place should know about that place and, in particular, how this applicant should express this knowledge. Furthermore, what this chapter has shown is not only evidence of how the emergence of register discrepancy gives way to misrecognition of identity claims, but also shows how identity is local knowledge dependent and how authenticity is being judged by a different institutional matrix of knowledge. It is the matching or mismatching of the above that determines who may speak, what they may speak about and, in particular, how they may speak about their own life history, their origins and their migration. For our case in point here, the denial of its interlingual as well as intra-lingual complexity has been shown to be a source of rather fundamental, although often invisible, injustice. It seems, in fact, that Bashir did not understand what was expected of him when it came to reporting to the officers and describing his home space, so he could not explain or understand the pre-textual gaps that were missing. In turn, one could infer that the officers did not understand these gaps either. Instead, as it results from the lack of knowledge reported in the textual artefact at hand, they sought resources that explained things in Bashir's origin location in terms that they would of course understand. It is these 'lacks' in mobility on both sides of the equation, in an interaction of unequal power dynamics, that led to the discounting of Bashir's case. Although aware that the straightforward anchoring of identity is a process fraught with complications even in imagined homogeneous communities of people belonging to a single national entity, here we see how the internet, its websites and the knowledge it gives access to, notwithstanding the immobility of those who consult it, appear to provide a further hook on which institutions happen to hold on tight in dismissing this asylum-seeking claim.

Notes

(1) The term ergoic is an adjectivisation of the Latin causative conjunction *ergo*, meaning in English 'therefore'.
(2) Conakry is divided into *communes*, with each *commune* consisting of more than one *quartier*.

References

Anderson, B. (1993) *Imagined Communities: Reflections on the Origins and Spread of Nationalism*. London: Verso.
Agha, A. (2003) The social life of cultural values. *Language & Communication* 23, 231–273.

Appadurai, A. (1996) *Modernity at Large: Cultural Dimensions of Globalization.* Minneapolis, MN: University of Minnesota Press.

Blackledge, A. and Creese, A. (2009) Meaning-making as dialogic process: Official and carnival lives in the language classroom. *Journal of Language, Identity & Education* 8 (4), 236–253.

Blommaert, J. (2005) *Discourse: A Critical Introduction.* Cambridge: Cambridge University Press.

Blommaert, J. (2009) Language, asylum and the national order. *Current Anthropology* 50 (4), 415–441.

Blommaert, J., Bock, M. and McCormick, K. (2006) Narrative inequality in the TRC hearings: On the hearability of hidden transcripts. *Journal of Language and Politics* 5 (1), 37–70.

Bohmer, C. and Shuman, A. (2011) *Rejecting Refugees: Political Asylum in the 21st Century.* London/New York: Routledge.

Copland, F. and Creese, A. (2014) *Linguistic Ethnography: Collecting, Analyzing and Presenting Data.* London: Sage.

Detailleure, J. and M. Spotti (2012) *Placing Shibboleths at the Institutional Gate: LADO Tests and the Construction of Asylum Seekers' Identities.* WPULL 99 https://www.academia.edu/6341603/WP99_Detailleur_and_Spotti_2013_Placing_shibboleths_at_the_institutional_gate_LADO_tests_and_the_construction_of_asylum_seekers_identities

Gee, J. (1999) *An Introduction to Discourse Analysis: Theory and Method.* London: Routledge.

Goffman, E. (1963) *Stigma.* London: Penguin.

Haas, B. (2015) Adjudicators, suspicion and the ambivalent production of authoritative knowledge. Paper presented at the Political Asylum and the Politics of Suspicion Symposium held at the Mershon Center for International Security Studies, Ohio State University, Columbus, Ohio, USA, 23 March.

Hall, S. (1992) The West and the rest: Discourse and power. In S. Hall and B. Gieben (eds) *Formations of Modernity* (pp. 275–331). Cambridge: Polity Press.

Haviland, J. (1989) "Tztamik ta lume, asta k'u cha'al bu chak' sat te' (Desde el suelo hasta la fruta): la migracion y la informacion en el discurso tzotzil." Paper presented to annual meetings of the Sociedad Mexicana de Antropologia, Merida, 18 Oct. 1989.

Jacquemet, M. (2005) Transidiomatic practices: Language and power in the age of globalization. *Language & Communication* 25, 257–277.

Jacquemet, M. (2013) Transidioma and asylum: Gumperz's legacy in intercultural institutional talk. *Journal of Linguistic Anthropology* 23 (3), 199–212.

Karrebaek, M. (2011) 'What's in your lunch-box today?': Health, ethnicity and respectability in the primary classroom. *Journal of Linguistic Anthropology* 22 (1), 1–22.

Maryns, K. and Blommaert, J. (2002) Pretextuality and pretextual gaps: On de/refining linguistic inequality. *Pragmatics* 12 (1), 11–30.

McDermott, R. (1988) Inarticulateness. In D. Tannen (ed.) *Linguistics in Context: Connecting Observation and Understanding* (pp. 37–68). Norwood, NJ: Ablex.

Ochs, E. (1996) Linguistic resources for socializing humanity. In J. Gumperz and S. Levinson (eds) *Rethinking Linguistic Relativity* (pp. 407–437). Cambridge: Cambridge University Press.

Rampton, B., Maybin, J. and Tusting, K. (2007) Linguistic ethnography: Links, problems and possibilities. Special issue of *Journal of Sociolinguistics* 11 (5), 575–695.

Shannahan, A. (2015) A narrative perspective on a well-founded fear: Officer stancetaking in a political asylum documentary. *Second Language Studies* 33 (2), 76–101.

Spotti, M. (2015) Asylum seeking, identity techniques and the paradox of web truths. *Border Criminologies* blog, 19 November. Oxford: University of Oxford Faculty of Law. https://www.law.ox.ac.uk/research-subject-groups/centre-criminology/centreborder-criminologies/blog/2014/11/asylum-seeking.

Spotti, M. (2018) 'It's all about naming things right': The paradox of web truths in the Belgian asylum-seeking procedure. In N. Gill and A. Good (eds) *Asylum Determination in Europe: Ethnographic Perspectives* (pp. 69–90). London: Palgrave.

Vertovec, S. (2007) Super-diversity and its implications. *Ethnic and Racial Studies* 30 (6), 1024–1054. doi:10.1080/01419870701599465

6 From Language to Politics: Communication, Power and Migration in the Central Mediterranean

Marco Jacquemet

Introduction

The Mediterranean is a transidiomatic environment: a multilingual space shaped by the communicative practices of groups of people, either territorially defined or deterritorialized, who communicate using an array of both face-to-face and long-distance media (Jacquemet, 2005). In the case of migration, these transidiomatic practices are activated by two sets of opposing players: those involved in border reinforcement and those engaged in border crossing.

European Union (EU) and state authorities operating in the Mediterranean area use various power technologies to manage the displacement and dispersal of migrants. On the other hand, migrants rely on their own technologies of mobility to navigate the Mediterranean passage. These dynamics of containment/displacement and their related power technologies have precipitated a dual discourse (in Foucault's sense of the term) on migration, organized around two poles: sedentary and mobile. This discourse has been constructed by Western policy makers and their allies – but to some extent also by migrants – to explain two different ways of being in the world: the citizen and the nomad (Nyers, 2015). This ideological discourse is used by Western nations (and nationalists) to justify the way they behave towards migrants: constructing sedentarity (and walls) to defend themselves against hordes of invaders. On the other hand, many migrant discursive formations focus on themes of exile, of unrootedness, of free movement, of no borders.

In exploring the discursive dynamics between these two agents, this chapter seeks to assess communicative practices and political discourses in the Mediterranean area resulting from the interaction between local populations, migrants and digital communication. After introducing the communicative landscape of the Mediterranean and reviewing the past decade of humanitarian and security missions in the Mediterranean (from Mare Nostrum to the EU-led Triton to EUNAVFOR MED), it discusses the Italian government's 2018 decision to close ports to international rescue operations, and looks at the responses of Italy's grassroots movement for migrant rights, which had emerged as a counterpoint to the government's strict border enforcement practices.

To support the decision by the Italian government of the time (composed of the populist Movimento 5 Stelle and the hard-right Lega) to close ports to rescue operations, populist leaders constructed and broadcasted a discourse whose central message was 'humanitarianism is a business.' This discourse reframed humanitarian search and rescue missions in Mediterranean waters as businesses profiteering from refugee flows. Because of this framing, 65% of Italians – already increasingly worried about their place in a rapidly mutating world and ready to blame their troubles on the migrants and refugees washing up on their shores – agreed with the government's anti-immigrant policy. But this framing was not universally accepted, and opposition coalesced in a movement that used clever mottos displayed on balcony banners and social media to poke fun at anti-immigrant politicians and to demand a more humanitarian approach to the crisis.

This chapter has two aims: (1) to explore the use of mainstream and social media by Italian populist leaders to frame their opposition to migration; (2) to document the use by migrant rights advocates of creative, non-standard usage of Italian (including mottos that featured intransitive verbs treated as transitive) to signal the existence of a different Italy, open to linguistic impurity, cultural mixing and political solidarity.

Communicative Technologies of Mobility/Immobility: Sedentary versus Mobile

This dual discourse was first provided with a theoretical framework by Gilles Deleuze and Félix Guattari in their discussion of nomadology and deterritorialization (1987). Central to this discussion is the structural difference between sedentary and mobile power. Deleuze and Guattari viewed sedentary sovereigns (kingdoms, city-states and free ports) as occupying a 'striated space' where these sovereigns use sedentary power technologies (frontiers, passports, moats and border guards) to counter the 'smooth space' activated by nomads in their endless move to new territories. Sedentary power reorders space and makes it measurable. Lines of division and demarcation serve to classify, measure and distribute striated space following political or economic imperatives. Borders, fortifications, land lots and city walls are all products of the striation of space – structures and constructs through which lines of flight can be harnessed and controlled. This striation is resisted by the turbulent, rhizomatic, smooth space of nomadic movement, where demarcating lines (roads, bridges, railway tracks) become vectors rather than units of measurement. Smooth space is 'a direction and not a dimension or metric determination' (Deleuze & Guattari, 1987: 478). As opposed to the gravitational space of a striated topography, a smooth topology of movement creates a deterritorialized space in which particular places are strictly subordinated to the paths crisscrossing them. This boundless space shifts with every movement. Like an ocean, it lacks the features that result in privileging one place over other places; it is therefore non-disciplined and cannot be controlled by sedentary means (Deleuze & Guattari, 1987: 480).

This dichotomy between sedentary power and nomadic movement provides a useful framework for examining the transidiomatic strategies used by migrants crossing the Mediterranean as well as the European response to these migrants. We can see these forces at work in shaping the communicative practices among authorities, migrants, human smugglers and fishermen. At the same time, we acknowledge that this dichotomy is a simplification of the complex phenomena of migration, in which there is a continuum between sedentary and mobile uses of technology on the part of migrants and authorities.

Government immigration agencies mostly operate in the striated space of the nation-state: gathering intelligence on migrants through the collection, coordination and analysis of multiple databases; probing intranets to gather additional evidence; relying on fixed digital infrastructures (such as networked office computers) during their interactions with migrants. The EU, the contemporary embodiment of sedentary power, seeks to stem the flow of people and control the traffic of knowledge. Central to the EU's border management strategy is the work of Frontex, the European agency for external border security. Frontex coordinates the activities of national border authorities to ensure the security of the EU's borders with non-Member States. The agency also assists in training national border guards, carries out intelligence gathering and risk analysis, monitors research relevant to the control and surveillance of external borders, offers technical and operational assistance at external borders, and supports Member States in organizing joint repatriation operations.[1] Frontex gathers intelligence about migrant movements across the Mediterranean through the collection, coordination and analysis of a battery of signal intercepts provided by national radar stations and by the EU-funded Sea Horse advanced satellite system (mostly used to track ships). This intelligence is then relayed to a fleet of ships and airplanes (managed both by the EU and by national governments) tasked with intercepting intruders – and at times sending them back (in so doing, these institutions violate migrants' rights to seek asylum; see *Hirsi Jamaa and Others v. Italy*, European Court of Human Rights, 2012; see also HRW, 2009). The EU's radio and satellite curtains, backed up by border patrols, are the dematerialized equivalents of the fortified walls of Medieval Europe. They are the late-modern solution for detecting undesirable subjects well before they enter protected territory.

On the other hand, returning to Deleuze and Guattari's concept of nomadology, migrants can be seen as occupying a smooth space (such as the sea) which they traverse using satellite and cellular mobile communication. This kind of communication offers three main technological affordances to subjects in transit: they can organize and coordinate activities 'on the fly'; they can use satellite technology to orient themselves and find their way in smooth, unmarked territories; and they can store valuable information (phone numbers of course, but also contact names, addresses, maps and meeting points) in minimal space. The cell phone allows interlocutors to make midcourse adjustments, to progressively refine an activity through repeated calls and to keep schedules and deadlines tentative (Ling, 2004; McIntosh, 2010).

Moreover, cellular satellite communication utilizes the Global Positioning System (GPS) to provide cell phone users anywhere with precise information on their physical location – thus layering a digital grid over the smooth space of the Mediterranean Sea. Each of 32 GPS satellites orbiting the globe broadcasts a continuous stream of radio signals about its changing position and time to the earth's surface. A cell phone's GPS receiver uses signals from at least four satellites to calculate its own position (in latitude and longitude), velocity and local time. GPS can be used as a navigational tool, a high-tech compass for orienting in unmapped or unchartered areas. Most deterritorialized subjects use mobile technologies, in particular smartphones, to maintain links with their social networks and navigate unfamiliar spaces, using images and maps stored on smartphones. Mobile phones enable mobile people to orchestrate their social and professional lives, to identify job opportunities, and even to send remittances – in fact, since 2002, mobile phones have been the main tool used by people around the world to send remittances (Sander, 2005).

It is not uncommon to see migrants disembarking from a Mediterranean crossing carrying nothing but a cell phone. In many detention centers for undocumented migrants, the cell phone is the only way to maintain contact with the outside world – as long as the battery lasts. Over a decade ago, Italian identification and expulsion centers (CIE, *Centri di Identificazione ed Espulsione*) began to routinely confiscate cell phones from their 'guests' (the official terminology for referring to detained migrants), causing migrants considerable anxiety. After the intervention of humanitarian agencies, the Italian state relented and started allowing migrants to keep their cell phones to access their contacts and address book, although phone chargers (and SIM cards in the case of a trafficking investigation) were still confiscated. This policy has been, however, in continuous flux: as recently as 2009, most detainees in the Bologna CIE were no longer allowed to keep their phones because a number had tried to commit suicide by ingesting the phone battery.

Migrants are not the only deterritorialized group that values cell phones – smuggling operations do, too. Not only can they use cell phones to keep tabs on traffickers' whereabouts, but the phones' storage capability allows easy access to local contacts. In August 2010 the Italian border patrol apprehended a Russian human smuggler near Riace (in southwestern Italy) as he was disembarking from a luxury yacht with 45 migrants, after crossing the Mediterranean from east to west in six days. He had with him a pair of binoculars and ten cell phones. One of these had Thuraya satellite service while the others were linked to various local carriers in the countries where he operated. These phones stored thousands of contacts. It took the Italian police months to piece together the criminal network that emerged from the phones (Di Nicola & Musumeci, 2014).

The strategies and technologies used by deterritorialized subjects and European authorities do occasionally overlap: the ethnographic reality does not always display the structural opposition between sedentary and mobile power discussed by Deleuze and Guattari. All agents involved in de- and reterritorialization processes use some hybrid strategies. While mobile phones have emerged as crucial tools for subjects in transit because of their technological affordances, state agents are tapping into these same affordances. Smartphones' advantages for migrants are clear, but migrants are not the only ones allowed to use them. State and international agencies use a combination of fixed infrastructures (radars, observation posts, communication control and command centers) and mobile technologies (ships, high-speed inflatable boats, surveillance camcopters, but also smartphones and other communication technologies) to search, intercept and at times rescue undocumented migrants and refugees crossing into state-controlled territory. On the other hand, migrants adopt at times strategies of striated space, such as securing national passports (real or fake), identifying secure departure and destination points or tapping into the resources of land-based organizations (such as relief agencies).

Nevertheless, at the ideological level, the clash between sovereign powers and purely mobile forces does shape the discourse on migration and communications among these agents – both carried out through transidiomatic practices. These practices lie in fact at the root of specific forms of subjectivation that the Mediterranean, as a border, contributes to produce. As such, they provide an effective angle for the analysis of the intense conflicts and struggles that today fill the Mediterranean borderscape.

This space is a highly political environment. One consequence of European unification has been the transformation of the Mediterranean Sea into a defensive moat to stop the flow of unwanted migrants. Contrary to the popular vision of the Mediterranean Sea as a homogeneous and lawless expanse lying outside the reach of state power, this maritime territory is, in fact, crisscrossed by variegated and at times conflicting jurisdictional regimes of 'unbundled sovereignty' (Sassen, 2006). This allows states to simultaneously extend their sovereign privileges through forms of mobile government and elude the responsibilities that come with it.

In this technopolitical moat, the communication networks of 'Fortress Europe' (the term used to refer to the way in which Europe controls its borders and detains immigrants, as well as to its negative attitudes towards immigration) have established a buffer zone surrounding EU territorial waters. These networks are set up to monitor and intercept people at sea, but often their actions result in serious and irreversible human rights violations, including imprisoning fishermen as human traffickers, blocking boats from docking and forcibly repatriating undocumented migrants. As Agamben (2005) pointed out, in these forceful acts an inherently unstable sovereignty is displayed through a series of violent, often unspeakably cruel performances. Furthermore, no single nation holds clear, self-evident authority over this territory. In effect, this violence leads scholars to conclude that the Mediterranean has become an extrajudicial area.

Yet tens of thousands of migrants, unable to enter the EU through safe and regular routes, nevertheless attempt to cross the sea. They tap into all sorts of mobile technologies to gain an advantage in this dangerous crossing. They try to be as light and invisible as possible, performing a disappearing act as they enter the sea on its southern shores, hoping to reappear safe and sound on the northern side (although many do not).

The EU and member nation-states have continued to restrict Mediterranean crossings using strategies that routinely show disregard for migrant lives. In summer 2013, escalating violence in Libya led a record number of people to attempt the crossing of the central Mediterranean.

This trend was exacerbated by what would become the largest refugee crisis since World War II: the Syrian exodus. The EU initially implemented a policy of non-assistance, which led to numerous tragic shipwrecks and drownings, mostly involving Syrians. Following these tragedies, EU politicians were swift to prescribe more of the same failed policies, including extra funding for Frontex and increased surveillance through the launch of Eurosur, the European Border Surveillance System (Heller & Jones, 2014).

On the other hand, a newly formed center-left government in Italy, faced with the impossibility of ignoring the public outcry caused by these shipwrecks, single-handedly launched what was by far the largest humanitarian and security operation in the Mediterranean: *Mare Nostrum* (MN). By prioritizing the task of saving lives at sea, MN constituted a considerable break with the EU practice of non-assistance at sea. At the same time, the Italian state extended its claim to rights and obligations at sea far beyond its normally accepted perimeter (even into Libyan territorial waters), effectively living up to the full, imperial meaning of *mare nostrum* ('our sea'), a Latin term first used by the Roman Empire and later by the Italian fascist regime. Moreover, as Martina Tazzioli pointed out in her recent work on MN (2015), this operation managed to focus public attention on the morality of the 'scene of rescue', recasting the role of the state and the military as that of a merciful savior.

However, this scene obscured other crucial aspects of the operation. First, it obscured the fact that, while a record number of people were rescued, a record number of deaths were also reported, and MN did not make the crossing less dangerous. MN assets deployed close to the Libyan coast came to operate as a 'half-way' bridge to Europe; migrants still resorted to the service of smugglers for the first stretch of their journey. Smugglers, in turn, provided this service with even more precarious and unseaworthy boats, counting on MN's assets to rescue migrants swiftly. Second, the flip-side of Italy's extension of its sovereign 'privileges' at sea was the retraction of its sovereign 'duties' on firm land – duties such as fingerprinting and assisting rescued migrants, thereby enabling their further movement across EU space. This in turn caused EU institutions and northern European states to ask Italy to end assistance at sea and reinstate orderly assistance on firm land.

In November 2014, MN was phased out in favor of the far more limited Frontex-led Triton operation. The aim of Triton was border control and not rescue at sea, and it thus involved a very different spatial and operational logic. Instead of proactively patrolling the waters immediately off the Libyan coast for migrants in trouble, Triton made search and rescue (SAR) missions subordinate in priority to border patrol.

Under Triton – rebranded in February 2018 as Operation Themis – SAR needs were partially met by a massive recourse to commercial shipping vessels as the agents of rescue operations. The commercial shipping community had already emerged as a crucial actor in rescue operations during MN. After MN ended, it took on an even more prominent role (Heller & Jones, 2015).

While commercial vessels have contributed to saving thousands of people, their involvement has also posed serious safety challenges. As Heller and Jones pointed out, commercial ships are not designed to safely approach boats that are much smaller, overcrowded and unstable. Furthermore, they often have a small crew that is not specifically trained nor equipped to carry out the extremely perilous operations (including communicating clear instructions) necessary to rescue migrants in the open seas. Without diminishing the important efforts of the shipping community, it is not surprising that the role of commercial vessels in rescue operations contributed to two major shipwrecks in April 2015, the largest to have occurred in the Mediterranean in recent history. In order to address this situation, a dozen non-governmental humanitarian agencies – Médecins Sans Frontières (MSF), the Maltese Migrants Offshore Aid Station (MOAS), SOS Mediterranée, Sea-Watch, Open Arms, Save the Children, LifeBoat and others – took the initiative to set up a system for rescue operations, assembling a veritable civilian rescue flotilla (Stierl, 2018).

Their impact was impressive on both symbolic and operational levels. Because the missions of MSF and other humanitarian organizations were associated with medical assistance in a war context, their intervention signaled that both the scale of migrant deaths and the militarization of borders that led to these tragedies had turned the Mediterranean into a war zone – a war zone created by the EU Member States and their policies.

For a while, the 'privatization' of rescue activities was actively encouraged by Italy and the EU, and the Italian media quickly dubbed these NGOs as *angeli del mare* (sea angels). Yet international legislation had established that Italy and other nation-states should maintain full control and coordination of SAR operations even in these cases of rescue by proxy. As a result, the scope of state intervention did not diminish; in fact, an additional EU operation, EUNAVFOR MED, was launched in 2015 to deploy Italian and other navies close to the Libyan coast with the goal of disrupting human smuggling networks. This time, however, rather than a 'humanitarian and military' campaign similar to MN, EUNAVFOR MED was 'a police operation with military means' (as Rear Admiral Hervé Bléjean, first deputy commander of the operation, described it), while the humanitarian mission was outsourced to non-governmental agencies. As a result, we witnessed a de-coupling of humanitarian and security agendas (Heller & Pezzali, 2016) which would eventually lead the EU and nation-states to take an increasingly antagonistic stance vis-à-vis humanitarian organizations.

Discursive Formations in Italy: Order-words and Passwords

Adopting Deleuze and Guattari's terminology, we can explore how the EU relies on order-words (interdictions/interpellations, examinations) to manage undocumented migrants. Order-words necessarily blend national languages with situational mixed languages. The EU deploys the heavy machinery of governmental control of territory, where displays of force are organized through multiple media, from faxes to radio transmissions, usually couched in the normative codes of territorial sovereignty. Meanwhile, migrants rely on multilingual passwords and linguistic creations to navigate uncharted territories, tap into the digital information infrastructure and maintain social connections. Migrants use fluid, massively multilingual and syncopated mobile communications, produced through the multiple technologies for territorial traverses (from cellular text messages to satellite phone calls) (see De Fina & Mazzaferro and D'Agostino, this volume, on fluidity and migration language).

Once an unknown presence in EU territorial waters is detected by Frontex or some other surveillance agent, the EU asserts its authority by deploying in full force its technolinguistic devices centering around three practices: interpellation/interdiction, examination and eventual acceptance/expulsion. In this context, every interaction between governmental agents and migrants conveys an implicit presupposition about who is in charge – a 'parenthetical imperative', in Deleuze and Guattari's (1987) words. Deleuze and Guattari called the production and repetition of this imperative function (immanent to language) the 'order-word'. 'Order' here should be taken in both senses: the statement gives an order (command) and establishes an order (by positioning people in a field of power). The order-word places people in a position to carry out implicit obligations or follow a preset direction. For Deleuze and Guattari:

> order-words do not concern commands only, but every act that is linked to statements by a 'social obligation.' Every statement displays this link, directly or indirectly – because every statement commits us to other statements through the rules of grammar, and ultimately to acts, which we are forced to carry out if we are not to be shown to be mad, or lying, or stupid, or otherwise unable to function socially. (Deleuze & Guattari, 1987: 479)

Deleuze and Guattari, however, lived within the secured borders of monolingual, metropolitan France, and did not consider what happens when subjects are unable to understand the order-words. While postcolonial theorists (as well as colonial administrators) faced the issue of incomprehension and misunderstanding head on (see, for instance, Bernard Cohn's (1996) work on 'the language of command and the command of language'), French intellectuals (including Foucault) were slow in adjusting to a world where shared knowledge and common languages could no longer be taken for granted.

In contrast to order-words are what Deleuze and Guattari called passwords. This concept refers to deviant, inventive, experimental uses of language during a passage (Deleuze & Guattari, 1987. 310–350). To produce passwords, migrants tap into their polyglot repertoires and create statements to enhance their chances of a successful crossing. We can observe these passwords in the interactions between migrants and migration authorities as well as between migrants and their contacts in Europe and abroad. The following section will analyze the discursive formations of EU representatives and undocumented migrants as two distinct fields of communicative phenomena, revealed through the lenses of two other concepts developed by Deleuze and Guattari in their discussion of nomadology: order-words (as used by authorities exercising sedentary power) and passwords (as used by mobile forces). While Deleuze and Guattari explored order-words and passwords in the context of the nation-state, an updated discussion of these terms must contextualize them in the transidiomatic spaces of contemporary communication.

In the next section we will discuss one example each of order-words and passwords: (1) the deployment of an order-word, an anti-immigrant trope, used by Italian populist leaders to frame their opposition to migration; and (2) the counter-move by migrant rights advocates to promote a password ('*scendeteli*', descend them*) to signal, through the ungrammatical use of an intransitive verb treated as transitive, the existence of a different Italy, open to linguistic impurity, cultural mixing and political solidarity.

Order-words: From 'Angeli del Mare' to 'Taxis del Mare'

As the relationship between NGOs and EU nation-states changed, so did the public discourse about the role of NGOs in rescuing migrants. This change in discourse can be traced back to a 15 December 2016 article in the *Financial Times* (FT) entitled 'EU border force flags concerns over charities' interaction with migrant smugglers' (Robinson, 2016). The article was based on confidential reports issued by Frontex which were shared among EU officials and diplomats.

These Frontex reports, in turn, had been prompted by research conducted over many years by Gefira, a European think-tank dedicated to 'economic and geopolitical analysis'. Starting in 2014, it had produced multiple demographic reports investigating 'ethnic substitution' (cf. Camus, *Le grand remplacement*, 2012). On 16 November 2016, Gefira published a report on the work of SAR NGOs, claiming that 'NGOs, the Italian Coast Guard, and human traffickers are coordinating their activities' and that, for NGOs, 'the real motive may be money'. In its report, Gefira relied on AIS (an automatic tracking system that uses transponders on ships monitored by vessel traffic services) to claim that NGOs were entering Libyan waters to pick up migrants.

The Frontex reports seen by the FT raised several alarming points: that criminal networks were smuggling migrants into Europe on NGO vessels; that migrants' boats received precise directions before departure on how to reach the NGOs' boats; and that people rescued by NGO vessels were often 'not willing to cooperate with debriefing experts at all' and 'were warned not to cooperate with Italian law enforcement or Frontex'.

The report from Frontex's intelligence-gathering arm, the Risk Analysis Unit, mentioned only one nonprofit by name: LifeBoat, a small German organization dedicated to picking up refugees stranded at sea between Libya and Italy. The report described one incident where two people were transferred to LifeBoat's rescue ship, *Minden*, by 'persons pretending to be fisherman' on a small boat flying the Libyan flag. The two rescued migrants said that the crew of the Libyan boat were 'people smugglers'. From this, Frontex asserted that this was 'the first reported case where criminal networks directly approached an EU vessel and smuggled the migrants directly into Europe using the NGO vessel'.

However, the report provided little evidence for the allegation, and what it did contain was contradicted by the rescue crew. Moreover, the sourcing was vague; at one point, the report cited 'Italian authorities', but it was not clear who – whether Frontex or Italian investigators, or both – actually debriefed the migrants, and when. Advocates pointed out that these debriefings sometimes took place in coercive situations, and refugees felt pressured to name smugglers or inform on other refugees, believing that it would help their asylum petitions.

Neither the FT article nor the Frontex reports on which it was based named any other NGOs, and the holes in the LifeBoat story were quickly revealed. Within a week, the FT issued a correction and Frontex declared that they never outright accused LifeBoat of colluding with smugglers.

Despite the walk-back, the story stuck. The charge that non-profits were directly involved in smuggling people into Europe swept through the conservative media and was used by Italian prosecutors to investigate a number of NGOs involved in SAR operations.

On the conservative media side, a communication studies undergraduate student at the University of Turin, Luca Donadel, published in March 2017 an 8-minute YouTube video in which he reconstructed SAR missions by analyzing commercially available data from the tracking devices of the NGOs' boats. In this video he championed the idea that migration was a business and questioned why the rescued migrants were brought to Italy and not to the much closer port of Zarzis, in Tunisia. In a very short time, the video was shared more than 60,000 times and viewed by more than one million users. Its viral reach skyrocketed when it was picked up by primetime TV show *Striscia la Notizia* (a Berlusconi-Mediaset program with more than 3.5 million viewers) in a report called *Profughi Take-Away* (Refugees Take-Away).

More substantially, in April 2017 the public prosecutor in Catania, Sicily, Carmelo Zuccaro, launched an investigation into a number of NGOs involved in SAR operations. On the basis of supporting evidence provided by the Italian secret service which was not admissible in court, the prosecutor alleged that SAR boats were operating in Libyan territorial waters, that there had been direct contacts and conversations in Arabic between people in Libya and the boats' crews, that these boats would turn off their transponders to avoid being detected, and that they were willing to pick up migrants at sea even before a SAR emergency had been declared by a Rescue Coordination Center (RCC). Since, however, none of these allegations could be proven in a court of law, Zuccaro elected to investigate the finances of some of these humanitarian organizations, especially MOAS. Founded in 2013, MOAS was financed by two Italian-American entrepreneurs using funds generated by their company, Tangiers Group, which provided insurance in conflict zones to US military subcontractors, NGO workers, journalists and missionaries, among others. In his statements to the media about the investigation, Zuccaro claimed that there was financial collusion between NGOs and the traffickers, and that there were phone contacts between the traffickers and the NGOs' boats.

A few days later, the Italian newspapers *La Stampa* and *Il Secolo XIX* both published a story by journalist Fabio Albanese, reporting on Zuccaro's claim that he had evidence of contacts between traffickers and NGOs. 'The prosecutor doesn't say how he obtained this information', Albanese wrote, 'but it's no mystery that the EU agency Frontex, in its report "Risk Analysis 2017", called some NGOs "taxis"' (*Come abbia queste informazioni, il procuratore non lo dice; ma che l'agenzia dell'Ue Frontex nel suo rapporto «Risk analysis 2017» abbia definito «taxi» alcune Ong non è un mistero*) (Albanese, 2017a).

One of the newspapers, *Il Secolo XIX*, even ran the article under the headline 'The Prosecutor of Catania: "Some NGOs are used as taxis by the traffickers"' (*La Procura di Catania: «Alcune Ong usate come taxi dagli scafisti»*) (Albanese, 2017b).

Frontex, however, never used the word 'taxi' in its original report and Zuccaro never cited the source of his allegation that NGOs were used as taxis. There were, however, two sources that had used the 'taxi' trope before the publication of Albanese's article on Zuccaro: one was an NGO representative featured in a *Breitbart News* article, and the other was Luigi Di Maio, the political head of the *Movimento 5 Stelle* (M5S, at the time in the opposition) and vice-president of the Chamber of Deputies (who would later become deputy prime minister of Italy).

In March 2017, *Breitbart News* published an article quoting Hans-Peter Buschheuer, spokesman for the NGO Sea-Eye, who contradicted the Frontex report alleging that many NGOs were unintentionally or intentionally helping people smugglers. 'We are definitely not a taxi for refugees', Buschheuer said (Tomlinson, 2017). He clearly never intended for 'taxi' to be used as a trope to disparage NGO rescue efforts.

Just before Albanese's story was published in *La Stampa*, Di Maio posted on Facebook: 'Who pays these taxis of the Mediterranean? Why do they do it? We'll raise these questions in Parliament, we'll get to the bottom of this story, and we hope that Minister Minniti will tell us all he knows'.

Luigi Di Maio
April 21, 2017 · 🌐

Chi paga questi taxi del Mediterraneo? E perchè lo fa? Presenteremo un'interrogazione in Parlamento, andremo fino in fondo a questa storia e ci auguriamo che il ministro Minniti ci dica tutto quello che sa.

Also in April 2017, during an interview with the Italian media, Di Maio declared, 'We are facing a phenomenon in which some boats pick up migrants at sea, but not because they are about to drown. For me these boats are taxis. We should just start a ferry service from Tripoli [Libya] to Trapani [Italy]' ('*Siamo di fronte a un fenomeno in cui delle imbarcazioni prendono dei migranti in mare, e non li salvano mentre stanno per affogare; per me sono taxi. Allora facciamo prima a mettere un traghetto Tripoli-Trapani*') (TGCom24, 2017).

Out of Di Maio's statements, Albanese's story with Zuccaro's quote and the Breitbart article with Buschheuer's quote, a trope was born: NGO boats as *taxis del mare* (water taxis). The circulation of this trope took on a feverish pitch with the release in July 2017 of a report from the Italian State Police on three SAR events involving *Iuventa*, the boat of the German NGO Jugend Rettet. Using eye-witness accounts, photographs and recordings of cell phone calls collected by two Italian secret service undercover agents who posed as security personnel on board another SAR boat (the *Vos Hestia* of Save The Children), the report accused the *Iuventa* of being involved in the trafficking of migrants.

The report was accompanied by a video posted on the website of the Italian State Police. The video told a story of collusion between the *Iuventa* and Libyan traffickers. Allegedly, over multiple days, there were phone calls and light signals between the two groups as they arranged a time and place to drop off and pick up migrants in the middle of the Mediterranean. The police recorded three events when the traffickers' passengers were simply transferred from their boats to the *Iuventa* even though the migrants' boats were not disabled or sinking.

In the first event, the police alleged that the *Iuventa* also helped the traffickers recover the boat used to carry the migrants. One segment of the police video claimed to show the *Iuventa*'s rubber rescue dinghy towing the traffickers' boat back to Libyan shores. It even included an image of three other traffickers on a dinghy waving goodbye to the *Iuventa*'s crew.[2]

In the second event, the police documented the proximity of traffickers and the *Iuventa*, with a picture showing the *Iuventa*, two *Iuventa*'s rescue dinghies, the migrants' boat and the traffickers' boat clustered together. They also provided a close-up of the traffickers removing the engine from the migrants' boat after the migrants were moved to the NGO's rescue dinghy, as well as an image of the traffickers leaving the scene and saying goodbye to the *Iuventa* crew and the migrants.

In the third event, according to the investigators, the traffickers again retrieved the engine from the migrants' boat; another photo was presented as evidence.

The police video featured, in addition, images of migrants being ferried to the *Iuventa*. These images were immediately seized upon by anti-immigration forces as proof that NGOs not only aided human trafficking but also encouraged this traffic by providing a 'half-bridge' to Europe.

A couple of weeks after the report and video came out, the *Iuventa* reached the Italian port of Lampedusa. Its entire crew was arrested for human trafficking, and the boat was impounded. Soon the same thing happened to other SAR NGOs, including Open Arms and Sea-Watch: personnel were indicted for trafficking and vessels were seized.

In August 2017, Di Maio again declared to parliament: 'While we're not clear about what's going on and don't have a law, we need to close our ports to all NGOs. Enough taxis. The Navy and Coast Guard will monitor these waters and save human lives, as it should be' ('*Quindi finché non ci vedremo chiaro e in assenza di una legge, bisogna chiudere i nostri porti a tutte le Ong. Basta coi taxi. A monitorare le acque e salvare vite umane ci penseranno la Marina e la Guardia costiera, come è giusto che sia*') (ANSA, 2017).

The diffusion of the *taxis del mare* trope made it possible for anti-immigrant forces in Italy to reframe the debate surrounding rescues at sea. They were no longer portrayed as necessary humanitarian missions but rather as for-profit transactions in which NGO boats, like Uber drivers, were standing by in international waters, waiting for the next client. The trope also played into the accusation that NGOs were acting as a driver in the decision to migrate, and served to increase migration via the Mediterranean in 2016.

This accusation was unwarranted. Analysis done on the correlation between the increase in migrant arrivals and the number of SAR operations suggested that SAR NGOs were not the main driver. This research demonstrated that the rate of increase in crossings registered along the Central Mediterranean route in 2016 was consistent with the increase in crossings by African migrants along the route between 2014 and 2015, a period in which the presence of SAR NGOs was more limited (see https://blamingtherescuers.org/).

Nevertheless, blaming SAR NGOs became the easiest way to divert public attention from the Italian and European authorities' own responsibilities and failures. In 2017, this framing had major consequences for Italy's management of migration, leading most notably to an Italian-Libyan agreement and a new code of conduct for NGOs operating in the Mediterranean.

Under the terms of the agreement with Libya, Italy agreed to train, equip and finance the Libyan coastguard as part of its effort to turn back vessels and return migrants to Libya. But Libya was not a stable government able to control the flow of migrants and provide credible options to the millions of desperate people still attempting to reach Europe from its shores. As a result of this deal, migrants attempting to cross to Europe were brought back to a country where they would frequently suffer torture and abuse.

Meanwhile, Italy developed a new code of conduct for all NGOs that might need to disembark rescued migrants in Italian ports. The code required the NGOs to: not enter the territorial waters of another country; allow police officers on board; not make trans-shipments; not use telephone communication or light signals; hold a certification of technical capability for rescues; declare all sources of financing; and collect the makeshift boats and the outboard engines used by migrant traffickers/smugglers. Those who did not agree to these conditions could not bring rescued passengers to Italian ports. But all the conditions made it impossible for the majority of NGOs to sign the code of conduct, which essentially terminated their missions in the Mediterranean.

At the beginning of 2018, in the midst of the social and political turbulence of a bitter electoral campaign (centered on populist stances and alternative facts), followed by two months of negotiations between the leading parties to form a new government, some Italian magistrates seemed to reevaluate the legal reasoning behind the prosecution of several SAR NGOs.

In April 2018, a judge in Ragusa, Sicily, released from seizure the SAR boat of Open Arms, declaring that there was insufficient evidence to support a trafficking charge against the crew. In June 2018, one day before the International Day of Refugees, a judge in Palermo, Sicily, agreed with the conclusions of the *Direzione distrettuale antimafia* that neither Open Arms nor Sea-Watch committed any crimes; the judge elected to end all proceedings against these two organizations.

These developments, however, were not picked up by the news media – unlike Prosecutor Zuccaro's accusations against SAR NGOs a year earlier, which received intense media exposure. On the other hand, politicians of the newly formed conservative government seized on the judges' decisions to revive the *taxi del mare* trope.

Maurizio Gasparri, a leader of the right-wing party Alleanza Nazionale, declared, 'The landings of illegal immigrants have resumed by the thousands! The Ragusa judge has given them the signal by releasing from seizure the boat of an NGO, thus sabotaging the excellent investigative work of the prosecutor in Catania. With the SAR NGO boats back in the waters, the water taxis have restarted their business with human traffickers' (*'Sono ripresi ormai a migliaia gli sbarchi di clandestini in Italia! Il gip di Ragusa ha dato il segnale dissequestrando la nave di una ong e vanificando l'ottima azione investigativa della procura di Catania. Rimesse in mare le navi delle Ong è ripreso l'operato dei taxi del mare che si mettono al servizio dei trafficanti di clandestini'*).

Giorgia Meloni, leader of Fratelli D'Italia, an extreme rightist and xenophobic party, stated, 'The invasion has started anew. In these hours the water taxis of the notorious SAR NGOs have disembarked another 1,500 illegal immigrants in Italy. We are no longer willing to tolerate this havoc' (*'È ricominciata l'invasione – rilancia Giorgia Meloni. In queste ore i taxi del mare delle famigerate Ong hanno sbarcato altri 1500 clandestini in Italia, non siamo disposti a tollerare ancora questo scempio'*).

As a result of their electoral success in March 2018,[3] the Lega and M5S formed a ruling coalition in June 2018, with the control of undocumented migration as one of their top priorities. With the *taxi del mare* trope flying high again, the new rightist government decided to take action against the SAR NGOs. Both leaders in Italy's new ruling coalition – Interior Minister Matteo Salvini for the far-right Lega and Di Maio for M5S – had pledged during the electoral campaign to adopt tough polices on migrants. One of Salvini's first moves was to close Italian ports to NGOs trying to disembark migrants rescued at sea, declaring that he would prevent their boats from operating as water taxis. In June 2018, Italy turned away the *Aquarius*, a rescue ship chartered by the NGO SOS Méditerranée carrying more than 600 rescued migrants. The *Aquarius* was diverted to Spain instead. In August, the *Ubaldo Diciotti*, an Italian coastguard ship, arrived at the port of Catania with more than 170 rescued migrants, but the government refused to let them land and sequestered them on board; 36 days passed before the passengers were allowed to disembark.

The port closures had the desired effect of sharply reducing NGO rescue missions in the Mediterranean. From the end of August 2018 to the summer of 2019, no NGO rescue vessel operated on the main migration routes between North Africa and Southern Europe. This achieved another goal of Italy's rightist government: preventing NGOs from serving as witnesses to the abuses of the Libyan coastguard, which continued to patrol the seas under the deal signed with Italy in 2017.

Yet, people seeking a better life are still attempting the risky Mediterranean crossing, and shipwrecks in the central Mediterranean have continued unabated, with significant loss of life. Frédéric Penard, the director of operations for SOS Méditerranée, said at the time: 'It is horrible what has been reported. This tragedy has been going on for years and is especially bad now. There are fewer boats, and with fewer boats there are fewer rescues, and there are more deaths' (Tondo & McVeigh, 2018).

Passwords: From language to politics

The attempt of the short-lived M5S-Lega government (June 2018–August 2019) at criminalizing SAR NGOs and its inhumane treatment of migrants did not go unopposed, however. Starting in summer 2018 and continuing through 2019, a wave of resistance and support for migrants and NGOs gained strength, mostly through the actions of '*il popolo dei balconi*' (the balcony people).

The origins of this movement date to the first war in Iraq, in 2004. At that time, Italians would display a rainbow flag – sometimes with the word *pace* (peace) overlying the rainbow – on the balconies and windows of their homes as a sign of opposition to the war. Since then, they maintained the habit of signaling political allegiances via similarly displayed banners.

In 2018, people all over Italy started displaying banners from their balconies that directly criticized Matteo Salvini for his anti-immigrant policies. Using the felicitous alliteration between the words *barconi* (large boats) and *balconi* (balconies), they coined slogans that contrasted Salvini's control over the migrants' and NGOs' boats with their own freedom of expression. The slogans, painted on huge white sheets, often used the informal (and somewhat impolite) *tu* pronoun to proclaim their authors' resolve:

'*Hai bloccato i barconi non bloccherai i balconi*'
(You blocked the boats but you won't block the balconies)

Some slogans warned Salvini in a more impersonal, indirect way of his inevitable downfall through a fanciful wordplay on the saying '*Chi di spada ferisce di spada perisce*' (he who lives by the sword dies by the sword):

'*Chi di barconi ferisce di balconi perisce*'
(He who lives by the boats will die by the balconies*)

Inserting themselves in the discourse about building walls to stop the flow of unwanted migrants, the *popolo dei balconi* metaphorically proclaimed their moral superiority vis-à-vis Salvini:

'*I nostri balconi + alti dei tuoi muri*'
(Our balconies [are] higher than your walls)

Or they used the opportunity to remind passing pedestrians of the moral superiority of building bridges over building walls:

'*Solo ponti, niente mura*'
(Only bridges, no walls)

When Salvini blocked the coastguard patrol ship *Ubaldo Diciotti* from disembarking the 170 migrants it had rescued in August, the *popolo dei balconi* issued their own appeal:

'*Fateli scendere*'
(Let them descend)

In January 2019, a Sea-Watch ship rescued 49 people off the coast of Libya and brought them to Syracuse, Sicily, where the mayor offered access to the city's port. The national government, however, prohibited the passengers from landing. With the ship anchored offshore in limbo for days, activists gathered at the coast to unfurl a banner with a surprising and creative linguistic twist:

'*Scendeteli**'
(Descend them*)

Near the end of the word, the banner's creators included an asterisk/star, used both by linguists to mark an ungrammatical sentence and by Italian left-wing radicals to display their political belonging.

The hashtag #scendeteli and the image of the banner immediately began trending on social media platforms; the protest was covered by print and broadcast media as well. The banner captured the social imagination of Italians across the nation for a number of reasons. In addition to addressing the blockade against NGO boats, it entered a high-profile debate occurring in Italy at the time about the transitive use of intransitive verbs – a practice until then considered ungrammatical in standard Italian and relegated to Southern Italian varieties.

In January 2019, Vittorio Coletti, an eminent linguist and member of the Accademia della Crusca (the most important research institution on the Italian language as well as the oldest linguistic academy in the world) wrote a post on the Accademia's website, in which he condoned, in rare cases, the transitive use of intransitive verbs, in particular with verbs of movement such as *scendere* (to descend), *salire* (to climb), *uscire* (to go out, leave) or *sedere* (to sit) (see Coletti, 2019).

This usage of the intransitive verb as transitive could be considered a case of ergativity, i.e. a verbal case that maintains an equivalence (such as the same word order or grammatical case) for the object of a transitive verb and the single core argument (or 'subject') of an intransitive verb, while treating the agent (or 'subject') of a transitive verb differently (Dixon, 1994).

Coletti pointed out that while in standard Italian these are all intransitive verbs (that is, they cannot be deployed in the passive form), in Southern Regional Italian, especially in Sicilian Italian, they can be used in a transitive form: '*scendi il cane*' (lit. descend the dog*, i.e. take out the dog), '*sali la spesa*' (ascend the shopping bag*, i.e. bring up the shopping bag), '*esci i soldi*' (exit the money*, i.e. take out the money) or '*siedi il bambino*' (sit the baby*, i.e. sit the baby down). He also pointed out that such transitive usages could be found in literary writing dating back to the 19th century and argued for a less puristic approach, allowing for contamination between standard and regional varieties.

This opinion was picked up by the Italian mainstream media, but they twisted Coletti's original comment into the sensationalistic claim that the Accademia della Crusca had authorized the supposedly ungrammatical transitive usage of intransitive verbs. For instance, the daily *La Repubblica* (29 January 2019) titled its article on the issue '*Esci il cane' si può dire*' ('It's proper to say: "take out the dog"').

The discussion in the mainstream press and social media of this seemingly obscure grammatical issue caused strong public reactions, both positive and negative. On the Accademia's Facebook page, comments were mostly negative: 'I hope this won't be accepted … I don't see the need for it. Expressions such as "*esci lo scatolo*" (take out the box) or "*scendi lo scatolo*" (bring the box down) give me the creeps', wrote Francesca. Teresa added: 'I cannot believe it! These are horrible grammatical mistakes, just like "*lo telefono*" (I'm calling him)'. Christian concluded: 'Damn you for having cleared "*esci il cane*" or "*siedi il bambino*". I had to take my "like" off of this page, unfortunately for you …' (*Il Post*, 29 January 2019).

Reactions on Twitter were more nuanced. Based on an analysis of comments on the issue, the Accademia della Crusca found that Italy was split in two, with a deep division along North/South lines: strong negative responses from people in the North and mostly positive comments from people in the South. Most comments generated from the North showed a clear animosity towards Southern Italian varieties (https://accademiadellacrusca.it/it/consulenza/entrare-uscire-salire-e-scendere-transitivi-a-furor-di-popolo/10).

The Accademia also generated two maps of the tweets, one highlighting positive comments, the other negative ones (see Figure 6.1). Perhaps the most impressive feature of these maps is that the areas of overwhelmingly negative comments match the political reach of the Lega, which remains quite popular in the north and the northeast, especially in Lombardy. Its presence in central and southern Italy, however, was (and remains) quite weak (Cataldi, 2018).

Language, Ethnonationalism and Social Movements

In *From Grammar to Politics*, Alessandro Duranti (1996) presented an 'ethnopragmatic' account of language use in Western Samoa that demonstrated the political and moral dimensions of grammatical choices. To conclude this chapter, I will advance a similar claim: that the non-standard expression '*scendete!*' uses its unsanctioned grammar and transitive load to point to the political nature of the struggle between pro and anti-immigrant forces. In this struggle, migrants and their allies on Italian shores are not puppets controlled by forces stronger than themselves but

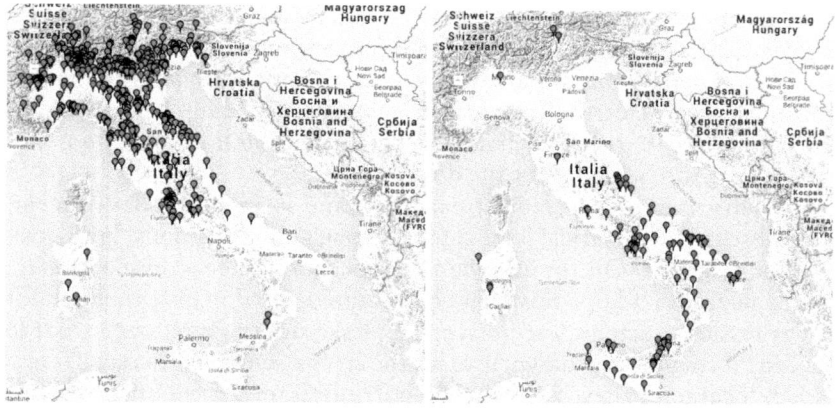

Against the transitive use   In favor of the transitive use

Figure 6.1 Pro/against the transitive use of intransitive verbs

rather have political strength and a progressive agenda. Because of its transitive force, '*scendeteli*' communicates a sense of imperative urgency to free the migrants, as opposed to the passivity of the plea '*fateli scendere*' (make them disembark). This transitive, ungrammatical usage spotlighted a segment of the Italian population willing to break the rules to help migrants.

This segment stood in opposition to the majority of Italian citizens, whose views were epitomized in the tweets about 'water taxis'. Many saw the transnational movement of people and flows of cultural practices not only as a threat to their social identity but also to their declining standard of living. During the Conte I government (the M5S-Lega coalition in power between June 2018 and September 2019), Italy saw its GDP fall by 0.5%, while GDP per capita was stuck at the same level as 20 years earlier. Overall unemployment remained high (at around 10%) and youth unemployment hovered around 30%. Long-standing social and regional inequalities continued. Public debt was 134% of GDP, providing a continuous source of financial risk (OECD, 2019). Moreover, the Conte I government proved unable to resolve major infrastructural failures (such as the collapse in Genoa of the Ponte Morandi freeway bridge or the impasse over the construction of the Lyon-Turin high-speed railway). In foreign policy, this government projected strong skepticism towards the EU and animosity towards its common policies. It opposed important European initiatives, such as the opening of EU markets to non-EU investment funds, sanctions against Russia after the Crimea invasion, and copyright laws for digital media. In this context, the EU took a tough stance towards Italy's proposed budget for this period, which had to be renegotiated twice in order to avoid European penalties, causing turmoil in Italian financial markets. Overall, the Conte I government appeared to be plagued by incompetence and internal bickering. To counter this impression, the government, driven by the Lega, pushed through a law and order program, aimed mostly against immigrants (such as the port closures for NGO boats or the *Decreto Sicurezza e Immigrazione, legge* 132/2018, which included slashing funds for migrant reception and integration). Regardless, the overall national sentiment remained that of a country teetering on the brink of economic collapse and cultural stagnation, ruled by a group of aggressive, intensely nationalistic but incompetent politicians.

The majority of the Italian population responded to this cultural and economic malaise by hardening the social boundaries of their 'community', strengthening in-group identities by raising the membership bar through practices of intolerance and exclusion. Nationalist resentment mixed with religious and racial aggressiveness was stoked by Italian 'sado-populist' politicians (in particular, Matteo Salvini, the Lega leader) to implement policies that were deliberately designed to cause pain (such as the *Decreto Sicurezza*). In his most recent book, *The Road to Unfreedom*, historian Timothy Snyder introduces the concept of sado-populism, in which 'to distract from their incapacity or unwillingness to reform, politicians instruct their citizens to experience elation and outrage at short intervals, drowning the future in the present' (Snyder, 2018: 8). By hurting people through their willing or unwilling incompetence, sado-populists create a reservoir of pain, anxiety and fear which is then directed against others, particularly migrants. As Snyder stated in an interview for Salon.com: 'In the long run, the way that you govern is by hurting people who don't mind being hurt because they think other people are hurting worse' (Devega, 2018: 2). As the majority of Italians became more and more impotent, incapable of stemming their downward mobility, their sense of national belonging came to be defined by a shared feeling of anxiety and fear of the future (see Berardi, 2019). This feeling found its outlet in the hate of migrants. At the root of all their anti-immigrant reactions, people felt threatened or hurt by increasing cultural diversity and economic disorder (among other unsettling changes) brought about by national and international forces. They activated an exclusive nativist ideology that generated a discourse of xenophobia hate, and violence – which found as one of its expressions the 'water taxi' trope.

However, as the case of *'scendeteli'* illustrates, not all Italian people responded in such a negative fashion to diversity and disorder. Interactions between migrants and local people produced a new form of reterritorialization that gave rise to experiments in communal living (see, for instance, the experience in Riace, where a forward-thinking mayor, Domenico Lucano, allowed 450 refugees to settle among the 1800 inhabitants of the town, preventing the closure of the local school and essentially revitalizing a moribund town). Although Lucano was later indicted on suspicion of abetting illegal immigration by then Minister of the Interior Matteo Salvini, his and others' practices of '*accoglienza*' (hospitality) produced racially mixed elective communities where Italians and migrants could find common ground and shared practices. In these spaces, we saw the emergence of recombinant identities, usually produced through encounters between minor codes of communication (such as Southern Regional Italian). '*Scendeteli*' along with the argument for the linguistic respectability of transitive uses of intransitive verbs, became a rallying cry to signal belonging to a social movement in favor not only of more permissive laws on immigration, but also of sharing a vision of Italy as a country open to linguistic impurity, cultural mixing and political solidarity.

Acknowledgements

An earlier version of this chapter was presented at the conference *Migration, Language, and Practices* at the Universitat Autònoma de Barcelona, Spain, June 2019. I particularly thank the panel organizers, Gerardo Mazzaferro and Anna De Fina, the conference organizers, Emilee Moore, Melissa Moyer and Gema Rubio, and conference participants Mike Bayhnam, Birgul Yilmaz and Marco Santello for their questions and comments. Finally, I want to thank Dawn Cunningham for her advice in the development of the final version of this chapter.

Notes

(1) In 2008 a broad coalition of humanitarian organizations expressed its concern that much of the rescue work by Frontex was in fact incidental to a deterrence campaign so broad and, at times, so undiscriminating, that asylum-seekers were being blocked from claiming protection under the 1951 Refugee Convention (HRW, policy reports).
(2) However, various NGO crews told news media that the Libyan men in the photo were more likely locals known as 'engine fishers', who make a living scavenging the engines from refugee rafts. Susanna Salm-Hain, the director of LifeBoat, said that it was 'quite a normal thing' to have engine fishers around during these rescues, most of which take place between 12 and 24 miles from the Libyan coast. The engine fishers – who were often at sea doing actual fishing when they were not scavenging – wait for

boats full of refugees to arrive in international waters and then steal their engines to sell back on land. 'When a migrant boat is sinking', said Christian Brensing, captain of the *Minden*, 'the engine fishers generally arrive much faster than the larger boats'. Engine fishers have helped to distribute life vests and, in a handful of cases, pulled people out of the water and transferred them to rescue ships.

(3) In the 4 March 2018 elections, the center-right coalition, led by Matteo Salvini's right-wing Lega, emerged with a plurality of seats in the Chamber of Deputies and in the Senate, while the anti-establishment Movimento 5 Stelle (M5S) led by Luigi Di Maio became the party with the largest number of votes. The center-left coalition, led by former Prime Minister Matteo Renzi, came third. However, no political group or party won an outright majority, resulting in a hung parliament. After three months of negotiation, a coalition was finally formed on 1 June between the M5S and the Lega, whose leaders both became Deputy Prime Ministers in a government led by the M5S-linked independent Giuseppe Conte as Prime Minister. This coalition ended with Conte's resignation on 20 August 2019 after the Lega pulled its support of the government.

References

Agamben, G. (2005) *State of Exception*. Chicago, IL: Chicago University Press.
Albanese, F. (2017a) Abbiamo le prove dei contatti tra scafisti e alcuni soccorritori. *LaStampa*, 23 April. See https://www.lastampa.it/cronaca/2017/04/23/news/abbi amo-le-prove-dei-contatt.-tra-scafisti-e-alcuni-soccorritori-1.34622607.
Albanese, F. (2017b) La Procura di Catania: 'Alcune Ong usate come taxi dagli scafisti'. *Il Secolo XIX*, 23 April. See https://www.ilsecoloxix it/italia/2017/04/23/news/la-procura-di-catania-alc_ne-ong-usate-come-taxi-dagli-scafisti-1.30793755.
ANSA (2017) Marina Libia, recupera e salva oltre 800 migranti. *Redazione ANSA*, 5 August. See https://www.ansa.it/sito/notizie/mondo/2017/08/04/marina-libia-fer mati-e-arrestati-oltre-800-migranti-_45a5d7be-9f4e-44bf-99ef-c56b3505f36c.html.
Berardi, F. (2019) Europe at Weimar. *Crisis and Critique* 6 (1), 49–54.
Cataldi, M. (2018) Crescita e nazionalizzazione della Lega di Salvini. In V Emanuele and A. Paparo (eds) *Gli sfidanti al governo: Disincanto, nuovi conflitti e diverse strategie dietro il voto del 4 marzo 2018*. Rome: LUP e CISE.
Cohn, B. (1996) *Colonialism and Its Forms of Knowledge*. Princeton, NJ: Princeton University Press.
Coletti, V. (2019) Siedi il bambino! No, fallo sedere! *Accademia della Crusca*, 11 January. See https://accademiadellacrusca.it/it/consulenza/siedi-il-bambino-no-fallo-sed ere/1575.
Deleuze, G. and Guattari, F. (1987) *A Thousand Plateaus: Capitalism and Schizophrenia*. Minneapolis, MN: University of Minnesota Press.
Devega, C. (2018) Historian Timothy Snyder on Trump's war on democracy: He is deliberately hurting white people. *Salon*, 9 May. See https://www.salon.com/2018/05/09/timothy-snyder-on-trumps-campaign-against-democracy-he-is-deliberately-hurting-white-people/.
Di Nicola, A. and Musumeci, G. (2014) *Confessione di un Trafficante di Uomini*. Milan: Chiare Lettere.
Dixon, R.M.W. (1994) *Ergativity*. Cambridge: Cambridge University Press.
Duranti, A. (1996) *From Grammar to Politics*. Berkeley, CA: University of California Press.

Heller, C. and Jones, C. (2014) Eurosur: Saving lives or reinforcing deadly borders? *Statewatch Journal* 23 (3/4), 15–34.

Heller, C. and Pezzali, L. (2016) Ebbing and flowing: The EU's shifting practices of (non-) assistance and bordering in a time of crisis. In W. Callison (ed.) *Europe at a Crossroads: Managed Inhospitality*. Near Futures Online. See http://nearfuturesonline.org/ebbing-and-flowing-the-eus-shifting-practices-of-non-assistance-and-bordering-in-a-time-of-crisis-part-2/.

HRW (Human Rights Watch) (2009) *Pushed Back, Pushed Around: Italy's Forced Return of Boat Migrants and Asylum Seekers, Libya's Mistreatment of Migrants and Asylum Seekers*. See https://www.hrw.org/report/2009/09/21/pushed-back-pushed-around/italys-forced-return-boat-migrants-and-asylum-seekers.

Jacquemet, M. (2005) Transidiomatic practices: Language and power in the age of globalization. *Language & Communication* 25, 257–277.

Ling, R. (2004) *The Mobile Connection*. San Francisco, CA: Kauffman.

McIntosh, J. (2010) Mobile phones and Mipoho's prophecy: The powers and dangers of flying language. *American Ethnologist* 37 (2), 337–353.

Nyers, P. (2015) Migrant citizenships and autonomous mobilities. *Migration, Mobility, & Displacement* 1 (1), 23–39.

Robinson, D. (2016) EU border force flags concerns over charities' interaction with migrant smugglers. *Financial Times*, 15 December. See https://www.ft.com/content/3e6b6450-c1f7-11e6-9bca-2b93a6856354.

Sander, C. (2005) Beam it across: Remittances via mobile phones. *Migrant Remittances* 2 (1), 1–3.

Sassen, S. (2006) *Territory, Authority, Rights: From Medieval to Global Assemblages*. Princeton, NJ: Princeton University Press.

Snyder, T. (2018) *The Road to Unfreedom*. New York: Tim Duggan Books.

Stierl, M. (2018) A fleet of Mediterranean border humanitarians. *Antipode* 50 (3), 704–724.

Tazzioli, M. (2015) The desultory politics of mobility and the humanitarian-military border in the Mediterranean: Mare Nostrum beyond the sea. *REMHU: Revista Interdisciplinar da Mobilidade Humana* 23 (44), 61–82.

TGCom24 (2017) Ang-migranti, Salvini: Un dossier le incastra, governo lo pubblichi. *TGCom24*, 30 April. See https://www.tgcom24.mediaset.it/politica/ong-migranti-salvini-un-dossier-le-incastra-governo-lo-pubblichi_3069290-201702a.shtml.

Tomlinson, C. (2017) Public anger growing at 'taxi' NGOs picking up migrants from Mediterranean. *Breitbart News*, 22 March. See https://www.breitbart.com/europe/2017/03/22/public-anger-growing-at-taxi-ngos-picking-up-migrants-from-mediterranean/.

Tondo, L. and McVeigh, K. (2018) No NGO rescue boats currently in central Mediterranean, agencies warn. *The Guardian*, 12 September. See https://www.theguardian.com/world/2018/sep/12/migrant-rescue-ships-mediterranean#:~:text=Fr%C3%A9d%C3%A9ric%20Penard%2C%20the%20director%20of,and%20there%20are%20more%20deaths.%E2%80%9D.

Virilio, P. (1986) *Speed and Politics*. New York: Semiotiext(e).

Part 3
Spaces of (Im)mobility and Resistance

7 Everyday Communicative Practices and Repertoires in Contexts of Involuntary and Enforced Immobility

Anna De Fina and Gerardo Mazzaferro

Introduction

The focus of this chapter is on a specific kind of immobility: the one experienced by refugees and asylum seekers in temporary reception centres (henceforth TRCs), a domain that has not received the attention it deserves in sociolinguistic studies. As migration increasingly turns into a privileged battleground for far-right governments and politicians, the importance of analysing and understanding the conditions of undocumented migrants, and particularly those of asylum seekers, for socially minded linguists also becomes more and more evident. Indeed, social scientists and human rights experts have been pointing to the many ways in which the handling of refugees by postmodern states represents a litmus test for democracies claiming to be based on respect for human rights by demonstrating their incapability to define such rights outside the territorial boundaries of the nation. Undocumented migrants and asylum seekers alike are more often than not denied the rights and protections to which ordinary citizens are entitled precisely by virtue of the fact that they are not seen as citizens of a specific nation (Wee, 2007). For this reason, Agamben states, for example, that the refugee represents the most disquieting figure in postmodern advanced societies precisely because 'by breaking the identity between the human and the citizen and that between nativity and nationality, it brings the originary fiction of sovereignty to crisis' (Agamben, 2000: 21).

In view of that, we argue that TRCs represent a very significant vantage point from which to observe the dynamics between mobility and immobility in highly globalised postmodern societies. Here we will focus on the representation of social and linguistic conditions within such environments in the discourse of participants in these institutions and on the role of language practices in the dynamics between mobility and immobility. In particular, we will attempt to provide some answers to the following research questions: How can spaces designed for the detention, containment and administration of migrants be described and characterised? How are these spaces related to mobility and immobility in the discourse and language practices of migrants? How are linguistic resources deployed within the different social spaces in which migrants carry out their everyday interactions both inside and outside institutionally regimented areas?

Before we present our data and analysis, we briefly discuss the theoretical methodological trends and constructs that underlie our approach. More specifically, we first expand on ways in which our work relates to and takes inspiration from the sociolinguistics of globalisation and the superdiversity movement. Then, we turn to our conception of the relationships between language, resources and language practices. Finally, we present a review of relevant theorisations about the dynamic connections between languages/identities and space-time coordinates and we briefly introduce our views on mobility/immobility.

Migration, Linguistic Resources and Repertoires, and Language Practices in Superdiverse Environments

As already mentioned, among our main theoretical methodological points of reference for this chapter are the sociolinguistics of globalisation (Blommaert, 2010) and superdiversity approaches (Arnaut *et al.*, 2015; Blommaert & Rampton, 2011; Creese & Blackledge, 2018; De Fina *et al.*, 2017).

Scholars that have animated both movements focused the attention of sociolinguists on mobility and diversity as central to understanding language practices and identities in the 21st century. The recognition of the centrality of mobility has implied a rejection of received notions about the stability of relationships between social categories, languages and communities seen as territorially bound, and a growing attention to virtual and disembodied communication, to the constitution of different kinds of transnational communities, to the shifting and complex definition and negotiation of hybrid sociolinguistic identities, and to the many ways in which communicative practices are shaped by the possibilities and affordances offered by the technological revolution.

One of the areas in which work on globalisation and superdiversity has been most important is the study of migration. Migration flows have dramatically intensified and diversified in the last three decades and, as a result of this, the composition and patterns of migrant groups nowadays are very different from those that characterised previous times. Indeed, early critiques against the essentialism and ethnocentrism of the 'nation-state-minded' mobilities paradigm had already been waged in this area by scholars of migration studies (see Glick-Schiller, 2010). Vertovec (2007, 2010) and others (Appadurai, 1996) point to the fact that, due to globalisation, the scale, speed and intensity of human mobility and world interconnectedness have reached unprecedented levels. The social economic conflicts that are continuously generated by the increasing centralisation of wealth and economic power, the redrawing of borders, the restrictive migratory policies of individual states and super-national entities, and the insurgence of war and conflict in different parts of the globe all contribute to these unprecedented flows and determine a great deal of unpredictability in the trajectories of migrants and the complexity of their groupings. The identities of migrants and their communicative practices can no longer be understood in terms of ethnic origins or territorial belonging, not only because of increasing transnational connections across countries, but also because many migrants go through complex mobile trajectories that profoundly influence the ways in which they use linguistic resources and the kinds of social networks in which they participate.

Work on superdiversity and globalisation has not only changed our view of migration but, more generally, our way of approaching language and culture, since it has been focused on understanding how conditions for communication and cultural encounter have changed and how these changes in turn affect the way we look at languages, identities and semiotic practices.

Within these perspectives there has also been a shift from languages as closed systems to communication as involving the deployment of a variety of linguistic resources from different named languages in conjunction with resources from a variety of other symbolic systems. These new understandings of languages as assemblages of resources underlie many of the constructs that have been proposed to capture, on the one hand, the fact that linguistic elements always work in conjunction with other kinds of semiotic resources in the achievement of communication and, on the other hand, the hybrid character of linguistic resources themselves. Such conceptions underlie, for example, the construct of translanguaging (henceforth TL) proposed by various authors (see Hua *et al.*, 2017; Li, 2018) or Jacquemet's (2005) construct of 'transidiomatic practices'. The latter refers to 'the communicative practices of deterritorialised groups that interact using different languages and communicative codes simultaneously present in a range of communicative media, both local and distant' (Jacquemet, 2019: 49).

However, in our analysis, linguistic and communicative practices are always imbricated with power-laden processes. Thus, TL and other linguistic practices need to be analysed within specific contexts and practices, so as not to reify them as necessarily free and creative. Scholars in linguistics and anthropology have underscored that the valorisation of languages is subject to change according to who does it, where and when (Prinsloo, 2017; Rymes, 2014). From this perspective, issues of power are always relevant to language usage and of course they turn out to be of fundamental importance in the study of language practices within spaces of immobility such as the ones that are the focus of our analysis. Sociolinguistic research on the profound imbrications of linguistic practices with space and time configurations, such as work on scales (Blommaert, 2010) or chronotopic identities (Blommaert & De Fina, 2017), is particularly relevant here. Indeed, TL and transidiomatic practices are not intrinsically creative but rather constitute resources whose function and value can change considerably according to scales and time-space-identity configurations. Power relations underlie ways in which resources are valued at different scales, thus revealing the existence of 'orders of indexicality', which:

> operate within large stratified complexes in which some forms of semiosis are systematically perceived as valuable, others as less valuable and some are not taken into account at all, while all are subject to rules of access and regulations as to circulation. (Blommaert, 2010: 35)

In that sense, as we will see, actual translinguistic TL talk is mostly seen as a dispreferred choice in communication between asylum seekers and authorities in a reception centre, while it will be regarded as the natural choice in amicable conversations among asylum seekers. Similarly, languages such as English or French will be subject to different valuations not only at different geographical scales but also, at a more micro level, within various chronotopic configurations. The notion of chronotope, proposed by Bakhtin to describe 'the intrinsic connectedness of temporal and spatial relationships' (Bakhtin, 1981: 84), in conjunction with the development of perspectives on the connections between chronotopes and identities (Agha, 2007; Blommaert & De Fina, 2017), allow for a description of ways in which different spaces relate to different temporal dimensions and identity presentations within the wider space of the TRC.

In order to capture the relationships between meaning-making, spaces and times in the cases that we are analysing we also incorporate in this chapter some of Foucault's ideas about the connections between spaces and social processes of inclusion and exclusion. In his work on governmentality, he highlighted the social function of spaces of surveillance and confinement, particularly in his notion of 'heterotopia' (Foucault, 2008 [1967]). Foucault was especially interested in the mechanisms through which governments exert their power and maintain control over the population. In his view, heterotopic spaces are kinds of 'counter spaces' where the normal order of things is suspended or inverted and where time acquires different dimensions. He talked about heterotopias as always presupposing 'a system of opening and closing that both isolates them and makes them penetrable' (Foucault, 2008 [1967]: 21) and as only functioning 'fully when people find themselves in a sort of absolute break with their traditional time' (Foucault, 2008 [1967]: 20). He further pointed to the existence of 'heterotopias of deviance' (Foucault, 2008 [1967]: 17) such as prisons. We see containment centres for migrants as belonging to that category of spaces. Indeed, going back to Agamben's insistence on the emblematic nature of the figure of the refugee, we can think of TRCs as places where 'deviants' are hidden from view, where traditional rights are suspended and where time comes to a halt, reducing people to forced immobility and to an exhausting waiting game. Agamben also talks about the absolute centrality of 'the camp' as 'the hidden matrix and nomos of the political space in which we still live' (Agamben, 2000: 37), while other authors (see, for example, Anderson & O'Dowd, 1999) have underlined how facilities created for migrants often constitute a barrier and a buffer between them and the society at large.

Underlying mobility and immobility are therefore power struggles and relationships; however, as we will see, mobility and immobility cannot be seen as bipolar oppositions, but rather as two processes dialectically linked in many ways. Just to give a few examples: migrants' mobility is punctuated by long periods of immobility; spaces of immobility can be transformed into spaces of mobility; and peripheral talk can become central among asylum seekers. At a higher level, the mobility of some peoples is premised on the immobility of others. Physical immobility does not prevent individuals and groups from experiencing virtual mobility. Mobility and immobility should be studied as processes rather than as states, and should be put in relation to one another. In other words, '[i]mmobility is never absolute because all people move to some degree or another in their everyday lives; rather, it is always relative to spatial and temporal frames' (Shewel, 2019: 2).

Indeed, the Foucauldian view of power, particularly as presented in his later work (Foucault, 1980) – which we take here as a starting point – is one in which strategies of domination always engender their opposite: resistance, such that in his analyses 'the history of government as the "conduct of conduct" is interwoven with the history of dissenting "counter-conducts"' (Gordon, 1991: 5). As we will see, therefore, migrants carve out spaces of resistance within the confines of their immobilities and use linguistic resources such as TL within 'safe houses' (Canagarajah, 2017: 29; Sabaté-Dalmau, 2014), or spatiotemporal frames constructed to exchange information and nurture sociability. In that sense, TL can be seen in many cases as a kind of 'heteroglossia of survival' (Busch, 2016).

The Reception System in Italy

Statistics on the number of migrants who arrive in Italy and are hosted in different reception structures are to be taken as indicative and certainly not exact. However, it is common knowledge that the years between 2016 and 2018 have seen a great number of arrivals by sea. According to the UNHCR (Colombo, 2020), 2016 was a peak year with 181,436 arrivals. In 2017 that number decreased to 119,369, while 2018 saw a dramatic reduction of arrivals to 23,370. This tendency was accentuated in 2019 given the hostile and aggressive policy of the Italian government at the time, dominated by the anti-immigrant postures of vice prime minister Salvini. Indeed, according to the same source in 2019, 11,471 migrants arrived by sea, a reduction of 51% with respect to the previous year. Migrants who get to Italy are mostly males (72%), with children representing 18% and women 10% of all arrivals. The most common nationalities of origin in 2019 were Tunisia (23%), Pakistan (10%), Algeria (9.8%), Iraq (9.1%), Ivory Coast (7.6%) and Bangladesh (6.8%) (Colombo, 2020).

In terms of the number of migrants hosted in reception structures, according to La Voce (2019), in 2018 there were 160,000. Of those, 440 were hosted in first aid and reception centres (CPSA/Hotspots), 132,000 in emergency reception centres (CAS) or private accommodation provided by church and voluntary associations, and about 27,000 within second-line reception centres (SPRAR), which after the enactment of the so-called Salvini Act (Decree Law no. 113/2018) were renamed as reception centres for refugees and unaccompanied children (SIPROIMI).

The legal, structural and functional characteristics of asylum in Italy are complex and differentiated (Puggioni, 2016: 159–207). Different kinds of centres, facilities and services operate. According to AIDA (2018), by the end of 2018 four Hotspots centres were located at the main places of disembarkation, that is, Taranto (Apulia), Lampedusa, Pozzallo and Messina (Sicily), where undocumented migrants are controlled, identified, fingerprinted and informed about the asylum procedure, relocation programme and voluntary return. Migrants who are entitled to international protection and unaccompanied minors are moved to second-line temporary reception structures, which consist of a network of small autonomous accommodation facilities, managed by local authorities, mainly municipalities, and third-sector associations, e.g. NGOs or cooperatives, aiming to offer reception, protection and integration services as well as personal programmes in terms of housing, employment, education and social life to migrants (SPRAR, 2016). Due to the massive migrant influx to Italy and Europe in 2015 and 2016 and the unavailability of reception structures, the CAS system was designed as a temporary solution to tackle these problems. De facto, CAS structures have gradually become part of the second-line reception system.

The enactment of the Decree Law no. 113/2018, elaborated by the Italian right-wing coalition government led by Salvini, undermined the legal framework governing the asylum system. The main changes introduced were the abolition of humanitarian protection, which limits the possibility of accessing the second-line protection system solely to unaccompanied children and beneficiaries of international protection, as well as the right for asylum seekers to residence registration (civil registration).

The Decree Law also introduced the possibility of detaining asylum seekers in Hotspots arbitrarily until the completion of identification procedures, while the maximum duration of detention for undocumented migrants awaiting repatriation within pre-removal centres (CPR) was extended to a maximum of 180 days. The Decree Law also changed the material reception conditions and services offered to migrants within second-line reception centres. Indeed, only basic needs such as personal hygiene, food or clothes can be guaranteed, while activities designed to develop so-called integrated reception, such as language courses, professional training, cultural mediation, legal assistance or leisure activities, can no longer be offered by managing bodies (AIDA, 2018). At the moment of our writing (May 2020), the immigration laws imposed by Salvini are still operative even though the new centre left coalition governing Italy has vowed to modify them.

Data and Sampling

We carried out our ethnography of language (Creese, 2008; Rampton *et al.*, 2004, 2015; Snell *et al.*, 2015) within different temporary second-line

CAS and SPRAR structures for refugees and asylum seekers in the cities of Genoa, Rapallo, Turin and Asti over a four-year period (2016–2019).

In order to achieve richer information and advance our understanding of situated language practices, resources and repertoires in contexts of forced immobility/mobility, we made use of triangulation of multiple data consisting of participant observation as well as 16 transcripts of audio-recordings of casual conversations, individual semi-guided interviews, and focus group discussions between operators, cultural mediators and migrants, as well as narratives of personal experience.

Our study is based on observations of interactions, conversations and interviews with a random sampling of 19 male asylum seekers, who at the time of our research were aged from 18 to 31 and came from Bangladesh, Cameroon, Ivory Coast, Gambia, New Guinea, Nigeria, Senegal and Somalia. Participants in our research show complex and differentiated life and migratory trajectories, cultural and educational backgrounds, individual linguistic repertoires, attitudes and ideologies as well as desires and imaginaries of mobility. They have been residing in Italy from one to three years, and have obtained a residence permit for humanitarian reasons, which under the Salvini Act can no longer be renewed. In addition, the majority of them were able to find temporary, seasonal and low-paid jobs, or alternatively perform voluntary service with local associations such as the Red Cross.

Furthermore, volunteering is a key component of TRCs; both unpaid volunteers and paid staff took part in our research, mainly through semi-guided interviews. TRC operators play a fundamental role in establishing, for example, mutual relationships within and beyond TRCs, learn and practise local language, understand the legal system of the country in which they are hosted, or respect the agreements that regulate everyday life within centres and which may cause moments of conflict or tension.

Temporary Reception Centres: Resources, Repertoires and Practices

TRCs represent unstable and unfinished social spaces, inhabited by a heterogeneous humanity, where new forms of sociality are constructed and negotiated in and through everyday interactions.

In TRCs, opening and closure towards the external world, namely urban environments, happen simultaneously. The conditions of movement, however, vary according to the types of reception structures as well as locally signed agreements between migrants and centres' managing bodies. Usually, migrants are able to exit and re-enter TRCs: they are authorised to work or to attend school or language and vocational courses during the daytime, although they are obliged to re-enter by the early hours of the evening. However, the possibility of exiting TRCs during the hours of the day as well as the organisation of social activities within zones of encounter in the city (Wood & Landry, 2007), involving local associations and population, do not necessarily translate into processes of recognition or conviviality, that is, 'low-intensity and apparently low-salience forms of interaction tailored towards a sense of commonness' (Blommaert, 2012: 10).

> Mobility may be unequal and, most importantly, may reproduce racial, ethnic and social class asymmetries enforcing migrants' immobilization. (Cresswell, 2006)

Asylum seekers and refugees may experience the city as a site of relations and exclusion as well as of marginalisation. In line with Blommaert, the city is:

> [...] a space that offers, enables, triggers, invites, prescribes, proscribes, polices or enforces certain patterns of social behaviour; a space that is never no-man's-land, but always, *somebody's space* [...] full of codes, expectations, norms and traditions; and a space of *power* controlled by, as well as controlling, people. (Blommaert, 2013: 3, emphasis in original)

Episodes of stigmatisation and discredit (Goffman, 1963) are typical of everyday life beyond TRCs. The experiences that asylum seekers go through are illustrated in Excerpt 1, a short passage from a long conversation between Jagger, an 18-year-old asylum seeker from Nigeria, and Vol. 2, a centre operator, who is trying to organise World Refugee Day events and activities. Note that in order to protect the anonymity of the subjects who took part in our research, this name and all names in the chapter are pseudonyms.

At the beginning of the fragment, Vol. 2 is proposing the organisation of a storytelling event in which people who are hosted in the centre may relate to the local population by telling of their experiences, and asks Jagger about his experiences:

Excerpt 1[1]

```
1  Vol. 2:   per la giornata del rifugiato / potremmo organizzare che ognuno racconta la sua
2             esperienza / con la gente del posto / com'è la gente fuori? / cosa avete sperimentato?
3  Jagger:   par example / io alle 12.00 finito allenamento pallone / io vado casa /
4             io vedo bimba sette anni / quando io visto lei dice 'mamma / mamma / guarda i neri /
5             [sua madre le dice] 'entra in macchina / vai' / ma perché così? (...) perché tu sei neri /
6             questo non lo so / questo non va bene.
```

1	Vol. 2:	for the world refugee day / we could organize that each of you tells his own
2		experience with local people / how are people outside? / what did you experience?
3	Jagger:	for example / I finished football training at 12 pm / I go back home /
4		I see a 7-year-old child / when I saw her she says / 'mummy / mummy / look the blacks' /
5		[her mother tells her] 'get into the car / go' / but why so? / because you are blacks
6		I do not know / this is no good.

Vol. 2's proposal gives Jagger the opportunity to talk about what seems to be a sensitive issue for him and most of the people within the centre. He tells a short story of his encounter with a mother and child coming back from soccer training. The complicating action of the narrative (Labov, 1972) is entirely presented through constructed dialogue in which the calling of attention of the child and the mother's reaction show both the singling out of people of colour as alien in Italy and the fear often associated with them. Indeed, the mother of the child in the story invites her to 'get into the car'. This anecdote exemplifies how often asylum seekers who are black acutely feel rejection in their encounters with people outside the reception centres. Their presence in the city exacerbates stigma, prejudices and stereotypes as well as reiterating and legitimising discourses of anger, social fear and anxiety about newly arrived migrants, rendering the latter as alien and strangers to the hosting community (lines 3–5) – as sociospatially un/misplaced. Jagger explicitly stigmatises this behaviour in the coda to his narrative where he qualifies the child's reaction as 'no good'.

However, processes of stigmatisation and discredit are also part of everyday life within TRCs. This is clearly demonstrated in Excerpt 2, a passage from a casual conversation between Bhargav, an asylum seeker from Bangladesh, and Vol. 1, a centre operator, who is taking Bhargav to task for breaking the agreement he signed when he arrived at the centre. The agreement provides that the people within the structure must carry out specific duties, including house cleaning. Those who do not respect the rules are obliged to leave the centre (line 4). Here both participants use English as it is their lingua franca.

Excerpt 2

1	Vol. 1:	[addressed to Rap_AB] *remember that you signed the contract / you must*
2		*follow the rules / tomorrow will be your turn / cleaning the bathroom.*
3	Bhargav:	[with reference to the Nigerian guests] *I no clean the bathroom for* i **negri*.*
4	Vol. 1:	*But you must / otherwise you are* fuori [out].
6		[Rap_AB leaves the room]

offensive, derogatory term for coloured people

By refusing to clean the bathroom (line 3), Bhargav attempts both to react to and resist techniques of government of everyday life within the centre (lines 1–2) and to reposition himself in opposition to black people, namely Nigerian migrants, by assigning them a fixed ethnoracial and social identity as 'black' (line 3). In this fragment, the racialised body, namely his skin colour attributes, becomes a site of struggle upholding racial inequalities and discrimination, which are conveyed through linguistic abuse, namely racial slurs or comments contributing to construct relations of power by delegitimising both individuals and groups.

As shown in this fragment, within TRCs ethnic and racial diversities may cause tensions, which complicate ordinary social relationships and may have consequences for how individuals position themselves and others in everyday encounters.

However, as we will discuss below, TRCs are not only spaces of conflict and tensions but rather complex and contradictory arenas, functioning as 'gateways and barriers to the "outside world", protective and imprisoning, areas of opportunity and/or insecurity, zones of contact and/or conflict, of co-operation and/or competition, of ambivalent identities and/or the aggressive assertion of difference' (Anderson & O'Dowd, 1999: 595).

Such complexities and ambiguities are also evident in the chronotopic organisation of TRCs which demonstrates that rather than being homogeneous and unitary spaces, they are apt to be transformed by different spatio-temporal combinations.

Indeed, different chronotopes are characterised by different timespace frames that in turn are associated with divergent communicative practices and identities. Thus TRCs can be seen as formal or institutional spaces, defined by temporalities of waiting and permanence, but they also harbour intimate, informal spaces of contiguity and proximity, or 'safe houses', where migrants may establish social relationships and networks, and create opportunities of exchange and sharing, contributing to subjectivity and identity repositioning, involving not only compliance within the 'exceptional' norms but also, interestingly, resistance to them.

It is within the latter that migrants show an orientation towards TL, which conveys their ability and possibility to engage with and draw on multiple linguistic and semiotic resources in combination to enhance understanding and meaning-making (Mazzaferro, 2018: 1–12). In 'safe houses', those chronotopic conditions, their group identities as translocal people with similar interests and problems are highlighted. Indeed, safe houses constitute relational and emergent spaces where migrants can adopt alternative and locally situated communicative practices, which oppose TRCs' dominant orientation to monolingualism or Italian-only literacies and policies and also present themselves to each other as cooperative. These practices are in direct opposition to official normativities in that TRCs' institutional agents evaluate multilingual practices, i.e. code-switching, as disabling, and leading to social immobility as well as enforcing cultural and linguistic asymmetries. Thus, TL is not everywhere, but rather where the 'dispositif' (Foucault, 1980), which controls and regulates human life within TRCs, allows migrants to access and deploy repertoires of language and semiotic resources for their purposes.

TL has been criticised for celebrating individuals' capacity to draw on and deploy repertoires of resources fluidly and dynamically, leaving power relations and structures unchallenged. Indeed it is true that TL does not necessarily imply the subversion of power relations or sociopolitical order. In fact, in the case of TRCs, it may be more accurate to see TL as an everyday practice of resistance and survival, that is, momentary, contingent and potentially transformative in micro counter-conducts enacted by migrants to oppose power relations and structures.

By analogy with Foucault's (Becker *et al.*, 1988: 298) later view of power and resistance, we can think of TL as 'a space where it is possible to play these games of power with as little domination as possible'. An example of this kind of resistance can be seen in Excerpt 3, taken from a conversation at dinnertime between migrants, who are complaining about the so-called pocket money they receive from centre management agents.

Excerpt 3

1	Kingsley:	*do you like dinner?*
2	Edu:	**oui c'est beau.** [yes, it's good]
3	Jaldar:	[addressing Kingsley] *go to* Genova *tomorrow?*
4	Kinsley:	*yes.*
5	Tamsir:	**no io studio.** [no, I study]
6	Edu:	**combien vous prenez?** [how much do they give you?] *how much?*
7	Kingsley:	*everytime a days / when I leave the house / 1.50 euros for each person*
8	Edu:	*only 1.50?*
9	Kingsley:	*yeah / this is no good.*
10	Deepesh:	**chi li dà? lui?** [who does give it (money) to you? him?]
11	Tamsir:	*no good / no good.*
12	Kingsley:	*we fight them / If they call the police / we fight them.*
13	Tamsir:	*no problem /* **oui mom ami /** [yes, my friend]
14	Kingsley:	**si** */ friend.*

We note that this excerpt starts with a convivial exchange about dinner. Migrants are using different named languages with each participant using their own preferred variety: French, Italian, English but also combinations of them in order to reach maximum communicability. In the course of the conversation Kingsley reveals his salary amount, provoking a reaction of disbelief by Edu (line 8). The subsequent conversation shows all the participants aligning with each other on Kingsley's fighting stance (line 12), and the convivial tone of the communication is underscored once again by the use of the expression 'mon ami' (my friend) by Tamsir in line 13 and the repetition of 'friend' in line 14 by Kingsley.

What this excerpt shows is that by drawing on and acting through all the available language resources, migrants are able to respond creatively and critically to an unjust situation related to their work pay. Through TL, migrants construct commonalities and solidarities in order to claim individual and collective rights. We can say that TL within TRCs is often practised within 'moments of action of resistance, mediation and collaboration which open up new possibilities for human agency, subjectivities and the (re)negotiation of speakers' identities, ideologies and repertoires' (Mazzaferro, 2018: 7).

The negotiation of repertoires of resources in and through TL is based on performative competence and its practice-based knowledge, or speakers' ability to manage appropriately, at a local scale, a plurality of resources in order to align with her/his interlocutors (Canagarajah, 2013). The mobilisation of language resources that migrants bring with them in mobility is constructed relationally; that is, the latter 'expand, change and overlap with others' (Rymes, 2014: 6), and by necessity. As explained by George, an 18-year-old Nigerian asylum seeker: 'people are forced to be within the same place sleeping, eating / and / they are forced to communicate and they do it by using different languages' if they want to communicate.

However, migrants show a deep linguistic, historical and political awareness as well as linguistic ideologies or orientations to repertoires of resources that circulate within TRCs. As already noted, language resources do not flow in a social vacuum, but rather acquire indexical meanings according to specific social, cultural and timespace domains or '[...] what the environment, as structured determinations and interactional emergence, enables or disables' (Blommaert *et al.*, 2005 198). For migrants on the move, the English language commonly represents a mobile and survival resource, which helps them to cross physical, geographical, bureaucratic and legal barriers along their journey to Europe. However, the use of English in everyday interactions within the TRCs, particularly in contacts between migrants and institutional agents, has deep cultural, ethnic, linguistic and ideological implications. Thus, language hierarchies and their ideological evaluation are also tightly connected with chronotopic conditions and scales. An example of this can be seen in Excerpt 4, in which the researcher (R) and Kamil, a 25-year-old asylum seeker from Mali, are talking about how people socialise within the centre.

Excerpt 4

```
1  Kamil:  fra noi anglofoni e francofoni è un problema / [nel centro] lingua inglese è
2           percepita [dagli operatori] come ((scandisce bene le parole)) come lingua migliore
3           / anche gli operatori (...) fanno più attenzione a quelli che parlano inglese rispetto
4           a quelli che parlano francese (...) per un nigeriano / per lui / un francofono non è
5           niente / perché l'inglese è una lingua internazionale / per questo loro si prendono
6           questa narrazione / l'inglese è mondiale.

1  Kamil:  there is a problem between English and French-speaking people [within the
2           centre] / the English language is perceived [by operators] ((choosing words
3           carefully)) as the best language / operators too (...) take care more of those who
4           can speak English than those who speak French (...) for a Nigerian / for him / a
5           French-speaking person has no value / because English is an international
6           language / they appropriate this narrative / English is a world language.
```

Kamil explains to R (researcher) that linguistic differences commonly cause tensions and conflicts within TRCs. In this excerpt, Kamil is opposing not languages, but at first widely defined groups of people characterised by different language dominance (lines 3–4). Later on he focuses his argument on 'Nigerians' as regarding Francophone speakers as 'nothing' and as buying the 'narrative' or ideology of the superiority of English because of the perception of it being an 'international' or a 'world' language (lines 5–6). There is a clear deictic (othering) 'us/they' opposition in the expression 'they appropriate this narrative' (line 6), which demonstrates the antagonism felt by Kamil in response to the differential treatment that Francophones like him receive in the centre.

As shown in both this expert and the following one (Excerpt 5), a short passage from a conversation between George and R (researcher) who is trying to elicit information about the use of English within TRCs, language resources associated with English undergo processes of re-indexicalization, or shifts in their indexical meaning according to the situations in which they are used.

Excerpt 5

```
1   R:       do you use English to communicate within the camp?
2   George:  we do not have English in Africa / we have a language which is more powerful /
3            which is broken / if you go around in the camp you will hear most of the Nigerian
4            people speaking that language / in contact here within the camp / we use English
5            most of the time / because the ospitis [guests] / the profugi [refugees] / the refugees
6            that are here / are English-speaking people and French-speaking people // so / in this
7            environment / in the Red Cross / in our job / with the / our ospitis [guests] we mostly
8            use English / without control / the English we use is broken / it doesn't have an
9            orthography / it doesn't have a grammatical accent / it is spoken as it come out of the
10           mouth / most of the time people understand each other.
```

George responds to R's question by saying: 'we do not have English in Africa / we have a language which is more powerful' (line 2). Two aspects of this response are important, first of all the identification of English as the colonial language and its opposition to 'broken English' (line 3) as the language of Nigerians. Interestingly, however, the expression 'broken English' has no negative connotation here, as it is presented as normal in its everyday uses. Rather, this variety is described as 'more powerful' (line 2) and it seems that its power is related by George to its ability to serve as the language of communication for people Broken English allows understanding and meaning-making among migrants ('most of the time people understand each other', line 10), as well as creating a sense of belonging to a shared history, culture and authenticity. By naming English as 'broken', George destabilises the view that speakers of English, who do not identify with the standard norms, are socially and linguistically inauthentic speakers, because they lack competence in what is regarded as the standard language. When George talks about using 'without control', not having an orthography and as 'spoken as it come out of the mouth' (lines 8–10), he highlights the indexical value of broken English as a language of communication. In that sense, the denial of English as a former colonial language represents a form of resistance to ideologies of cultural and linguistic normativity, authenticity and appropriateness. Nigerian migrants within TRCs speak broken English commonly evaluated as a socially, culturally and ethnically 'minoritized' form of semiosis (Blommaert, 2010: 38) and are happy to do so.

Thus, and as already observed, '[...] what counts as appropriate, high-status, or inferior language is a situated, placed, or localised judgement, because language norms are ecological or contextual and they operate on scale levels' (Prinsloo, 2017: 364–365). However, in order to better understand how repertoires of resources are indexically evaluated and deployed in everyday language practices within chronotopic frames of temporary enforced (im)mobility, it may be useful to compare the TRCs under investigation here with detention camps in Libya. Indeed, most of the migrants who took part in our research spent some months, in some cases years, trapped within Libyan detention camps where, despite the grave conditions of detention, they learned enough Libyan Arabic to survive the dehumanising encampment conditions. Asylum seekers and refugees associate Libyan Arabic with traumatic events, including physical violence, killings and loss of friends, leading to a sort of linguistic amnesia, or a defense and coping strategy, which protects them from the emotional consequences of distressing events, and forces them to deny any knowledge of Libyan Arabic.

However, the language of the camp is not dialogical or relational; that is, it does not include or accept any kind of mediation. Conversely, it aims to isolate and immobilise migrants both physically and communicatively. See, for example, Extract 6, a short fragment from a conversation between Jax, an 18-year-old Nigerian asylum seeker, and the researcher (R) who is trying to elicit information about communication with local people in Libya:

Excerpt 6

1 **R:** come facevi a comunicare in Libia?
2 **Jax:** per comunicare in Libia è difficile / in Libia tu non devi parlare / tu non parli niente /morto /
3 devi stare tranquillo / non parla.

1 **R:** how did you communicate in Libya?
2 **Jax:** it is difficult to communicate in Libya / in Libya you are not allowed to speak / you must not say
3 anything you must not say anything otherwise you are dead / you must stay calm / you must not speak

In this fragment Jax explains how interactions between migrants and their captors are not oriented towards mutuality, but rather are limited to the establishment and exercise of power and control (lines 2 and 3). There is, in other words, a direct nexus between the spoken word, or what migrants are ordered to do, and action, or what they are expected to do. The lack of knowledge of Libyan Arabic put migrants' lives at risk. Thus, silence represents both an alienation strategy (line 2), contributing to both migrants' estrangement and, in most cases, acceptance of what happens around them, and a survival practice (line 3).

It is evident that detention camps in Libya differ from the TRCs under investigation here, where contingent communicative or TL practices of resistance may be enacted and human agency restored. Detention camps for transiting migrants in Libya are liminal, invisible spaces, 'born out of the state of exception', where individuals are degraded to voiceless, silenced, unauthorised and non-agentive subjects, and reduced to 'bare life' (Agamben, 2000). They represent the elaboration of the biopolitics of immobilisation of migrants through strategies and techniques of surveillance, reinforced by monologic and hierarchical communicative practices.

Conclusion

The aim of this chapter has been to investigate the interconnectedness between forms of mobility and immobility in global migratory processes, namely those involving undocumented migrants, asylum seekers and refugees within TRCs. More precisely, we have focused on how migrants, who are embedded in spatio-temporal frames of control, surveillance and enforced immobilisation, are able to access and circulate repertoires of linguistic resources for their purposes, according to the different chronotopic frames, organisation and conditions of TRCs. Thus, we have argued that the possibility of drawing on and deploying repertoires of linguistic resources that migrants bring with them in mobility is subject to spatio-temporal scales, chronotopic identities and indexical orders.

We have illustrated how migrants are able to resist the conditions of TRCs by creating relational zones or safe houses, in which they can construct communicative or TL practices of resistance by mobilising repertoires of language resources that are linked to their identity enactments in a situation where they are racialised and profiled. TL in this case represents a potentially transformative communicative mode, through which migrants are able to engage with cultural and linguistic diversity and social and economic asymmetries. More generally, we have shown the intimate links between the use and evaluation of linguistic resources and the spatio/temporal conditions within which they are deployed.

Note

(1) Transcription key:

AB:	speaker
/	a short pause
//	a pause
(…)	omitted text
(( ))	other details
[…]	section excerpted
Roman	Italian
Italics	English
Bold	French

References

Agamben, G. (2000) *State of Exception*. Chicago, IL: University of Chicago Press.
Agha, A. (2007) Recombinant selves in mass mediated spacetime. *Language & Communication* 27, 320–335.
AIDA (Asylum Information Database) (2018) *Country Report Italy*. See http://www.asylumineurope.org/.
Anderson, J. and O'Dowd, L. (1999) Borders, border regions and territoriality: Contradictory meanings, changing significance. *Regional Studies* 33 (7), 593–604. doi:10.1080/00343409950078648
Appadurai, A. (1996) *Modernity at Large: Cultural Dimensions of Globalization*. Minneapolis, MN: University of Minnesota Press.

Arnaut, K., Blommaert, J., Rampton, B. and Spotti, M. (eds) (2015) *Language and Superdiversity*. New York: Routledge.
Bakhtin, M. (1981) Forms of time and of the chronotope in the novel: Notes toward a historical poetics. In *The Dialogic Imagination: Four Essays* (M. Holquist, ed.; C. Emerson and M. Holquist, trans.) (pp. 84–258). Austin, TX: University of Texas Press.
Becker, H., Fornet-Betancourt, R. and Gomez-Müller, A. (1988) The ethic of the care for the self as a practice of freedom: An interview with Michael Foucault on 20th January 1984. In J. Bernhauer and D. Rasmussen (eds) *The Final Foucault*. Cambridge, MA: MIT Press.
Blommaert, J. (2010) *The Sociolinguistics of Globalization*. Cambridge: Cambridge University Press.
Blommaert, J. (2012) Complexity, accents and conviviality: Concluding comments. AAAL 2012 Panel on Constructing Identities in Transnational Spaces. Tilburg Papers in Culture Studies No. 26. See https://pure.uvt.nl/ws/portalfiles/portal/30357079/TPCS_26_Blommaert.pdf.
Blommaert, J. (2013) *Ethnography, Superdiversity and Linguistic Landscapes: Chronicles of Complexity*. Bristol: Multilingual Matters.
Blommaert, J. and De Fina, A. (2017) Chronotopic identities: On the timespace organization of who we are. In A. De Fina, D. Ikizoglu and J. Wegner (eds) *Diversity and Superdiversity: Sociocultural Linguistic Perspectives* (pp. 1–15). Washington, DC: Georgetown University Press.
Blommaert, J. and Rampton, B. (2011) Language and superdiversity. *Diversities* 13 (2), 1–21. See http://newdiversities.mmg.mpg.de/?page_id=2056 (accessed 22 May 2020).
Blommaert, J., Collins, J. and Slembrouck, S. (2005) Spaces of multilingualism. *Language & Communication* 25 (3), 197–216.
Busch, B. (2016) Heteroglossia of survival: To have one's voice heard, to develop a voice worth hearing. Working Papers in Urban Language and Literacy No. 188. London: King's College.
Canagarajah, S. (2013) *Translingual Practice: Global Englishes and Cosmopolitan Relations*. New York: Routledge.
Canagarajah, S. (2017) *Translingual Practices and Neoliberal Policies: Attitudes and Strategies of African Skilled Migrants in Anglophone Workplaces*. Cham: Springer.
Colombo, F. (2020) Quanti migranti sono arrivati nel 2019? *Le Nius*, 13 January. See https://www.lenius.it/migranti-2019/.
Creese, A. (2008) Linguistic ethnography. In K.A. King and N.H. Hornberger (eds) *Encyclopedia of Language and Education, Vol. 10: Research Methods in Language and Education* (2nd edn) (pp. 229–241). New York: Springer.
Creese, A. and Blackledge, A. (2018) *The Routledge Handbook of Language and Superdiversity*. London/New York: Routledge.
Cresswell, T. (2006) *On the Move: Mobility in the Modern Western World*. New York: Routledge.
De Fina, A., Ikizoglu, D. and Wegner, J. (eds) (2017) *Diversity and Superdiversity: Sociocultural Linguistic Perspectives*. Washington DC: Georgetown University Press.
Dehaene, M. and De Cauter, L. (eds) (2008) *Heterotopia and the City: Public Space in a Postcivil Society*. New York: Routledge.
Foucault, M. (1980) *Power and Knowledge: Selected Interviews and Other Writings 1972–1977* (C. Gordon, ed.; C. Gordon, L. Marshal, J. Mepham and K. Sober, trans.). New York: Pantheon.

Foucault, M. (2008 [1967]) Of other spaces. In M. Dehaene and L. De Cauter (eds) (2008) *Heterotopia and the City: Public Space in a Postcivil Society*. New York: Routledge.
Glick-Schiller, N. (2010) A global perspective on transnational migration: Theorising migration without methodological nationalism. In R. Bauböch and T. Faist (eds) *Diaspora and Transnationalism: Diaspora, Methods and Theories* (pp. 109–129). Amsterdam: Amsterdam University Press.
Goffman, E. (1963) *Stigma: Notes on the Management of Spoiled Identity*. Englewood Cliffs, NJ: Prentice-Hall.
Gordon, C. (1991) Governmental rationality: An introduction. In B. Graham, C. Gordon and P. Miller (eds) *The Foucault Effect: Studies in Governmentality* (pp. 1–52). Chicago, IL: University of Chicago Press.
Hua, Z., Li, W. and Lyons, A. (2017) Polish shop(ping) as translanguaging space. *Social Semiotics* 27 (4), 411–433
Jacquemet, M. (2005) Transidiomatic practices: Language and power in the age of globalization. *Language & Communication* 25 (3), 257–277.
Jacquemet, M. (2019) Beyond the speech community: On belonging to a multilingual, diasporic, and digital social network. *Language & Communication* 68, 46–56. doi:10.1016/j.langcom.2018.10.010
Labov, W. (1972) The transformation of experience in narrative syntax. In W. Labov (ed.) *Language in the Inner City: Studies in the Black English Vernacular* (pp. 354–396). Philadelphia, PA: University of Pennsylvania Press.
La Voce (2019) *Ecco le cifre dell'accoglienza in Italia*. See https://bit.ly/2IsQPWO.
Li, W. (2018) Translanguaging as a practical theory of language. *Applied Linguistics* 39 (1), 9–30.
Mazzaferro, G. (2018) *Translanguaging as Everyday Practice*. Cham: Springer.
Prinsloo, M. (2017) Spatio-temporal scales and the study of mobility. In S. Canagarajah (ed.) *The Routledge Handbook of Migration and Language* (pp. 364–380). London: Routledge.
Puggioni, R. (2016) *Rethinking International Protection: The Sovereign, the State, the Refugee*. London: Palgrave Macmillan.
Rampton, B., Tusting, K., Maybin, J., Barwell, R., Creese, A. and Lytra, V. (2004) UK linguistic ethnography: A discussion paper. See https://www.lancaster.ac.uk/fss/organisations/lingethn/documents/discussion_paper_jan_05.pdf.
Rampton, B., Maybin, J. and Roberts, C. (2015) Methodological foundations in linguistic ethnography. In J. Snell, S. Shaw and F. Copland (eds) *Linguistic Ethnography: Interdisciplinary Explorations*. Houndmills: Palgrave Macmillan.
Rymes, B. (2014) *Communicating Beyond Language: Everyday Encounters with Diversity*. New York: Routledge.
Sabaté-Dalmau, M. (2014) *Migrant Communication Enterprises: Regimentation and Resistance*. Bristol: Multilingual Matters.
Schewel, K. (2019) Understanding immobility: Moving beyond the mobility bias in migration studies. *International Migration Review* 54 (2), 328–355.
Snell, J., Shaw, S.E. and Copland, F. (eds) (2015) *Linguistic Ethnography: Interdisciplinary Explorations*. Basingstoke: Palgrave Macmillan.
SPRAR (2016) Rapporto Annaule Sprar: Sistema di Protezionbe per Richiedenti Asilo e Rifugiati. Atlante Sprar 2016. Prato: SPRAR. See https://www.retesai.it/wp-content/uploads/2017/06/Atlante-Sprar-2016-2017-RAPPORTO-leggero.pdf.
Vertovec, S. (2007) Super-diversity and its implications. *Ethnic and Racial Studies* 30 (6), 1024–1254.

Vertovec, S. (2010) Towards post-multiculturalism? Changing communities, contexts and conditions of diversity. *International Social Science Journal* 199, 83–95.
Wee, L. (2007) Linguistic human rights and mobility. *Journal of Multilingual and Multicultural Development* 28 (4), 325–338.
Wood, P. and Landry, P.W. (2007) *The Intercultural City: Planning for Diversity Advantage*. Sterling, VA: Earthscan.

8 Beachspaces: Racism and Settler-Colonial (Im)mobilities at the Shoreline[1]

Ana Deumert

> The beach marked the beginning of conquest and subsequently became the playground for white leisure seekers.
> Isabel Hofmeyr, *Oceans as Empty Spaces?* (2018)

> I have tried to see everything keenly, nakedly, despite the fact that human motives are always mixed, at best of times a very complicated affair.
> Lewis Nkosi, *Mating Birds* (2005 [1983])

Introduction: Settler-Colonial (Im)mobilities

This chapter differs from the other chapters in this volume: the focus is not on international or transnational migration, but on (im)mobilities within a given polity – apartheid and post-apartheid South Africa. Colonialism and apartheid made Black people into strangers in their own lands: they were uprooted and displaced, their lands were stolen, their bodies turned into labour and subjected to surveillance. Zarina Chiba's poem 'Migrant in My Own Land' (1975) speaks about 'condemnation', about tightly controlled forms of partial mobility that were exploitative, imprisoning, violent and dehumanising. She writes about the many places in South Africa that are forbidden to her, that she may not even 'touch'. And she continues:

> Muizenberg beach with its shocking blue sea
> sundrenched
> but denied to me
> migrant labourer passing through,
> from my bantustan home to the cities of work
> milked by my warders

> who bar me from gazing
> the lushest per cent of my land
> Sixteen million dispossessed
> condemned to the arid per cent
> – thirteen to be exact –
> neatly ensconced from four million
> who've snatched
> eighty-seven per cent of my land.

Dispossession, labour exploitation and segregation ('neatly ensconced') were the cornerstones of apartheid, a violent and inhumane political order that was grounded in settler-colonial ideologies (Kelley, 2017). After 1994, the advent of democratic rule notwithstanding, many of the old structures remained in place. Land, for example, is still mostly in the hands of whites: in 1975, when Chiba's poem was published, whites owned over 80% of the land; in 2017 – over two decades after the legal-political end of apartheid – they still owned 72% (Department of Rural Development and Land Reform, 2017). And yet, they constitute less than 10% of the population of South Africa. This privately owned land is inaccessible to the majority of the country's people. The *Trespass Act* of 1959 (last amended in 1997) makes sure of this: fines or imprisonment are stipulated penalties for entering privately owned land, even if the land is vacant and 'unimproved' (i.e. land without buildings or standing crops; see Sawers, 2011, on settler-colonial restrictions on the 'right to roam'). Yet, it is not only private land that the former settlers claim as 'theirs'; I will show that public space – using the example of the shoreline and the ocean – is equally claimed.

Land ownership is central to spatial politics, and it is because of this that settler-colonial formations are of particular interest for understanding (im)mobilities. Settler colonialism is, as has been noted by Patrick Wolfe (2006), a structure-of-domination that is shaped by *repeated* acts of spatial, economic *and* symbolic dispossession, control and erasure. Thus, it is not only lands and labour that are taken, but Indigenous structures and institutions are destroyed, and Indigenous people are forcefully assimilated into colonial ways-of-being (see Piazza, this volume).[2] This includes language as well as Indigenous knowledges and art. And since these acts are repeated – continuously and habitually – the structure-of-domination is reproduced and re-instantiated, time and again: it is a structure-of-domination that is also a structure-of-repetition.

South Africa as a settler-colonial state exists within a complex transnational network of similar formations. Settler colonialism was one of the core political and ideological manifestations of Empire, instantiated around the globe, in different locales that were, and are, connected by routes across the ocean. This created, and continues to create, intercolonial mobilities. Examples of this are the quite regular mobilities between the United Kingdom, South Africa and Australia: these mobilities occurred in the past (when missionaries and colonial officials moved between these places of Empire), and are continuing today (with large numbers of white South Africans settling, permanently or temporarily, in Australia and the UK; Andrucki, 2010; Flahaux & De Haas, 2016; Rule, 1994; see Steel, 2015, on oceans as the 'medium' for settler-colonial mobilities). The structure of these mobilities is chronotopic: linking past and present, stretching across the globe.

In this chapter, I look at a particular spatial constellation in the settler colony: beachspaces. Chiba wrote in 1975 about the beauty of Muizenberg beach, a beach that was denied to her, a beach where she could not swim or be. I argue that beachspaces are salient ideological formations that link race[3] and space in ways that are persistent and enduring, and that shape everyday (im)mobilities, affects and discursive formations. I start ('The Beach and the Ocean: Settler Colonialism as a Transnational Regime') by reflecting on the shoreline and the ocean as sites of arrival and control in various settler-colonial states (the United States, Australia, Brazil and South Africa). This is followed ('South Africa's Apartheid: Macro and Micro') by a discussion of the history of beach apartheid in South Africa. In the section titled 'Visceral Movements-Moments and Affective Pathologies' I look at the psychological dispositions that underpin settler colonialism, its anxieties and desires. The following section, 'A Nervous State – Even When on Holiday', turns to the present and looks at public social media debates about 'the right to the beach' that took place in early January 2020. I conclude with some reflections on decolonisation: Can settler-colonial societies decolonise? And what, if any, is the role of beachspaces in this process?

The Beach and the Ocean: Settler Colonialism as a Transnational Regime

South Africa is bordered by two oceans: to the east and to the west, the Atlantic Ocean and the Indian Ocean, respectively. The coastline stretches over almost 3000 kilometres, from the border with Namibia to the border with Mozambique. Along these 3000 km we find a multitude of beaches: some rocky and some sandy, some easily accessible and some almost inaccessible, some with treacherous waters and some with gentle waves.

The beach is a borderland between land and ocean, unsettling categories and inviting us to embrace a sense of liminality; to recognise natureculture entanglements (Preston-Whyte, 2004; see Malone & Ovenden, 2017, on naturecultures). One can think of the beach as a third space (Bhabha, 1994): it is simultaneously part of social and natural worlds. As a social space the beach is also a public place: although beach privatisation is increasingly common, many beaches remain – at this point in time – open to the public, free for anyone to visit. As a social space the beach has – from the early 20th century onwards – emerged as a place of modern leisure culture. For many it is also a space of spirituality and emotional well-being (Wheaton et al., 2019), as well as a space that helps to secure livelihoods (Maharaj, 2017). Along the African coast, the beach also reminds one of history. It was a place of conquest and colonisation. It was on the beach that the first ships landed in the 15th century, and that initial encounters between Indigenous peoples, soon to be colonised, and Europeans, soon to subjugate and oppress, took place. Given such contrasting meanings of 'the beach', it is perhaps not surprising that beaches are also 'contested sites where power is exercised', and in settler colonies across the world, beachspaces have been heavily racialised (Wheaton et al., 2019: 3).[4] Racial segregation, whether legally enforced or habitually reproduced, has long been inscribed on the sandy shores of diverse settler colonies, from the United States to Australia, from Brazil to South Africa.

To transgress racial boundaries and borders could have deadly consequences: in 1919, on a sweltering hot day in Chicago, Eugene Williams, a Black teenager, was stoned to death when he swam in what was perceived as a 'whites-only' area. A white man began throwing rocks at him, hitting him on the head and causing him to drown. When the police refused to arrest the white man responsible for Eugene Williams' murder, the outrage of local residents boiled over and culminated in the 1919 Chicago 'race riot', bringing into the open the sweltering tensions between Black and white residents. Unlike in Alabama or Mississippi, Jim Crow laws were not legally enforced in Illinois, and the Chicago beaches were not 'officially' segregated. Yet, white and Black spaces were nevertheless divided by an invisible line, an imaginary and exclusionary white spatiality across which African Americans moved at their peril. The beach at Lake Michigan was a pertinent symbol of larger sociopolitical processes: of racism and segregation, of a desire to control Black movements and mobilities at a time when the Great Migration meant that approximately 1.5 million of Black people had moved from the southern to the northern cities (Hartfield, 2018; McWirther, 2011).

Almost a century later – in December 2005, at Sydney's Cronulla Beach – white youths wrapped themselves in Australian flags, abused Lebanese Australians and shouted anti-Islam messages. Again, the beach – its sandy shores, the hot weather and the blue of the ocean a constant and evocative presence – was central to displays of white supremacy (Kabir, 2015; on Australian beachspaces, see also Kamaloni, 2019: 87ff.; Moreton-Robinson, 2015: 33ff.). Such displays of whiteness are persistent in the everyday, and are not limited to isolated events and sudden ruptures. Rather, they shape everyday mobilities. Going-to-the-beach requires not only mobility (that is, the ability to walk, or access to transport, private or public), but also – if one wishes to stay undisturbed and without surveillance – a certain demeanour and way-of-being. This is evident in Michele Lobo's (2014: 103–104) ethnography of beachspaces in Darwin, Australia. She narrates the following incident that happened when she, a woman of Indian heritage, spent an evening with a group of Aboriginal men and women on the beach, watching the sunset:

> I was invited by strangers on the bus to come and see how they enjoy sunset at Mindil beach, Darwin ... The atmosphere is convivial ...we talk loud and laugh ... argue and joke, mimic each other, as well as nudge and push each other in jest ... Before long, however, a policeman arrives and talks in a condescending manner to the men and a patronising manner to the women. I hear, 'Sweetheart, you're not talking on a megaphone' ... In this moment ... *a living Aboriginal culture is erased through actions that clean the beach of difference.* (Emphasis added)

Brazil, another settler-colony, is often believed to be different due to long-standing national narratives that celebrate racial mixing and hybridity. However, these celebrations of hybridity are accompanied by a 'whitening imperative' and avoidance of Blackness (Moraes Silva *et al.*, 2019; Rahier, 2003). Ben Penglase (2007: 305), for example, argues that the myth of a 'racial democracy' notwithstanding, boundaries are 'increasingly impermeable', and the beach, especially, is a highly racialised place. Jennifer Roth-Gordon (2016) describes Rio's famous beaches – Ipanema, Copacapana and Leblon – as structurally 'white beaches'. Only from the mid-1980s onwards, when public transport improvements made it possible for residents from impoverished outlying areas to visit the beach on weekends and public holidays, did Black beachgoers arrive in larger numbers. Responses from white residents in the south zone of the city typically avoid explicit reference to racial difference, yet remain grounded in discourses permeated with what Roth-Gordon calls 'racially tinged language', and express persistent fears of 'racial contact'. She quotes from a magazine article that was published in 1996 in the Brazilian magazine *Veja* (similar to *Time* or *Newsweek* in the United States; I cite the English translation – the original Portuguese can be found in Roth-Gordon,

2016: 188). Without ever mentioning race, the text is nevertheless permeated by racialised ways of thinking about democracy, public spaces and mobilities:

> In areas [where the beaches] democratized by force, privileged sons and daughters guarded in buildings and condominiums surrounded on all sides by fences now live side-by-side with funk fans who are used to the violent day-to-day reality of the *favelas*. It's a shock.

'Funk fans' is code for Black beachgoers, and sharing space with them is 'a shock' to the entrenched structures of racialised spatiality in Rio de Janeiro.

The beach is also a troubled space in post-apartheid South Africa. For many, it is an escape from the drudgery of work, and a space for relaxation and recuperation. As elsewhere, it is also a space where livelihoods are maintained (through fishing and collecting), and various forms of Indigenous spirituality are practised (Leboloane & Madise, 2006). And it is a space where the racialised practices of the past continue to be present, and whites, especially, reproduce the old patterns of apartheid. As noted by the South African journalist Ferial Hafajee (2019): 'Beaches are places of fun, but also of pain'. Consider the well-known case of a Durban estate agent. In January 2016, she took to Twitter to voice her views. She posted an image of the crowded Durban beachfront on New Year's Day, and called those celebrating the New Year 'monkeys', drawing on a longstanding racist trope of anti-black dehumanisation. In December 2016, a resident of Hout Bay, an affluent seaside suburb in Cape Town, called Black beach dwellers 'stupid animals'. The year 2017 started no better when African beachgoers at Amazimtoti, south of Durban, were referred to as 'cockroaches' (Lujabe, 2017). A year later, a South African holidaymaker posted a video from a beach in Greece where – to his delight – he was among white people only. In his racist rant, celebrating the beach's whiteness, he used the k-word (South Africa's equivalent to the n-word). In most of these cases legal action has been taken and cases of *crimen injuria* have been opened – yet similar incidents continue to happen (see section titled 'A Nervous State – Even When on Holiday').[5] They spring up with sad regularity around the December/January holiday season, when the weather is hot and the beaches full. Howard Feldman (2018), a South African social commentator, noted: 'somehow it is a trip to the beach that seems to be the trigger for some South African racists'. The beach, one may say, is 'racially volatile' (Kamaloni, 2019: 91).

Beaches are, as noted above, public spaces. The beach as a commons could be an equaliser, a place that everyone can enjoy, where people from different walks of life can, in principle, intermingle freely. And this could – if one believes in Gordon Allport's (1954) contact theory – over time improve intergroup relations and reduce negative prejudice. Yet, as the South African scholar Zimitri Erasmus (2010) has argued, sharing space does not end racism. The reason why contact theory – which is ultimately premised on the belief that mobilities are free, unconstricted and enabling – does not work is its lack of attention to what Erasmus calls 'the pathologies of white privilege': 'innocence, entitlement, denial, benevolent patronage, oppressive courtesies, and arrogance'. To this one may add the more specific pathologies of settler colonialism, and the threat that Indigenous presence poses to the future of the settler-colonial project, an ideological-political project that claims control of *all* land – not only of privately owned land, but also of public spaces (Moreton-Robinson, 2015). I will return to these pathologies in the section titled 'Visceral Movements-Moments and Affective Pathologies'.

South Africa's Apartheid: Macro and Micro

South Africa's apartheid laws – as a direct continuation of earlier settler-colonial legislation – were a blatant exercise in spatial control. Following colonial dispossession and oppression, the apartheid state created, and legislated, racially structured experiences of space. The basic principle of apartheid (Afrikaans, 'apartness') was spatial segregation: the country was carved up into self-governing Bantustans, which were declared to be the 'homelands' of Black South Africans, and the only place where they had the right to own land. Cities were firmly divided along racial lines. Black South Africans were allowed in the white urban suburbs only for purposes of work, and forced to carry identity documents – known colloquially, and subversively, as *dompas*, 'stupid or cursed pass' – at all times. This was known as *groot*, grand or macro apartheid, mapping race onto space and creating lived cartographies of racism. Race was spatialised and, consequently, space was racialised.

Central to apartheid legislation was the *Group Areas Act* (1950/1957) which regulated where people might live, settle and where they might own property. The Act divided people into racial categories, and given the centrality of these classifications in South African life it is expedient to quote the act in full:

[T]here shall be the following groups:

(a) a white group, in which shall be included any person who in appearance, obviously is, or who is generally accepted as a white person [...]

(b) a native group in which shall be included –
   (i) any person who in fact is, or is generally accepted as a member of an aboriginal race or tribe of Africa [...]
   (ii) any woman to whichever race, tribe or class she may belong, between whom and a person who is in terms of sub-paragraph (i), a member of a native group, there exists a marriage or who cohabits with such a person;
(c) a coloured group in which shall be included –
   (i) any person who is not a member of the white group or of the native group; and
   (ii) any woman to whichever race, tribe or class she may belong, between whom and a person who is in terms of sub-paragraph (i), a member of the coloured group, there exists a marriage or who cohabits with such a person. (Section (2), Act No 41 of 1950)[6]

While racial classifications in, for example, the United States relied on notions of descent (the notorious 'one-drop rule') and pseudo-scientific reasoning, South African law was based on appearance (*seeing race*) and social convention (*being raced*). It was grounded in the practices of everyday racialisation and racism that defined colonial whiteness, and every white person was essentially 'an expert on the subject of race' (Posel, 2001: 96), assigning racial categories to others, determining their life-changes in a racist state, shaping their social and spatial (im)mobilities, and creating non-overlapping categories of unitary whiteness and Blackness. In addition, the legislation contained a strongly gendered aspect: any woman will become 'native' or 'Coloured' if she lives with someone thus classified. The fear of sexual intimacy, of undesirable bodily contact and the end of whiteness haunts the legal text. I will return to this in the section titled 'Visceral Movements-Moments and Affective Pathologies'.

The *Group Areas Act* of 1950 led to a series of forced removals as inner-city areas and seaside suburbs were declared white, and Black residents were transported to distant townships. In addition, many Black South Africans were sent to the, largely rural, Bantustans. Altogether around four million Black people were forcefully resettled (Field, 2001; Platzky & Walker, 1985). Nevertheless, urbanisation continued: people came to the (white) cities in search of work – sometimes as registered migrants recruited to work in the mines, at other times individually, trying their luck in a deeply hostile environment, seeking domestic work, doing so-called 'piece-jobs' or working in the township economy.[7] They moved to the cities so that they could send remittances to their kin who struggled to for survival in the impoverished Bantustans (Mabin, 1992). It was mobility driven by necessity and survival, defiant of apartheid mechanisms of control. This mobility created illegal shacklands on the outskirts of apartheid's white cities, and with it unique forms of modernity and urbanity (Bank, 2011). It was also a mobility that was largely invisible to 'white eyes'. Charles van Onselen (2019: 10) notes how over 400,000 Black workers entered Johannesburg every year to work in the mines, a substantial presence that existed at the margins of society, disposable and unacknowledged.

In 1953, the *Reservation of Special Amenities Act* was passed to ensure that not only residential areas, but all public facilities would be racially segregated. This included trams, buses and trains, hotels and movie theatres, parks and sports fields – all public space was thus placed under white control. The act forms part of a string of legislation that has been referred to as *klein apartheid*. In English this is usually translated as 'petty apartheid', yet as Alan Paton (1958: 254) noted, 'there is nothing petty about it. It is unspeakable'. A more appropriate translation would be 'micro apartheid', drawing attention to the ways in which such legislation regulated the minutiae of everyday life: it was no longer possible for friends to share a meal together, or to sit next to one another on a park bench; restrooms were segregated as were post offices and bars; relationships across the colour line were illegal, punishable by imprisonment (*Prohibition of Mixed Marriages Act* 1949, *Immorality Act* 1927/1950).

Beaches, however, provided a bit of a legislative problem. The 1953 Act refers only to land: 'public premises includes any land, enclosure, building, structure, hall, room, office or convenience to which the public has access'. This does not include the ocean, and swimmers could – in principle – move freely across the seascape, without violating apartheid legislation. For a few years the ocean provided a freedom of movement that the land no longer did. But not for long. The Act was amended in 1960: 'the sea and the bed of the sea within the three miles limit' was now explicitly included (Rogerson, 2017: 98). Twelve years later, the *Seashore Amendment Act* (1972) ensured that the matter of beaches was solved once and for all. Full control was established over the ocean. An article by Kim Prochazka and Lisa Kruger (2001) on beach apartheid contains an image, taken in Kalk Bay, Cape Town on Christmas Day 1977, during the height of beach apartheid. Across a high concrete wall one sees, from the vantage point of a well-maintained and sparsely occupied white beach, another beach, crowded with people, cheek by jowl, with only limited amenities. This is the Coloured beach. Steps go up to the wall and on top of the steps stand two law enforcement officers. Their job is to ensure that no-one crosses over to the white beach. Signs with the inscription 'white persons only/net blankes' demarcate the space for everyone to see.

All the best beaches in Cape Town were designated 'white'. There were four small Coloured beaches, one Indian beach, one Chinese beach and one African beach (Rogerson, 2017: 100). The African beach was called Mnandi Beach. *Mnandi* is isiXhosa and means 'nice' or 'pleasant' – yet the beach was anything but 'nice'. Sindiwe Magona remembers Mnandi Beach in her autobiography *Forced to Grow* (1992: 12) as follows: 'Uninviting. Unappetising. Bleak and desolate. Barren. And not safe'. The pattern was repeated across the country. In Durban, for example, more than 2 km of beach were reserved for whites (at the time 22% of the population), 650 metres were granted to Africans (46% of the population), 550 metres to Indians (28% of the population) and 300 metres to Coloureds (4% of the population). And the order of beaches was always the same: *never* would a white beach border an African beach directly. The white beach would border the Coloured beach, which would border the Indian beach, which would border the African beach. And sometimes, as was the case in Port Elizabeth, there would even be a 'buffer zone' between the white and the Coloured beach. At the beach, 'ecologies' of contact (cf. Durrheim & Dixon, 2005) were tightly controlled, projecting racial hierarchies and anxieties onto spatial arrangements.

The white beaches were safe, with public amenities, shark nets and lifeguards; the Black beaches were unprotected and treacherous, often located next to sewage outlets (Rogerson, 2017). A short extract from *Sechaba* (March 1969: 16) shows not only the absurdities of implementation, but also how micro apartheid controlled and surveilled everyone's movements.

BEACH APARTHEID
Can a White angler cross a Coloured beach to reach a fishing spot on the other side? And can a Coloured angler cross a White beach? [...] [A] White angler was stopped by a Coloured lifesaver as he set out to cross the newly-zoned Coloured beach, King Neptune, to fish beyond it. [...] A Divisional Council spokesman said that anyone entering an area zoned for a different race could be fined a maximum of R100.

Beach apartheid was strictly enforced. When an Afrikaans newspaper compared President P.W. Botha to Winston Churchill in the early 1980s, cartoonist Tony Grogan evoked Churchill's WWII speech from 1940, which included the lines 'we shall fight on the beaches [...] we will never surrender' (Figure 8.1).[8] In apartheid South Africa this took on a very different meaning: the people to be fought were not the Nazis, but a mother and her child,

Figure 8.1 We will fight them on the beaches. We will never surrender! (Tony Grogan 1981)
Source: Special Collections, University of Cape Town Libraries. Reproduced with permission from the artist, Tony Grogan.

arrested simply because they tried to swim at a beach. As Paton (1958) noted: micro apartheid was 'unspeakable', inhumane and violent.

During the 1980s, beach protests challenged the persistent whiteness of South Africa's coastline. Slogans such as 'Drown apartheid' and 'All of God's beaches for all of God's people' accompanied multi-racial picnics that were held at whites-only beaches. Best known is probably the swim-in by Labour Party leader Allen Hendrickse which took place in 1987 at a whites-only beach in Port Elizabeth. Hendrickse was later ordered by Botha to issue an apology (Lloyd, 2016). In 1989, after F.W. De Klerk had assumed the office of president, beach apartheid was officially ended. A year later, Nelson Mandela was released, political organisations unbanned and the *Separate Amenities Act* was repealed. Four years later, the first democratic elections took place and the legal-political system of apartheid was finally abolished. Yet, as argued in the section titled 'The Beach and the Ocean: Settler Colonialism as a Transnational Regime', the beach remained part of the settler-colonial project and its white imaginary did not disappear with the end of colonialism or apartheid. I will return to the present in the section titled 'A Nervous State – Even When on Holiday', after reflecting on the affective dimensions, and motivations, of settler colonialism and apartheid. Why create – and maintain – such a costly system of cruel inhumanities?[9]

Visceral Movements-Moments and Affective Pathologies

The most insightful descriptions of the psychology of whiteness and settler coloniality have been formulated precisely by those who have suffered from its violence. As noted by bell hooks (1992: 165):

> [B]lack folks have, from slavery on, shared in conversations with one another 'special' knowledge of whiteness gleaned from close scrutiny of white people.

In addition to such vernacular knowledges, which circulate across generations, there is also scholarly work on the psychology of colonisers, and a psychological-psychiatric register has shaped, for example, the writings of Frantz Fanon, W.E.B. du Bois, Aimé Césaire, Steve Biko, Chabani Manganyi, Albert Memmi, Homi Bhaba, Ashis Nandy and Fredrick Hickling. These scholars have argued that psychological states are shaped by the collective-historical experiences of colonialism, dehumanisation, exploitation and oppression, leading to lasting pathologies and traumas. Albert Memmi (2003 [1974]: 13) observed that 'if colonization destroys the colonized, it also rots the colonizer'. Césaire put it even more strongly in his *Discourse on Colonialism* (2000 [1950]: 39): 'no one colonizes innocently, no one colonizes with impunity either', the coloniser is 'sick' and 'morally diseased'.

In addition to vernacular knowledges and scholarly discussions, literature provides another window for understanding the psychological dimensions of settler colonialism. *Mating Birds* (2005 [1983]) by Lewis Nkosi is a novel that addresses precisely these psychologies by centring the beach as a space of impossibility and violence. *Mating Birds* tells the story of Ndi Sibiya, accused of having raped a white woman, Veronica Slater, whom he had met at the beach, each of them lying on their side of the colour-line, looking at one another, never touching, never speaking. Nkosi's novel speaks to the visceral nature of racism, the fear of bodies moving towards one another, touching one another – and the forbidden desire for just this touch (on the visceral, not merely discursive, nature of racism, see Hook, 2012). It is a fear that is enshrined in the *Immorality Act* and the *Prohibition of Mixed Marriages Act*, outlawing any form of sexual intimacy between 'Europeans' and 'non-Europeans'. Beachspaces are such a powerful site because on the beach spatial segregation and the prohibition of intimacy merge and join forces: with skin exposed (wearing nothing but a swimming costume), Blackness/whiteness become hypervisible, infusing interpersonal encounters with a 'fleshiness' that is absent in other spaces (Lobo, 2014). While some contact was unavoidable to meet the labour needs of the colonial economy (including domestic work), this contact was minimized as much as possible.[10] The mere possibility of an intimate union between settlers and Indigenous people was the ultimate threat to the colonial order – a threat that, because of its love-lust entanglements, was also dangerously uncontrollable. As noted by Kopano Ratele (2004: 148) in his reflections on 'kinky politics' and race as a sexual fetish: 'sex came to mean so much in South Africa' – it had the potential to destroy the colonial order, and it was because of this that white women who cohabited with Black or Coloured men legally lost their 'whiteness', their racial privileges. In a paper written in 1960, the sociologist Pierre Van den Berghe notes that in South Africa one finds 'a morbid fear of miscegenation unparalleled in intensity anywhere else in the world' (Van den Berghe, 1960: 68). Intimate contact challenges the 'logic of elimination' that is at the core of settler colonialism (Wolfe, 2006), and shakes the very foundations of white supremacy. It makes 'the other' not only visible, but also returns their humanity, which repeated acts of dispossession, subjugation and oppression had denied them. And in doing so it challenges the grounds on which the settler-colonial polity is built: How can settler colonialism continue if we recognize it as unjust and immoral? How can one keep one's land after recognizing those from whom it was taken? Instead, in order to maintain one's ill-gotten property and wealth, one has to avert one' eyes, disavow, recoil and lash out, whenever Indigenous presence makes itself felt (Henderson, 2017).

In 2005, when *Mating Birds* was re-issued, Nkosi explained that he wanted to write 'a story of an obsession in which the sea, the sun, and bodies on the beach combine to form an image' (Nkosi, 2005 [1983]: 5). This is reminiscent of another story set in a settler-colonial context, involving the sea, the sun, bodies and the beach: Albert Camus's *L'Étranger* ('The Stranger' or, in a more recent translation '*The Outsider*', 1942).[11] Camus's novel culminates in a murder on the beach, committed by the protagonist, Meursault. European readers have quite consistently interpreted the story as an exemplification of 'the absurd'. Yet this a reading that jars; it elides the fact that Meursault was not just anyone, but an Algerian settler (a *pieds noir*), and that the person he murdered remains faceless and unnamed, simply referred to as 'the Arab'. More than 70 years later, the Algerian writer Kamel Dahoud (2015) published his novel *The Meursault Investigation*: 'the Arab' now has a name (Musa) and a brother (Harun) (on the historical-political complexities of reading of Camus and Dahoud, see Isaac, 2016; for a postcolonial reading of Camus, see Said, 1993). In an interview in the *Los Angeles Review of Books*, Dahoud comments:

> Ever since the Middle Ages, the white man has the habit of naming Africa and Asia's mountains and insects, all the while denying the names of the human beings they encounter. By removing their names, they render banal murder and crimes. (Zaretsky, 2015)

Not seeing the other, not knowing their name, is a another symbolic instantiation of 'the logic of elimination' (see also Deumert, 2018). Nkosi describes white South Africans in *Mating Birds* as follows: 'a people so accustomed to regarding blacks as nothing but pegs on which to hang their hats' (Nkosi, 2005 [1983]: 89). The other is nothing but an object, without name or humanity. These psychological dispositions are 'strongly etched into the social unconscious and institutional legacy' (Amin, 2010: 3), creating chronotopic habits of thinking and acting, a 'race-inflected sensory/affective culture' (Amin, 2010: 8), and a 'psychosocial ontology of spatiality' that is based on exclusion (Henderson, 2017: 45). And these dispositions are sedimented in institutions and the legal system and transmitted across generations. Jean-Paul Sartre (2011 [1956]: 138) called this 'the colonial system', a system of being-and-thinking that persists through time and space:

> And when we talk of the 'colonial system', we must be clear about what we mean. It is not an abstract mechanism. The system exists, it functions; the inferal cycle of colonialism is a reality. But this reality is embodied in a million colonists, children and grandchildren of colonists, who have been shaped by colonialism and who think, speak and act according to the very principles of the colonial system.

Mating Birds is set not in the 1980s, when the first tentative steps were taken to dismantle micro apartheid, but during the heydays of apartheid: the 1950s. White South African critics took exception to this (Graham, 2005). The writer André Brink, even though a vocal critic of the apartheid regime, accused Nkosi in 1992 of being obsessed with 'race and colour' and continues:

> *Mating Birds* is a return to a past distorted by subjective memory, anger and distance ... the text bears the weight of the author's desperate need to vindicate its own exile ... [Nkosi is] the expatriate preying on the carcass of the land he has abandoned – as rapacious as any colonizer plundering virgin territory. (Brink, 1992: 16–17)

These are astonishing words. Nkosi, upon winning a scholarship to Harvard, was granted an exit visa by the South African state in 1961, a visa that allowed him to leave, but never to come back. He was one of the many Black South Africans driven into exile by a racist state, so anger would be quite an expected, and understandable, emotion. But Brink goes further, likening Nkosi – one of the many dispossessed, violated and oppressed South Africans – to the 'coloniser', the settler who takes and destroys the land. Where does Brink's anger come from? How can a novel about beach apartheid and its sexual politics – the paranoid fear of the 'black peril' – turn a writer who opposed apartheid into someone who attacks one of its victims? I believe that at the heart of Brink's own anger with Nkosi's novel is his inability to understand – like other South African critics before him – that the colonial/apartheid/racist past continues into the present, that micro apartheid did not end some time in the 1980s when the legislation was slowly and partially dismantled, but that it continued in the minds of people, in habits and everyday practices. Nkosi set his novel in the past, because this past still matters: the racial present is always chronotopic, with 'racial legacies close enough to the surface to spring back with force' (Amin, 2010: 3).[12]

In this context it is worth taking a look at an event that took place in Durban, where Nkosi's novel is set: in 1982, one year before the novel was published, Battery Beach II, a small beach located between the white beaches and the Coloured beach, became the first (and only) mixed beach. Two social scientists, Valerie Møller and Lawrence Schlemmer (1982), followed this event and conducted various surveys at the time to study 'attitudes towards beach integration'. The proposal to create just one, small, integrated beach led to widespread public debate in the media, in numerous council meetings and in meetings organised by white ratepayers' associations; petitions against integration were submitted, signed by thousands of white South Africans. The surveys carried out by Møller and Schlemmer show that close to 80% of white respondents supported beach apartheid. Highly sexualised anxieties about Black men looking at and meeting white women were prominent among the concerns expressed. Some respondents made a firm distinction between sharing space for walking and sharing space for swimming: the first was a possibility one could consider, the second fundamentally undesirable. White beachgoers felt physically uncomfortable and anxious at the thought of a shared beachspace. One of the respondents noted: 'whites will feel threatened, it [the beach] won't have a peaceful atmosphere anymore' (Møller & Schlemmer, 1982: 133). Quite similar sentiments were articulated in 'letters to the editor' in the 1990s, after the beaches had been desegregated and Black beachgoers became a visible presence: 'Never in my life have I experienced such a fearful feeling after being swamped by so many unruly black youths' (1991; cited in Durrheim & Dixon, 2001: 446).

Thus, the logic of elimination – the making-invisible-through-controlling-the-movement-of-racialised-bodies – that informed the *Immorality Act* of 1927 and the *Reservation of Separate Amenities Act* of 1953 was still present in 1982, in 1991, in 2016, 2017 and 2018 (see section on 'The Beach and the Ocean: Settler Colonialism as a Transnational Regime'). It is the chronotopic quality of settler-colonial racism that inspired Nkosi to set his novel in the past – because the past is still with us today. The spectre of the past-in-the-present is a well-known trope in postcolonial and decolonial theory (see, for example, Gordon, 1997). South Africa is not exceptional in this respect.

A Nervous State – Even When on Holiday

Mobilities continue to be denied and restricted. Sunshine Kamaloni (2019: 85–86), a Black Zambian woman, reflects on her experiences in South Africa in the 2000s:

> My experience of racism in South Africa was always overt and visible ... the more I socialised I became to know *instinctively* which places I could go [to] and the spaces to avoid. (Emphasis added)

Writing about the racialisation of space in Cuba, Kristina Wirtz (2017) refers to these everyday ways of moving within one's immediate environment as *micro-mobilities*. These are movements within one's city or town, distinguished from mobilities that transverse larger distances (such as transnational or regional migration).

December and January are holiday season in South Africa: the weather is hot, the schools are closed and public holidays allow for many South Africans to take a much deserved break. The feeling of enjoyment, of good times ahead, is captured in the commonly uttered phrase *ke dezemba boss!*, 'guys, it's December!'. The atmosphere is festive; people are looking forward to a nice time, to enjoy themselves, to end the old year in style and to welcome the new year. Atmospheres are difficult to capture in words – their affective resonances need to be felt; their texture, ephemeral and often not quite graspable, can only be experienced. Nevertheless, they matter to social life (Stewart, 2011). In the sections on 'The Beach and the Ocean: Settler Colonialism as a Transnational Regime' and 'Visceral Movements-Moments and Affective Pathologies', I noted that, somehow, it is the happy and relaxed atmosphere of beachspaces that brings racist sentiments to the surface, without fail, every year – a chronotopic reality in the South African summer.

As I am editing this chapter, on 10 January 2020, my Twitter feed informs me about yet another racist incident: a case of hate speech was opened against a businessman who, while complaining about litter on a beach in KwaZulu-Natal, compared, like the estate agent four years earlier, Black beachgoers to 'monkeys'.[13] And just as the new year started, a resident of Camps Bay, a wealthy seaside suburb, complained on a public Facebook group about holiday makers and beachgoers at the beach on the first of January, celebrating the new year.

Going to the beach on New Year's Day has a long tradition in Cape Town, and since the end of apartheid residents from across the city visit former white beaches on this day, beaches with good amenities and in beautiful settings. Camps Bay is one such beach. Yet, the resident did not appreciate the festive atmosphere, the enjoyment of people, the holiday feeling. Instead the post is a lament about crowds and litter, traffic and noise. The text is accompanied by 14 photographs. Of particular interest are two images:

(i) People picnicking on the broad pavement, resting under palm trees on blankets, or sitting in chairs. The caption reads: 'Blocking pedestrian walking space'.
(ii) People sitting under a tree on the lawn next to the beach – some have beach chairs, some sit on blankets, a young child is jumping. The caption reads: 'Too much'.

Example (i) relates directly to the question of micro-mobilities: the mobilities of racial 'others' into the symbolically white space of Camps Bay are positioned as hindering the mobility of those who consider this public space to be 'their space', and who expect that their (white) mobilities will always be smooth, uninterrupted and easy, never striated (Andrucki, 2010). Example (ii) is deliberately ambiguous in its reference, and shows that not all racism is overt: while a case of hate-speech was opened against the above mentioned businessman, this anonymous post avoids overt racial references, but nevertheless draws on the longstanding racist tropes, defining Blackness in terms of behaviour rather than phenotype. Roth-Gordon (2016) referred to these kinds of discourses in Brazil as 'racially-tinged' language (see section titled 'The Beach and the Ocean: Settler Colonialism as a Transnational Regime'). In the Facebook comment sections, readers-writers talk about 'racist innuendo', 'a racist undertone'. One reader-writer referred to it as 'apartheid 2.0'. Combined with images of only Black beachgoers, the lament is a coded comment about 'too much Blackness' in Camps Bay, chiming with similar comments on other social media sites, as well as the discourses reported in Møller and Schlemmer (1982) and Durrheim and Dixon (2001). Reader-writers are certainly not fooled:

> Seems as though some Yt people are upset ... I mean let's be honest this isn't about fkin pollution or litter, now is it? ;-) mxim.[14]

Of course, racist discourses are not fully stable, and there is both change and repetition. Noticeable in this Facebook discussion was that old discourses about 'too much litter' and 'overcrowding' were reframed – in the context of global debates about climate change – as 'destroying the environment', 'not caring for the environment', not being committed to 'the conservation of our natural environment'. This is an example of 'grafting', a concept developed by Susan Gal (2018) to capture the way in which signs can be repurposed in ways that invert their original political meaning, and allow racist discourses to continue (without mentioning race, see also Bonilla-Silva, 2006, on 'racism without racists'). In other words, they are grafted onto a positive concept (in this case, 'care for the environment'), but continue to communicate messages that stand in direct opposition to the seemingly progressive ethos that is communicated (see also Ochs, 1990, on double indexicality). In earlier work (Deumert, 2019b), I have shown how global minority rights discourses are used to construct South African whiteness as vulnerable and in need of protection. This not only invisibilises the persistent power and privilege of whiteness, but also draws on the moral authority of the original discourse. It indexes, overtly, a commitment to a human-rights-based ethos, while following a political project that is nationalistic, racist and exclusionary. In this case the legitimacy of environmental discourses is used to hide the racist force of the utterance.

Yet, 'in the final analysis' – as struggle stalwart Neville Alexander used to say – whether in Durban or Cape Town, whether in the 1960s, 1980s, 2000s or 2020, the freedom of 'the racial other' to 'do as they like' and 'move as they wish' rattles the settler-colonial order. Drawing on Michael Taussig (1991), Denis Byrne (2010) described racist spatial regimes as 'nervous systems': tense, fearful, filled with paranoia and longing, always on edge, never fully at ease, shot through with racial anxiety, always ready to explode into rage and anger or, alternatively, withdrawal, retreating to private and secluded beaches that are only accessible to those with money (Bank, 2011). The 2019 *South African Reconciliation Barometer* speaks directly to the unresolved issues of the past and a whiteness that remains unapologetic, unwilling to address the past-in-the-present so that the future can look different (Potgieter, 2019).[15] In 2019, around 15% of South Africans surveyed did not believe that apartheid was a crime against humanity (including those who were 'undecided'), and around 25% did not believe that the apartheid government oppressed the majority of the population. Apartheid denialists were, and this is not surprising, mostly white. As Ralph Ellison (2016 [1952]: 3) writes in the prologue to the *Invisible Man*, what one sees – or doesn't see – with one's physical eyes is a 'matter of the construction of their *inner* eyes, those eyes with which they look through their physical eyes upon reality'. The inner eye, as noted by Sartre (2011 [1956]), is passed on from generation to generation. The inner eye creates mental representations of 'the world' that are saturated with affect, and that, in turn, produce and re-produce the settler-colonial subject and the particular brand of spatialised racism that defines it. The past is not 'long gone and buried' (as one of those commenting on the Facebook post remarked), it is right here, and the struggle, now and then, is for a future that is different from the colonial-apartheid past. The original post received over 1200 comments and was shared almost 700 times, sometimes with approval, more often to expose the racism to a wider audience. Readers-writers consistently asserted their right to be in any public space, at any beach, at any time, thus unmapping the apartheid cartography of race:

> Bottom line #asiyindawo ['we are not going anywhere']. Next year we will be back!!

Conclusion

Settler colonialism carries with it a restlessness, a deep-seated nervousness: mobility is foundational to its formation, embedded in its history, and to control the resilient mobility of the racialised 'other' is central to its continuation, necessary to maintain the fiction that colonial settlement is possible, that the colonised, the dispossessed will, ultimately, not chase the settlers away and reclaim their sovereignty of land and livelihoods. And with this I return to the question I asked at the beginning: is it possible to decolonise settler colonialism? The answer is simple: unless questions of land and space, which are at the heart of the settler-colonial project, are addressed, settler-colonialism will stay and decolonisation will be halted in its tracks.

Beachspaces link past and present in an imaginary that is not only that of white supremacy and settler coloniality, but also of anticolonial struggle and freedom. In 1975, the Jamaican poet Andrew Salkey published a poem called 'Rays of Hope'. The poem is set at an unnamed South African beach and starts with the return of 'the wretched':

> You should have seen
> who struggled out of the sea,
> today: a tired, rock-sliced

miner, with clogged pores,
who'd given up the race,
foxing them completely,
locking his hands into the sand!

And as the wretched arrive at the shore, the 'Boer ghosts, scrambling, land-crazed, diamond-swipers' understand 'deep down' that 'they've got to hit that southern water' and 'swim all the way out, to the wide, quiet Antarctic'. Here, the poet tells what is necessary for settler colonialism to end: the settler needs to disappear *'qua* settler' (Henderson, 2017: 40). And this means talking about the question of land, public and private, and about enforced and surveilled (im)mobilities across such lands.

Salkey's poem brings to mind the prophesy of uNongqawuse, where it is said that the 'ancestors ... will rise from the dead after we have killed our cattle. They will emerge from the sea' (Mda, 2000: 272). It also brings to mind the ritual slaughter of a sheep on Clifton Beach in Cape Town. This was done – in December 2018 – to cleanse the beach of its racist past, and to allow for new futures: futures that are located outside of the settler-colonial imaginary.[16] The beach is past, present and future.

Notes

(1) Parts of this chapter draw on a short column that I published in November 2019 on *diggit.com* (Deumert, 2019a). This version constitutes the expanded argument and pays attention not only to 'the politics of the beach', but also to 'the psychology of the beach'. As always I am greatly indebted to my partner and colleague Nkululeko Mabandla for discussion and debate, for challenges and critique, for suggestions and encouragement.

(2) I use the term Indigenous to point to global continuities across settler-colonial formations. It could be replaced with Black (which I tend to use in the sense envisioned by Steve Biko), or African.

(3) Since race is a social construct, some scholars opt to put it into inverted commas (Erasmus, 2010), or to 'put it under erasure' (i.e. Ratele, 2004). I sympathise with these decisions, but decided to leave it unmarked. Despite being socially and historically constructed, it has real effects (like age, disability, gender and sexuality).

(4) Thus, I disagree with Durrheim and Dixon (2005: 11), who argue that beach relations present 'but a "thin slice" of social life'. Rather, the beach is central to understanding how settler-colonial spatialities (and affects) are instantiated in public space.

(5) In South African common law, *crimen injuria* refers to cases of 'unlawfully and intentionally impairing the dignity or privacy of another person' (https://www.saps.gov.za/faqdetail.php?fid=9; see also Phelps, 2018).

(6) The classification 'Indian' was included around 1960. Up until then Indian South Africans were grouped as Coloured. For a summative overview of the various acts that defined the apartheid state, see Landis (1957).

(7) Piece-job is a South African term which refers to various forms of casual labour.

(8) See digitalcollections.lib.uct.ac.za/islandora/object/islandora%3A6151.
(9) South Africa was not unique in passing such legislation. The Jim Crow laws in the United States similar regulated the segregation of public facilities (see Dixon et al., 2009; for a comparative discussion; also Massey & Denton, 1993).
(10) As Hook (2012) argues, the Black body was positioned as abject, and any form of direct contact had to be avoided. He cites from J.M. Coetzee's (1997) memoir *Boyhood*: 'The custom, it appears, is that after a person of colour has drunk from a cup, the cup must be smashed' (cited in Hook, 2012: 45).
(11) The 1989 translation by Matthew Ward uses the well-established title '*The Stranger*', while the 2012 translation by Sandra Smith uses '*The Outsider*'.
(12) Such vitriolic reactions are not unusual. When I first presented aspects of this chapter at a workshop, a white colleague adopted a similar style of critique – aggressive and personalised.
(13) See https://www.iol.co.za/news/south-africa/kwazulu-natal/businessman-in-hot-water-over-facebook-post-likening-black-people-to-baboons-monkeys-40302684?utm_source=twitter&utm_medium=social.
(14) 'Mxim' (also 'mxm') is a South African social media expression, indexing a clicking sound similar to 'tsk', dismissive.
(15) The *South African Reconciliation Barometer Survey* is conducted annually by the Institute for Justice and Reconciliation. The first survey was conducted in 2003, and from 2009 onwards survey reports are available online.
(16) See https://www.dailymaverick.co.za/opinionista/2018-12-30-clifton-4th-beach-of-slaughtered-sheep-drowned-slaves-and-collective-rituals/.

References

Allport, G. (1954) *The Nature of Prejudice*. Cambridge, MA: Addison-Wesley.
Amin, A. (2010) The Remainders of Race. *Theory, Culture & Society* 27, 1–23.
Andrucki, M.J. (2010) The visa whiteness machine: Transnational motility in post-apartheid South Africa. *Ethnicities* 10, 358–370.
Bank, L. (2011) Frontiers of freedom: Race, landscape and nationalism in the coastal cultures of South Africa. *Anthropology Southern Africa* 38, 248–268.
Bhabha, H.K. (1994) *The Location of Culture*. London: Routledge.
Bonilla-Silva, E. (2006) *Racism Without Racists: Color-Blind Racism and the Persistence of Racial Inequality in the United States*. Lanham, MD: Rowman & Littlefield.
Brink, A. (1992) An ornithology of sexual politics: Lewis Nkosi's 'Mating Birds'. *English in Africa* 19, 1–20.
Byrne, D. (2010) Nervous landscapes: Race and space in Australia. In B. Mar and P. Edmonds (eds) *Making Settler Colonial Space: Perspectives on Race, Place and Identity* (pp. 103–128). Basingstoke: Palgrave.
Camus, A. (1989 [1942]) *The Stranger* (M. Ward, trans.). New York: Vintage.
Camus, A. (2012 [1942]) *The Outsider* (S. Smith, trans.). London: Penguin.
Césaire, A. (2000 [1950]) *Discourse on Colonialism* (with a new introduction by R.D.G. Kelley). London/New York: Monthly Review Press.
Chiba, Z. (1975) 'A Migrant in My Own Land'. *Sechaba* 9, 10.
Dahoud, K. (2015) *The Meursault Investigation*. New York: Other Press.
Department of Rural Development and Land Reform (2017) *Land Audit Report*. See https://www.gov.za/sites/default/files/gcis_document/201802/landauditreport13feb2018.pdf

Deumert, A. (2017) The multivocality of heritage: Moments, encounters and mobilities. In A. Creese and A. Blackledge (eds) *The Handbook of Superdiversity*. London: Routledge.

Deumert, A. (2018) Settler colonialism speaks. *Language Ecology* 2, 91–111.

Deumert, A. (2019a) Racism and the politics of the beach. *Diggit Magazine*, 28 November. See https://www.diggitmagazine.com/column/politics-beach-racism.

Deumert A. (2019b) Sensational signs, authority and the public sphere: Settler colonial rhetoric in times of change. *Journal of Sociolinguistics* 23, 467–484.

Dixon, J., Tredoux, C., Durrheim, K., Finchilescu, G. and Clack, B. (2009) 'The inner citadels of the color line': Mapping the micro-ecology of racial segregation in everyday life spaces. *Social and Personality Psychology Compass* 2, 1547–1569.

Durrheim, K. and Dixon, J. (2001) The role of place and metaphor in social exclusion: South Africa's beaches as sites of shifting racialization. *Ethnic and Racial Studies* 24, 433–450.

Durrheim, K. and Dixon, J. (2005) *Racial Encounter: The Social Psychology of Contact and Segregation*. London: Routledge.

Ellison, R. (2016 [1952]) *Invisible Man*. London: Penguin.

Erasmus, Z. (2010) Contact theory: Too timid for 'race' and racism. *Journal of Social Issues* 66, 387–400.

Feldman, H. (2018) On white South Africans being racist on the beach. *Howard Feldman* blog, 22 August. See https://howardfeldman.co.za/on-white-south-africans-being-racist-at-the-beach/.

Field, S. (ed.) (2001) *Lost Communities, Living Memories: Remembering Forced Removals in Cape Town*. Cape Town: David Philip.

Flahaux, M.L. and De Haas, H. (2016) African migration: Trends, patterns, drivers. *Comparative Migration Studies* 4, 1–25.

Gal, S. (2018) Registers in circulation: The social organization of interdiscursivity. *Signs and Society* 6, 1–24.

Gordon, A. (1997) *Ghostly Matters: Haunting and the Sociological Imagination*. Minneapolis, MN: University of Minnesota Press.

Graham, L. (2005) 'Bathing area – for whites only': Reading prohibitive signs and 'black peril' in Lewis Nkosi's 'Mating Birds'. In L. Stiebel and L. Gunner (eds) *Still Beating the Drum: Critical Perspectives on Lewis Nkosi* (pp. 147–166). Amsterdam/New York: Rodopi.

Hafajee, F. (2019) I swim where I like? Or does beach apartheid linger on? *Daily Maverick*, 8 January. See https://www.dailymaverick.co.za/article/2019-01-08-i-swim-where-i-like-or-does-beach-apartheid-linger-on/.

Hartfield, C. (2018) *A Few Red Drops: The Chicago Race Riot of 1919*. New York: Clarion.

Henderson, P. (2017) Imagined communities: The psychosocial space of settler colonialism. *Settler Colonial Studies* 7, 40–56.

Hofmeyer, I. (2018) Oceans as empty spaces: Redrafting our knowledge by dropping the colonial lens. *The Conversation*, 6 September. See https://theconversation.com/oceans-as-empty-spaces-redrafting-our-knowledge-by-dropping-the-colonial-lens-10 2778.

Hook, D. (2012) *A Critical Psychology of the Postcolonial: The Mind of Apartheid*. London: Routledge.

hooks, b. (1992) *Black Looks: Race and Representation*. Boston, MA: Southend Press.

Isaac, J.C. (2016) Camus on trial. *Dissent* 63 (1), 145–150.

Kabir, N.A. (2015) The Cronulla riots: Muslims' place in the white imaginary spatiality. *Contemporary Islam* 9, 271–290.
Kamaloni, S. (2019) *Understanding Racism in a Post-Racial World: Visible Invisibilities*. London: Palgrave.
Kelley, R.D.G. (2017) The rest of us: Rethinking settler and native. *American Quarterly* 69, 267–276.
Landis, E.S. (1957) Apartheid legislation. *Africa Today* 4, 45–48.
Lebeloane, L. and Mokhele, M. (2006) The use of different types of water in the Zion Christian Church. *Studia Historiae Ecclesiasticae* 32, 143–152.
Lloyd, J. (2016) The much-debated swimming excursion of the late Rev Allan Hendrickse. *Litnet*, 8 March. See https://www.litnet.co.za/the-much-debated-swimming-excursion-of-the-rev-allan-hendrickse/.
Lobo, M. (2014) Affective energies: Sensory bodies on the beach in Darwin, Australia. *Emotion, Space and Society* 12, 101–109.
Lujabe, N. (2017) 2017 started just like 2016, with racist rants on social media. *City Press*, 6 January. See https://city-press.news24.com/News/2017-started-just-like-2016-with-racist-rants-on-social-media-20170106.
Mabin, A. (1992) Dispossession, exploitation and struggle: An historical overview of South African urbanization. In D.M. Smith (ed.) *The Apartheid City and Beyond: Urbanization and Social Change in South Africa* (pp. 12–24). London: Routledge.
Magona, S. (1992) *Forced to Grow*. Cape Town: David Phillip.
Maharaj, B. (2017) Contesting displacement and the struggle for survival: The case of subsistence fisher folk in Durban, South Africa. *Local Economy* 32, 744–762.
Malone, N. and Ovenden, K. (2017) Natureculture. In A. Fuentes (ed.) *International Encyclopedia of Primatology* (pp. 848–849). Chichester John Wiley & Sons.
Massey, D.S. and Denton, N. (1993) *American Apartheid: Segregation and the Making of the Underclass*. Cambridge: Harvard University Press.
McWirther, C. (2011) *Red Summer: The Summer of 2019 and the Awakening of Black America*. New York: Henry Holt.
Mda, Z. (2000) *Heart of Redness*. New York: Picador.
Memmi, A. (2003 [1974]) *Colonizer and Colonized* (with a new introduction by N. Gordimer). London: Earthscan.
Møller, V. and Schlemmer, L. (1982) *Attitudes Towards Beach Integration: A Comparative Study of Black and White Reactions to Multiracial Beaches in Durban*. Durban: Centre for Applied Social Sciences, University of Natal.
Moraes Silva, G., Souza Leão, L. and Grillo, B. (2019) Seeing whites: Views of black Brazilians in Rio de Janeiro. *Ethnic and Racial Studies* 43 (4), 632–651. doi:10.1080/01419870.2019.1585897
Moreton-Robinson, A. (2015) *The White Possessive: Property, Power and Indigenous Sovereignty*. Minneapolis, MN: University of Minnesota Press.
Nkosi, L. (2005 [1983]) *Mating Birds*. Cape Town: Kwela Books.
Ochs, E. (1990) Indexicality and socialization. In J.W. Stigler, R.A. Shweder and G. Herdt (eds) *Cultural Psychology* (pp. 287–308). Cambridge: Cambridge University Press.
Paton, A. (1958) *The Long View*. Minneapolis, MN: University of Michigan.
Penglase, B. (2007) Barbarians on the beach: Media narratives of violence in Rio de Janeiro, Brazil. *Crime, Media, Culture* 3, 305–325.
Phelps, K. (2018) South African law needs a zero tolerance approach to racist utterances. *The Conversation*, 3 October. See https://theconversation.com/south-african-law-needs-a-zero-tolerance-approach-to-racist-utterances-104078.

Platzky, L. and Walker, C. (1985) *The Surplus People: Forced Removals in South Africa.* Johannesburg: Ravan Press.

Posel, D. (2001) Race as common sense: Racial classification in twentieth century South Africa. *African Studies Review* 44, 87–113.

Potgieter, E. (2019) *SA Reconciliation Barometer Survey: 2019 Report.* Cape Town: Institute for Justice and Reconciliation. See https://www.ijr.org.za/south-african-reconciliation-barometer-survey-2019.

Preston-Whyte, R. (2004) The beach as a liminal space. In A.A. Lew, C.M. Hall and A.M. Williams (eds) *A Companion to Tourism* (pp. 349–359). Oxford: Blackwell.

Prochazka, K. and Kruger, L.M. (2001) Trends in beach utilisation on the Cape Peninsula, South Africa, during and after apartheid. *Transactions of the Royal Society of South Africa* 56, 25–40.

Rahier, J.M. (2003) Introduction: Mestizaje, mulataje, mestiçagem in Latin American ideologies of national identities. *Journal of Latin American Anthropology* 8, 40–50.

Ratele, K. (2004) Kinky politics. In S. Andred (ed.) *Re-thinking Sexualities in Africa* (pp. 139–157). Uppsala: Nordic Africa Institute.

Rogerson, J.M. (2017) 'Kicking sand in the face of Apartheid': Segregated beaches in South Africa. *Bulletin of Geography: Socio-Economic Series* 35, 93–110.

Roth-Gordon, J. (2016) *Race and the Brazilian Body: Blackness, Whiteness, and Everyday Language in Rio de Janeiro.* Oakland, CA: University of California Press.

Rule, S.P. (1994) A second-phase diaspora: South African migration to Australia. *Geoforum* 25, 33–39.

Said, E.W. (1993) *Culture and Imperialism.* New York: Knopf.

Salkey, A. (1975) 'Rays of Hope'. *Sechaba* 9, 15.

Sartre, J.-P. (2011 [1956]) Colonialism is a system. *Interventions* 3, 127–140.

Sawers, B. (2011) The right to exclude from unimproved land. *Temple Law Review* 83, 665–696.

Steel, F. (2015) The 'missing link': Space, race, and transoceanic ties in the settler-colonial Pacific. *Transfers* 5, 49–67.

Stewart, K. (2011) Atmospheric attunements. *Environment and Planning D: Society and Space* 29, 445–453.

Taussig, M. (1991) *The Nervous System.* New York: Routledge.

Van den Berghe, P.L. (1960) Miscegenation in South Africa. *Cahiers des Études Africaines* 1, 68–84.

Van Onselen, C. (2019) *The Night Trains.* Johannesburg/Cape Town: Jonathan Ball.

Wheaton, B., Waiti, J., Cosgriff, M. and Burrows, L. (2019) Coastal blue space and wellbeing research: Looking beyond western tides. *Leisure Studies* 39 (1), 83–95. doi:10.1080/02614367.2019.1640774

Wirtz, K. (2017) Mobilizations of race, place, and history in Santiago de Cuba's Carnivalesque. *American Anthropologist* 119 (1), 58–72.

Wolfe, P. (2006) Settler colonialism and the elimination of the native. *Journal of Genocide Research* 8, 387–409.

Zaretsky, R. (2015) Insolence, exile, and the kingdom. *Los Angeles Review of Books*, 9 June. See https://lareviewofbooks.org/article/insolence-exile-and-the-kingdom/.

9 Language and Humanitarian Governmentality in a Refugee Camp on Lesvos Island

Birgul Yilmaz

Introduction

Separated from Turkey by a 10-kilometre channel, Lesvos island received 45% of the refugees who arrived in Europe in 2015. An agreement called the EU-Turkey Statement signed in March 2016 led to the containment of refugees in hotspots, camps and shelters. Through this statement, the so-called Balkan route has been closed and the refugees, including children and young people, have been immobilised in refugee camps. Drawing on a eight month ethnography on Lesvos island, this chapter investigates how language teaching and learning become part of the immobilisation of the refugees in a camp that I call Eastside camp (all names used here are pseudonyms from here onwards) and the tensions that emerge when refugees are 'stuck' in the asylum procedures. To do this, I problematise the logics of humanitarian governmentality namely how the deployment of moral sentiments such as 'compassion', normalises children's exclusion from public schools and push them towards non-formal education provided in the camps. In my analysis, I question the ambivalent techniques based on 'compassion', namely feelings for the suffering and misfortunes of others (Fassin, 2012), in 'conducting' the refugees' conducts, i.e. the rationalisations and prescriptions of rules, and I introduce Foucault's (2007) notion of 'counter-conduct' (see also Uria, 2012), that is, complex layers of refusals, questioning and struggles that emerge as a reaction to the ways in which refugees are governed in a humanitarian setting. By using Fassin's work on humanitarianism and Foucault's notion of counter-conduct as my analytical tools in analysing how refugees are managed, I demonstrate how the logics of humanitarian governmentality obscured in discourses of suffering and misfortune entail legal, spatial and social immobility. In order to do this, I move away from the power/resistance dichotomy (Urla & Helepololei 2014) that underlies much of the sociolinguistics literature and instead focus on how subjects 'struggle' diagonally, namely the ways in which they move away from direct confrontations to create new forms of conducting themselves 'otherwise', which become evident in the struggle around language teaching and learning. By focusing on the entanglements occurring in language education, I demonstrate the contradictions of this type of governmentality (Tazzioli, 2020), which is underpinned by immobility, political economic, biopolitical and security choices and which, in return, denies refugee children's legally enshrined right to education.

In what follows, I first give an overview of the refugee context on Lesvos island and briefly explain the relationship between humanitarian governmentality and the immobilisation of refugees on the island. Second, I provide an overview of contradictory discourses, namely the compassion towards refugees' suffering on the one hand and normalising refugee children's exclusion from public schooling on the other. In my analysis, I present a report published by the Ministry of Education and Religious Affairs in Greece (MERA, 2017) as well as providing snapshots from my overall fieldwork including field notes (9 sets), visual materials including photos (168 photos), vignettes, audio-recordings collected via interviews (5 hours), semi structured interviews (10 participants) and my reflections to account for three key findings that emerge from the practices of the humanitarian actors. More specifically I explain: (a) how humanitarian governmentality normalises the exclusion of the refugee children from public schooling; (b) how it conducts refugees' conducts, that is, how the 'rules' of living in a camp are set out; and (c) the counter-conducts and entanglements that emerge within the constraints of living in a refugee camp.

'Refugee education' on Lesvos island

War and instability in the Middle East, especially in Syria, have brought 821,008[1] refugees to Greece since 2015. About a quarter of this figure comprises children, with or without guardians. An agreement signed between the EU and Turkey in March 2016 restricted the arrivals of refugees in Europe and entailed stricter border controls, leading to the containment of thousands of refugees, including children and young adults, on the Greek island of Lesvos in an infamous hotspot called Moria. Referring to Moria as the 'the prison' or 'the hell', the refugees have continued to experience horrendous living conditions, including threats of violence, sexual violence, fires, and lack of water and toilets. While some refugee children self-harm and attempt suicide (MSF, 2018), six refugees in Moria died at the time of this research. Moria functions as a 'hotspot' technology (Pascucci & Patchett, 2018), in other words as a detention centre where biometric information and procedures including identification, registration and fingerprinting of asylum seekers and migrants arriving in the EU by sea (EPRS, 2018) are taken. Those who qualify as 'vulnerable families' are then sent to the Eastside camp where this ethnography took place. I will use the term 'refugee' to denote those who seek international protection and assistance (Geneva Convention, 1951),[2] waiting to be registered and identified (see Dublin III Regulation),[3] and who have/have not applied for asylum. In fact it is reported that only 5% of refugees out of 800,000 have applied for asylum since 2015 (Carlson et al., 2018: 671) in Greece. Many refugees stay informally and are forced to continue their journeys to Western Europe via smugglers rather than legal routes. On Lesvos island, refugees cannot leave the island unless authorities such as the United Nations High Commissioner for Refugees (UNHCR) or the Greek authorities decide to relocate them, and this is reinforced with temporary identification cards that restrict geographical mobility within Greece. Living under such uncertain conditions means experiencing a tremendous amount of waiting (Khosravi, 2017), confusion, lack of information and immobilisation, while being diligently sorted and categorised as children, adults, family, vulnerable and sick, and being partially 'tamed' (Pascucci et al., 2018) by supranational organisations such as the European Asylum Support Office (EASO), an agency of the European Union, and other governmental and non-governmental organisations.

As the EU-Turkey statement had an impact on the mobility of refugees, the Ministry of Education in Greece needed to find a formula to address the question of refugee education and integration, especially for those who fall into the category of children (and/or minors aged below 16) requiring compulsory education in public schools. Greece agreed to create special education structures in the reception centres, and to develop bridging programmes in order for refugee children to access public schooling (Simopoulos & Alexandridis, 2019: 27).

When addressing the issue of refugee education in Greece, a report written by the Ministry of Education Research and Religious Affairs (MERA, 2017) highlighted the importance of language learning in refugee settings. In the report, the Ministry addresses mobility, fluidity and the 'refugees' ignorance of the Greek language' (MERA, 2017: 36). The report added that the Greek language was of little use for the refugee population as they did not plan to stay in Greece and, while their lives were on hold or in transit, English and German lessons provided by the non-governmental organisations (NGOs) attracted them more than Greek language classes (MERA, 2017). These conflicting statements about which languages refugees learn or wish not to learn were the result of the unexpected immobility and possible mobility or relocation to mainland Greece or other EU countries that the ministry had to consider. Refugees aspired to continue their journeys, mainly to Germany, but as their stay on Lesvos island continued for an undetermined period of time, learning the Greek language became necessary according to the Ministry of Education – despite the fact that asylum procedures and public health concerns as well as negative reactions from the local population hindered refugee children's access to public schools.

The report also highlighted that 'the more relaxed pedagogical methods of the Greek school' did not meet the expectations of the refugees because they had 'experience of educational systems that are governed by traditional and authoritarian pedagogical logic' (MERA, 2017: 58). On reading the report, two assumptions become clear: that the refugees need 'special' education because it is assumed that they have been out of school and need preparatory classes; and that the educational backgrounds of refugees are regarded as authoritarian whereas the Greek education system is seen as relaxed. These assumptions appear to establish a compassionate, but also a patronising, outlook on the refugee population and the knowledge they bring, while their reluctance, and refusal, to learn the Greek language is associated not only with their mobility but, more importantly, with their 'ignorance'. Following Foucault's (2007) notion of 'conduct', namely rationalisations and prescriptions of rules and rituals, and 'counter-conduct', that is, the 'struggle against the processes implemented for conducting others' involving 'border elements' where the individuals are neither inside nor outside the pastoral care (Foucault, 2007: 268, 282), which he developed in his lecture series, Security, Territory, Population, given at the Collège de France in 1977–1978, I will explain how frictions and struggles emerge as a result of how the exclusion of refugee children is justified or, rather, demystified.

When conceptualising the notion of counter-conduct, Foucault asks: 'How can we designate the type of revolts, or rather the sort of specific web of resistance to forms of power that do not exercise sovereignty and do not exploit, but "conduct"?' (Foucault, 2007: 200). The difference between counter-conduct and resistance, revolt and insubordination is that it 'turns one's attention to the difficult and complex layers of mutual implication, contradiction and ambiguity that emerge (even) in radical spaces' (Rossdale & Stierl, 2016: 163). Some examples of counter-conduct are 'refusing to be a soldier [...] refusal of civic education, of society's values, a refusal of a certain obligatory relationship to the nation [...]' (Foucault, 2007: 265). In the body of this chapter, counter-conducts involve refusal to learn the Greek language, which was imposed on the refugees due to their prolonged stay in the camps. For the refugees, learning the Greek language meant that they were going to be 'stuck' in Greece. Although the Ministry of Education and the other humanitarian actors involved in the education of the refugee children were aware that the refugees were in limbo, I argue that language teaching and learning became part of the management and immobilisation of the refugees, which in turn resulted in 'counter-conducts' as direct revolts were not possible in Eastside camp (but violent incidents often took place in Moria). The humanitarian actors' endeavour to 'normalise' the containment of refugees within the ambivalent discourses of 'normalisation' as taken up by the Greek Ministry of Education and other national and supranational actors such as the European Commission for Governance of Migrant Integration in Greece in turn led to tensions in language teaching and learning. Thus, I deal with the humanitarian actors' role in conducting refugees' conducts via specific procedures, techniques and activities including language education, and also give an account of how individuals question, confront, change and struggle to escape certain ways of being conducted (Rossdale & Stierl, 2016: 160). Focusing on the issue of language learning and teaching in the camp, I argue that the struggles of the asylum seekers are not vertical or horizontal as suggested by dichotomic views of power/resistance, but are rather diagonally or tangentially shaped. The latter enable individuals to find 'lines of flight', a 'nomadic creativity' (Deleuze & Guattari, 1987 [1980]), and discover other ways of escaping the normalisations in the cracks of the asylum process. I discuss both conducts and counter-conducts of humanitarian actors and refugees where there is blurriness between care, morality, political economy and immobility, ambivalently entangled in language learning and teaching.

Humanitarian Governmentality: Morality, Political Economy and Immobility

Humanitarian governmentality is a mode of governing 'precarious lives', that is, 'the lives of the unemployed and the asylum seekers, [...] of sick immigrants [...] of disaster victims and victims of conflict' (Fassin, 2012: 4), with moral sentiments such as compassion (Muehlebach, 2012) and care logics. Sociolinguistic literature on language and migration that focuses on governmentality (Del Percio, 2016; Martin Rojo & Del Percio, 2019) conceptualises language and communication as 'moralized forms of conduct' (Del Percio, 2016: 2). In the same vein, humanitarian work is 'morally driven, politically ambiguous, and deeply paradoxical' (Fassin, 2012: xii) and the term humanitarian is full of 'semantic sedimentation' (Fassin, 2012: 6). Its lexicon is misleading, as 'inequality is replaced by exclusion, domination is transformed into misfortune, injustice is articulated as suffering, and violence is expressed in terms of trauma' (Fassin, 2012: 6). What is more, humanitarian governmentality camouflages the business aspect of its ethos through compassion. It employs techniques of care imbued in compassion through moral sentiments obscuring the political economy involving philanthropists' investments and immobilities that it implements. While morality first appears to be at odds with capitalism, it is in fact an apparatus for the functioning of capitalist agenda, especially where voluntarism, solidarity, charity and work done out of love disguise the fact that states have withdrawn resources from the public services (Muehlebach, 2012). The morality of humanitarianism, however, involves fences, barbed wire, containers, precarity, uncertainty and the disciplining and education of individuals.

Humanitarianism necessitates immobilisation, as the latter is not only part and parcel of the logics of care or aid but it is also necessary for the securitisation of borders and control, especially on an island such as Lesvos which shares the Aegean sea with Turkey. For example, because the border in the sea between the island and Turkey is blurry, the Greek government has been discussing to place a 'floating'[4] sea border to push back the refugees. The interventions of humanitarian actors, from the securitisation of the borders to education, create 'an intimate relationship to the border but also to im/mobility' (Pallister-Wilkins, 2019: 372). The logics of humanitarian borderwork involve 'mobile care' for the suffering bodies in spaces of im/mobility (Pallister-Wilkins, 2019). This mobility is one of the principles of humanitarianism, in that 'independence' allows NGOs like MSF (Medicine San Frontier/Doctors Without Borders) to move aid workers and their resources from one place to another to provide care for those who are immobilised in places such as camps (Agier, 2011). The immobilisation apparatus that is put into practice in humanitarian settings involves sets of procedures such as detention during identification and registration, legal and spatial restrictions such as containing refugees in closed or semi-closed camps, and activities such as language teaching and recreational activities. In other words, this apparatus involves 'spatial, infrastructural and institutional moorings that configure and enable' (Hannam *et al.*, 2006: 3) or disable individuals in their inclusion in or exclusion from certain spaces and activities. This apparatus creates possibilities and impossibilities in terms of refugees' everyday physical and geographical motilities as well as in their conduct, including the rules and how they are expected to conduct themselves in asymmetrical contractual relationships with authorities, borders and legal procedures. What immobility does is that it excludes refugees from particular social, spatial, legal and discursive spaces by setting out rules or rationalisations.

In what follows, I explain how Eastside camp, where this ethnography took place, operated as a space of exclusion, where refugees' lives were separated from the locals through the reinforcement of rules, social relations and other everyday conducts such as receiving aid in the camp and other exclusionary practices that immobilised them in the camp.

Doing Fieldwork in a Container and Seeing Things

I arrived on Lesvos in October 2016 to work as a sociolinguist and field researcher as part of a large multi-sited, interdisciplinary project called project P.R.E.S.S. (Provision of Refugee Education and Support Scheme), funded by the Hellenic Open University. After a few days of training on how to do research in refugee camps, organised by the project coordinators in Athens, I landed on the island together with a colleague with whom I worked closely during the course of the project. As we drove from the airport, passing the port in the centre of the island, towards my hotel in a village called Thermi on the northeast side of the island, I saw a big grey FRONTEX (European Border and Coast Guard Agency) vessel with the EU and UK flags on it. I started taking strolls around the seafront side of the island in the coming days to familiarise myself with the place. I saw confiscated boats that had smuggled refugees from Turkey to Lesvos. I saw objects left behind such as children's lifejackets, hats, baby clothes, shoes, and black plastic dinghy pieces scattered on the shores of the island. Wondering who might have owned these objects, I could not stop thinking about the violence that I saw during my work for a BBC documentary called *Exodus: Our Journey to Europe*, where refugees filmed their journeys, including their crossing of the sea. As I gradually met people on the island, they told me, 'there were so many dead people here', 'some people died when they were only two meters away from the shore', 'the fish in the sea probably eat dead bodies, try not to eat fish', 'you should have seen the island in 2015'. Having heard these disturbing experiences from people, I felt quite lucky that I only saw the objects left behind instead of dead bodies. What is left now, however, is a lifejacket graveyard on the island.

The project allowed me to spend a year on the island as it aimed to identify and implement programmes addressing refugees' educational needs in Greece. I was to spend the year conducting a team ethnography together with two colleagues – Nadina Leivaditi, who had an MA in Social Anthropology, and Efstratia Kallintzi, who had an MA in Educational Approaches to Multilingualism. Although we conducted fieldwork in various places on the island such as a language and support school and a shelter for unaccompanied minors, the field site that I will concentrate on in this chapter is a refugee camp run by the local government which I will call Eastside camp. This camp hosted around 1000 refugees, as families selected in Moria qualified to stay there. The asylum seekers were mainly from Afghanistan, the Kurdistan Region of Iraq, Syria and other parts of South Asia, the Middle East and North Africa.

The camp management called the camp a 'village' and referred to the refugees as 'guests' in order to give them a sense of 'dignity'. In fact, the word *camp* is not used in the Greek language and often the term 'hospitality structure' is invoked under the concept of *philoxenia*, 'broadly meaning hospitality to foreigners and strangers more generally' (Cheliotis, 2013: 725). Hospitality, an invisible pact signed between the 'host and hostage' (Fassin, 2012: 136), however, always entails inequalities. The camp was surrounded by barbed wire. It was located on the periphery of the centre of the island, looking like an 'other' place covered with white isobox containers, separating the refugees from the city centre (and not far from a brothel) (see also De Fina & Mazzaferro, this volume, on this point). Although refugees were allowed to go to the centre of the island, many of them felt intimidated because some cafés and restaurants would not allow refugees to sit in their premises, as I was told by many asylum seekers. At the entrance to the camp there was a map showing all the organisations operating in it and the locations of the containers with numbers on them. The camp was divided into two sections: educational and residential areas. The educational area had several containers designated for educational activities run by NGOs, providing language lessons as part of their humanitarian missions as well as their aim to give a sense of 'normality' and 'psychosocial support' to the refugee children and adults. The residential area was separated from the educational area, and had containers in which refugees lived together with their families.

The architecture of the camp was panoptical. Nobody could see what the others were doing in their containers and only the managers knew what everyone did. The containers did not have kitchens or bathrooms, and bathrooms were shared. Although this place was called a 'village' by the management to give a more 'dignified' sense to the space, it did not resemble a village as it had military-like architecture such as barbed wire fencing, neat divisions between spaces and security at the door. In addition, members of NGOs were walking around with IDs and vests with their logos on them. In the containers where the families lived, there were bunk beds, grey blankets and plastic sheets on the floors with UNHCR's logo. Families in the camp received precooked food in a medico-military style at certain hours of the day. This military style also involved other semiotic elements such as the clothing chosen by the management. Both female and male managers often wore green military combat trousers, military belt buckles, commando sweaters with shoulder patches, aviator sunglasses and military boots, occasionally combined with more casual garments such as flamboyant scarves and make up.

The barbed wired 'village' had an entrance with multilingual security guards. Visitors had to sign a notebook or show their ID cards to go in and out. Alcohol and fires for cooking were prohibited. All conduct, including that involved in education, health, security and the researchers' work, was 'expertised'. When my colleagues and I negotiated our entrance to the camp, the management told us that we were the 'experts' and that we had to prepare an education programme in order to enter the camp. Although our access had already been granted by the project coordinators, we had to renegotiate it. So, after further discussions with the management, we were asked to teach geography lessons to children because it was stated that the refugees were 'disoriented' and that they did not know their whereabouts. We were asked to prepare an educational activity and email it to the managers, who were to decide whether we would be allowed to conduct our fieldwork in the camp or not. Although none of us was a geography expert, we were able to comply because Efstratia had experience in teaching geography to children. Our conversation with the management was rather unpleasant because we were reminded of the 'serenity in the village' as if we were potential 'trouble makers' who might disrupt the rules of the camp.

Ms Papa from the management team especially attracted my attention because of her attire: she wore military (cargo) combat trousers and a green military belt with a military buckle. She also wore postal/military boots and walked with great confidence when she showed the camp to me and my colleagues. Her chest was upright and her torso straight, just like a soldier. She was very firm and vigilant, informing the male manager about any decision to be taken. While we were walking with her, she said that in the West the first thing children do in the morning is to go to school and that the children in Eastside camp needed to get used to this through their educational activities.

Compassioning and Normalising the (Non-)education of Children

As I discussed earlier, humanitarian work involves logics of compassion and immobility that obscure categories such as legitimate/illegitimate, normal/pathological which result in the inclusion or exclusion of individuals in specific spaces such as public schools. Children's schooling and language education were seen as moral and legal obligations, as children below the age of 16 are obliged to go to school, and also their trajectories such as their experiences of war were acknowledged with compassion. While the actors tried to normalise the refugees' containment, their undermining of children's educational backgrounds was justified as follows:

> Refugee children are in a transition phase from a war situation to normality and, therefore, what they want from education is different. [...] They may have more knowledge compared to other children of their age in western societies, they know how to survive, how to overcome obstacles and how to get adjusted but they do not have the knowledge which is positively assessed in schools. (MERA, 2017: 65)

Although the 'normality' implied here is not 'normal', as living in containers surrounded by barbed wire is not 'normal', the quote implies that refugees' psychosocial circumstances of know(ing) (the knowledge about how to survive) is less valued than the kind of knowledge that is assessed in the Greek education system. What is clear, however, is that there is a politics of difference (Flubacher & Yeung, 2016), as illustrated by the exclusion of refugee children from public schools because of their non-Western backgrounds combined with a compassionate understanding of their experiences of war. The same argument goes for language education. UNESCO reports that 'language and literacy barriers are deemed to be one of the main obstacles preventing refugees from accessing and attending school, especially outside camp settings'.[5] Despite the fact that many children on the island should have been in school by law, protected by the Greek Constitution and by Article 13 L 4540/2018 that states 'asylum-seeking children have access to the education system under similar conditions as Greek nationals',[6] child refugees on Lesvos could not access schools (only 36 children attended public schools at the time of this research) due to negative public opinion around their vaccination status (Trubeta, 2018), which 'turned children into dangerous bodies legitimising their exclusion from their obligation to go to school' (correspondence with Alfonso Del Percio). The discourse of disease legitimises conceptualisations of (the lack of) vaccination as an 'existential threat' (Milani, 2020), estranging, manipulating and nesting this issue in asylum seekers' 'ignorance' (of the Greek language). Although it is highlighted in the report that 'the right to education is a fundamental human right which is respected, protected and promoted by the Greek state' (MERA 2017: 5), refugees are blamed for not learning the Greek language.

This suggests that the 'normalisation' efforts of actors such as the Ministry of Education and the humanitarian workers comprise specific conducts expected from the refugees, that is, to attend the lessons provided in the camp and to behave in a way that is anticipated or assumed by those who have the authority to set the rules. However, these contradicting anticipations and the unrecognition of refugees' linguistic resources led refugee children to 'struggle' for their language learning choices and for possible or aspired geographical mobility, for employment or simply as a reaction to how their level of education was defined by the actors.

These struggles and entanglements, as I will demonstrate, were related to how humanitarian actors envisioned managing refugees' immobilities (legal and spatial), the issue of language teaching and learning related to these immobilities, and possible future mobility anticipated by the refugees.

Conducting Refugees' Conducts

The UNHCR and also local NGOs struggled to teach Greek to the refugees. Learning the Greek language was part of conducting the refugees while they stayed in Eastside camp. Although English lessons were also provided, entanglements occurred between the demands of the refugees and humanitarian actors in relation to language learning. Despite many refugees' final destination of re/settlement not being an officially English speaking country, they still wanted to learn English as it was associated with future mobility and flexibility as an international language and/or the lingua franca of the humanitarian settings in Greece. In a meeting, Lito, a Senior Protection Assistant from the UNHCR, working closely with the Ministry of Education on the island, emphasised that most refugees were 'reluctant to learn Greek as they planned to go to other EU countries, especially Germany'. Lito noted that the UNHCR had run educational sessions in Eastside camp and had tried to 'raise awareness' of provision in camps by 'convince[ing] the refugees to learn Greek since they lived in Greece for now'. Interestingly, Lito used compassionate language such as 'raising awareness' to coerce the refugees by 'convincing' them to learn the Greek language, as there were no prospects of their leaving the country any time soon.

Often, English lessons are offered to refugees by the national and international NGOs,[7] UNICEF or partners of the UNHCR. The provision of lessons depends on whether an NGO is an international or a local one. Many local NGOs that operate in the camps prioritise Greek lessons as their funds depend on the provision of particular language teaching.

For the refugees, English has a valued status (Moyer, 2018), as highlighted during the fieldwork, in that it increases their chances of communicating with humanitarian actors, staff, fellow refugees and locals. The role of English was associated with increased mobility and the Greek language was associated with immobility. Under such uncertain conditions about their relocation and future journeys, learning Greek meant that they were going to be 'stuck' in Greece. Decisions that refugees make in terms of their language choices are often in conflict with what humanitarian actors provide in relation to refugees' overall well-being and speculative future integration in the wider society. For example, most refugees who had a desire to go to Germany had positive attitudes towards English and also wanted to learn German. The Greek language was associated with staying in Greece, whereas German was associated with hope and represented a speculative investment (Tabiola & Lorente, 2017) for the future. In recent correspondence with a member of staff from UNICEF, I asked why requests about German classes were declined. 'It is part of child protection', he stated. So, the denial of asylum seekers' demands for learning German is rationalised as child protection and a code of conduct in order to prevent false expectations and disappointment. But asylum-seeking children are not convinced and they find their own creative ways of escaping Greek language learning.

What are the specific practices of NGOs in terms of language education? What exactly do they do when they teach English in the containers of the camps? Our request to observe NGOs' language lessons was declined, but because we shared the same container with the NGOs who provided education in the camp, artefacts such as the following image hanging on the plastic walls of the container are noteworthy in terms of how language teaching and learning meant that specific conducts were expected from the refugees attending their lessons.

English was not only valued by the asylum seekers: its domination was visible in the linguistic landscape of the camp. The small kiosks at the entrance had predominantly English signage with Persian, Arabic and Greek translations. In the container, the juxtaposition of two images on the same wall (see Figure 9.1) shows how language teaching and the general conduct expected from the refugees coexisted. Note how the first image demonstrates the role of the teacher as an active agent who does the teaching and the role of the student as the receiver of this teaching. However, the ultimate goal does not seem to be only teaching sets of rules about English grammar but teaching sets of rules in terms of individuals' conduct during the lessons. The expected conduct enforces punctuality, bringing the required tools, listening and asking questions in an orderly

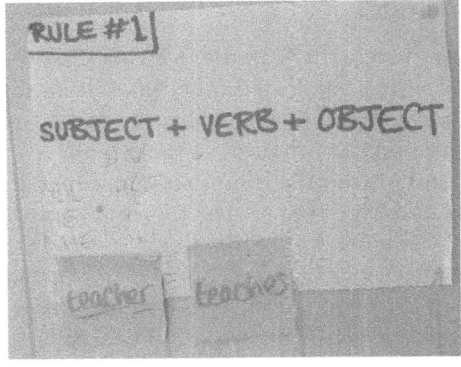 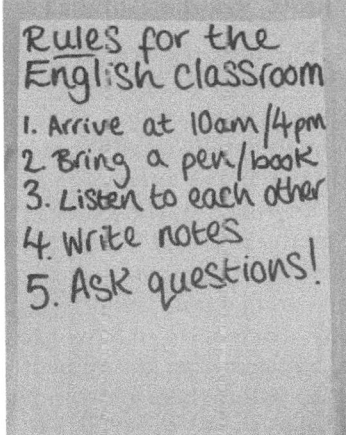

Figure 9.1 Container in Eastside camp
©Birgul Yilmaz ©Project P.R.E.S.S.

fashion, as demonstrated in the second image. The juxtaposition of these two images on the same wall shows how language teaching and general conduct expected from the refugees coexist at the same time.

To extrapolate these rules to general conduct in the camp, I give an example from one of the meetings I attended there. These meetings took place in the amphitheatre of the camp every two weeks and they were occasions for the manager to give a talk and discuss issues in the camp. The manager greeted us with 'hello family' and continued, 'maybe you are specialist, expert but you must remember you're in a family'. This 'pastoral metaphor' (Foucault, 2007) which applied to the relationships in the camp resonated in the manager's theatrical speeches when everyone gathered for regular meetings. The manager continued: 'Eastside camp is different from all the other camps [usually referring to Moria]. We respect all NGOs but we have a different mentality. It is we, not me. It is we, not me. Welcome home. Follow the official way. Follow the law if you want to take the children to museum and etc. Make my day I want to make my day. Continue. Shoes, hats, gloves etc. [pointing at a child who had no shoes on]'. Now, as Foucault (2007: 131) argues, the art of governing involves 'a household, souls, children, a province, a convent, a religious order, and a family'. However, these expectations about the conducts of humanitarian workers and refugees, as well as the researchers, identified as 'family' led to tensions, entanglements and, more importantly, struggles on the ground.

'Counter-conduct' and Entanglements

The notion of counter-conduct I presented earlier in this chapter entails struggle or the possibility of 'being conducted otherwise'. In other words, while 'conduct' is about normalising power, counter-conduct is about destabilising power, authority and the conducts of the others.

On the way to Eastside camp and also to the infamous Moria camp, an ex-military base used as a camp and detention centre, there was a wall of graffiti that said 'Fuck your rules' (Figure 9.2). Although it is not clear whether refugees, volunteers or solidarity groups had put this graffiti on the road that goes from the centre of the island to the two refugee camps, these words seem to have a relationship to all the rules that everyone in the humanitarian government has to follow. Refugees as well as humanitarian aid workers and solidarity groups working with them were subjected to sets of rules, from their sexual activities to the distribution and consumption of food. For example, aid workers were encouraged to wear clothes that were not sexually revealing. In this respect, Figure 9.2 is counter-conduct par excellence, where we see how the rules of humanitarian governance are challenged and destabilised.

To give a second example, the following episode happened when my colleagues and I attended a Christmas celebration for children in the camp. We were asked by Ida, who worked there, to help with the activities and we agreed to watch the kids while they participated in the activities in the playground. We met Bejya, a young girl from Hewler, in the

Figure 9.2 On the way to Moria 'the prison' and Eastside camp
©Birgul Yilmaz ©Project P.R.E.S.S.

Kurdistan Region of Iraq. She was 16 years old and attended some of the lessons in the camp. She was with her little brother and was taking care of him. Many young girls were responsibilised for this type of care, looking after younger siblings, helping their mothers with cooking and cleaning. Bejya attended the lessons in the camp and helped the family with their asylum papers using the English she learnt. Later, Bejya's father and eight-year-old Rajo joined the conversation. Rajo was happy to speak to me in English. He said 'If you just go to school you don't learn a language. I went to school for seven years and didn't learn English. But here I speak with people in English. I learn outside. I like English because I can talk to people from everywhere'. Many young people were interested in English and they learned in the playground or playing football or other sports. It was very interesting that an eight-year old had awareness of how he learned English better outside of the classroom, while his sister learned in the container. Rajo implied that he learnt better than his sister by trying to show me how good his English was. Although the NGOs made efforts for every child to attend the lessons provided in the camp, this did not always happen. Rajo narrative demonstrates how he created a possibility of learning English otherwise and by refusing the lessons provided in the containers.

Similarly, at the gates of the camp, I met Avan (aged 16) from the Kurdistan Region of Iraq. He lived with 13 or 14 members of his family and had not been to school since they left Iraq. He did not attend the lessons because he found learning English in conversation was more practical for him as he needed to work. Hanging out at the entrance to the camp gates, where the camp security and various NGOs were having lunch or coffee, Avan learned English and a bit of Greek and Farsi and improved his Arabic. This enabled him to begin to interpret for the Red Cross and other NGOs, translating from Arabic to English. In my encounters in the camp and in general on the island, many refugees told me that they wanted to learn English and work as interpreters. Most of them were either young people or educated people and were multilingual. Undoubtedly, most refugees on the move want to learn English, partly to invest in their futures and find jobs but also because English is important in terms of survival while navigating in uncertainty. Although the learning and teaching of languages in this specific context can be understood from the humanitarian logic of compassion for the suffering of the unfortunate, the economic consequences and ambivalence they create is noteworthy. While as indicated in the Ministry's report, the refugees need to be 'integrated' step by step, the refugees had their own reasons as to why they did not want to attend the Greek lessons, hence rationalising their choices and refusals.

A ten-year-old refugee boy, Menan, who came to our geography sessions regularly, said: 'This teacher don't know. She doesn't know *tableau* in French [whiteboard]. Look no good teacher. They play [referring to children]. Maths easy. English easy. This people don't know. Look this class no good. Just play'. A lot of the NGOs' teaching activities involved psychosocial components such as playing. Sometimes, in what were called 'safe spaces' designated for children's activities, I had the opportunity a glimpse of how children were gathered together singing or playing games prior to or during the lessons. This learning through playing did not work for Menan, who spoke French, Arabic and English. He expected the lessons to be more advanced and he found them too easy and not up to his level, challenging the assumption that refugees are assumed to have no education or a lack of literacy skills. His narrative comes as a counter-conduct, challenging what is offered in the camp.

While this observation may have relevance to some, as their education may have been interrupted by war and conflict, there are also refugees who are very well educated and do not receive education that meets their expectations. Afsoon, the mother of two Afghan girls who came to our geography sessions, was a dentist in Kabul where her husband was assassinated (she reported). She complained that all that the children learnt in the camp was A, B, C, while tears dropped from her eyes. Afsoon complained that there was no colour in their container as everything was either white or grey. Paradoxically, despite the general humanitarian discourse indicated in a UNESCO report highlighting the 'lack of the language skills required in host settings' and 'high degree of geographical mobility [...] expos(ure) to a multitude of languages in and outside of education settings' as obstacles to asylum seekers' schooling, Afsoon's narrative demonstrates that the education provided in the camp was not satisfactory and as a result she saw no point in sending her children to the lessons despite the uncertainty about their future mobility.

These stories show that asylum seekers immobilised in the Eastside camp find different ways and spaces for learning the English language and struggle to be conducted otherwise. Although the efforts demonstrated in these episodes are partly speculative investments (Tabiola & Lorente, 2017) for future mobility, they are also part of refugees' counter-conducts in escaping from container teaching and the Greek language that they associate with immobility.

Conclusion

By exploring Foucault's notions of conduct and counter-conduct in a humanitarian context, I showed how refugee children and their families are being conducted by various actors in a refugee camp on Lesvos island. Focusing on these two conceptualisations, I have illustrated the techniques of humanitarian governmentality, that is, the role of compassion and immobilisation in normalising refugee children's exclusion from public schooling. I showed the entanglements emerging in the context of conducting the asylum seekers by concentrating on their counter-conducts, which do not manifest as total revolts, disobedience or resistance but as questioning, justifications and problematisations. As total escape from a camp is not possible, I have tried to show how individuals partially escape from the conducts of the humanitarian governance 'being conducted'. In this sense, if governmentality is governing souls, households and family, counter-conduct is destabilising, delocalising, deterritorialising this type of logic by creating an affect of entanglement which manifests as questioning, refusal or diagonal escapes from the specificities of humanitarian conducts. One of the effects of these entanglements is how language learning and teaching give birth to counter-narratives, counter-realities and otherwise becomings (Rossdale & Stierl, 2016). Counter-conduct should be understood as explained by Foucault: 'the will not to be governed is always the will not to be governed thusly, like that, by these people, at this price' (Foucault, 1997: 72).

More specifically, through the report of the Ministry of Education, I tried to show how mobility and immobility are at the heart of the 'problem' of teaching English, German and Greek. While English was preferred by the refugees in terms of their aspired mobility, German was associated with their resettlement in Germany which humanitarian actors identified as a 'false expectation' and a problem in terms of child protection. The Greek language, on the other hand, was acknowledged as a non-desirable language as it was associated with being stuck in Greece and hence further immobility.

Through vignettes, visual material and my reflections, I have sought to show how the notions of conduct and counter-conduct as analytical tools could help us to understand the logics of humanitarian governmentality that is imbued in an im/mobility apparatus. This apparatus demystifies refugees' legally enshrined rights to education.

Acknowledgements

I wish to thank my mentor Alfonso Del Percio for his feedback and thoughtful suggestions on an earlier version of this chapter. I would like to thank Betty Merchant at the University of Texas at San Antonio who listened to me patiently right after this fieldwork was completed. I also would like to thank Anna De Fina and Gerardo Mazzaferro who commented on an earlier version of this chapter. Many thanks to all the children in this study, without whom I would not have been able to complete such a difficult task. Special thanks to the two reviewers whose feedback contributed to this chapter immensely. Finally, many thanks to Emma Brooks and Cat Tebaldi who proofread this chapter. Many thanks to Michiel Leezenberg.

Funding

This paper is funded by the British Academy Postdoctoral Fellowship and Research Grant PF2\180052. The ethnographic material was produced in the framework of Project P.R.E.S.S. (Provision of Refugee Education and Support Scheme) funded by the Hellenic Open University in Greece.

Notes

(1) IOM, UN Migration. See https://www.iom.int/news/irregular-migrant-refugee-arrivals-europe-top-one-million-2015-iom.
(2) Geneva Convention, 1951. See https://www.unhcr.org/4ca34be29.pdf.
(3) Hellenic Republic, Ministry of Migration and Asylum. See http://asylo.gov.gr/en/?page_id=81.
(4) The New York Times. See https://www.nytimes.com/2020/02/01/world/europe/greece-migrants-floating-barrier.html.
(5) UNESDOC Digital Library 2018. See https://unesdoc.unesco.org/ark:/48223/pf0000261278.
(6) AIDA (Asylum Information Database). Access to Education: Greece https://www.asylumineurope.org/reports/country/greece/reception-conditions/employment-and-education/access-education.
(7) Activities of international NGOs were terminated towards the end of fieldwork in July 2017 as the Greek government took over the management of the refugees which implied more jobs for the Greek nationals who often did not have any experience of working with refugees. There were also disputes between the local government, police, including counter-terrorism services about some of the activities of the NGOs. European Parliament (30 May 2018). See https://www.europarl.europa.eu/doceo/document/E-8-2018-002966_EN.html.

References

Agier, M. (2011) *Managing the Undesirables*. London: Polity Press.
Carlson, M., Jakli, L. and Linos, K. (2018) Rumors and refugees: How government-created information vacuums undermine effective crisis management. *International Studies Quarterly* 62 (3), 671–685.
Cheliotis, L. (2013) Behind the veil of philoxenia. *European Journal of Criminology* 10 (6), 725–745.

Deleuze, G. and Guattari, F. (1987 [1980]) *A Thousand Plateaus* (B. Massumi, trans.). Minneapolis, MN: University of Minnesota Press.

Del Percio, A. (2016) The governmentality of migration. *Language & Communication* 51, 87–98.

European Commission (2020) *Governance of Migrant Integration in Greece: Migrant Integration Information and good practices.* See https://ec.europa.eu/migrant-integration/governance/greece.

EPRS (2018) Hotspot at EU external borders: State of play. Briefing. European Parliamentary Research Service. See https://www.europarl.europa.eu/RegData/etudes/BRIE/2018/623563/EPRS_BRI(2018)623563_EN.pdf.

Fassin, D. (2012) *Humanitarian Reason* (R. Gomme, trans.). Berkeley, CA: University of California Press.

Flubacher, M. and Yeung, S. (2016) Discourses of integration. *Multilingua* 35 (6), 599–616.

Foucault, M. (1997) What is critique? In S. Lotringer and L. Hochroch (eds) *The Politics of Truth: Michel Foucault* (pp. 23–82). New York: Semiotext(e).

Foucault, M. (2007) *Security, Territory, Population – Lectures at the Collège de France, 1977–78* (G. Burchell, trans.). New York: Palgrave MacMillan.

Hannam, K., Sheller, M. and Urry, J. (2006) Editorial: Mobilities, immobilities and moorings. *Mobilities* 1 (1), 1–22.

Khosravi, S. (2017) *Precarious Lives.* Philadelphia, PA: University of Pennsylvania Press.

Martín Rojo, L. and Del Percio, A. (eds) (2019) *Language and Neoliberal Governmentality.* London: Routledge.

MERA (2017) *Scientific Committee in Support of Refugee Children: Refugee Education Project.* Athens: Ministry of Education Research and Religious Affairs.

Milani, T. (2020) No-go zones in Sweden: The infectious communicability of evil. *Language, Culture and Society* 2 (1), 7–36.

Moyer, M. (2018) Language, mobility and work. *Language and Intercultural Communication* 18 (4), 357–361.

Médecins Sans Frontières (MSF). (2018). Self-harm and attempted suicides increasing for child refugees in Lesbos. Retrieved March 11 2021, from https://www.msf.org/child-refugees-lesbos-are-increasingly-self-harming-andattempting-suicide

Muehlebach, A. (2012) *The Moral Neoliberal.* Chicago, IL: University of Chicago Press.

Pallister-Wilkins, P. (2019) Im/mobility and humanitarian triage. In K. Mitchell, R. Jones and J.L. Fluri (eds) *Handbook on Critical Geographies of Migration* (pp. 372–383). Cheltenham: Edward Elgar.

Pascucci, E. and Patchett, E.J. (2018) Hotspots. *Journal of Contemporary European Research* 14 (4).

Pascucci, E., Häkli, J. and Kallio, K.P. (2018) Delay and neglect. In A. Paasi, E.-K. Prokkola, J. Saarinen and K. Zimmerbauer (eds) *Borderless Worlds for Whom?* (pp. 93–107). London: Routledge.

Rossdale, C. and Stierl, M. (2016) Everything is dangerous: Conduct and counter-conduct in the occupy movement. *Global Society* 30 (2), 157–178.

Simopoulos, G. and Alexandridis, A. (2019) Refugee education in Greece. *Forced Migration Review* 60, 27–29.

Tabiola, H. and Lorente, B. (2017) Neoliberalism in ELT aid: Interrogating a USAID ELT project in southern Philippines. In M-C. Flubacher and A. Del Percio (eds) *Language, Education and Neoliberalism: Critical Studies in Sociolinguistics* (pp. 122–139). Bristol: Multilingual Matters.

Tazzioli, M. (2020) Governing migrant mobility through mobility. *Environment and Planning C: Politics and Space* 38 (1), 3–19.
Trubeta, S. (2018) Vaccination and the refugee camp: Exercising the free choice of vaccination from an abject position in Germany and Greece. *Journal of Ethnic and Migration Studies* 46 (15), 3370–3387. doi:10.1080/1369183X.2018.1501269
Urla, J. (2012) *Reclaiming Basque: Language, Nation, and Cultural Activism*. Reno: University of Nevada Press.
Urla, J. and Helepololei, J. (2014) The ethnography of resistance then and now. *History and Anthropology* 25, 431–451.

Part 4
(Im)mobilities, Subjectivity, Identity and Agency

10 Estrangement and Home in Queer Asylum Stories

Mike Baynham, Bahiru Shewaye and Gomes O. Kayode

لاانت انت
و لا الديار ديار
[أبو تمام]

> You are not you
> and home is not home
> [Abu Tammam]

لاينظرون وراءهم ليودعوا منفى
فان أمامهم منفى
[محمود درويش]

> They don't look behind them to say goodbye to exile
> as they are facing exile
> [Mahmoud Darwish]

Introduction

Linguistic studies of oral narrative emerged in the late 1960s and early 1970s with the foundational work of Labov. The narratives studied, like the urban sociolinguistics of that period (Baynham, 2012), were firmly located in a time/place, in the neighbourhood/barrio. The shift in sociolinguistics away from spatially located community towards a sociolinguistics of mobility/globalisation (Blommaert, 2010) was mirrored by a corresponding turn in narrative studies (Baynham & De Fina, 2005) towards the narratives of mobile subjects and spatial dislocation/relocation with a growing literature on migration narratives, including queer migration narratives (Cantú, 2009; Carrillo, 2017; Gray & Baynham, 2020). It has been argued (Baynham, 2017; Mai & King, 2009) that migration narratives, along with migration studies more generally, have underestimated the push/pull of affect and desire in migration processes in general (cf. also Koven, 2019, on this matter). This is particularly highlighted in queer migration narratives. In this chapter we examine stories told in a small corpus of interviews with those who have successfully gained asylum because of persecution based on their sexuality.

Juffermans (2018) shows how the backstory of migration is important in making sense of migration trajectories. Nowhere is this more evident than in the case of those whose sexuality drives the decision to migrate/seek asylum. Many of those interviewed spoke of a growing sense of estrangement and displacement, often from a very young age, as they realised that their emotional and sexual responses, even before they could name them, did not match those around them. They were already out of place. As they grew up, this inchoate feeling of being out of place became a form of immobilisation: they were unable to live their lives freely. They reported the experience of homophobic violence, verbal and physical, creating further estrangement and fear for personal safety: a radical sense of not being at home in their own home, leading eventually to the decision to seek asylum. These narratives unsettle unquestioned assumptions in narrative studies of nostalgic regret for the homeland and desire to return. Queer narratives, as Mole (2018) has pointed out, writing about Russian LGBTQ migrants in Berlin, problematise the meaning of home. The paradoxical relationship between these queer migration stories and the theme of im(mobility) lies in the fact that to stay requires a denial of themselves, embracing a chronotope of concealment, while to be free to live their lives openly requires leaving, embracing a chronotope of flight. In a further irony: having embraced flight, the asylum process in most cases cuts off the possibility of return, creating a further cycle of (im)mobility.

Stories of queer asylum trajectories involve issues of sexual orientation and identity and the risks associated with visibility and activism. These combine, leading to a situation where someone no longer feels safe and is driven to seek asylum. For a number of those we interviewed, their backstory started at a very early age, when they began to perceive themselves as responding differently from those around them, not yet having a name for what they were feeling. Ahmed from Somalia was early aware of same sex attraction:

> I knew it when I was 6 years old but I knew it that I like men. Because when I see marriage you know marriage in Africa I was dreaming one day I will get married like that but not a man. I will ask myself if you be a women you can get a man that can be married to you. After that I was asking always myself, why you are a man. You know when we was young the mom says after lunch we must sleep and my mom says you have to

sleep and I can't, I wanted to go outside but my mom she told me that I have to when I go to bed and when I want to sleep I always dream someday I will get married that I am woman.

In this chapter, using concepts from the work of Bakhtin, the narrative chronotope and ideological becoming, as well as the concept of performativity and activism derived from recent work by Judith Butler (2015) on the performativity of assembly, we present initial findings from a small-scale project designed to explore the drivers for (im)mobility in queer asylum stories.

Methodology

The research team consisted of myself (Mike), as well as Bahiru Shewaye (Bahi) [online nickname Beki] and Kayode Gomes, both queer activists. Based on conversations with Bahi, Kayode and others, I drafted an interview schedule for an open-ended ethnographic interview. Having circulated the draft for comments, I trialled it with Bahi and Kayode, interviewing them about their lives leading up to their decisions to seek asylum. This phase gave them experience in this type of interviewing. With Bahi and Kayode as insiders and Mike as an outsider to the asylum process, we were able to combine insider/outsider perspectives, leading me (Mike) on many occasions to revise crude and simplistic assumptions. For example, my initial interest focused simply on asylum on the basis of sexuality. As the research continued, it became clear that almost everyone interviewed had been involved in various forms of queer activism, so the intersection between sexuality and activism became part of the investigation. We continue to problematise this relationship in ongoing work.

Bahi and Kayode transcribed their own interviews, providing them with experience in transcribing interview data and offering the first data for the project. Bahi and Kayode then made contact with people in their networks who had been through the asylum process and who were prepared to be interviewed, and then conducted and transcribed the interviews, further contributing to our data set of nine interviews:

Name	Home country	Country of asylum
Abiola	Nigeria	The Netherlands
Ahmed	Somalia	Austria
Beki	Ethiopia	UK

(Continued)

Name	Home country	Country of asylum
Cuchi	Ethiopia	Austria
Gomes	Nigeria	The Netherlands
Jessica	Jamaica	The Netherlands
Judith	Nigeria	The Netherlands
Noel	Ethiopia	Austria
Shevon	Syria	The Netherlands

In this chapter we draw on the interviews with Abiola, Ahmed and Jessica, going into more detail about Beki's interview.

We then went through the interviews, identifying two themes for further investigation: (1) how participants became aware of their sexuality and how this awareness changed and developed as they grew up; and (2) how they became involved in different kinds of activism related to their sexuality. We separately went through the data, coding for these themes but also for others. For example, it became apparent that those who conformed to gender norms – boys who behaved and presented like 'boys', girls who behaved and presented like 'girls' – had an easier time than 'boyish' girls or 'girly' boys.

Our Analytic Approach

The interviews elicited rich and vivid narrative data, corresponding to the lifestory genre identified by Linde (1993). To do justice to this richness, we quote some relatively long extracts from the data. For Linde, the lifestory presents and evaluates the life trajectory of an individual and is open-ended and episodic in structure, often involving shifts in timespace. Our aim was to explore with our interviewees the circumstances leading up to their asylum claim. Asylum stories connect with the broader category of migration stories, involving radical shifts in timespace. In such narratives, Baynham (2003: 351) argued that 'orientation/disorientation/reorientation in space and time, far from being a simple contextual backdrop *is* the story'.

Understanding how the elements of the queer life trajectory identified here hang together and are recognisable suggests the relevance of the notion of the Bakhtinian chronotope, originally developed for literary narrative. As Bakhtin puts it:

> We will give the name chronotope (literally, 'time space') to the intrinsic connectedness of temporal and spatial relationships. (Bakhtin, 1981: 84)

As he makes clear in Bakhtin (1981: 84–85), for Bakhtin the notion of chronotope is closely connected with that of genre. He distinguishes simple 'primary' genres from complex 'secondary' genres, composed of simple primary genres. The oral life story is clearly a complex secondary genre. Similarly, the scope of the chronotope spans complex episodic secondary genres such as, in his case, travel novels, in our case lifestories. It can also be applied to smaller elements of such complex, open and episodically extensive stories, which he calls 'motifs', such as a meeting or a quarrel. Such motifs, according to Bakhtin, are also constituted in their distinctive timespace and are thus chronotopic. Although Bakhtin's focus was on literary texts, he clearly envisaged the extension of the chronotope to everyday interaction in the social world. This aspect, undeveloped in his work, was taken up by Agha (2007) and by others such as Blommaert and De Fina (2017), Divita (2019), Koven (2019) and Perrino (2015). As well as the emphasis on time/space, Agha emphasises a third dimension crucial to the Bakhtinian chronotope, that of personhood (Blommaert and De Fina emphasise identity in a similar way). Agha (2007: 322) also points out tellingly that 'the concept of chronotope is of vanishingly little interest when extracted from a frame of contrast'. So, what is the cross-chronotopic contrast in this study? Surely it lies in the gradually emergent difference between the chronotope of heteronormativity and queer selves, growing up against its grain, formulating and inhabiting as they grow with increasing awareness and explicitness a queer chronotope that will put them in conflict with dominant heteronormativity and in the end will drive them towards the chronotope of flight (towards mobility rather than immobility).

So, what is the chronotope of the queer asylum story? Perhaps the most striking aspect overall, as the title of this chapter suggests, is that from a very early age there is a sense of spatial dislocation, of estrangement in apparently familiar spaces, such as the home and the social life of the school. Madden (2013: 63) writes similarly of 'a range of chronotopes in which heteronormative space and time undergo queer revision'. Interviewees talked about experiences initially in the spaces of childhood and adolescence, typically home and school, each with their chronotopic distinctiveness. Even within the home there are chronotopically distinctive spaces: for Ahmed his bed during an enforced afternoon sleep as a young child is a timespace governed by both constraint (being put to bed by his mother) and the freedom to dream of being married to a man, imagining another life, as do the subjects in Dick (2010).

Within the narrative constraints and affordances of the chronotope, Bakhtin goes on to consider the ways in which these timespaces shape and enable the actions of protagonists and their development. Here another Bakhtinian notion, that of 'ideological becoming' or 'ideological development' (cf. also O'Connor 2018), becomes relevant:

> Our ideological development is just such an intense struggle within us for hegemony among various available verbal and ideological points of view, approaches, directions, values. (Bakhtin, 1981: 346)

Growing into the queer chronotope involves just such painful struggles.

The notion of ideological becoming also enables us to say something about the idea of activism which, as suggested above, became a central emphasis in our analysis. So how can we understand activism as a theoretical construct? We see activism as a range of ways, verbal and embodied, of speaking back to dominant normativities, here heteronormativity. So, specifically, queer activism is a performative speaking back to heteronormativity. In so doing we draw on Judith Butler's notion of performativity as articulated in Butler (2015). As Butler points out, in activism expressed, for example, through a large-scale demonstration: the body speaks. Activism can be organised through visible means, through NGOs for example, of the sort that Judith, Gomes and Shevon were involved in, or it can be a clandestine, underground organisation, of the sort created by Bahi and his friends in Addis. It can be a grassroots community organisation as in the case of Jessica. What all these activisms have in common is that they bring risk to the protagonists. Standing up against powerful interests, here standing up against heteronormativity, is a risky business. The consequences of making themselves visible, or being made visible by being outed, lead them to seek asylum. This is not just the case of those who are organised into groups. In some contexts, simply living your life openly is a form of speaking back to heteronormativity, and thus running the risk of harm. In the case of Ahmed and Abiola, finding a voice and telling their story is a form of activism, of speaking back to the powerful forces that have othered them, part of their ideological becoming.

Characteristic Phases in the Queer Asylum Story

There seemed to be a similarity between the stages reported and the consequent ideological becoming of those we interviewed. The earliest phase is an awareness of same sex attraction, without having a name for it, although perhaps with an inchoate sense that it might be better not to make too much of it. The next phase, in the early teens, is a coming to awareness of sexuality and difference, often through a painful othering from peers, the wider community or religious teaching. For a few of those we interviewed, school enabled them to find fulfilling love and friendship; for others it was an experience of exclusion and loneliness, leading in the later teens to a reaching out to find others like themselves. This conscious reaching out towards queer others and communities is often reported as online. In terms of ideological becoming, they start to take hold of their life, beginning to explore and express their queer sexuality and identity through developing a queer social and love life. Along with these explorations of queer sociality in different ways seemed to come various types of involvement in activism. Increasing visibility attracts persecution or censure from family, neighbours and the wider society as well as from police, clergy and other agents of the state – creating a tipping point and the decision to leave and seek asylum. The majority of those we interviewed followed this trajectory; however, Abiola didn't.

Abiola's story

Abiola found a partner at school, and successfully concealed their relationship from the eyes of others. However, her foster father found her diary, surprised her at home with her friend, and took it upon himself to 'correct' her sexual orientation by subjecting her to rape:

Abiola: I think he read my diary because everything I was doing from the beginning from 14, how I started everything, I was writing everything down on my diary so he read it. The day I invited my girlfriend to my house, that day, because normally he comes late from work, everyone, my foster mum, everyone comes home late from work, so my sisters, I took them to my mother in the market, so I could have my privacy at home with her, but I didn't know my foster dad was going to come early because he read my diary, he was monitoring me for a long time, so and that day, he caught us together which his expression was really really bad, so yeah, he was really angry, he didn't say it to my foster mum because he wanted to use the opportunity to abuse me, he was having sex with me, like I can not refuse him anytime he comes because he always like beat me when he does the shit, yeah so that was his reaction.

The chronotope of a time and a place for intimacy is cruelly interrupted, leading to sustained abuse in which the house becomes no longer safe. In chronotopic terms, Abiola lives the chronotope of the unsafe house, a place of abuse not protection.

In the next phase of her life she is on the streets in another Nigerian city, and then is trafficked to Germany before escaping to the Netherlands and claiming asylum:

Abiola: Yea, I actually left Nigeria for safety because of my sexuality, yea, how should I say this? Because I was living with my foster parents, so I got caught on my sexuality, so I flee the house ... not that I flee immediately, I was there been assaulted, been used because my foster dad was using me, having sex with me because he thinks that will bring my imagination back or that's gonna stop me from being who I am. So from then I was patient because I had to finish my secondary school, so after my secondary school, I went from Ketu to Ojuelgba where I stayed on the street for 2 years. ... So yeah, that's when I met the person who brought me to Germany, Mr Williams, so I got to Germany, though he didn't know about my sexuality, though he told me I will come here, he will help me to come here, maybe go to school or look for a job meanwhile I didn't know he was actually trafficking me here for prostitution, which I got to Germany I found that it was prostitution then I had no choice because I had no one in Germany and he told me if I should go to the police, I would be deported, so that scared me a lot that I didn't go to the police, that I had to work as a sex worker for a year and 4 months or 3 months yeah, he charged, I had to pay him €55,000 which I paid €40,000 already before I running away from Germany to Netherlands. ...

Abiola, sexually abused and trafficked, had no experience of activism, but by the end of the interview she recounts her sense of having a story, of being someone who has learnt that she is a survivor and she is strong:

Abiola: I want my story to inspire people if it can, I just hope it will [...] General, for me I love to talk to people about my situation, and when I talk to people about my situation, lot of people, the response I get, is like wow you are strong. How can you go through all this and you are still smiling like this? Because I talk to people about it that's why I can smile, if I keep everything to myself, it's gonna eat me up because I know I have gone through a lot even stuffs that I can't even say out.

Abiola, through sharing her ideological becoming, affirms the value of having a story, of having come through violence, abuse and suffering as a strong person. Simply speaking up, having a story to tell and telling it is a form of activism.

Jessica's story

Jessica, a Jamaican trans woman, kicked out of home in her teens, spent her formative years on the street. She does her growing up on the street and her activism emerges from the relationships she forges 'under the mango tree':

Jessica: So back at home in Jamaica *Colour Pink* group started under a mango tree and basically, it was just me, couple of friends, under mango tree and we talk and gossip about people and we got bored because we didn't have tv, so we gossip about everything and who did sex work and the condom break and who didn't… All of those stuffs. But what happened, what was really shocking was that, we were dying, so when the group got bigger because we started up with 3 then it becomes 4 and then I was like the little ring leader and people use to come to me. And then all though, because I started at 16, and now I reach like 17, so there was younger ones coming in, they become my child, so they start calling me Mummy because I had more experience and so we gossip and I had children and we gossip, and I had husband, technically, husband with children but (laughs) at 17 and then we gossip, but then we realized the group got bigger and then we realized that we were dying. People were dying because of sex work. Person were dying because of HIV, illnesses and not just HIV but opportunist infections. But and also during sex work, because a lot of the girls, they use to drag, they put on female clothes and they use to go out and men, when men found out that they were men, which they are transwomen but cot n cot, Jamaica will say men, they kill them and some use to come pretending to buy sex, and they didn't come to buy sex, they come to rob us money and kill if they can.

For Jessica, home is the street. Embodying the queer chronotope, she recreates a queer family – a kind of queer parallel to the straight family that rejected her. She makes a home and her queer life unfolds 'under the mango tree' with other homeless young people. Making a life for herself under the mango tree, her literally grassroots activism evolves into a queer activist organisation, *Colour Pink*, bringing visibility that will eventually make Jamaica untenable, leading her to seek asylum, to embark on the chronotope of flight.

Beki, a Queer Activist From Addis Ababa: The Performativity of Naming and Shaming

Beki, a queer activist from Ethiopia in his early 30s (interviewed by Mike), successfully gained asylum in the UK based on his sexuality and activism in December 2016. What I (Mike) learnt by talking to him over the months when he was seeking asylum, and which changed my thinking on the topic, was how interconnected his sexuality was and is with his activism. It will be clear from the discussion of the asylum process above that the story of what leads up to the decision to seek asylum is crucial.

So queer asylum stories, like queer migration stories, always start with and only make sense in terms of the story of what went before. Beki in his late teens grows into his queer identity, with social media providing the crucial safe space for exploring his developing sexuality and as an organising space for his activism. This safe space is cruelly breached in the circumstances that led to his decision to leave Ethiopia and seek asylum.

Before naming: 'I didn't know the name of it then'

Asked when he first became aware of his sexuality, Beki, like Ahmed, starts by talking about a time before he had a name for the feelings and desires of attraction to other boys. He counts himself lucky that his attraction didn't slip out innocently, with unforeseeable consequences:

Beki: I don't know the name of it then, I don't know what I was. It was like when I was 13 I knew already. Because that was the time when my friend start talking about sexual attraction, we just developed this puberty age right so people start talking about it. Girls were talking about boys, boys were talking about girls. There is no one talking about boys about boys (Mike and Beki laugh)
Beki: and I knew where my feeling was... that I like boys because I didn't know at that time if it was wrong or right

Beki recounts a chronotope of innocence: feelings did not have names yet; there was no censure.

Au commencement il y avait l'injure/In the beginning was insult

In his early teens, Beki is brought face to face with social and religious censure. He sees himself named. This process is what Althusser calls interpellation or hailing. The first sentence of Eribon's (2004) *Insult and the Making of the Gay Self* asserts that the first time the young queer person will find themselves named will be through insult and verbal abuse. So it is with Beki, although he is at first unaware that the abuse terms he hears connect with his non-normative sexuality. He describes the terms he hears around him – '*busheti*', meaning faggot; '*setaset*', feminine – not understanding the implications:

Beki: I mean nobody told me, I never heard of the word gebresedom (act of sodomy) before that. Of course the word busheti I have heard it never asked what it was, I don't understand it. Am like why didn't I say it I don't understand. I still don't understand. ... I use to be very feminine. Especially my very early ages I use to be really you know. They use to call me names Setaset (feminine) you know
Mike: What is setaset?
Beki: Like feminine or sissy, that is what it meant.

Gebresodom: Naming, interpellation, shame

It is only at the age of 14, in religious instruction class, that Beki comes across the prescription against sodomy in Leviticus and suddenly finds himself named, interpellated by the associated shame:

Beki: But the thing is this is what I did, when I knew that I was different. You get at a certain age and there are Sunday schools at the the Ethiopian orthodox church you start that bible study or whatever so at one of the sessions that Sodom and Gomorrah from Leviticus came to the page and for the first time I knew what I was. It was horrifying; it destroyed everything in my head
Mike: The religion concept that did it
Beki: Yes because that is the first introduction I had to the same sex thing. As I said I heard the word busheti in school but I did not know what it was. And the word Gebresedom I have never heard of it because from the age of 6 till 13 there is no sexual content discussion around the church teachings or preachings. That specific time they start talking about a word from Leviticus and gebresedom something I was Oh my god that is what I am, I am the sinner, I am this, I am that. All the negative introductions to your own kind of true self was like. Anyway that is how I knew anyway about myself.

Beki comes to know himself through the prescription of Leviticus. It is hard to imagine a more graphic illustration of the interpellation and subjection of the young subject by a patriarchal heteronormative discourse, which of course, as Lacan points out, occurs through language: at its most primitive level the performative of being named. Chronotopically, he comes up against the painful intersection between human timespace and the timespace of judgement and eternity. Struggling out of this knot through constructing and inhabiting a queer chronotope is his struggle, his process of ideological becoming.

Social media: A space of play

In his older teens and 20s, initially constrained by his increasing visibility in the media and entertainment industry in Addis Ababa, Beki is driven by curiosity and the desire to meet others who share his feelings. He googles 'gay Ethiopians' and discovers many possibilities to develop, despite the social repression around him, a social circle where he can feel at home, a safe queer space:

Beki: I knew for a long time those people existed in my country the community existed in my city. But I didn't act on it at that time I was working in the film industry so it is easy to be targeted. Even though I don't do acting everybody knows my name, you call my name and everybody knows my name
Mike: So you were kind of visible
Beki: Yes.
[…]
Beki: (laugh) so 2011 I was like you know what am just going to do this. Two years back I think 2009 I started googling on my phone Ethiopian gays and there was a website that pops up on the page *gay datanata* something on the site there a whole lot of Ethiopian names I was like wow people actually you know
Mike: Are this people in Ethiopia or
Beki: Most of them in Addis there are a few numbers who are living abroad at the time. It's an international dating site, I didn't even know how to use it and then I didn't have the interest I was just curious. I just wanted to know if actually Ethiopians were living in Addis. So I kind of have the information. So 2011 I sent a face book message from my registered name to this guy's name

Curiously, however, naming again becomes an issue. Beki naively uses his registered name to contact the man, which brings the swift advice to use a pseudonym. The chronotope of online dating in a homophobic environment does not favour personal disclosure:

Beki: The guy calls me he is very nice the first thing he said was don't ever use your registered name.
Mike: Really?
Beki: Ya that is the first thing he said don't
Mike: It's a good idea very good advice

Beki: Then he was like you have to have this a pseudonym, so I created the pseudonym
Mike: Ya
Beki: So once I created the pseudonym account I followed on his friends and start requesting people.
Mike: So then you have access to his friends.
Beki: Exactly. I started adding friends from his list.
Mike: And then what?
Beki: After that I joined the underground but visible in a way kind of community in Addis.
Mike: What sort of social when you say underground but visible, was it like meeting in people's houses or cafes?
Beki: Ehh ya. They have informal meetings in people's houses, their friends you know they go to bars together, restaurants they go to cafes together and they have parties very private but they use to have parties and stuff.

Chronotopically, he is learning something about the timespace of online dating and the potential of being someone else online.

Queer activism: Sexual health for gay men

Beki's participation in the house parties of the underground gay scene in Addis develops his activism. He notices a tendency for sexual recklessness among the young gay men, many of whom who have migrated to Addis for its relative openness. We see the important role of Facebook as a means of networking and communication in a socially repressive context:

Mike: So Facebook is really important as a kind of support?
Beki: Yes it is very much, because that is the only thing we have. There is no other option. Through that I started meeting people out of my comfort zone you know, people I would never normally run into because we won't be spending time in the same kind of area. I have met a group of guys went to their place somewhere in 2012 I think, I met this guy and invited me to his place every Saturday they have an informal gathering to chew chat it was a group of 9/8 young gay people, am not I was not an expert am not a health officer or a doctor but I was just curious and one conversation led to another and I saw how vulnerable they were to being exposed to HIV/STI and STD and I ask them about lubricants and condoms, condoms of course they know about because of all the advertisement and availability there is. Most of they don't know about lubricant and the availability in the

country because it was not allowed to be advertised or to promote it in anyway. So people don't have knowledge on lubricant. So that was that time I said oh my god there actually is a need to do something. Am in position to do something all of my gay friends around me there in good position. Everyone earns money, so I went to my friends and told them these group of people they have no clue about HIV, STI STD forget it they have no clue about that so why don't we start by contributing money 100 birr per month buy condoms and lubricant we can send or give away to such kind of informal gatherings

Beki and others see the need for safe sex education in these scenes, leading to the formation of an underground network offering safe sex advice and materials to vulnerable gay men. This has to be highly secret, organised through a closed Facebook page, with all members of the network using pseudonyms.

Networking as danger

While remaining highly secret within Ethiopia, the network starts to develop a profile outsides Ethiopia, both within Africa and further afield. And this creates danger:

Beki: Visibility made it dangerous.
Mike: How did it become visible?
Beki: We become very strong as a group, as I said when I joined Facebook there were few pages but they were not that active, so once we come together we made it strong and became visible, we also invite people to have a discussion on and then the timing also was bad western countries specially US was pushing the gay agenda to different African countries so Nigeria, Uganda legislation put everything up in front. At that time we did an interview with Newsweek and we talks about group of people who are doing this and this, that shocked the government because they have been denying throughout the years saying we don't have gays in the country.

With visibility goes audibility – a voice that counteracts the government policy that gays do not exist in Ethiopia. Beki describes a conversation going beyond borders with other activists in Africa and beyond. By 2015, the network gets news of a coming crackdown:

Beki: 2015 there was an election coming up, we got an information that says the government is make list of names of active LGBT advocates on facebook or any social media platform. So we are like what do we do and all sort of discussions because at that time most of us were exposed to the gay community so if you catch one of the gay guys intimidate them by police, they can easily point us out saying this is one is Beki this one is blah blah because everybody knows me as Beki that is my pseudonym.

Again, a focus on naming: we see the fragility of the pseudonym as protection against aggression. If everyone knows you well, it is not hard to connect your pseudonym with your registered name and hence to your offline life.

Betrayed

Despite the build-up, Beki describes the day that their network was betrayed on Facebook, with the details of all members listed, accompanied by threats, as one of shock and disbelief:

Beki: I think somewhere around 2nd week of March someone send us a message on our page we have an online page where we give clinical counselling too on that page somebody send a message saying 'we know who you are, we know what you are doing you need to stop blah blah' I was like you got to be kidding me, well what happens know last year yes election you have an excuse and a minute later he/she whoever sent a whole list of names Dana members.
Mike: Real names?
Beki: Yes registered names. But I was still thinking this is some kind of a cruel joke practical joke that someone we know is doing. Honestly that was what in my head. It goes again 'Stop advocating for gay rights in Ethiopia blah blah blah' these is another message, we are not replying mind you. The next message that comes up was a photo of individuals, a photo we took in groups she/he sent that and said we are going to reveal your identity. Where you live, where you work blah blah simultaneously so that you have no control over it.

Beki's decision to leave

At the conclusion of the interview, Beki describes how this betrayal of the network led him to leave Ethiopia and seek asylum in the UK:

Beki: So I told them I am done living in people's mercy, am going to take control of my life, if I have to start from scratch and be miserable so be it. I'm like I'm done. So ya April 13th I left to the UK.

Conclusion

We have been discussing the chronotope in terms of significant life stages and their timespace coordinates, childhood, puberty and early adolescence, late adolescence and young adulthood, linking these to processes of ideological becoming and an increasingly explicit emergence of queer identities. However, we must not forget that chronotopes can occur in much more momentary contexts, corresponding to Bakhtin's motifs category, as Blommaert and De Fina point out:

> There is no reason why chronotopic cultural practice would be confined to the 'big' stages of life only, because even within narrower timespans we can see non-random co-occurrences of timespace configurations and forms of cultural practice and identity enactment. (Blommaert & De Fina, 2017: 5–6)

Let us revisit two examples from the data: little Ahmed is forced to have an afternoon sleep by his mother and, within the timespace constraints of his bed and the afternoon, dreams of being able to marry a man; 14-year-old Beki in the religious instruction class is brought face to face with the Leviticus definition of sodomy, recognising himself in that distorting mirror as '*gebresodomaween*'. Both of these instances are chronotopically distinctive moments. But neither timespace is entirely constrained by the chronotopic moment of telling (now) or of the situation told (then). Ahmed's dream brings into his bed both a longing and future possibility; the invocation of Leviticus for Beki brings in sin and damnation, the longue durée of eternity. Chronotopic timespaces intersect and in the intersection is their poignancy. Nor are these the only examples. The data are rich with startlingly captured instances: Jessica, with the other trans teens thrown out onto the streets in Kingston and living as sex workers, finds her activist self with her queer family under the mango tree. A space. A time. A formative space and time. Abiola, at the moment when her stepfather returns to find her together with her girlfriend. The safety of a love nest invaded. These are accounts of identity formation in action, Bakhtin's 'ideological becoming'. Ahmed has no way of knowing what trouble his childish dream of marrying a man will lead to for him. For the schoolgirl Abiola, discovery leads to years of abuse out of which she is eventually able to reclaim her voice. But what is also crucial is that this is identity formation *à rebours*, against the grain of normativities. Here we remember Agha's emphasis on chronotopic contrast. But here the contrast is not simple; it involves a struggle, involving real danger. And this is what makes these data on the one hand utterly unique and on the other hand utterly commonplace. Such things happen all the time and most often pass unnoticed. So these data are seeded with moments that are both unique and commonplace, perhaps uniquely commonplace. Perhaps indeed everyone has stories like this. But it is arguably easier to capture those moments of ideological becoming that are in synch with prevailing normativities; these are less painful and easier to talk about.

In conclusion, we come back to what Blommaert and De Fina (2017: 5) term the 'big stages of life', the chronotope of the lifestory, to answer the question that drives this chapter: What is the backstory of those who finally choose or are driven to seek asylum based on their sexual identity? The perception of difference comes early, even before it has a name. Young people in their early teens can be interpellated by heteronormative discourses that other them. Later they start to take hold of their own lives, engaging with and creating queer community, which can then lead, in interesting ways, to visibility and different kinds of activism. Finally, there comes a tipping point: life becomes unliveable, simply too dangerous, triggering the decision to leave. For Abiola, the trigger is the abuse she suffers in secret in the family home, which drives her out onto the streets and thence to Germany. For Beki it is the busting of the cover of his Facebook activist network, which is also his friendship group. In both cases, the safe becomes unsafe: the familiar chronotopic security of home, the friendship group, become unsafe and threatening. What is perhaps distinctive about these queer asylum stories is how early this sense of difference, of estrangement from the social mainstream, can start: daydreaming in bed when your mother has forced you to have an afternoon sleep; as an early teenager in a religious instruction class; when as a young adult your Facebook group is infiltrated and busted. All of this funnels the queer subject towards a decision to leave. To embark on the chronotope of flight.

References

Agha, A. (2007) Recombinant selves in mass mediated spacetime. *Language & Communication* 27, 320–335.

Bakhtin, M. (1981) Forms of time and of the chronotope in the novel: Notes toward a historical poetics. In *The Dialogic Imagination: Four Essays* (M. Holquist, ed.; C. Emerson and M. Holquist, trans.) (pp. 84–258). Austin, TX: University of Texas Press.

Baynham, M. (2003) Narratives in space and time: Beyond 'backdrop' accounts of narrative orientation. *Narrative Inquiry* 13 (2), 347–366.

Baynham, M. (2012) Cultural geography and the retheorisation of sociolinguistic space. In S. Gardner and M. Martin-Jones (eds) *Multilingualism, Discourse and Ethnography*. Abingdon: Routledge.

Baynham, M. (2017) Intersections of necessity and desire in migration research. In S. Canagarajah (ed.) *The Routledge Handbook of Language and Migration*. London: Routledge.

Baynham, M. and De Fina, A. (eds) (2005) *Dislocations/Relocations: Narratives of Displacement*. London: Routledge.

Blommaert, J. (2010) *The Sociolinguistics of Globalization*. Cambridge: Cambridge University Press.

Blommaert, J. and De Fina, A. (2017) Chronotopic identities: On the timespace organization of who we are. In A. De Fina, D. Ikizoglu and J. Wegner (eds) *Diversity and Super-diversity* (pp. 1–14). Washington, DC: Georgetown University Press.

Butler, J. (2015) *Notes Towards a Performative Theory of Assembly*. Cambridge, Mass.: Harvard University Press.

Cantú, L. (2009) *The Sexuality of Migration: Border Crossings and Mexican Immigrant Men*. New York: New York University Press.

Carrillo, H. (2017) *Pathways of Desire: The Sexual Migration of Mexican Gay Men*. Chicago, IL: University of Chicago Press.

Dick, H. (2010) Imagined lives and modernist chronotopes in Mexican nonmigrant discourse. *American Ethnologist* 37 (2), 275–290.

Divita, D. (2019) Discourses of (be)longing: Later life and the politics of nostalgia. In R. Piazza (ed.) *Discourses of Identity in Liminal Places and Spaces* (pp. 64–82). London: Routledge.

Eribon, D. (2004) *Insult and the Making of the Gay Self*. Durham: Duke University Press.

Gray, J. and Baynham, M. (2020) Queer migration narratives. In K. Hall and R. Barrett (eds) *Oxford Handbook of Language and Sexuality*. Oxford: Oxford University Press.

Juffermans, K. (2018) Micro-landscapes and the double semiotic horizon of mobility in the global South. In A. Peck, C. Stroud and Q. Williams (eds) *Making Sense of People, Place and Linguistic Landscapes* (pp. 201–222). London: Routledge.

Koven, M. (2019) Narrating desire for place: Chronotopes of desire for the Portuguese homeland before and after 'return'. In R. Piazza (ed.) *Discourses of Identity in Liminal Places and Spaces* (pp. 42–63). London: Routledge.

Linde, C. (1993) *Life Stories*. Oxford: Oxford University Press.

Madden, C. (2013) 'I contain multitudes': The queer chronotopes of Annie Proulx' 'Brokeback Mountain'. *Short Fiction in Theory & Practice* (3) 1, 63–75.

Mai, N. and King, R. (2009) Love, sexuality and migration: Mapping the issue(s). *Mobilities* (4) 3, 295–307.

Mole, R.C.M. (2018) Identity, belonging and solidarity in the Russian-speaking queer diaspora in Berlin. *Slavic Review* 77 (1), 77–98.

O'Connor, B. (2018) 'Too much cream on the tacos': Narrative and moral personhood in transfronterizo experience. *Association of Mexican American Educators Journal* 12 (2), 153–181.

Perrino, S. (2015) Chronotopes: Time and space in oral narratives. In A. De Fina and A. Georgakopoulou (eds) *Handbook of Narrative Analysis* (pp. 149–159). Oxford: Blackwell.

11 The Power of (Im)mobility: Irish Travellers' Agentive Identities in Transit and Permanency

Roberta Piazza

Introduction

In the UK, mobile Irish Travellers are a minority group marginalised and stigmatised by sedentary mainstream society. This ethnographic case study focuses on a female Irish Traveller in southern England who was interviewed in a condition of semi-mobility in a transit camp and, a few years later, in a state of immobility in an adjoining permanent site. The focus is on how she constructed her identity differently in the two moments and contexts.

As a female Traveller, she has the role of custodian of her children, their culture and values. Compared to the transit camp (Piazza, 2014) where she lived intermittently for years, in the permanent site this woman gained a stronger voice and greater awareness of her condition. Through interviews and ethnographic observation, the study observes the woman's 'material agency' (Lahlou, 2017) in the new condition of immobility and her persistent want for an 'institutional agency' (Lahlou, 2017) that will grant her authority and recognition in the wider world.

The concept of place-identity refers to the 'located nature of subjectivity' and answers questions about 'who we are' in relation to 'where we are' (Dixon & Durrheim, 2000: 27). Physical 'space' and discursively constructed 'place' (Liebscher & Dailey-O'Cain, 2013: 16) usefully differentiate between the materiality and emotionality inherent in the notion of space, although Giesekeing *et al.* (2014: XXIII) advocate a more integrated notion of place 'embodied' with a materiality that is metaphoric, discursive and physical. Place is integral to self-construction and at the basis of 'place attachment' (Speller, 2000), but people also mould place according to their individual personae.

Recent ethnographic and sociolinguistic research investigates place as mobile and deterritorialised (Kabanich, 2012), for example in the context of migration (e.g. Baynham, 2009; Pujolar, 2009). Due to a capitalism-induced crisis, space has become a scarcity and a precious commodity (Cross & Karides, 2007), resulting in an unequal access to it. Space is usually managed and socially constructed in a hegemonic (Gramsci, 1971) way by majoritarian society, generally according to an ethos of immobility, with the consequent exclusion of groups that challenge this dominant ideology. A case in point is nomadic groups, such as the Irish Travellers, whose mobile tradition is continuously threatened by society's laws. These, on the one hand, impose sedentarism on itinerant groups by chastising them for moving around the country and causing disruption and dirt (Piazza, 2021), while on the other hand they force them into continuous mobility by not providing a sufficient number of serviced sites and limiting their stay in them to short periods.

This chapter presents a case study of a female Irish Traveller in the south of England who was first interviewed in 2013 in a transit camp and three years later when she moved to the adjacent permanent encampment. Based on interviews and ethnographic observation and framed within social constructivism and Lefebvre's (2014 [1991]) notion of space as socially constructed, this study observes how the woman's sense of 'agency' (Duranti, 2006; Lahlou, 2017) and identity changed in the different contexts. In the interview, understood as a social and cultural practice (De Fina, 2019), two aspects of her life appear closely intertwined: her role as guardian of her children and her longing for choice.

Identity, Agency and Spatial (Im)mobility

Lefebvre's (2014 [1991]) notion of space as always embodying a meaning rather than being neutral or 'empty' can be usefully connected to issues of (im)mobility. Bourdieu's (1977, in Gieseking *et al.*, 2014: XXIII) claim that 'meaning and action, or practice, interact in interdependent ways to inculcate and reinforce cultural knowledge and behaviour' similarly relates to immobility at the basis of dominant groups' ethos.

Analyses of (im)mobility and space can uncover systems of exclusion that are hidden and naturalised (Low, 2014: 34). As will be discussed, Travellers' limited access to space is symptomatic of a hegemonic spatial ideology that excludes this nomadic community.

Past research on identity construction in migratory contexts strongly indicates how displacement affects identity (see De Fina, 2003) and how spatial mobility, whether chosen or forced, impacts identity maintenance (e.g. Baynham & De Fina, 2005; Canagarajah, 2017; Delanty *et al.*, 2008; Vertovec, 2001). This case study, therefore, contributes to such research. However, following Deleuze and Guattari (1999), it focuses on 'nomads', who are very different from 'migrants':

> The life of the nomad is an intermezzo. (...) The nomad is not at all the same as the migrant; for the migrant goes principally from one point to another, even if the second point is uncertain, unforeseen, or not well localized. But the nomad goes from point to point only as a consequence and as a factual necessity; in principle, points for him are relays along a trajectory. (Deleuze & Guattari, 1999: 443)

As identity is discursive, situated (Bucholtz & Hall, 2005) and performative, individuals can create 'different versions of self' (Benwell & Stokoe, 2006: 138) which are even contradictory at times (Billig, 1996; Ladegaard, 2011; May, 2004). Within a social constructivism framework, '[t]alk is (...) the site in which identity is instantiated' (Ladegaard, 2012: 452) in opposition to a pre-discursive and essentialist view of identity. Ladergaard (2012), however, notes how often studies attempt to combine the constructionist and the essentialist approach along 'a weak-strong continuum, with identity as a fixed entity at one end, and identity as a fluctuating process at the other' (Ladegaard, 2012: 453). In constructing one's identity through talk, a subject confronts the existing discourses that circulate in society about space and (im)mobility, generally produced by individuals with recognised expertise and status (planners, engineers, architects) (Lefebvre, 2014 [1991]; Soja, 1996).

This study's contention is that agency is predicated on access to landscape and (im)mobility. Culturally, Irish Travellers believe in an ethic of mobility, which historically has been the basis of their exclusion; however, paradoxically, it is mainstream society that forces them to be mobile. Settled society's social and legal constraints, it is claimed, have a clear impact on Travellers' agency. As it incorporates material, intellectual and emotional components, agency involves complex issues, most notably intentionality and the role of the subject or actor (Duranti, 2006: 453). Similarly, for Ahearn (2001: 112), agency is the 'socio-culturally mediated capacity to act' in order to reach a particular goal. Duranti's definition of agency includes the important element of power:

> Agency is (...) the property of those entities (i) that have some degree of control over their own behaviour, (ii) whose actions in the world affect other entities' (...), and (iii) whose actions are the object of evaluation (...). (Duranti, 2006: 453)

Ahearn largely conflates agency with free will, which empowers an individual to resist numerous consolidated discourses and practices, while Duranti focuses on the distinction between agency as performing and agency as encoding, although he sees the two as 'mutually dependent' (Duranti, 2006: 467).

Bucholtz and Hall's (2005: 606) understanding of agency as 'the accomplishment of social action' relates to the degree of autonomy of the subject vis-à-vis the role of social structure. This point is very relevant to the present analysis of how a marginal woman subjected to the dominance of social structures finds a way to her own agency. Block (2012) situates the discussion of agency and identity within Marxist work in the social sciences (Durkheim, Lev-Strauss, etc.) and specifically engages with the work of Sherry Ortner (from the 1990s to the 2000s) and Margaret Archer (in the 1960s and 1970s), who recognise the objective impact of social structures and how these profoundly limit the degree of individual agency. From Ortner, Block takes the emphasis on subjectivity or 'cultural and historical consciousness' as a state of awareness of one's agency. From Archer, however, Block takes the notion that social structure is independent of agency until the individual enters into contact with it (Block, 2012: 53–54).

Some identity studies emphasise the performative aspect of agency and see it as the ability to confirm one's self through actions, and encoding as the linguistic realisation of agency through semantico-syntactic patterns like transitivity or 'any aspect of language (...) from phonological variables to individual words, to complex discourse structures such as patterns of actions in narratives' (De Fina et al., 2006: 15).

A more recent approach to agency proposed by Lahlou (2017) provides a suitable framework for the interpretation of the Traveller's talk in this study. Lahlou locates agency within his 'installation theory', which sees the outside environment as a series of built settings with 'affordances planted in' it (Lahlou, 2017: 226) (from the road to the kitchen or cockpit), within which individuals with their own culturally developed skills and competences operate. Within such a framework are three different types of agency: material, embodied and social. As the term suggests, material agency refers to the ability to access the material resources in the environment, from one's kitchen to one's car'. However, such access to affordances is not sufficient as a subject needs embodied agency based on education, experience and the capacity to reflect on her context in the past, present and future. Finally, social agency is the individual's capacity to deal with community's rules 'in their local domains of control' (Lahlou, 2017: 227). Social agency is often mediated through what Lahlou terms 'institutional agency', which is granted to the person or group in response to their activities and actions, which are allowed and even praised or, vice versa, condemned. For Lahlou, the three layers of agency – material, embodied and social – cooperate simultaneously to construct agency as a 'situated notion' (Lahlou, 2017: 228).

Lahlou's conceptualisation of agency is in line with the Bakhtinean notion of the chronotope that intersects the axes of time and space. Blommaert and De Fina (2017: 5) interpret chronotopes as 'socially shared, and differential, complexes of value attributed to specific forms of identity [...] enacted in specific timespace frames', and suggest that most identity work can be interpreted as 'being chronotopically organized' (Blommaert & De Fina, 2017: 1). In a subsequent study of minor asylum seekers in a school of Italian in Sicily, De Fina *et al.* (2020: 72) observe how integral to the children's identities is the chronotope of Odysseus as a 'social type' located in a certain place and time rather than an 'abstract representation'.

The construct of agency lends itself well to the analysis of the Traveller's situated identity within her community in the transit and mobile condition first and permanent and immobile site later, in which she is interviewed. When discussing this woman's talk, it is important to bear in mind that any consideration of agency is limited to her relation to a space and an (im)mobile condition she has been denied. It is only in terms of these elements that her sectorial agency, whether material, embodied or social, is considered. Other agentive aspects of her identity may, of course, exist in relation to other spheres of her life, from the material possession of her caravan to the control over her children, her partner or her relationships with the community, which are beyond the remit of the present discussion.

Contextualisation

Irish Travellers are one of the largest nomadic groups living in the UK. While they moved freely between Ireland and Britain for generations, the current groups migrated in the 1950s and 1960s and settled in well as attested by their Irish-English bilingualism and their emotional attachment to the British soil. Tracy, the pseudonym for the woman interviewed in this study, shows her successful control of both domains in her first talk in 2013.

Excerpt 1[1]

Interviewer:	(...) so you're not Irish are you?
Tracy:	*No I was born in England.*
Int.:	You were born in England?

Tracy: I'm Irish descent.
Int.:   You're Irish descent, okay because you have less of an accent than the other women.
Tracy: *I kind of calm it down* when I talk to English people because they use to say, 'what?'
         What was that?' *So I usually calm it down a little bit.*

Tracy is in control of her language and able to instrumentally 'calm down' her Irish accent in order to, she claims, ease communication with outsiders; as in a situation of diglossia (Fishman, 1967), she sways between a private, less prestigious code (Irish) and a public, more widely accepted one (English). Similarly, she prevaricates between her two identities, as she dismisses her Irish membership ('No I was born in England') to then retrieve it and inscribe herself in a community of Irish mobility by heritage.

As persons 'of nomadic habit' (Caravan Sites Act, 1968), Irish Travellers have a deeply embedded need to be mobile. In the past, they were allowed to roam freely in the UK in their caravans, making and selling goods (e.g. wooden pegs), tinkering, picking up seasonal work, hawking and horse dealing. From the early 1600s, previously common land was increasingly privatised as a result of a series of Enclosure Acts, which made it nearly impossible for itinerant communities to pursue their traditional mobile lifestyles. After decades of marginalisation and exclusion, in 1989 Gypsies, Romani and Travellers (GRT), who totalled about 63,000 (*c*.0.1% of the British population according to the 2011 Census), were recognised as a distinct ethnic group.

Echoing Foucault (1980), every society creates discourses in support of their 'regimes of truth'. Stability and permanency are the regimes of truth or core tenets of the majoritarian settled society. As a consequence, Travellers' access to and use of space are continuously challenged and they are frequent victims of racism, discrimination and even hate crime (James, 2007).

Nowadays, in contrast to total mobility, most Travellers prefer to live on council or private serviced sites; however, due to the scarcity of these spaces, they often have no alternative but to keep moving.

The Case Study

I began my ethnographic fieldwork with Irish Travellers in 2012, at a council owned and managed Traveller transit site on the outskirts of a coastal town in southeast England, where the maximum stay was three months. Observational data were collected about all relevant information including school attendance and the community's activities. The local council was happy with my gathering information about the site community since this could help to improve their support services and their relationship with the residents. Generally, the women at the site seemed pleased to talk to me and welcomed me into their caravans.

The interviews were semi-structured and had an informal style and flexible format with the interviewees occasionally receiving sympathetic feedback. 'This nonhierarchical, dynamic, and fluid frame (...) was important in establishing trust and rapport with the participants' and was successful with initially reluctant participants (Levinson, 2007: 18). Through the interviews, the women managed to 'mediate' their experiences and 'put them "out there" at arm's length, and in doing so, create[d] some emotional and reflective distance' from them (Medved & Brockmeier, 2015: 87).

In July 2016, a permanent site, contiguous to the transit site, was opened. The 12 so-called 'amenity blocks' on the new site were bungalows consisting of an open-plan kitchen, a toilet and a separate shower room, with adjoining outside space for caravans and vehicles. The families sleep in their caravans while spending most of the day in their newly built bungalows. Most of the women originally interviewed at the transit camp moved to the permanent section. Once they had settled, a second round of interviews was then undertaken in 2017.

Out of a total of 20 women interviewed between 2012 and 2018, Tracy was chosen due to her powerful personality. Like most of the women who were interviewed in a larger research on Irish Travellers (Piazza, 2021), Tracy constructs herself as the guardian of her family and custodian of her community's beliefs and traditions. This emerges in different guises in her conversations in which the two elements of space, mobile and immobile, and time, before and after the fulfilment of her desire (Whitehead, 2002) for a secure accommodation, are integral to Tracy's construction of her subjectivity.

Agency in Semi-mobility

This section analyses the first interview with Tracy in 2013 at the transit site. She had three children then and lived in a caravan like all other Travellers. As the guardian of her family, Tracy does not express volitions for herself but mainly in the name of her son, who requires stability due to his special needs. Despite being a very able woman, Tracy was denied material agency by regulations that only allow limited stays at the transit site.

Modality and war metaphors

Tracy constructs herself as a soldier dealing with obtuse institutions, through her use of war metaphors (Lakoff, 1991) and the word 'hope'. The following excerpts show Tracy struggling to make local institutions appreciate the hardship involved in being a mother in an enforced mobile and precarious situation.

Excerpt 2

Interviewer:	So tell me what is this – why this place? Why here? What is it that attracts you besides of course the fact that you are =
Tracy:	=To be honest, that is the only reason.
Int.:	Really?
Tracy:	That is the only reason for me *to be honest* because *I wouldn't I wouldn't put with it* if you know what I mean? *I wouldn't put up with the torture* it's not worth it.
Int.	What do you mean put up with it?
Tracy:	It's not worth it. Like having to *fight constantly* – having to *constantly* say why you need to stay and *constantly trying to get your point across*, do you know what I mean? Whereas if (son's name) wasn't autistic, I'd just travel. *I have to fight for him.*

Excerpt 3

(Tracy has been explaining the difficulty of finding a space outside the site she is in at the moment where she can stay a maximum of 12 weeks)

Tracy:	It's just a case of the same thing every year. We come in that school and you *fight* to get as long as you possibly can so you *don't have* to take him out of the school, and then *you have* to take him out of the school because eventually *you have* to go, and then *hope* that the school will hold his place until you can come back in again. Because they won't allow him to go to school from a camp.
Int.:	They won't?
Tracy:	No, because they said that if he, if I leave, say if we stay here in (place name), if I leave and I to (.) say (place name) for a week, well he's no longer in the catchment. Even though the chances are I'd be pulling back here to (place name) after that week I- it still wouldn't be classed the same. So they said they can't look at it that way, *they've got* to look at it the way that he's out of catchment and *they have* to take the place back. So then when I'd come back after the week *I'd have* to reapply which would be a load of hassle.

In England, children are eligible to enrol at schools in their local geographic or 'catchment' area. If they intermit, even for reasons beyond their control, there is no guarantee that they will be allowed to re-enrol at the same school as the place will go to another eligible child. Given this lack of institutional flexibility, Tracy's use of metaphoric language is not surprising. The dormant conduit (Lakoff & Johnson, 1980: 10–12) metaphor ('get your point across'; communication is sending/words are objects/linguistic expressions are containers), reflecting Tracy's difficulty in communicating with the council, sets the frame of the irreconcilable rupture between the authorities and Travellers. Subsequently, her use of the verb 'fight', accompanied by the repeated adverb 'constantly', and the reference to 'torture' suggest a conceptual scenario (Musolff, 2006) associated with the target domain (dealing with the council/laws) of hardship that she elucidates by conjuring up the image of struggle and fight, as source domain (Chilton & Ilyin, 1993). In other words, the relationship with the authorities is war and providing stability and education for her children is a painful (like torture in a war context) and often useless attempt.

Tracy's resentment about depending on others' decisions and institutional regulations is encoded in her reference to her lack of choice through the consistent use of 'have to'. Such use of deontic modality is 'a form of participation of the speaker in the speech event' (Halliday, 1970: 335), which plays a discursive role (Gonzálvez García, 2000) in the meaning negotiation between Tracy and the interviewer, centred on the Traveller's inhumane life condition.

However, in spite of an absence of space-related material agency and lack of choice, Tracy showed a considerable degree of embodied agency through her ability to reflect on her situation. Within Lahlou's vision of the context as an installation that wraps up individuals' life as in a 'bundle', the various layers of agency are not independent (Lahlou, 2017: 227). Being agentive, therefore, comprises the capacity to carry out activities that pertain to the three areas of material, embodied and social (often via institutional) agency. Lahlou's model does not envisage the situation of an individual deprived of material agency but still able to reflect on her situation. This is the case of Tracy, who lacks agency over her physical space, but is still able to analyse critically her family's condition and plan her future ('we have to follow the rules in case the site is built so that we're allowed to have a pitch on it').

Embodied agency

The above exchanges highlight Tracy's longing for spatial stability for herself and her family although in the context of a severely constrained material agency. The fragments below, however, reveal a different Tracy.

Excerpt 4

Interviewer: So you really still experience this reaction against you ↑
Tracy: Yeah, because everybody it's a it's a it's a known fact, everybody knows it. It's like when we took the kids to school it's a known fact between the teachers and the kids at the school that these kids are travelling kids. It's not like which I don't understand, I don't know why that has to be made as a point. Do you know what I mean? like I don't know why that has to be—
Int.: Is it because you reckon because they know the teacher knows that she's gonna stay or he's gonna stay a short period of time?
Tracy: Yeah. And *I think* that's what it is. And I had the teacher at here the other day and I was saying to her, the teacher comes from by the school, like 'why isn't she coming back' and 'are you gonna put her back in?' And I said *'to be honest it just feels like because some parents don't care, you think that no parent cares'*. Like there was parent's evening, and I said, 'I got no parent evening slip' which *I would have wanted to go to that*, I go to (son's name), do you know what I mean? I said *I would have wanted to know.* And I said *'she needs extra help'* (referring to her daughter) because she's obviously behind, so I said *'I want to help or tell me how to do it'* I said *'and I'll do it with her'*. Like I went to erm WH Smith the other day and I got like all like and stuff, you know tracing stuff and all that, to help her at home. I said *'and if you tell me how to help her'*, I said *'I'll help her'*, do you know what I mean? I said, *'if he can't do it'*, I said *'send out the paperwork to me and'* I said, *'and I'll do it with her at home'*. It's just the downside of it is that you've just basically got to make the choice between their education and their lifestyle do you know what I mean? *Which shouldn't really be have to be a choice.* But obviously at the minute it is because as you can see they don't let anybody on here.

Even in a condition of spatial deprivation, Tracy manages to analyse her context critically and discern between her responsibilities and her rights; the reference to having to choose between allegiance to the Travellers' traditional lifestyle and education encodes her frustration. In the above excerpt, the reporting of the encounter with the teacher through self-voicing, while dramatising the narrative, indexes the speaker's stance towards the institutional power and her reflective ability. The accusation that the teacher tars all Travellers with the same brush, both those who are not committed to their children's education and others who are, is direct and only seemingly modulated ('to be honest'), as is her blaming the teacher for not sending out the slip for the parents' evening. 'I would have wanted to go to that' and 'Which shouldn't really be have to be a choice' reflect a 'situation [that] was/is not actualized, [therefore it] conveys criticism' (Huddleston & Pullum, 2002: 186). Although devoid of one type of agency, Tracy's reconstruction of the failed communication with the school suggests she is agentive in other subtler ways, when she constructs herself as a parent determined to assist her children by providing them with the necessary equipment. Agency therefore emerges from the opposition between a deserving 'us' or 'me' and an insensitive and racist 'them' or 'you'.

Social and institutional agency

As a Traveller, Tracy's social agency derives from knowing her group's rules well and being able to negotiate her own independent female role within her collectivity. However, being 'constrained by other people' (Lahlou, 2017: 227), she has very limited social and institutional agency with regard to a stable space for her family.

In what follows, Tracy establishes another opposition between the Traveller support council staff and the people high up in the institutional hierarchy.

Excerpt 5

Interviewer: Yeah, he's such a nice person and (name) as well yeah.
Tracy: He really, really would [help] and so would (name). But it feels like *the ones higher up that don't know us, we're just a name on a paper*. It feels like they're judging your life and *they're they're making the decisions* and *they don't realise how important* the decision is that they're making, for instance about me leaving me having to leave here. They don't realise that the consequences of that is that (son's name) has to come out of school, he won't get speech therapy, he won't get the help he needs and he might lose his place like he did before do you know what I mean? *They don't look at the consequences, it's just like, 'oh well they can't stay'*. And in reality we could because I've stayed here for two and half years before. So they try and say 'it's because of the planning permission', I don't care, the 12 weeks for planning permission, but yeah, I was on here for two and a half years, so why didn't the planning permission come into it then? Because (son's) specialist doctor got involved.
Int.: But I think things have changed ↑
Tracy: They haven't.
Int.: No?

Tracy: That happened, the new law come in two years ago and yet last year I come in in September and I didn't leave 'til the end of April and I left of my own accord. So do you know what I mean?
Int.: Yeah.
Tracy: They try and tell you this like you're (.) because obviously most travellers are uneducated. *Unfortunately for them, I know everything about it because I read everything.* So as I turned around I said to them, the other day, and they said they want to ban me off it, I said, *'you can't, there's no law to say that you are allowed to ban me off here for 12 months, it's a transit site'.* Do you know what I mean? *'And if you ban me off it I'll only pull out to camp out there anyway so it doesn't make a difference to me'.* But of course it just feels like you're meant to just give up but unfortunately I can't just give up so you know what I mean?

Tracy's dramatic tone in the above graphically conveys her bitterness about the lack of recognition and the social exclusion she experiences on a daily basis. Pronouns are crucial indicators of 'specific speakers in specific contexts' (De Fina *et al.*, 2006: 4) but also of 'interlocutory' and 'social identities' (Ochs, 1993: 302). The recurring use of 'they' indexing an anonymous entity oblivious to her family's needs encodes Tracy's distress about her lack of choice and ties in effectively with her previous war metaphors. Tracy 'dissociates' (van Leeuwen, 2008: 38) from the institutions by following the generic 'they' with a negative and blaming predicate. She positions herself critically 'in a Bakhtinian dialogic universe of voices other than (her) own' (Lauerbach, 2006: 198) by insistently 'ventriloquizing' or 'mock-representing' the insensitive and even illogical institutions' discourse ('oh well, they can't stay') (Goffman, 1974: 536). Such a recurring strategy expresses the irreconcilable hiatus between her community and the authorities. Once again her agentive self emerges in this acute dissection of the situation.

Agency in Immobility and Permanency

The previous discussion of Tracy's identity construction in relation to a denied space revolved around a lack and a consequent want. As a mother of young children, one of whom requires special attention, Tracy talked about the moral imperative to protect her family and voiced her material and institutional deprivation. She constructed herself as 'at war' with the insensitive, inattentive institutions. Social structures are responsible for her diminished agency; however, her ability to carefully analyse the situation and the institutions' mistakes endows her with a different kind of agency.

At the end of 2016, Tracy's aspiration to secure stability for her family came true when the construction of the permanent camp was completed and the new Travellers' space opened. The Council's 'local connection' rule[2] recognised Tracy's entitlement to one of the bungalows. In the permanent site where many of the earlier transit respondents had now transferred, I resumed my interviews with the aim of recording the impact that the new space may have had on the women.

The questions in the second round of interviews centred on the change in the women's lives and any still existing issues and aspirations. The key hypothesis was that the new situation of safe immobility would give the women a new sense of self-efficacy and stronger agency. This was, in part, confirmed, although some issues still emerged in Tracy's narratives.

Tracy's material and embodied agency

Once again, Tracy is not completely free to construct and express her agency in a context in which she is in direct contact with the social structures (Block, 2012). She is now in a much more satisfactory situation, the details of which, however, still escape her control. While Tracy expressed satisfaction at finally having her own 'shed', as she called the bungalow, a critical tone is still detectable in her talk.

Excerpt 6

Interviewer:	I'd really like to know how you feel about this place.
Tracy:	This place?
Int.:	Yes
Tracy:	Ahm (0.3) *honestly it's lovely it's it's lovely* but the only difference is that we've got a kitchen and a bathroom because it still feels like a transit site it doesn't feel like (0.1) because everybody we were staying with is still here and there's still a transit site behind us you don't you don't feel remote if you know what I mean.
Int.:	Yes, yes, but are you happy with it?
Tracy.:	Yeah ↓
Int.:	But, you're not terribly happy ↑
Tracy:	*I'm not too happy no because it could be a little bit more secure I think.*
Int.:	Ah
Tracy:	Because you've got the transit site so close
Int.:	Right

260 Part 4: (Im)mobilities, Subjectivity, Identity and Agency

Tracy: And it's *it's still like a caravan with a shed*, do you know what I mean?
Int.: Yes and do you like that?
Tracy: I do and I don't. I do because I wouldn't like to feel too (.) closed in but *it's nice to get a bit of privacy* as well
Int.: Yes it's interesting (...)
Tracy: This transit site is ok it's lovely they couldn't have done no better but it's still (0.3) I don't know
Int.: How would you change it? How would you change it?
Tracy: How would I change it? I'd start by putting a fence the all way round ah. ~ THERE ARE TWO THINGS I'D CHANGE~. I'd put I'd block the transit site off and I'd have a road going up this way instead of driving through the transit site to get out because it's awkward when you're driving up there I don't know (...)
Int.: So you feel that the two sites are very close?
Tracy: Yes they are yes.
Int.: Do you feel that the people who live in the transit site are bothered by you?
Tracy: No! No no I don't feel they're bothered by us because Travellers are used to living like that it's just when you're settled (.) when you're travelling around everywhere you pull on it's not your home so you can't, *people can't really choose* where you go where you can't go *when you're settled and you are in a home and it's your home and you like to keep it look nice* and whatever it's hard when you get so many people around you know what I mean? I looked out of my back window this morning there was a man picking up all rubbish from them bushes. *I wanna to close that blind.*

Tracy answers my question with hesitation, signalled by a long pause, but followed by a reassuring repetition ('it's lovely it's, it's lovely') and a discourse marker ('honestly') which delay the dispreferred (Pomerantz, 1984) reductionist statement about her new home ('it still feels like a transit site'). Later, she differentiates between her past as a Traveller and her present situation in a home she tries to 'make look nice'. In her recently acquired immobility, Tracy expects to lead her own life and have greater agency; however, she realises she is still unable to make her own choices mainly because of the new site's adjacency to the old transit site, again a decision that reflects the impact of social structures on her life. Tracy has certainly acquired material agency as she no longer needs to move away from the site every three months and find another council or private space to pull up on; moreover, her children's education is ensured. The long 'fight', as she called it, for the permanency she described in the first interview is now won.

However, the permanent site is a 'striated' or 'metric' space, in other words a regimented, structured, orderly landscape, 'for which it is possible to assign constant directions' (Deleuze & Guattari, 1999: 566), like a motorway, which someone else has created for her community according to criteria that are foreign to her. (Interestingly, Tracy reinvented her own space in a guise mostly in line with her traditions, as some time later she acquired a massive four-room mobile home, which she parked outside the council-built bungalow, to which she transferred her family.) As she is now in an immobile arrangement, she does not want to share her space with those mobile residents still allowed a three month stay, a community to which she feels she no longer belongs; she asks for a separate road and does not want to be reminded that a temporary, unhappy site still exists when looking at it from her window. As before, Tracy shows strong embodied agency as she is able to reflect on her condition and critically analyse the alternatives (separating the two sites and having different access to them), besides being very vocal in expressing them (as the faster pace and higher pitch in the excerpt above suggest).

Still negotiating social agency

In her new living arrangement, Tracy has acquired a degree of agency and is in a better position to negotiate her identity as her children's guardian. Yet, she doesn't stop defending her Traveller identity in the newly acquired immobility.

Excerpt 7

Tracy: I think the good thing of living this way is *you're never alone never you're never alone. You'd never want for anything*, never in life if you- my sister lives in a house
Interviewer: Oh does she?
Tracy: Yeah, there are no travellers on the road where she lives and if she runs out of sugar she wouldn't dare knock on her next door neighbour and say 'have you got sugar' or anyone along that road or if she ever needed anything ANYTHINK from dinner to soap powder anything to a pair of shoes- you'd never want for anything.

While her previous talk contained several references to her needs and desires ('And you want them to be half normal/hope that the school will hold his place until you can come back in again/having to constantly say why you need to stay'), in her new immobile settled status Tracy defines her community as making individuals free from wants and loneliness.

Not even in immobility is everything positive, however. Tracy has now achieved more embodied agency and, as a result, has become more vocal about her new needs, one complaint being the excessive vicinity of the permanent site to the old transit area (see Excerpt 6 above). Another concern emerges in response to the question about how much Travellers were involved in designing the new site. With regard to this point, the information from the council seems to suggest that the Traveller community had a say, and this is supported by conversations I had with the charity Friends, Family and Travellers, which closely supports the community. However, Tracy's reply in Excerpt 8 suggests otherwise.

Excerpt 8

Interviewer:	Did you have any did you contribute to designing this place? Did you have a voice? Could you say, 'We will like it this way.'
Tracy:	We did and we didn't.
Int.:	Why?
Tracy:	They asked us what we (Overlapping Background Noise) (To her child) Be quiet for a minute because I'm talking. They asked us what we thought we'd like. Um, because when they when *they've done the plans for this, obviously, it was done by architects, so.*
Int.:	By who sorry?
Tracy:	Architects, isn't it?
Int.:	Yeah, yeah. Of course, yes.
Tracy:	*So, when they have a plan for something, you can't really change the structure of things.*
Int.:	No, of course.
Tracy:	But inside, they asked us would we prefer a bath or a shower. We asked for a bath instead of a shower, well, they gave us both. And what else? The colouring.
Int.:	Oh, all right.
Tracy:	The kitchens and that. But apart from that, *it was literally just done by the council.*

Tracy recognises the minimal role of her community in the site designs, although she bows to the experts' competence. Her acquiescence to the council's and architects' decisions, albeit understandable, indicates her awareness that her community has not yet achieved an institutional recognition from settled society and is subject to others' decisions.

One more urgent concern supports this conclusion about Tracy's agency. Being very conservative and traditionalist, Travellers are extremely serious about controlling their children. The schooling most of them want for them is generally only at the lowest levels and their eschewal of education is a form of resistance to (Levinson, 2007) and fear of settled society and its lax moral norms.

In the following excerpt, Tracy's argument about education shows her determination to perpetuate the divide between her community's ethos and that of mainstream settled society in spite of the efforts of staff and case workers to convince the Travellers of the necessity of education.

Excerpt 9

Tracy:	Because especially when you put your children into primary school you start to understand why the people before us didn't want to put their children. Because when they start getting to last years of school, it's when *the children start learning things I don't think children should know about.*
Interviewer:	Mm-hmm.
Tracy:	Children... *children should be children.* I don't think they *should know* about sex education and =
Int.:	= Sex, yeah, yeah.
Tracy:	boyfriends and periods for girls. They *shouldn't know* about that until they're at the age where they *should start know*ing about it. (...) When they're this age at school, it doesn't matter because there's no (0.1) there's no badness there at this age. They go and they learn and they learn how to read and write and play. And all the children at their age it's all one understanding. But when it comes to year 6, it's completely different.

Tracy's use of deontic modals encoding a sense of moral obligation to preserve youth's innocence betrays her fear of the outer world and indexes her identity construction as guardian of her children's integrity. In her words, mainstream reality appears as oozing immorality from which her community needs to shield its children. Preserving the separation between her ingroup where children are kept as children and the outer world is therefore the essential task of a parent like Tracy who has partial but not yet complete agency.

Excerpt 10

Interviewer:	Mm-hmm. What is your relationship with, um, you know, the other people, the settled people?
Tracy:	Well, I've got some friends.
Int.:	Really?
Tracy:	But *we're so different.* It's hard to (.) I've got some friends at the school that I chat to. They're nice girls but they're so, *such different ways of living* that I couldn't, um (.) *such different. So different.*

Int.:	Yeah, very different. It's hard.
Tracy:	*Very different. Different ways of upbringing their children, different ways of speaking* in front of people.
Int.:	Yeah.
Tracy:	*Different ways of (.) different completely* ↓

Here the insistent repetition of the qualifier 'different', describing the way of living, bringing up children and even speaking, reinforces the 'us' and 'them' and the polarity between Travellers' permanency and the lifestyle of Gorja people, or non-Travellers. However, it is in the last excerpt that Tracy pictures herself as a woman still devoid of social agency. She now has her own permanent space (hence she is endowed with material agency), and she is insightful enough to reflect on her condition (hence she has developed embodied agency); however, due to the outside world not recognising her community's customs and ideology and denying it institutional agency, she still is an incomplete social actor subject to the external pressure of social structures.

Excerpt 11

Tracy:	(Talking about an education adviser) And she's got this, uh, view on life that, 'Oh the travellers, the travelling girls miss out so much on life.' Well they do, but they don't neither because *we still all end up being okay and we enjoy our life. It's not a horrible life, it's an enjoyable life. We enjoy our life.* But anyway, she thinks that they're missing out so much on life that she wants them to go to school. I said, 'along with you thinking they're missing out on life, we think that when we put them to school we're (0.2) not putting them into danger because you're not really putting them into danger but you're also showing them another side of life that they don't need to see'.
Interviewer:	Mm-hmm.
Tracy:	I said 'they can...yeah they can get education at home' and she says that (city name) got a law against education at home. *I said I'd google* it and look at it but I never did because I was too busy. And she's, um (.) I don't like her because she's too forceful. She's too, um *She's got her way on our w*ay. She got a thing in her mind and you aren't changing it, you know.

Tracy describes the pressure she often feels in the new space when educational advisers try to convince her to keep her children in school. She defends Travellers' life as 'enjoyable' and justifies their eschewal of education. Her reply 'I'd google it' shows again her embodied agency, but at the same time her struggle to get social agency that can only be achieved if her way of life is recognised by settled society. Looking at this issue from a non-biased perspective, what is of relevance is not who is right and who is wrong; rather it is the opposition between two very different ways of seeing the world that is at stake here. Tracy certainly has agency in many domains of her life. However, when entering into contact with the majoritarian group and its social structures, she loses that agency and is unable to function socially. In conclusion, in this situation of still partial agency, her desires and wants remain unfulfilled and cannot be transformed into intention to perform actions (Malle & Knobe, 2001).

Conclusion

This study reflects on a representative member of an Irish Traveller group who suffers from problematic access to living space and a contradictory relation with (im)mobility. It was within a vision of space as not neutral but always politically meaningful that Tracy's talk was analysed in two distinct contexts of partial and forced mobility and permanent immobility.

Throughout the two interviews, Tracy defended her mobile lifestyle as the 'systematic product of habitus', resulting from those socialised norms or tendencies that guide behaviour and thinking, which are 'internalized and converted into a disposition that generates meaningful practices and meaning-giving perceptions' (Bourdieu, 1984, in Gieseking et al., 2014: 139–140). Her nomadic habitus that functions as a system of signs organises all other aspects of life in her community, including education and morality. However, Tracy's lifestyle is not understood or granted any form of recognition by the majoritarian settled community, which, by abiding by very different socialised norms, continues to constrain her agency. She is unable to make her own choice of an itinerant life if she wants to ensure her children's basic education; however, she cannot stay in any given space for longer than three months, which forces her to resume mobility. When permanency is finally bestowed upon her, it is in a shape that is, at least partly, foreign to her.

This case study, therefore, contributes to the discussion about the relationship between agency and social structures and underlines the crucial role that these have in reducing the individual's free will at least when she comes in contact with them. Drawing on Block (2012: 54), it is argued that there is 'a temporal/historical frame to all acts of agency in subject positioning'. In the particular story of Tracy, the Traveller, the historical frame is that of society's racist disposition towards itinerant groups, to which she refers in her identity construction and which undeniably impinges on her agency, still moulded by a society whose social norms she does not endorse. By using Lahlou's tripartite division of material, embodied and social (and institutional) agency, this study has shown the importance of access to space and the difficulty encountered by those people whose spatial interpretation is not consonant with and is therefore refuted by mainstream society. While in line with others, this study emphasises the crucial function of social structures, it highlights that agency is entirely a context-dependent notion; in light of this, a person can have low agency in some domains and high in others. Even in a context of precarious immobility and forced mobility, Tracy constructs herself as agentive and capable of engaging critically with the social structures of a society she does not respect or believe in. Later on, she shows that having one's own immobile space ensures self-efficacy and a sense of dignity and security to which she aspired for nearly 20 years in her wanderings across the south of England. However, permanency within a situation of lack of social and institutional recognition is still not sufficient to grant full agency to an individual. In this situation of only partial agency, therefore, Tracy's wants are still unfulfilled in spite of the immobility mainstream society has granted her.

Notes

(1) Transcription symbols:
(…) deleted text
(non-verbal information)
[transcriber's notes]
(.) pause
(1.0) long pause indicated by seconds
Italics for easy identification of relevant elements
CAPS for higher pitch
↑ for rising intonation in a non-interrogative context
↓ for falling intonation
= latching
~xxx~ for faster delivery
(2) Local connection means that someone lives or works in the area, has close family in the area or lives in the area for other special reasons. In this case, the council can be of assistance.

References

Ahearn, L. (2001) Language and agency. *Annual Review of Anthropology* 30, 109–137.
Baynham, M. (2009) 'Just one day like today': Scale and the analysis of space/time orientation in narrative displacement. In J. Collins, M. Baynham and S. Slembrouck (eds) *Globalization and Language in Contact: Scale, Migration, and Communicative Practices* (pp. 130–147). London/New York: Continuum.

Baynham, M. and De Fina, A. (eds) (2005) *Dislocations/Relocations: Narratives of Displacement*. London/New York: Routledge.

Benwell, B. and Stokoe, E. (2006) *Identity and Discourse*. Edinburgh: Edinburgh University Press.

Billig, M. (1996) *Arguing and Thinking: A Rhetorical Approach to Social Psychology* (2nd edn). Cambridge: Cambridge University Press.

Block, D. (2012) Unpicking agency in sociolinguistic research with migrants. In S. Gardner and M. Martin-Jones (eds) *Multilingualism, Discourse and Ethnography* (pp. 47–61). New York/London: Routledge.

Blommaert, J. and De Fina, A. (2017) Chronotopic identities: On the timespace organization of who we are. In A. De Fina, D. Ikizoglu and J. Wegner (eds) *Diversity and Super-diversity* (pp. 1–14). Washington, DC: Georgetown University Press.

Bourdieu, P. (1977) *Outline of a Theory of Practice* (R. Nice, trans.). Cambridge: Cambridge University Press.

Bourdieu, P. (1984) The habitus and the space of life-styles. In J. Gieseking, W. Mangold, C. Katz, S. Low and S. Saegert (eds) *The People, Place, and Space Reader* (pp. 139–144). New York/London, Routledge.

Bucholtz, M. and Hall, K. (2005) Identity and interaction: A sociocultural linguistic approach. *Discourse Studies* 7 (4/5), 585–614.

Canagarajah, S. (2017) *Translingual Practices and Neoliberal Policies*. New York: Springer.

Caravan Sites Act (1968) See https://www.legislation.gov.uk/ukpga/1968/52/contents.

Chilton, P.A. and Ilyin, M. (1993) Metaphor in political discourse: The case of the 'Common European House'. *Discourse and Society* 4 (1), 7–31.

Coleman, S. and Collins, P. (eds) (2006) *Locating the Field: Space, Place and Context in Anthropology*. Oxford/New York: Berg.

Cross, J. and Karides, M. (2007) Capitalism, modernity, and the 'appropriate' use of space. In J. Cross and A. Morales (eds) *Street Entrepreneurs: People, Place, & Politics in Local and Global Perspective* (pp. 19–35). Abingdon: Routledge.

De Fina, A. (2003) *Identity in Narrative: A Study of Immigrant Discourse*. Amsterdam/Philadelphia, PA: John Benjamins.

De Fina, A. (2019) Narrative and identities. In A. De Fina and A. Georgakopoulou (eds) *The Handbook of Narrative Analysis* (pp. 351–368). Malden, MA: Wiley Blackwell.

De Fina, A., Schiffrin, D. and Bamberg, M. (eds) (2006) *Discourse and Identity*. Cambridge: Cambridge University Press.

De Fina, A., Paternostro, G. and Amoruso, M. (2020) Odysseus the traveler: Appropriation of a chronotope in a community of practice. *Language & Communication* 70, 71–81

Delanty, G., Wodak, R. and Jones, P. (2008) *Identity, Belonging and Migration*. Liverpool: Liverpool University Press.

Deleuze, G. and Guattari, F. (1999) *A Thousands Plateaus*. London: Bloomsbury

Dixon, J. and Durrheim, K. (2000) Displacing place-identity: A discursive approach to locating self and other. *British Journal of Social Psychology* 39, 27–44.

Duranti, A. (2006) Agency in language. In A. Duranti (ed.) *A Companion to Linguistic Anthropology* (pp. 451–473). Malden, MA: Blackwell.

Fishman, J. (1967) Bilingualism with and without diglossia. Diglossia with and without bilingualism. *Journal of Social Issues* 2, 29–38.

Foucault, M. (1980) *Power/Knowledge*. Brighton: Harvester Press.

Gieseking, J.J., Mangold, W., Katz, C., Low, S. and Saeger, S. (eds) (2014) *The People, Place, and Space Reader*. New York/London: Routledge.

Goffman, E. (1974) *Frame Analysis – An Essay in the Organization of Experience*. Boston, MA: Northeastern Press.

Gonzálvez García, F. (2000) Modulating grammar through modality: A discourse approach. *ELIA* 1, 119–136.

Gramsci, A. (1971) *Prison Notebooks*. New York: International Publishers.

Halliday, M.A.K. (1970) Functional diversity in language as seen from a consideration of modality and mood in English. *Foundations of Language* 6, 322–361.

Huddleston, R. and Pullum, G. (2002) *The Cambridge Grammar of the English Language*. Cambridge: Cambridge University Press.

James, Z. (2007) Policing marginal spaces: Controlling Gypsies and Travellers. *Criminology & Criminal Justice* 7 (4), 367–389.

Kabachnik, P. (2012) Nomads and mobile places: Disentangling place, space and mobility. *Identities: Global Studies in Culture and Power* 19 (2), 210–228.

Ladegaard, H. (2011) Stereotypes in the making: Stereotypes and cultural generalizations in Hong Kong students' discourse. *Journal of Asian Pacific Communication* 21, 133–158.

Ladegaard, H. (2012) The discourse of powerlessness and repression: Identity construction in domestic helper narratives. *Journal of Sociolinguistics* 16 (4), 450–482.

Lahlou, S. (2017) How agency is distributed through installations. In N.J. Enfield and P. Kockelman (eds) *Distributed Agency* (pp. 221–232). Oxford: Oxford University Press.

Lakoff, G. (1991) Metaphors and war: The metaphor system used to justify war in the Gulf. Paper delivered at Berkeley University. See https://escholarship.org/content/qt9sm131vj/qt9sm131vj.pdf.

Lakoff, G. and Johnson, M. (1980) *Metaphors We Live By*. Chicago, IL: University of Chicago Press.

Lauerbach, G. (2006) Discourse representation in political interviews: The construction of identities and relations through voicing and ventriloquizing. *Journal of Pragmatics* 38, 196–215.

Lefebvre, H. (2014 [1991]) The production of space. In J. Giesekin, W. Mangold, C. Katz, S. Low and S. Saegert (eds) *The People, Place, and Space Reader* (pp. 289–293). New York/London: Routledge.

Levinson, M. (2007) Literacy in English Gypsy communities: Cultural capital manifested as negative asset. *American Educational Research Journal* 44 (1), 5–39.

Liebscher, G. and Dailey-O'Cain, J. (2013) *Language, Space and Identity in Migration*. Basingstoke: Palgrave Macmillan.

Low, S. (2014) Spatialising culture. In J. Giesekin, W. Mangold, C. Katz, S. Low and S. Saegert (eds) *The People, Place, and Space Reader* (pp. 34–38). New York/London: Routledge.

Malle, B. and Knobe, J. (2001) The distinction between desire and intention: A folk-conceptual analysis. In B. Malle, L. Moses and D. Baldwin (eds) *Intentions and Intentionality* (pp. 45–67). Cambridge, MA: MIT Press.

May, V. (2004) Narrative identity and the re-conceptualization of lone motherhood. *Narrative Enquiry* 14, 169–189.

Medved, M. and Brockmeier, J. (2015) On the margins: Aboriginal realities and 'white man's research'. In R. Piazza and A. Fasulo (eds) *Marked Identities* (pp. 79–97). London: Palgrave.

Musolff, A. (2006) Metaphor scenarios in public discourse. *Metaphor and Symbol* 21 (1), 23–38.

Ochs, E. (1993) Constructing social identity: A language socialization perspective. *Research on Language and Social Interaction* 26, 287–306.

Piazza, R. (2014) '… might go to Birmingham, Leeds … up round there, Manchester … and then we always come back here …': The conceptualisation of place among a group of Irish women travellers. *Discourse and Society* 25 (2), 263–282.

Piazza, R. (2021) *The Discursive Construction of Identity and Space among Mobile People*. London: Bloomsbury.
Pomerantz, A. (1984) Agreeing and disagreeing with assessments: Some features of preferred/dispreferred turn shapes. In J. Maxwell Atkinson and J. Heritage (eds) *Structures of Social Action: Studies in Conversation Analysis* (pp. 57–101). Cambridge: Cambridge University Press.
Pujolar, J. (2009) Immigration in Catalonia: Marking territory through language. In J. Collins, M. Baynham and S. Slembrouck (eds) *Globalization and Language in Contact: Scale, Migration, and Communicative Practices* (pp. 85–108). London/New York: Continuum.
Soja, E.W. (1996) *Thirdspace: Journeys to Los Angeles and Other Real-and-imagined Places*. Malden, MA: Blackwell.
Speller, G. (2000) A community in transition: A longitudinal study of place attachment and identity processes in the context of an enforced relocation. PhD thesis, University of Surrey.
van Leeuwen, T. (2008) *Discourse and Practice*. Oxford: Oxford University Press.
Vertovec, S. (2001) Transnationalism and identity. *Journal of Ethnic and Migration Studies* 27 (4), 573–582.
Whitehead, S. (2002) *Men and Masculinity*. London: Polity Press.

12 Postscript: Immobilities Normalized

Jan Blommaert

Salazar's (2018: 154) caution against over-celebrations of mobilities and their self-evident benefits has rarely been borne out to such a painful extent as now, at the time of writing this postscript. I am writing it from the depth of the COVID-19 crisis of 2020 and its worldwide restrictions on mobility. This exceptional global condition was compounded by a personal one, in which the side-effects of cancer confined me to a wheelchair recently. These sobering conditions make it overly clear that we live in a world in which mobility is still selective and conditional, not an inevitable extension of a set of other conditions. As a footnote, I should note that these global and personal realities add to something I thought I would not witness any more in my lifetime: European politicians boasting their record of curtailing (and rendering impossible) the free movement of people within the EU, celebrating hard borders, and winning elections on platforms advocating such restrictions. For those who believe that mobility is the simple defining condition of the 21st century, these are times that prompt reflection and reconsideration. This collection of essays does precisely that: it brings to the issue of mobilities its inevitable antithesis, immobilities, and examines the very diverse conditions and constraints that generate a complicated dynamic between both poles. Having said that, I can offer a couple of general reflections on this wonderful collection of studies.

I have to start from something extraordinarily trivial: all the studies in this book actually operate from within a sociolinguistics of mobility – they have taken on board all the ontological and methodological premises developed within that strand of sociolinguistics – and, consequently, they all accept that there is nothing stable or static about the sociolinguistic phenomena they describe. Whenever people move, their sociolinguistic repertoires get affected, and this has effects in the most palpable sense on what it is they can achieve in actual moments of interaction.

I am making this trivial point because it excludes several lines of argument in this book: lines, for instance, that would explain institutional misunderstanding between – say – an asylum applicant and an immigration official working through an application procedure interview as sociocognitively or cognitive-psychologically generated. No, the direction taken in this collection of essays is towards a number of very different factors of explanation. We can summarize them with some keywords: power-knowledge, governmentality, distributed agency and distributed access to agency depending on access to scales and chronotopes, immobilization not as a given but as an intervention and an effect of (usually unilateral) agency, and as an intervention that has determining effects – they cannot be simply reversed by the immobilized party. To summarize this: the direction of explanation taken by the authors in this collection is one of socially and institutionally enacted power, not – I underscore – an explanation in which more sophisticated measurement or testing tools can bring about change.

Observe how in the same breath – and several authors did not miss that point – a pretty popular sociolinguistic discourse needs to be surrendered: one in which mobility and its 'trans'-phenomenology of seemingly unrestricted innovativeness and creativity are perceived (and celebrated) as primarily a possibility. Evidently, what we see in this book is that strategies of immobilization shape impossibilities; they disqualify much of what could be valuable as problem-solving resources in complex interaction situations and render voiceless people who, otherwise, would be eminently capable of voicing their own interests and concerns. It is essential that we see the relationship between mobility-as-possibility and immobilization-as-impossibility as twins, as dimensions that are invariably present – latently or actively – in a sociolinguistics of mobility.

The more complex and fascinating the possibilities of sociolinguistic mobility have proven to be, the more complex and fascinating we must expect their negation to be. Strategies of immobilization, of disqualification and de-voicing, we can read in the pages of this book, are at once simple and complex. They are simple because, often, they emerge from unilateral and pretty brutal acts of power. But they are complex because this power is played out in a Foucaultian field of power-knowledge, in which particular language ideologies – those of literate standardization, usually – and sociolinguistic imaginations – those of sedentary homogeneism, usually – are deployed and enforced. Needless to say that this deployment occurs in spite of the existence of overwhelming and crippling disqualifications of such ideologies and imaginations. Their deployment is axiomatic, and as such a key element of the governmentality overwhelmingly brought down on the field of language and mobility – read, language and migration, with resulting forms of multilingualisms and multiliteracies.

And it is at this point that we face the burden of precision and accuracy in analysis. I consider the widely shared awareness, articulated throughout this book, of the critical relevance of notions such as scales and chronotopes an analytical advantage here, for both concepts force us towards utmost explicitness in our work. There is no way of understanding mobilities without a notion of scales, that forces us to look into the precise zones affected by processes of mobility and to consider the specific dynamics of access to particular scales. Not every refugee, obviously, has access to the scale-level of officially regulated and fully legal migration. Detecting the rules of access to different scale-levels is, I am convinced, a major analytical task for all of us. And the same goes for chronotopes: the concept compels us to extreme precision in specifying what 'context' actually is when we consider situated moments and processes of communication. Both concepts, in that sense, protect us from facile overgeneralizations and poorly grounded forms of critique. When we use them well, they benefit the punch of our critique and create a bedrock of robust empirical arguments in our favor.

There is, finally, one empirical feature of the studies collected here that struck me. It is about the smallness of the world for those who have been the victims of immobilization strategies. People who have seen the most productive parts of their (often impressive) repertoires disqualified or stigmatized are condemned to painfully difficult trajectories between very small spaces of agency – we can call them (COVID-19-wise) 'bubbles'. Often, online infrastructures are crucial facilitators in this. Other than that, their mobility is heavily restricted to small congregations, many of which bear low prestige and legitimacy. The power-knowledge regime of immobilization, we can see, reduces the size, scope and social impact of the social world in which its victims live. And we can imagine the difficulties facing those who wish to break out of the smallness of such a regimented world, in which most of what defines you, as a fully 'integrated' person, is considered to have no value or legitimacy.

It is easier for many of us – the hypermobile elites of this world – to imagine this now, because for most of 2020, many of us lived under lockdown and were subject to severe restrictions on mobility due to the COVID-19 crisis. Immobilities became normalized in 2020. Online tools were the prescribed alternative. And while we now inevitably must realize that we live in an online-offline nexus, all of us have experienced the limitations of a social system exclusively operating through online tools.

The loss of access to erstwhile self-evident forms of mobility, ranging (across scales and chronotopes, note) all the way from air travel across the globe to even visits to our neighborhood supermarkets or family members came as a terrific shock and wake-up call to many of us. A world of severely restricted mobility is an ordeal, something we can only experience in terms of loss and restriction, even punishment. It is good, however, to have gone through this experience. It is now part of our social imagination – we can imagine how life is under immobilization measures. Those measures are and have been applied, we know, to millions of other people in the context of restrictions on movement – to migrants, refugees, asylum seekers, name it. And they have been politically weaponized by politicians and parties in so many parts of the world, often with great electoral effects.

It is good, I believe, that a book such as this one will enter the public domain at a time when the public has experienced the rigors of a heavily sanctioned and policed life of immobility usually administered to the Other, the unwanted Other, and cannot any longer fake ignorance about how it feels, how it reduces all of us as human beings, and how it should never be a social or political ambition. While this book may have been perceived as militant and radical a year ago, it may now be read as a much-welcomed explanation of the weird predicament so many of us experienced just recently. And of the unbearable injustices that motivate it.

Reference

Salazar, N. (2018) Theorizing mobility through concepts and figures. *Tempo Social* 30 (2), 153–168. doi:10.11606/0103-2070.ts.2018.142112

Index

Page numbers in bold refer to information in figures, those followed by n refer to notes.

Abiola (pseudonym) 232, 234, 235–236, 244–245
abuse 235, 236
  linguistic 173, 199–200, 238–239
Accademia della Crusca 154–155
activism 234, 238, 241
advertising discourse 89–93, 96–105, 108–109
affiliative agency 38, 53
African languages 27–29, 31–35, 127–129
African migrants 18–19, 22–23, 26–27, 41, 66, 74
Afsoon (pseudonym) 222
agency 8, 247, 248–251, 257–259, 265–266, 271
  embodied agency 250, 255, 261, 262, 264
  institutional agency 250, 255, 264
  material agency 250, 253, 255, 259
  social agency 250, 255, 257, 261–265
Ahmed (pseudonym) 230–231, 232, 234, 244
Albanese, Fabio 147
Alleanza Nazionale 151
Amadou (pseudonym) 32–33
apartheid 183–185, 186–191
  on beaches 191–194, 195, 197–198
  post-apartheid 183, 188–189, 197–198, 200–202
  see also racism; segregation
Aquarius (ship) 152
Arabic languages 70–72, 106–107
  Libyan 32–33, 34, 177–178
  Sudanese 43, 44
asylum seekers
  'asylum speakers' 119
  education 20–21
  institutional contexts 70–74, 121–122, 131–133, 209
  rejection of 118, 122–129
  sexuality 231–232, 243
  see also migrants; refugees
asymmetric contact zones 61–62
Australia 41, 43, 50–52, 57n
  racism 186–187
authenticity 119–120, 133
Avan (pseudonym) 221

Bakhtin, Mikhail 166, 232–234
balcony people 152–154
Bambara language 31
Bashir (pseudonym) 118, 122–129, 131
beaches 184, 185–189, 201–202
  apartheid 191–194, 195, 197–198
Bejya (pseudonym) 220–221
Beki (pseudonym) 237–245
Belgium *see* Flanders
belonging 5, 19, 51, 54–56
  linguistic 48
  political 154, 158
Bengali migrants 22
Bhargav (pseudonym) 172–173
borders 1–2, 8, 9, 40, 136
  beaches 185–189
  and language 33, 52, 56

Mediterranean Sea 137–138, 141–143, 146
reinforcement 91, 136, 138–139, 144, 212, 270
Bossi-Fini Law (Law No 189, 2002), Italy 35–36n
Brazil, racism 187–188
Brink, André 196–197

camps/centres 167, 212, 219–222
  architecture 214–215
  detention centres 139–140, 177–178
  hotspots 168–169, 208–209
  Irish traveller permanent sites 247, 253, 259, 262
  Irish traveller transit camps 247, 252–253, 258, 259–260, 262
  reception centres 34, 163, 168–178, 209–210
Camus, Albert 195–196
capitalism 212, 248
cartographic representations 100–102
CAS (emergency reception centres), Italy 168–170
Catalonia 90, 93, 106, 109
categorization 62–65, 80–81
  migrants 23, 25, 74, 104, 209
  mobility based 90–91
  racial 189–190
cell phones 19, 139–140
CGVS/CGRS (Commissioner General for Refugees and Stateless Persons), Belgium 70–72, 122–124, 131
chronotopes 6, 251, 272
  and identity 166
  language repertoires 175
  and migration 56, 173
  queer asylum stories 230, 232–233, 244–245
church 53, 239
CIE (*Centri di Identificazione ed Expulsione*) 140
citizenship 90, 136, 163
  gatekeeping 88, 91, 93, 94–95, 109
coastline *see* beaches
Coletti, Vittorio 154–155

colonialism 183–186, 194–198, 201–202
  languages of 28, 31, 177
Colour Pink 237
communicative practices 2, 5, 19, 165–166
  in Mediterranean Sea 138
  in temporary reception centres (TRCs) 173–176, 177, 179
communities 3, 35, 51–53
  see also Irish Travellers
compassion 207–208, 212, 215–216, 219, 223
comprehension *see* mutual understanding
conduct 168, 210, 222–223
contact theory 189
contact zones 3, 61–62
contextualization practices 79–80
counter-conduct 168, 207–208, 210–211, 220, 222–223
Covid-19 7, 270, 272–273
CPSA/Hotspots 168–169
Cuba 198

Dahoud, Kamel 196
data collection 22, 24, 26–27, 65–66, 122–126, 169–170
De Klerk, F.W. 193
Decree Law no. 113/2018, Italy 168–169
detention centres 139–140, 177–178
deterritorialization 97–102, 137–138, 139–140, 166
Di Maio, Luigi 148–149, 150, 152, 159n
Digi.Mobil 96
digital technology *see* ICT (Information & telecommunication technologies)
discourses
  dual discourses 137, 138
  multimodal discourse analysis 92–93, 99–104
disruption 40
Donadel, Luca 147

Eastside Camp, Lesvos 207, 209, 213, 214, 219–220
economic migrants 2, 7–8, 99

education 212
  asylum seekers 20–21
  informal 221–222
  Irish Travellers 254–257, 260–261, 263–264
  refugees 209–211, 215–219, 222–223
  see also teaching
elective affinity 38, 53
ELF (English as a lingua franca) see global English
embodied agency 250, 255, 261, 262, 264
emergency reception centres (CAS), Italy 168–170
English language 174–177, 217–219, 221–222
  global English 60–63, 74, 77, 78, 82, 106, 217–218
  learning 209–210, 221–222
  migration experiences 31, 32, 34, 43–44
enregisterment 4, 116–117, 119–120, 130–131
entitlement 65, 81, 259
  medical prescriptions 74–77
ethical issues 25–26
Ethiopia 44, 49–50, 239–245
ethnographic studies 120–122, 231–232, 247–248, 252–253
EUNAVFOR MED 137, 143
European Asylum Support Office (EASO) 209
European Union (EU) 91, 117, 145, 270
  agreement with Turkey 207, 208–209
  Mediterranean Sea 136–137, 138–139, 141, 142, 143–144
  see also government policies
Eurosur 142
exclusion 167, 248
  child refugees 216–217
  extranjeros 91, 93, 96–97
  Irish Travellers 249, 252, 258, 263–264
  of migrants 18–19, 171–172, 212–213
  settled migrants 50–52
  see also othering
exclusive (negative) immobility 53–55
Exodus: Our Journey to Europe (TV show) 213

experiential orientation 71, 73
extranjeros 91, 93, 96–97

Facebook 22, 26, 241–243
  racism 199–201
family relationships 102–105, 107–108
first language 26–27, 38–39, 43, 118
Flanders
  asylum applications 70–74
  institutional contexts 60–65, 77–78, 81–82, 118, 121–122
  refugees' entitlements 74–77
  university applications 66–70
flight 138, 211, 230, 233, 237, 245
fluidity 18, 34, 39, 45, 51–52
Foucault, Michel 167–168, 207, 210, 223
Fratelli D'Italia 151
French language 31, 35, 127–128, 132, 174, 176
Frontex 138–139, 142, 144, 146, 147–148, 158n, 213
Fula (Pular) language 31, 32

Gasparri, Maurizio 151
gatekeeping 8, 62, 72
  citizenship 88, 91, 93, 94–95, 109
Gefira 146
German language 209–210, 218
Germany 236
global English 60–63, 78, 82
  institutional contexts 74, 77, 78
  in marketing 106
  teaching 217–218
globalization 2, 4, 20, 87, 164–165
Go Back Where You Come From (TV show) 51, 57n
government policies 88–90
  Flanders 70, 122
  Greece 209–211
  Italy 150, 168–169
  Spain 90–91, 94–95
  see also European Union (EU)
governmentality 9–10, 89–90, 167, 223, 271–272
  humanitarian governmentality 211–213

neo-liberal governmentality 88–90, 108–110
GPS (Global Positioning System) 139
Greece
 government policies 209–211
 Lesvos Island 207, 208–209, 213, 214–222
Greek language 209–211, 216, 217–218
Group Areas Act (1950/1975), South Africa 189–190
Guinea Conakry 118, 123–125, 127–128

Happy Móvil 96
Hellenic Open University, Greece 213
Hendrickse, Allen 193
heteroglossia 17, 29, 168
heteronormativity 233
heterotopia 167
home language *see* first language
horizontal language situation 45, 51–52
hospitality 214
humanitarian aid 137, 211, 215–217
 search and rescue missions 137, 142–144, 146–153
humanitarian governmentality 207–208, 211–213
hybridity 2, 164, 165, 187
Hymesian narrative inequality 119

Ibrahim (pseudonym) 32
ICT (Information & telecommunication technologies) 5, 18–20, 35, 87–89, 108–110, 136, 138–139
 language policies 106–107
 marketing 89
 mobile communications 5, 139–140
 Spain 90
 see also internet based information; telecommunications industry sector
identity 2, 5, 6
 and agency 248–249, 250
 chronotopic identity 166
 construction of 258
 migrant identities 51–52, 54–55, 91–92
 place identity 247–248
 proofs of 117–118, 119, 132–133

sexuality 230
ideological becoming 234, 240
illegality 24–26
immigrants *see* migrants
(im)mobilities 40–41, 43, 117, 260
 dynamics 6–8, 163–164
 enforced 20–21, 24, 34, 163, 177–179
 (im)mobilization 98, 207, 209–210, 212, 271
 language and space 38–39, 52–56, 248
 multi-layered 41–43
 normalization 272–273
 and power 167–168
 settler-colonial (im)mobilities 183–185
 see also mobilities
Immorality Act (1927/1950), South Africa 191, 194–195
inarticulateness 129
inclusion 82, 167, 212
 pathways for 23–24
inclusive (positive) mobility 53–55
indexical meanings 11, 99, 175–177, 200
indigeneity, proof of 125, 131
indigenous people 119–120, 184, 186, 188, 189, 195, 202n
installation theory 250
institutional agency 250, 255, 264
institutional contexts 8, 61, 65, 173
 asylum seekers 70–74, 121–122, 131–133
 categorization processes 25, 63–65, 168–169
 enregisterment 94–95, 116–117, 130–131
 institutional literacy 73–74, 81–82
 Irish Travellers 258–259
 matrix of suspicion 118, 119
 racial profiling 89
 residence permits 74–77
 university applications 66–70
 use of global English 62–63, 65, 77, 78
integration 19, 98
interactional alignment 62, 64, 70–71, 79, 80–82
interactional skills 79, 80–81
International Telecommunications Union (ITU) 111n

internet based information 117, 120, 125, 129, 131
  see also ICT (Information & telecommunication technologies)
Irish Travellers 247
  education 254–257, 260–261, 263–264
  exclusion 262, 264
  identity 251, 261
  traditions 249, 251–253, 255–257, 262–263
  isolation 20–21
  see also segregation
Italian Coastguard 146, 152, 153
Italian language 174
  #scendeteli controversy 154–158
  teaching 21–22, 26
Italy 20
  ItaStra workshops 21–24
  media coverage 143, 147–149, 151, 154–155
  political situation 137, 142, 147–155, 156–158, 159n
  reception centres 163, 168–178
Iuventa (boat) 149

Jagger (pseudonym) 171–172
Jamaica 237
Jessica (pseudonym) 232, 234, 237, 244
Jugend Rettet 149

Kamil (pseudonym) 176

L1 language see first language
languages
  boundaries 39
  informal learning 31, 221–222
  as resource 3–4, 165–166, 174–177, 179
  shaping spaces 41–42, 46–52, 56
  socialization 28
  teaching 208, 209–211, 215–219, 222–223
Lebara 96, 99–100, 107
Lega 137, 152, 155, 156–157, 159n
legal assistance 65, 70–74
legality 24–26, 88

Lesvos Island, Greece 207, 208–209, 213, 214–222
l'Étranger (Camus) 195–196
Ley 25/2007 (2006), Spain 94–95, 105
LGBTQ migrants see queer life trajectories
Libya 26
  agreement with Italy 150
  Arabic language 32–33, 34, 177–178
  engine fishers 158n
  and migrants 20, 141, 146, 177–178
LifeBoat 143, 146, 158n
lifestory genre 232–233, 245
Lingua (pseudonym) 42
  multilingualism 43–46, 48–52
lingua franca see global English
linguistic spaces 35, 46–52
  borders 18
  linguo-spatial triad 46–48
  maps 30
literacy skills
  institutional contexts 122–123, 126, 128
  and language learning 21, 26, 44, 53
Lucano, Domenico 158

M5S (*Movimento 5 Stelle*) 137, 148, 152, 156, 159n
Malidi (pseudonym) 118, 126–128, 131
Malinka language 124, 127, 129
Mamadou (pseudonym) 31–32
Mande language 129
Mandela, Nelson 193
Mandinka language 31, 32, 34
Manjako language 32
Mare Nostrum (MN) 137, 142
marginalisation 8, 171, 252
market segmentation 104
  of migrants 90, 95–96
market spaces 48–49
material agency 250, 253, 255, 259
Mating Birds (Nkosi) 194, 196–198
meaning, construction of 8, 61–62, 92–93, 116, 167
Médecins Sans Frontières (MSF) 143, 212
media coverage, Italy 143, 147–149, 151, 154–155

medical prescriptions 74–77
Mediterranean Sea 212
    as border 137–138, 141–143, 146
    search and rescue missions 137, 142–144, 146–153
Meloni, Giorgia 151
Menan (pseudonym) 222
methodologies *see* research methods
migrants
    categorization 23, 25, 74, 104, 209
    containment 167
    as customers 97–102
    economic migrants 2, 7–8, 99
    flows of 117, 165
    as guests 121–122, 140, 176, 214
    insecurity of 24–26
    languages 18, 107–108
    migrant identities 91–92
    stereotypes 35, 93, 96–98, 99–101, 107–108, 109–110, 172
    use of ICT 19, 87–88
    see also asylum seekers; refugees
migration experiences 18, 24–26, 30, 42
    in Africa 26–27, 48–51
    in Australia 51–53
    English language 31, 32, 34, 43–44
    language skills 33–35
    queer asylum stories 229–231
militaristic camps 214–215
military metaphors 254–256, 261
Minden (ship) 146, 159n
mixed methods 41
MOAS (Maltese Migrants Offshore Aid Station) 143, 147
mobile communications 9, 139–140
mobilities 40–41, 270
    bounded 20
    dynamics 3, 4, 6–8, 163–164
    forced 24, 265
    mobility turn 1–8
    and sedentary power 137–138, 167–168
    and segregation 18–21
    virtual mobility 167
    see also (im)mobilities
monetization, family relationships 102–105

monolingualism 40, 105–106, 108, 109, 111n
Moria Camp, Lesvos 208–209, 219–220
Moroccans 99–100
mother tongue *see* first language
Movimento 5 Stelle (M5S) 137, 148, 152, 156, 159n
Movistar 106
multilingualism 33, 39
    Africa 18, 26–27, 27–29, 127–129
    fluidity 45–46
    mobilities 5, 38–39, 42, 82
    repertoires 30–35, 43–46, 127–129
    segregation 34–35
multimodal discourse analysis 92–93, 99–104
Muslims
    advertising discourse 98
    Qu'ranic schools 33–34, 123, 125
mutual understanding 61–62, 68–69, 79, 80–81
    problems of 72–73, 76–77

naming practices 118, 130–131, 132–133, 196, 240, 243
nation states 8, 89–90, 97–98, 107, 165
    control by 102, 104, 109, 138
native language *see* first language
neo-liberal governmentality 88–90, 108–110
NGOs 212, 214
    language teaching 214, 217–218, 221–222
    Mediterranean Sea 143, 145–152, 158n
Niger 20, 26–27
Nilotic languages 45
Nkosi, Lewis 194, 196–198
nomads 136, 248–249
    nomadic habit 252, 265
    nomadology 137–138, 139
normalization
    of exclusion 207–208
    (im)mobilities 272–273
    non-education of children 215–217

Open Arms 143, 149, 151
Operation Themis 143

Orange 95–96, **104**, 106
order-words 144–152
othering 97, 98, 109, 200, 201, 273
   see also exclusion; segregation

Pakistanis 99–100
particularization 63–64
passing 48, 49
passwords 10, 145
Peircean grid 47
Penard, Frédéric 152
peripheries 2, 3, 5, 82
Peul people 124
place see spaces
political situation
   Greece 209–211
   Italy 137, 142, 147–155, 156–158, 159n
   Spain 90–91
popolo dei balconi 152–154
populism 137, 148–152, 168
   sado-populism 157
porosity 39
post-apartheid 183, 188–189, 197–198, 200–202
power 5, 6, 8, 10, 271
   inequality 133
   and language 39–40, 51–52, 55, 119, 166
   mobilities 167–168
   political 88
   sedentary 137–138
   technologies 136
Prohibition of Mixed Marriages Act (1949), South Africa 191, 194–195
Pular language 31, 32

queer life trajectories 232–235, 244–245
   Abiola 235–236
   Beki 237–243
   Jessica 237

racism 173, 183
   on beaches 186–189, 197–200
   Irish Travellers 252, 257, 265
   racial profiling 89, 104–105
   see also apartheid
reception centres
   Greece 209–210
   Italy 163, 168–178
receptive language 34
reciprocity 79, 82
refugees 163
   camps 44, 50, 208–209, 214–222
   education 208–211, 215–219, 222–223
   entitlements 74–77
   immobilization 207–209
   informal learning 221–222
   status 65–66, 68–69, 122
   see also asylum seekers; migrants
registers 18
   discrepancies 129–131, 132–133
   expectations of 118–119
relational zones 173, 179
remittances 2, 139, 190
Renzi, Matteo 159n
repertoires 9, 17–18, 270
   African languages 28–29, 30–34, 46, 127–129
   communicative practices 174–175, 177, 179
   language choice 31–34, 48–52, 78
research methods
   data collection 22, 26–27, 65–66, 122–126, 169–170
   ethical issues 25–26
   ethnographic studies 120–122, 231–232, 247–248, 252–253
   mixed methods 41
   multimodal discourse analysis 92–93, 99–104
Reservation of Special Amenities Act (1953), South Africa 191
Romanians 97, 106

safe houses 168, 173, 179
Salvini, Matteo 152–153, 157, 158, 159n, 168, 169
Salvini Act (Decree Law no. 113/2018) see Decree Law no. 113/2018
Save the Children 143, 149
scales 4, 166, 272
scapes 1, 4
   see also spaces
#*scendeteli* controversy 154–158

schools *see* education
Sea Horse satellite system 139
search and rescue missions 137, 146–153
Seashore Amendment Act (1972), South Africa 191
Sea-Watch 143, 149, 151, 153
securitisation 212
sedentarism 1, 248
sedentary discourses 137, 138
segregation 18–19, 20–21, 184, 189–194
  multilingualism 34–35
  United States 186
  see also apartheid; isolation; othering
self-governmentality 89–90
semiotic resources 5, 6, 7, 163
settler-colonial polities 189, 195, 201–202
  (im)mobilities 183–185, 194
sexuality
  and apartheid 190, 191, 194
  queer 229–231, 234–235
SIPROIMI 168
smooth space 137–138, 139
smugglers *see* traffickers
social agency 250, 255, 257, 261–265
social networks 2
  family relationships 102–105
social structures 250, 258–259, 260, 264–266
  social inequality 39–40
SOS Méditerranée 143, 152
Soussou (Susu) language 127, 129
South Africa
  apartheid 183–185, 189–194
  beaches 185–186, 188–189, 191–194, 195, 197–198
  (im)mobilities 198–201
  post-apartheid 183, 188–189, 197–198, 200–202
South Sudan 41–42, 43, 44, 48–49
  diaspora 53, 55
spaces 5, 6, 39–40
  exclusion 212–213
  heterotopic spaces 167
  (im)mobilities 38, 233
  institutional 173
  place identity 97, 247–248
  political aspects 167, 184, 247–248, 265
  public spaces 186, 188–189, 191, 197–198, 201–202
  racialisation 198–200
  shaping languages 41–42, 46–48, 48–52, 56
  striated and smooth spaces 137–140, 199, 261
  third space 186
  virtual spaces 3, 5, 7, 272–273
  see also apartheid; scapes
Spain
  attitudes to migrants 97, 111n
  immigration policies 90–91
  Ley 25/2007 (2006) 94–95, 105
  telecommunications industry 93–96, 105–109
Spanish language 105–108, 111n
SPRAR (secondary reception centres), Italy 168, 170
stances 62, 64–65, 78–79
stasis 40, 55
striated space 137–138, 140, 199, 261
Striscia la Notizia (TV show) 147
superdiversity 3–4, 117, 164–165
Susu (Soussou) language 127, 129
Syria 142
  refugees 70–72

task focus 68–69, 79
taxis del mare trope 147–150, 151–152, 156
teaching
  data collection through 29–30
  languages 208, 209–211, 215–219, 222–223
  teacher training 26
  see also education
telecommunications industry sector 90, 111n
  Spain 95–96, 105–109
  see also ICT (Information & telecommunication technologies)
Telefónica 94, 95–96, 105, 106–107
temporary reception centres (TRCs), Italy 163, 170–178

Territorial Commissions for the Recognition of International Protection, Italy 25, 35–36n
terrorism 94
third space 186
Tracy (pseudonym) 251–265
traffickers 236
  networks of 142, 146
  and NGOs 141, 149, 151, 158n
  tracking 140
transidiomatic practices 165–166
transit camps 247, 252–253, 258, 259–260, 262
translanguaging 4, 39, 78, 165–168, 173–176, 179
translation 78, 107
transnational networks 19–20, 102–105
Travellers *see* Irish Travellers
Trespass Act (1959), South Africa 184
Triton 137, 142–143
Turkey, agreement with EU 207, 208–209

Ubaldo Diciotti (coastguard ship) 152, 153

unaccompanied foreign minors (UFMs) 22–23, 25, 122, 168–169
UNHCR (United Nations High Commissioner for Refugees) 36n, 209, 217
United States, racism 186, 203n
university applications 65, 66–70
urban areas 3, 190

virtual spaces 3, 5, 7, 272–273
visual imagery 98–104
Vodafone 95–96, 98
Vos Hestia (boat) 149

war metaphors 254–256
welfare support 65
  medical prescriptions 74–77
white supremacy *see* apartheid; racism
Williams, Eugene 186
Wolof language 31, 32, 35

YouTube videos 44, 147

Zuccaro, Carmelo 147–148, 151

For Product Safety Concerns and Information please contact our EU Authorised Representative:

Easy Access System Europe

Mustamäe tee 50

10621 Tallinn

Estonia

gpsr.requests@easproject.com

www.ingramcontent.com/pod-product-compliance
Ingram Content Group UK Ltd.
Pitfield, Milton Keynes, MK11 3LW, UK
UKHW021822220426

5349IPUK00003B/42